# Kent

# Kent

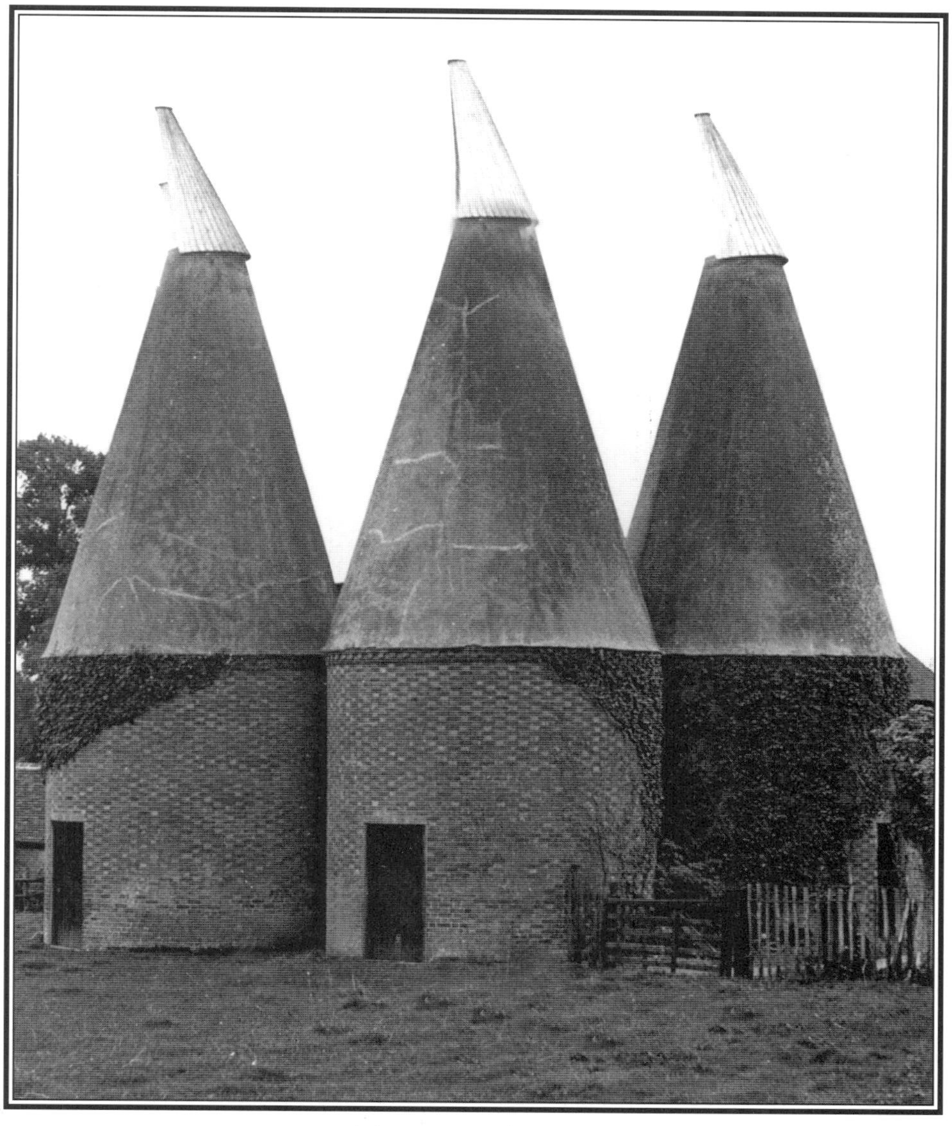

Helen Livingston

Waterton Press Limited

First published in the United Kingdom in 1998 by
Frith Publishing an imprint of Waterton Press Limited
Reprinted in 1999



British Library Cataloguing in Publication Data

Helen Livingston
Kent

ISBN 1-84125-028-7

Reproductions of all the photographs in this book are available as framed or mounted prints. For more information please contact The Francis Frith Collection at the address below quoting the title of this book and the page number and photograph number or title.

The Francis Frith Collection,
PO Box 1697, Salisbury, Wilts SP3 5TW
Tel: 01747 855 669
E mail: bookprints@francisfrith.com

Typeset in Bembo Semi Bold

Printed and bound in Great Britain by
WBC Limited, Bridgend, Glamorgan.

# Contents

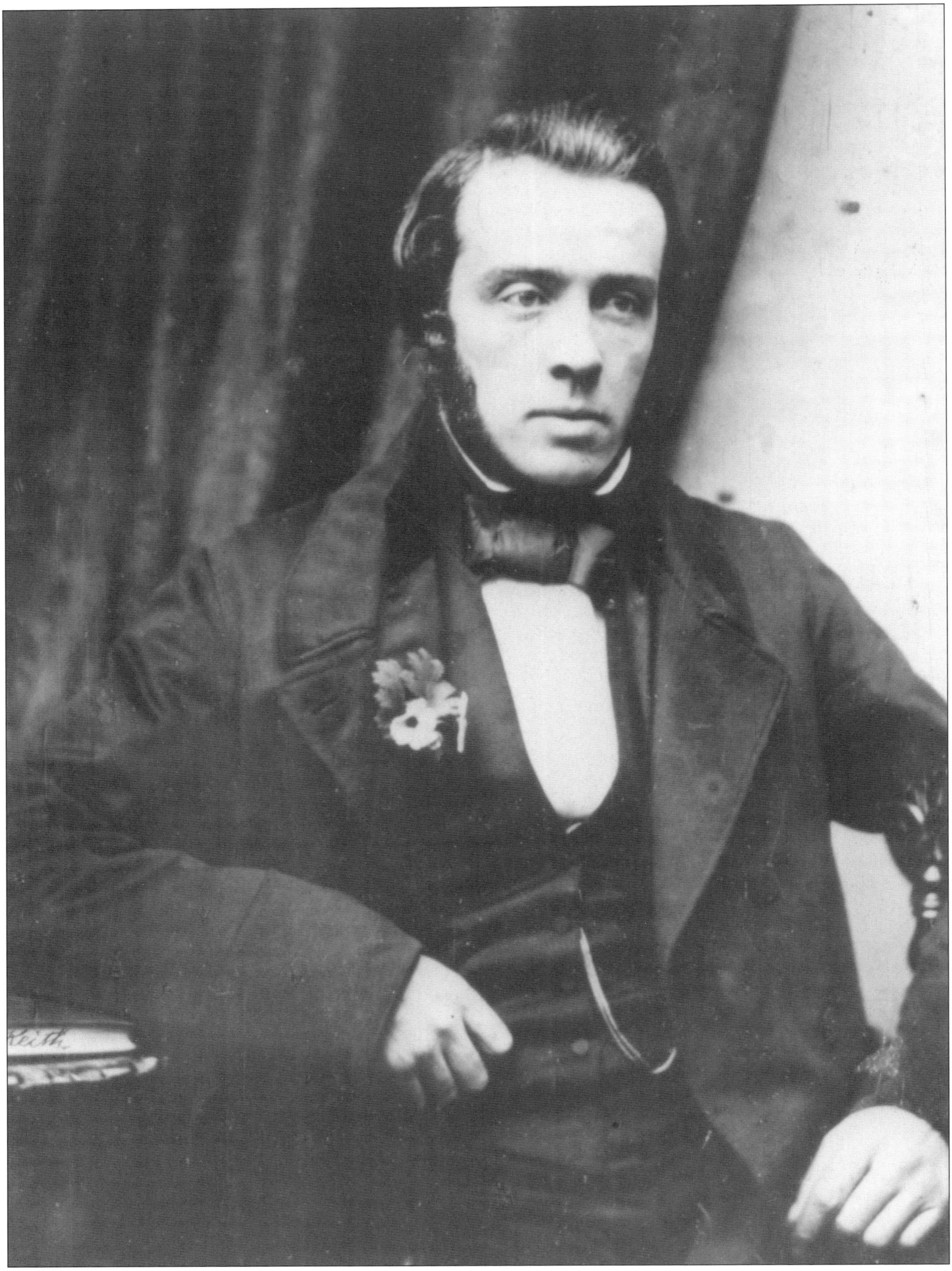

Francis Frith 1822-1898

# Introduction
# Francis Frith: A Victorian Pioneer

Francis Frith, the founder of the world famous photographic archive was a complex and multitudinous man. A devout Quaker and a highly successful and respected Victorian businessman he was also a flamboyant character.

By 1855 Frith had already established a wholesale grocery business in Liverpool and sold it for the astonishing sum of £200,000, equivalent of over £15,000,000 today. Now a multi-millionaire he was able to indulge in his irresistible desire to travel. As a child he had pored over books penned by early explorers, and his imagination had been stirred by family holidays to the sublime mountain regions of Wales and Scotland. "What a land of spirit-stirring and enriching scenes and places!" he had written. He was to return to these scenes of grandeur in later years to "recapture the thousands of vivid and tender memories", but with a very different purpose. Now in his thirties, and captivated by the new science of photography, Frith set out on a series of pioneering journeys to the Middle East, that occupied him from 1856 until 1860.

He took with him a specially-designed wicker carriage which acted as camera, dark-room and sleeping chamber. These far-flung journeys were full of intrigue and adventure. In his life story, written when he was sixty-three, Frith tells of being held captive by bandits, and fighting "an awful midnight battle to the very point of exhaustion and surrender with a deadly pack of hungry, wild dogs". He bargained for several weeks with a "mysterious priest" over a beautiful seven-volume illuminated Koran, which is now in the British Museum. Wearing full arab costume, Frith arrived at Akaba by camel seventy years before Lawrence of Arabia, where he encountered "desert princes and rival sheikhs, blazing with jewel-hilted swords".

During these extraordinary adventures he was assiduously exploring the desert regions of the Nile and recording the antiquities and people with his camera, Frith was the first photographer ever to travel beyond the sixth cataract. Africa, we must remember, was still the "Dark Continent", and Stanley and Livingstone's famous meeting was a decade into the future. The conditions for picture taking confound belief. He laboured for hours on end in his dark-room in the sweltering heat, while the volatile collodion chemicals fizzed dangerously in their trays. Often he was forced to work in tombs and caves where conditions were cooler.

Back in London he exhibited his photographs and was "rapturously cheered" by the Royal Society. His reputation as a photographer was made overnight. His photographs were issued in albums by James S. Virtue and William MacKenzie, and published simultaneously in London and New York. An eminent historian has likened their impact on the population of the time to that on our own generation of the first photographs taken on the surface of the moon.

Characteristically, Frith spotted the potential to create a new business as a specialist publisher of photographs. In 1860 he married Mary Ann Rosling and set out to photograph every city, town and village in Britain. For the next thirty years Frith travelled the country by train and by pony and trap, producing photographs that were keenly bought by the millions of Victorians who, because of the burgeoning rail network, were beginning to enjoy holidays and day trips to Britain's seaside resorts and beauty spots.

To meet the demand he gathered together a team of up to twelve photographers, and also published the work of independent artist-photographers of the reputation of Roger Fenton and Francis Bedford. Together with clerks and photographic printers he employed a substantial staff at his Reigate studios. To gain an understanding of the scale of Frith's business one only has to look at the catalogue issued by Frith & Co. in 1886. It runs to some 670 pages listing not only many thousands of views of the British Isles but also photographs of most major European countries, and China, Japan, the USA and Canada. By 1890 Frith had created the greatest specialist photographic publishing company in the world.

He died in 1898 at his villa in Cannes, his great project still growing. His sons, Eustace and Cyril, took over the task, and Frith & Co. continued in business for another seventy years, until by 1970 the archive contained over a third of a million pictures of 7,000 cities, towns and villages.

The photographic record he has left to us stands as a living monument to a remarkable and very special man.

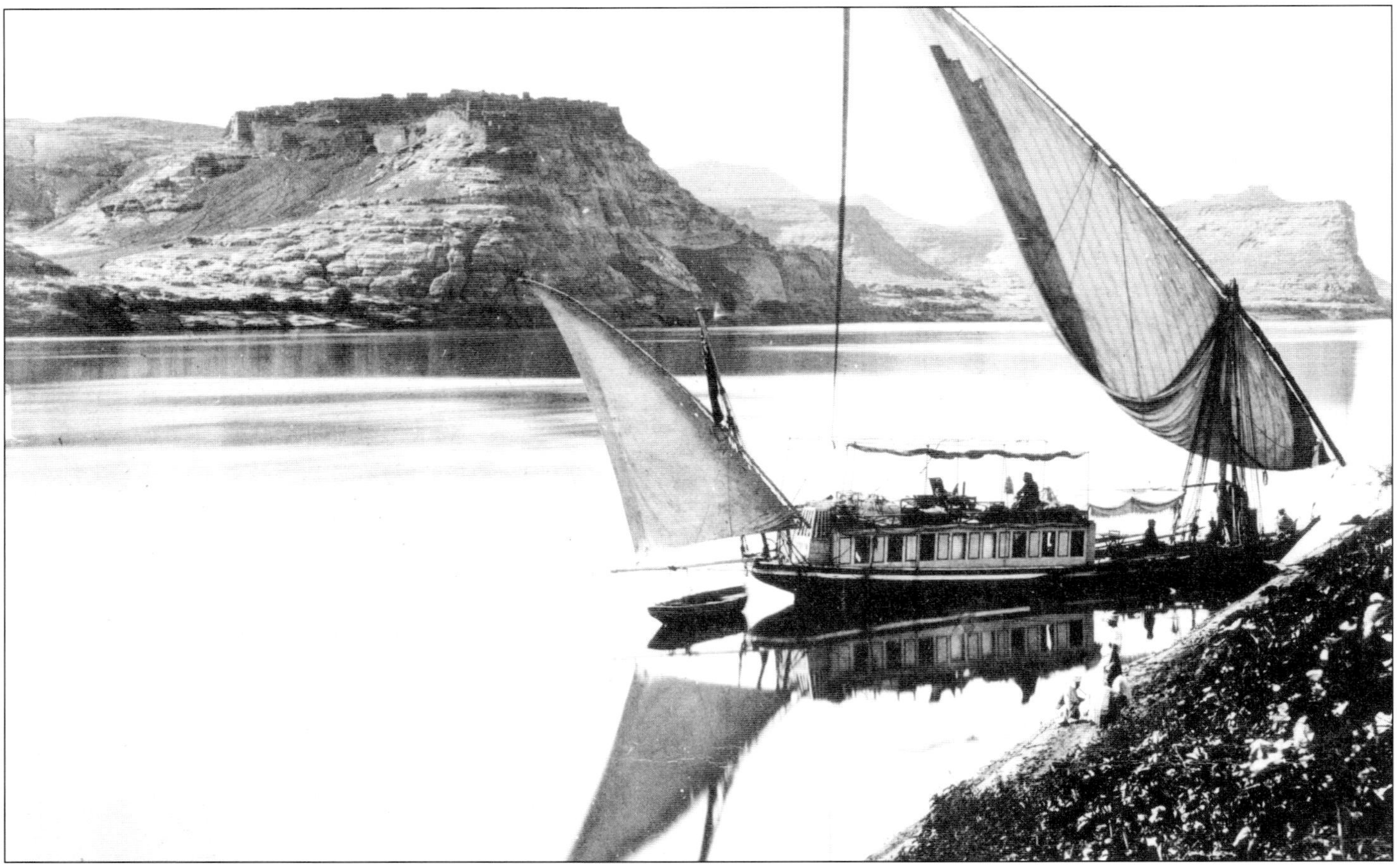

Frith's dhow in Egypt *c.*1857

# Ashford

Ashford is a bustling modern town that developed with the railway, but it is also mentioned in the Book of Doomsday. The old established market town is dominated by the great pinnacled tower of its fifteenth century church, which is pleasantly situated in a square. Today, offices jostle near to the railway, Ashford International Station and the motorway.

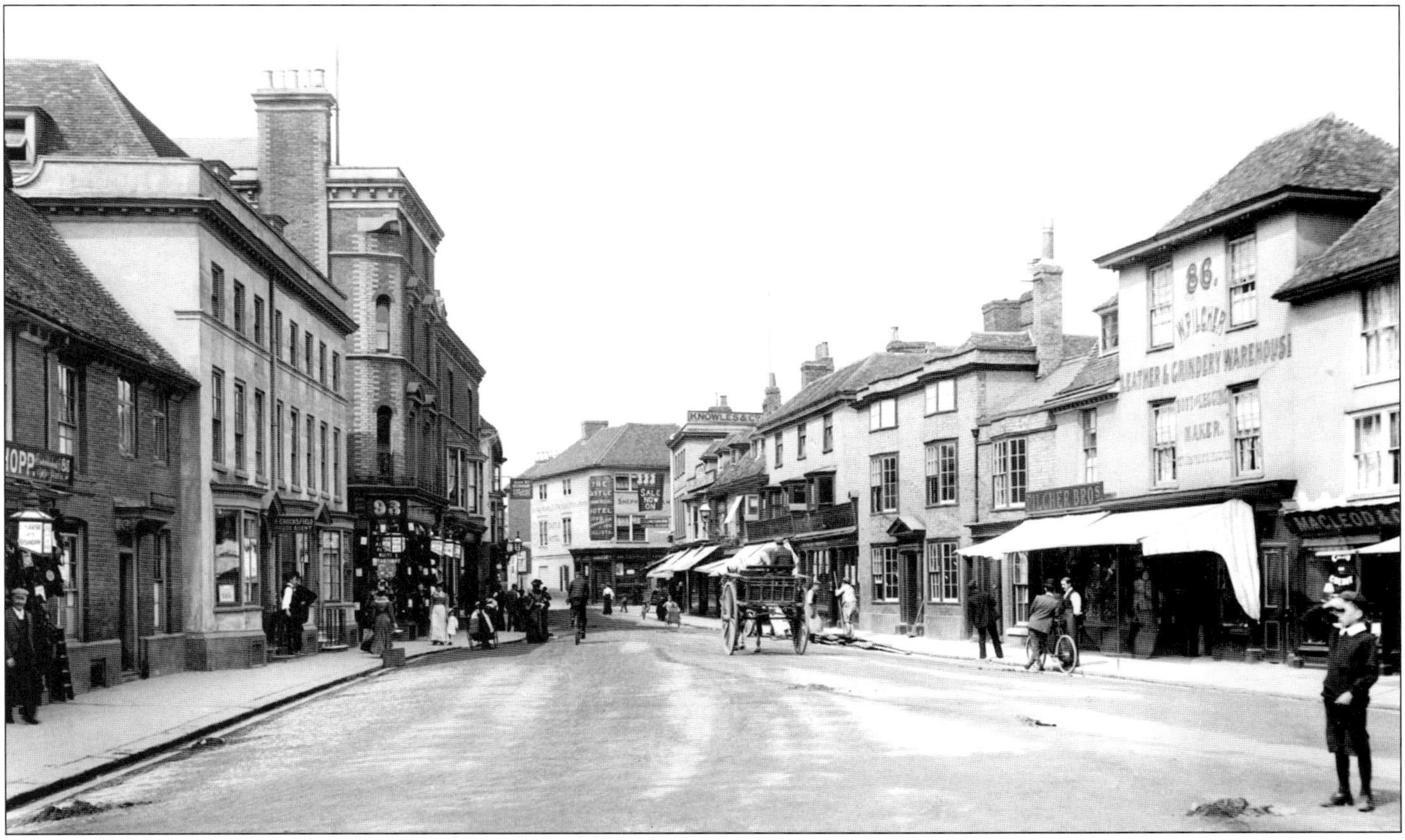


47523
An excellent view of Ashford High Street, taken in 1901. The only traffic is a horse-drawn cart and a bicycle. By this date, Ashford was also an important railway town, with a major carriage works.

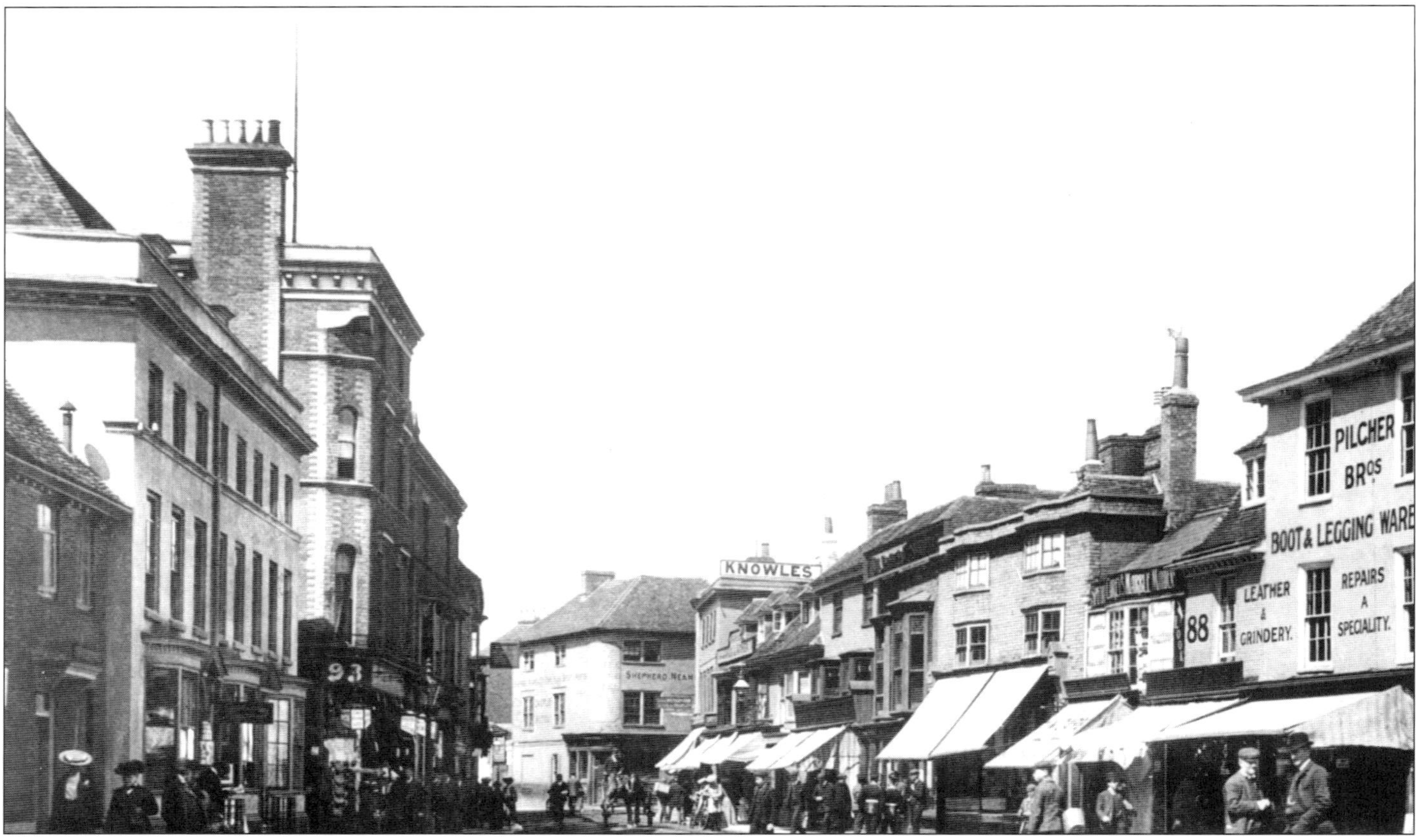


53443
This view of the High Street is taken five years later, and shows little change and even less wheeled traffic. The double bowfronted house has acquired an awning. The camera does not seem quite such a novelty to the bystanders.

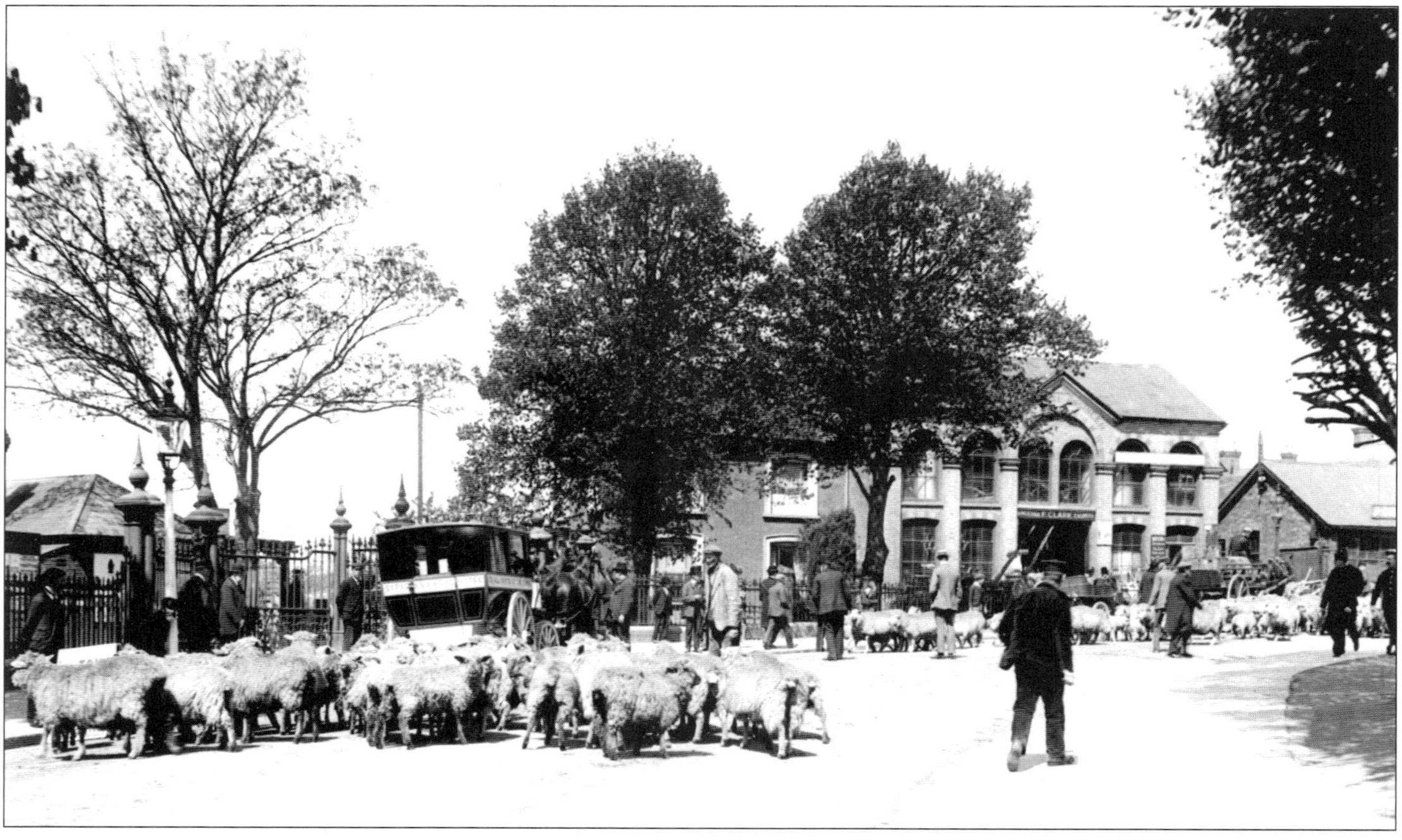

53445
A once familiar scene, the sheep sales at the Ashford Market in 1906. Ashford has for centuries been an important market town, and scenes such as this, with the sheep in the middle of the street, were once a familiar sight. The cattle market was on the left.

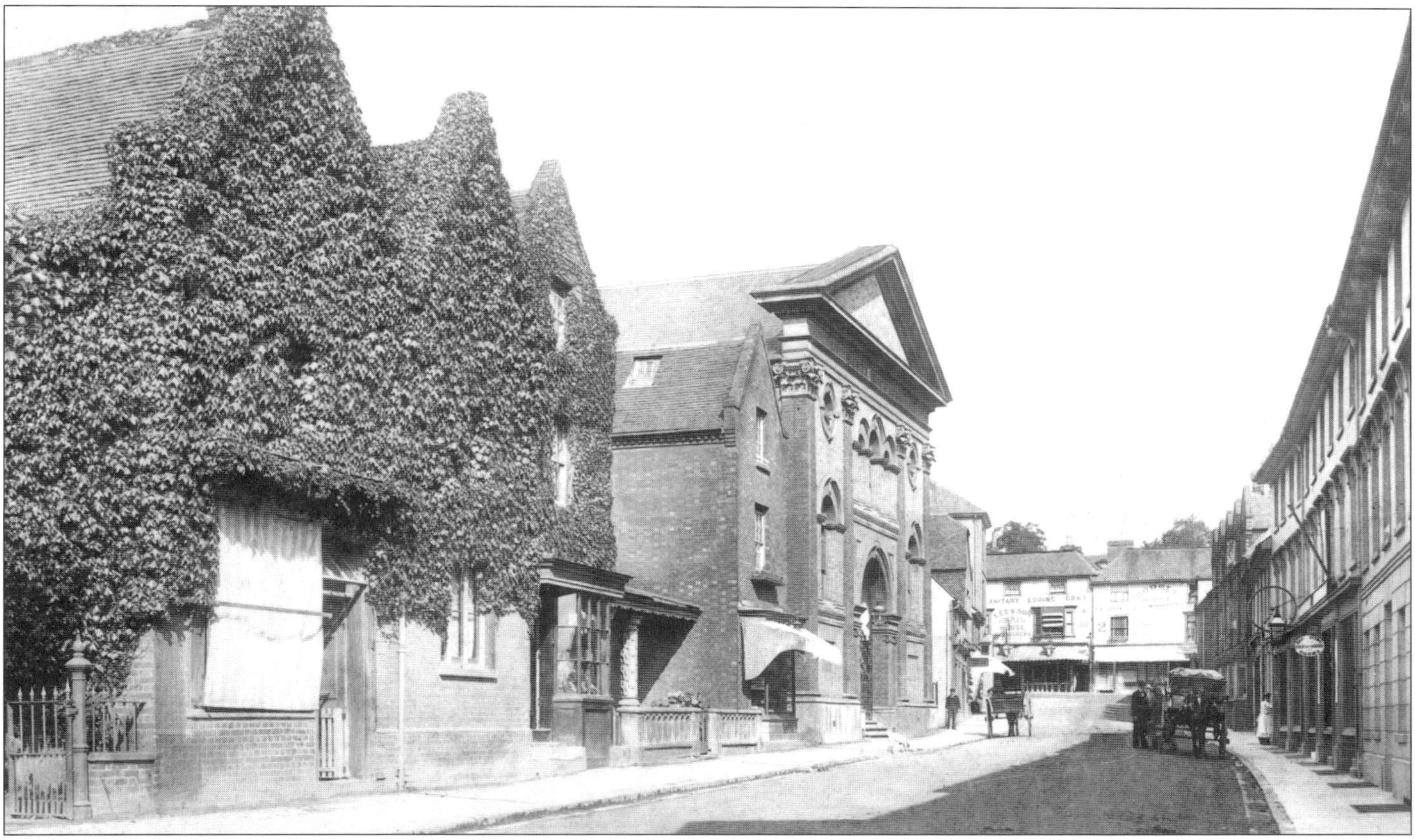

50330
A fine view of Ashford, this time taken in Marsh Street in 1903, with its fine ivy-clad buildings and chapel. Again, only horse-drawn carts can be seen and all seems quiet.

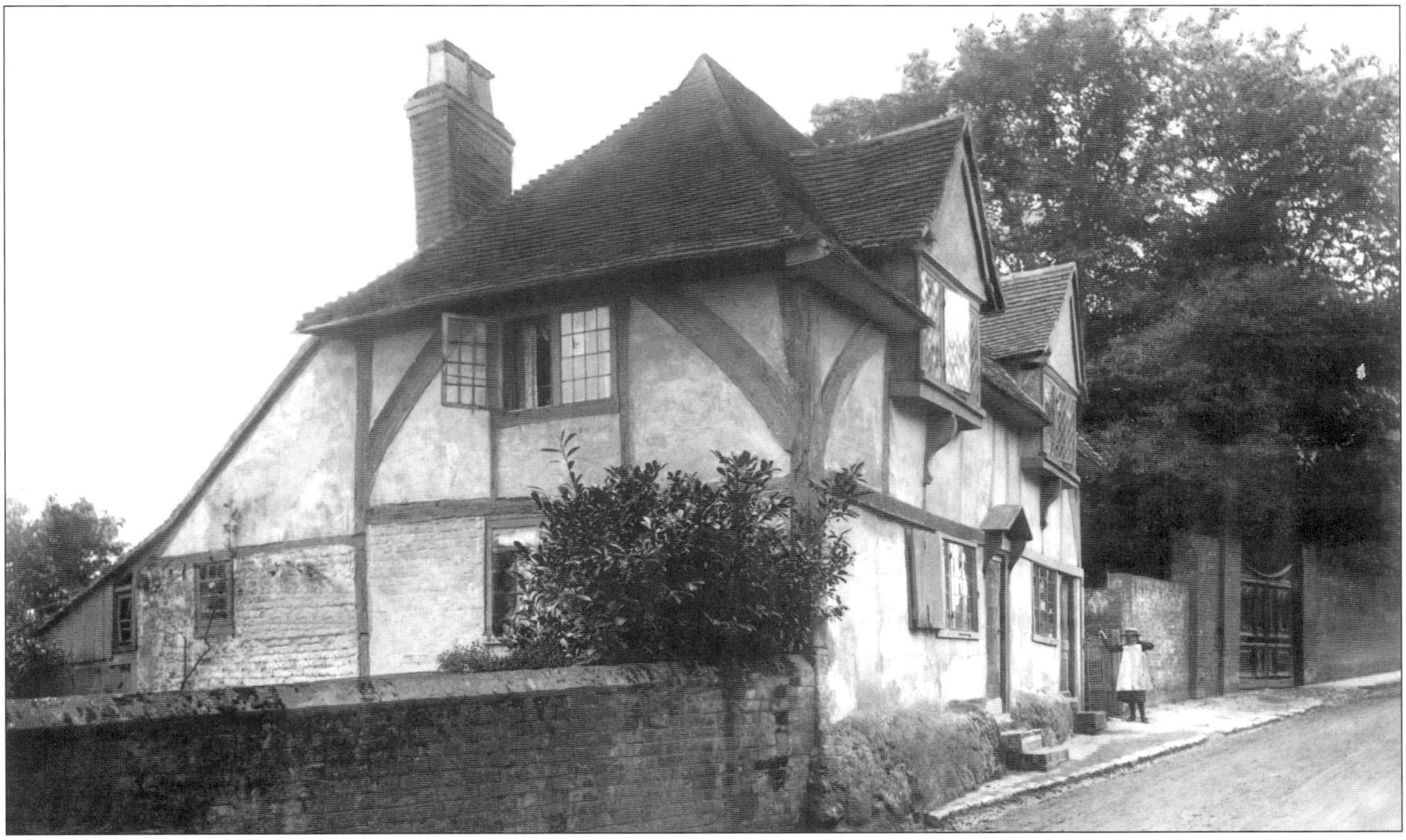

50333
A study of some attractive old cottages at East Mill, Ashford, taken in 1903. A little girl is staring suspiciously at the camera. Note the unmetalled surface of the road. The cottages are now demolished.

# Aylesford

A perfectly sited village by the River Medway. The scene of many battles in ancient years. The medieval bridge is on the site of an ancient ford, once the only crossing between Rochester and Maidstone. The Carmelite friary, rededicated in 1949, is now a place of pilgrimage.

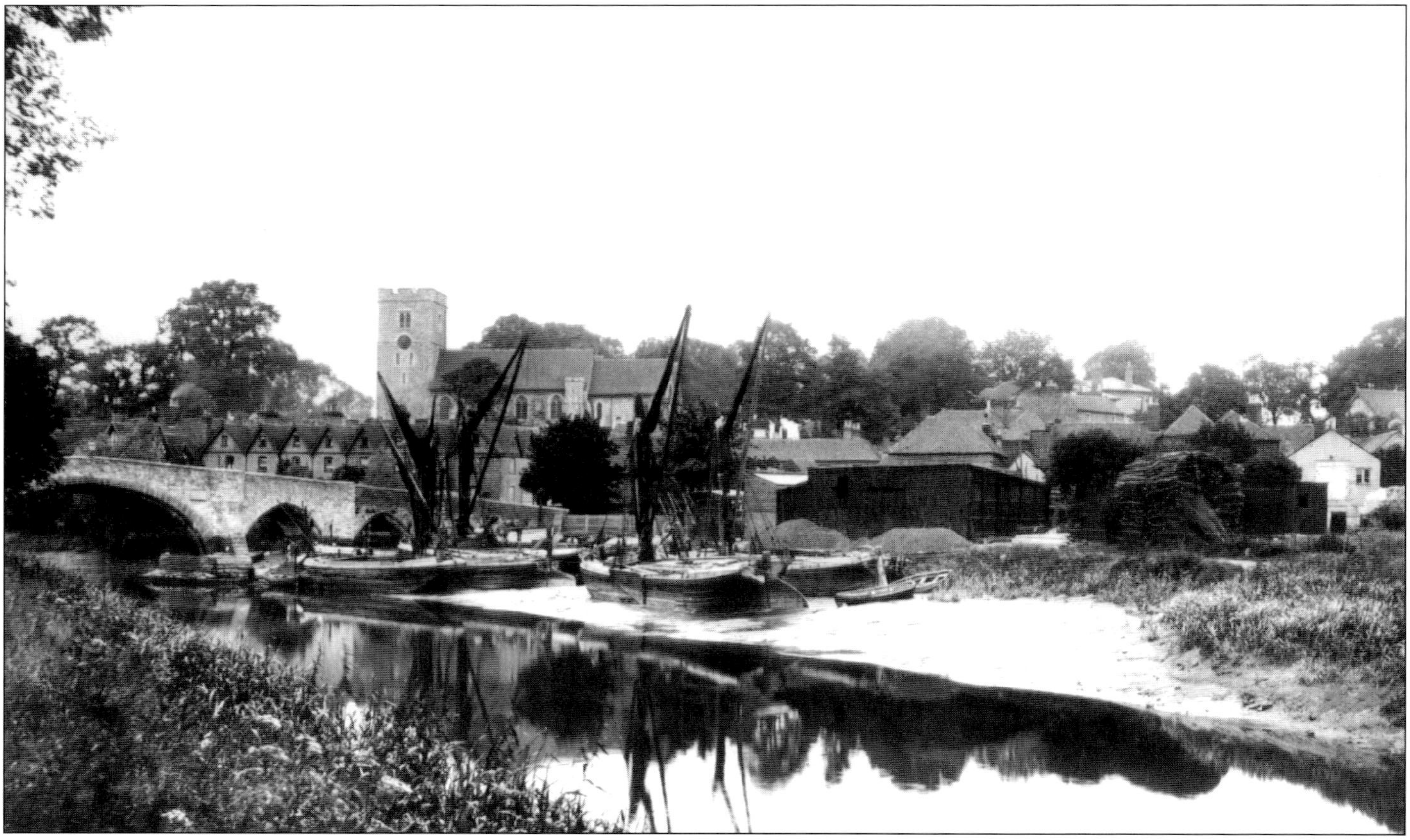

41549
A view from the west bank of the River Medway, looking to the medieval bridge and Aylesford. It is superbly proportioned, with one wide central span and three smaller arches on the approach. Sailing barges are beached on the far shore.

# BEARSTED

Bearsted is an attractive village that nestles around its ancient village green. Formerly the scene of Civil War skirmishes, it is now famous in cricket history. The church is Norman, its tower crowned with some curious sculptures of lions. It also has a massive timbered roof.

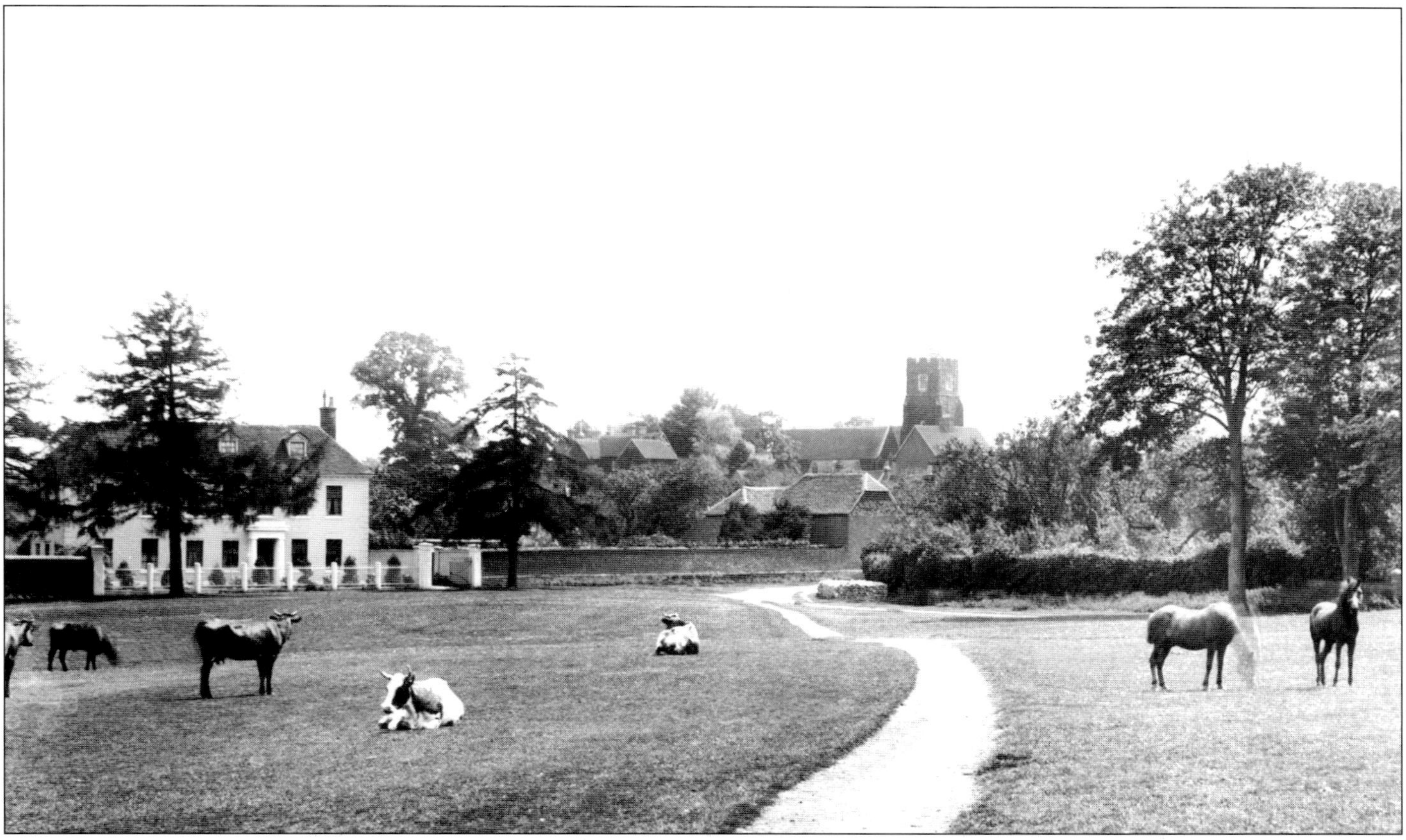

41565
This 1898 view shows the attractive nature of Bearsted's village green, with cattle and horses grazing contentedly. The winding path across the green leads the eye to the distant tower of the Norman church.

# Broadstairs

A well-known resort on the Isle of Thanet between Margate and Ramsgate, it retains a village atmosphere. Charles Dickens once lived here, and today there is an annual Dickens festival. It has quaint streets, a promenade, cliffs and a harbour, together with a fine old church. The tower of St Peter's was used as a signalling station is Napoleonic times.

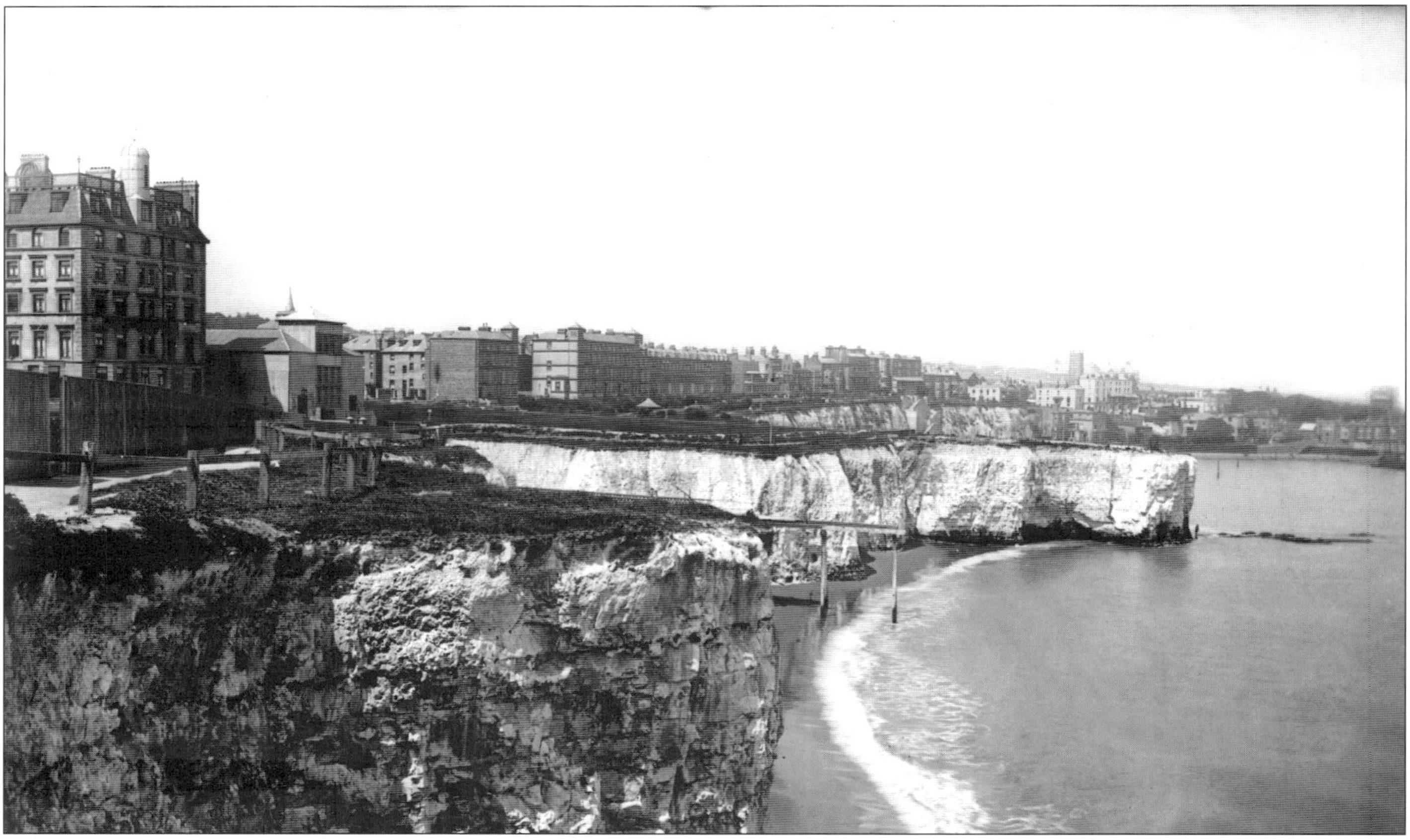

19708
A magnificent view of the cliffs taken in 1897, the light catching the white chalk. The handsome skyline of Broadstairs, with its fine clifftop establishments and hotels, sweeps round the bay to St Peter's church.

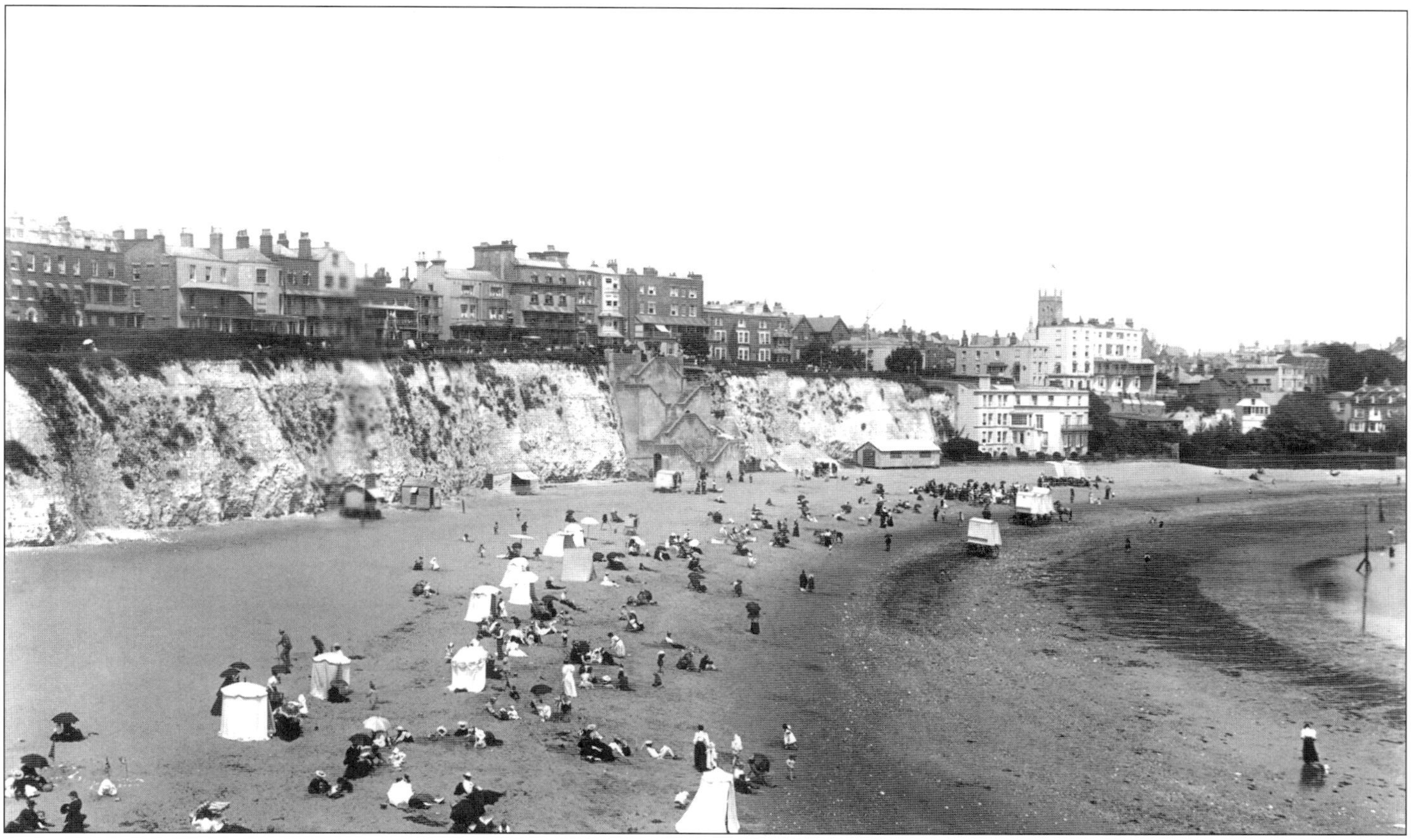

39589
An 1897 view of the beach at Broadstairs, taken from the cliff seen in the foreground of the previous picture. On the beach are bathing tents and a few bathing machines. In the centre are the stairs down to the beach.

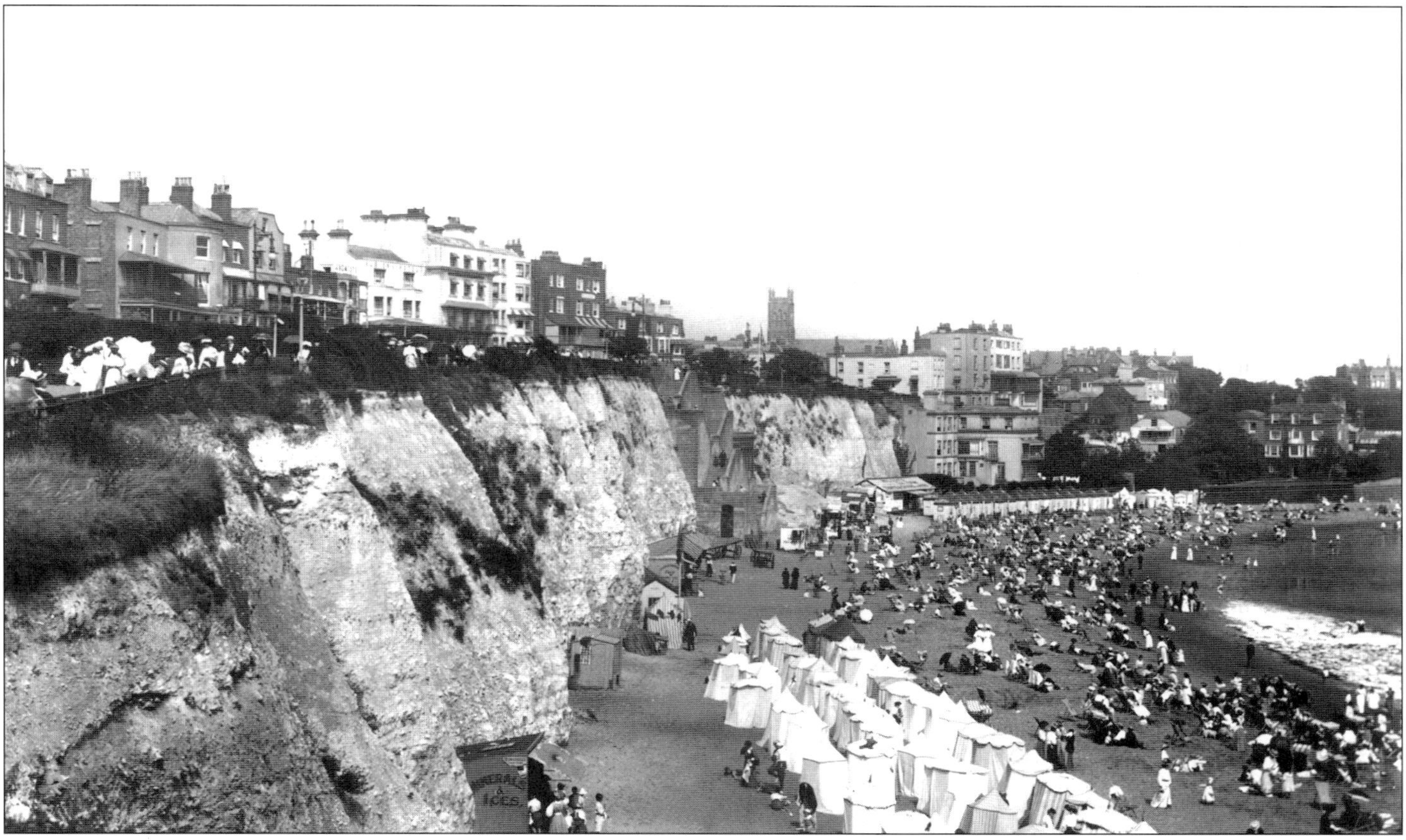

58325
This picture taken ten years later shows a holiday crowd thronging the sandy beach. The bathing tents have now multiplied beneath the cliffs: meanwhile promenaders stroll on the clifftop.

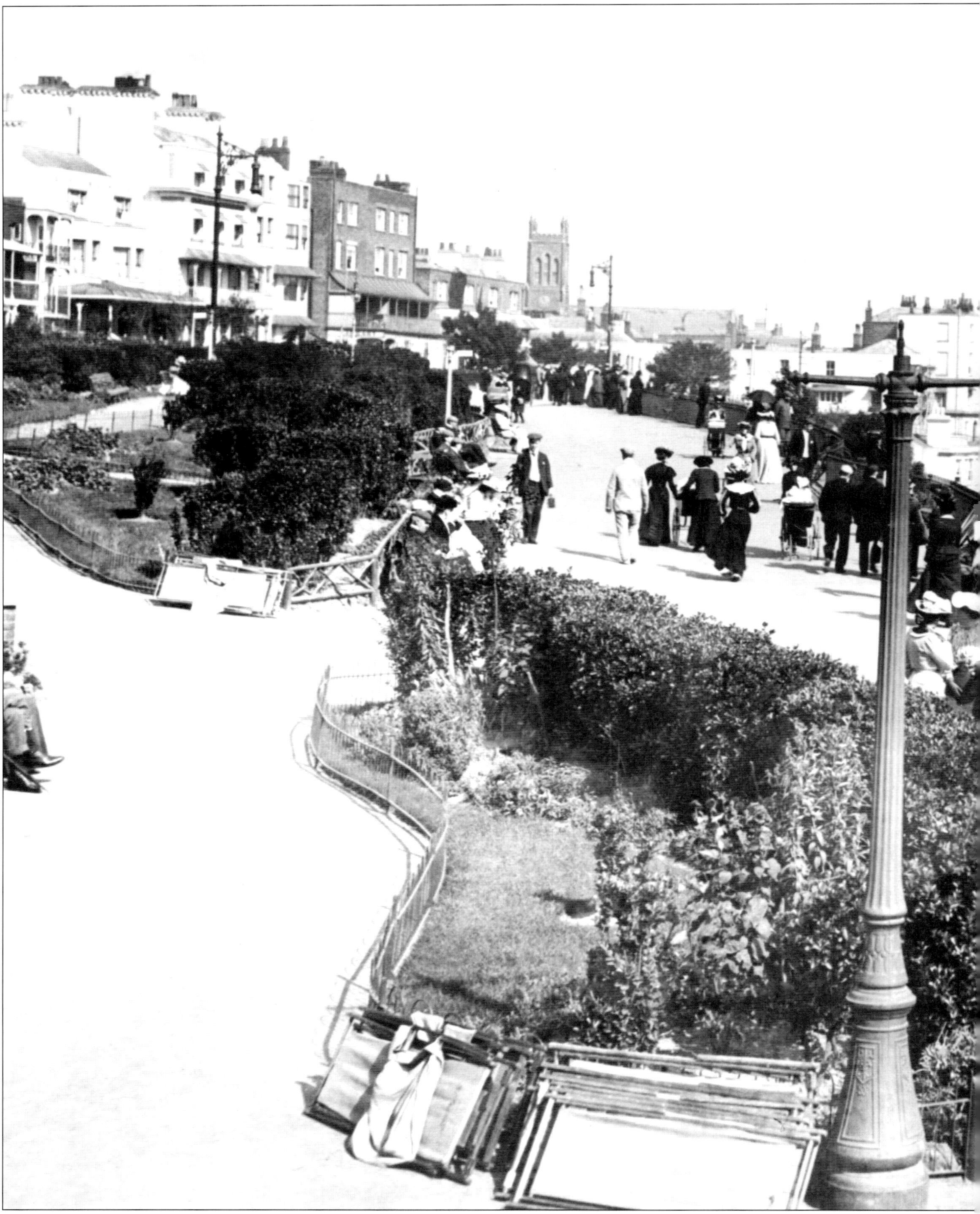

48842
A turn of the century view of the promenade, showing St Peter's Church, Bleak House and the harbour. Note the deckchairs stacked up against the railings ready for use, and the child sitting on a toy pedal-train.

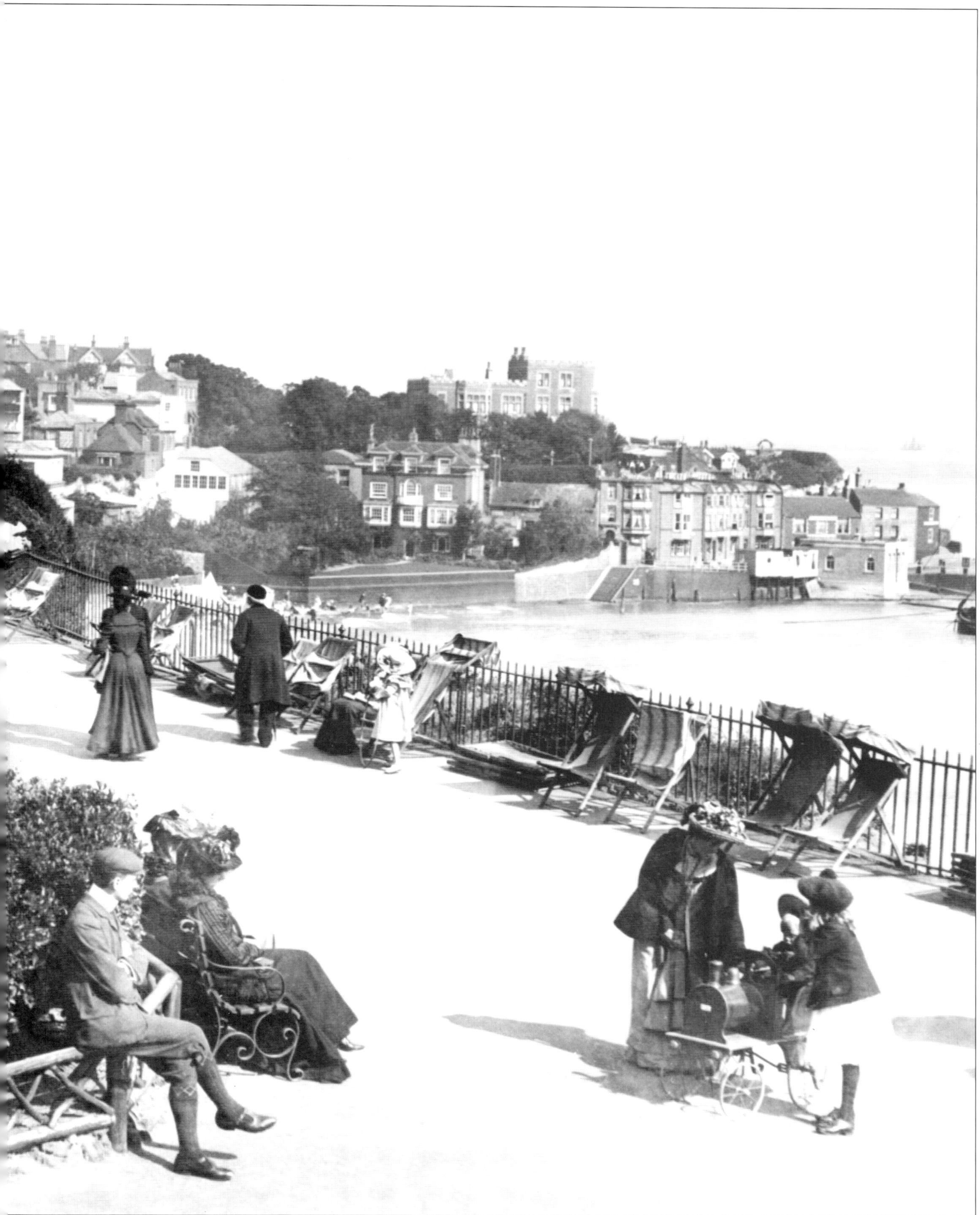

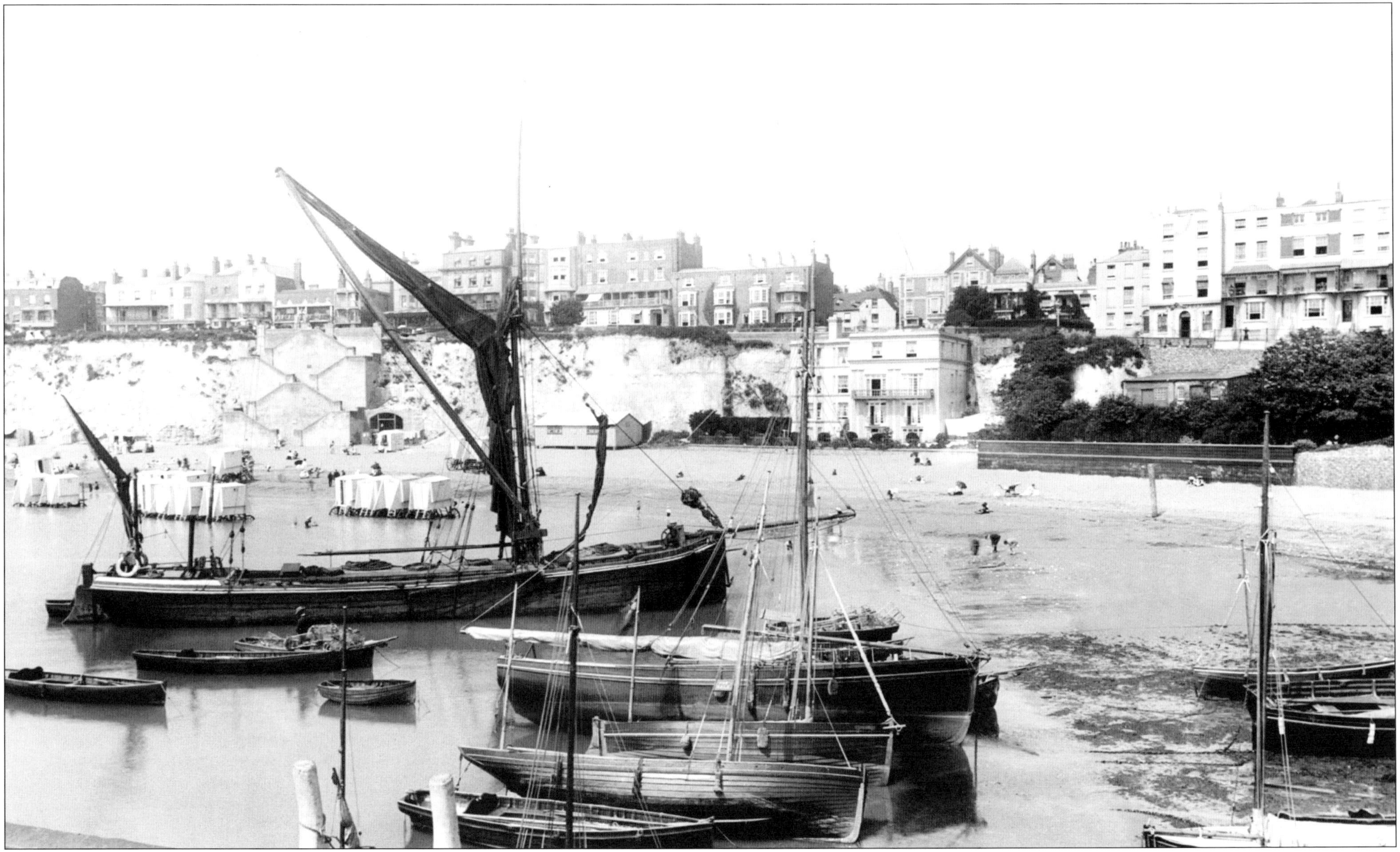

39592
A superb 1897 view of Broadstairs Harbour. This shows part of the fishing fleet and a spritsail sailing barge beached in the shallow waters at low tide. White painted bathing machines are visible behind the barge.

# Canterbury

An historic city dominated by its famous cathedral, which since Saxon days has been the spiritual capital of England. The cathedral was rebuilt in the twelfth century, and began to assume its modern form. It was here that Thomas à Becket was murdered in 1170, and the city has been a place of pilgrimage ever since. The crypt is the finest of its type in the world.

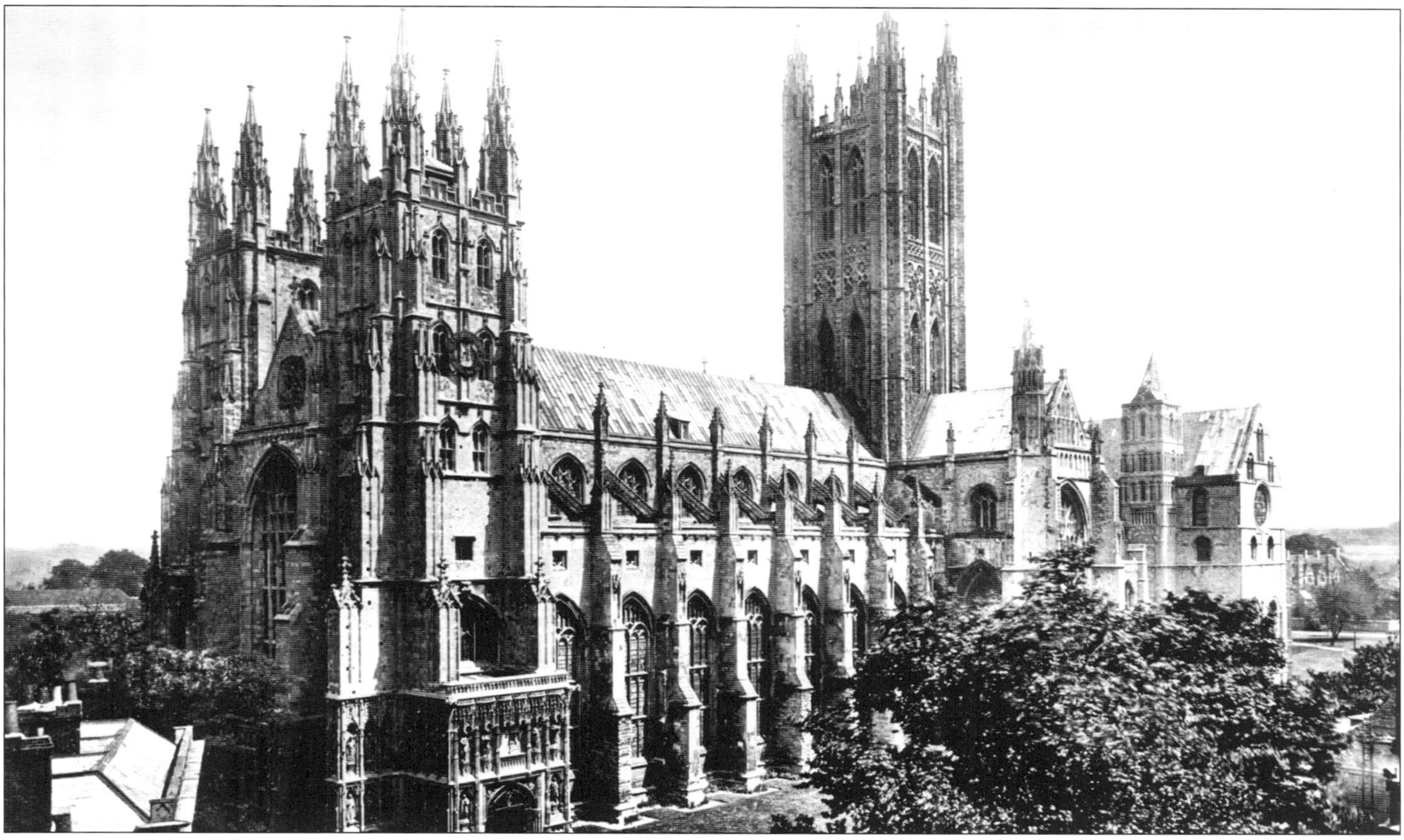

21350
A fine study of the cathedral taken in 1888. The huge west front dominates the picture, perhaps the most famous symbol of the Anglican church, and a landmark for many miles around.

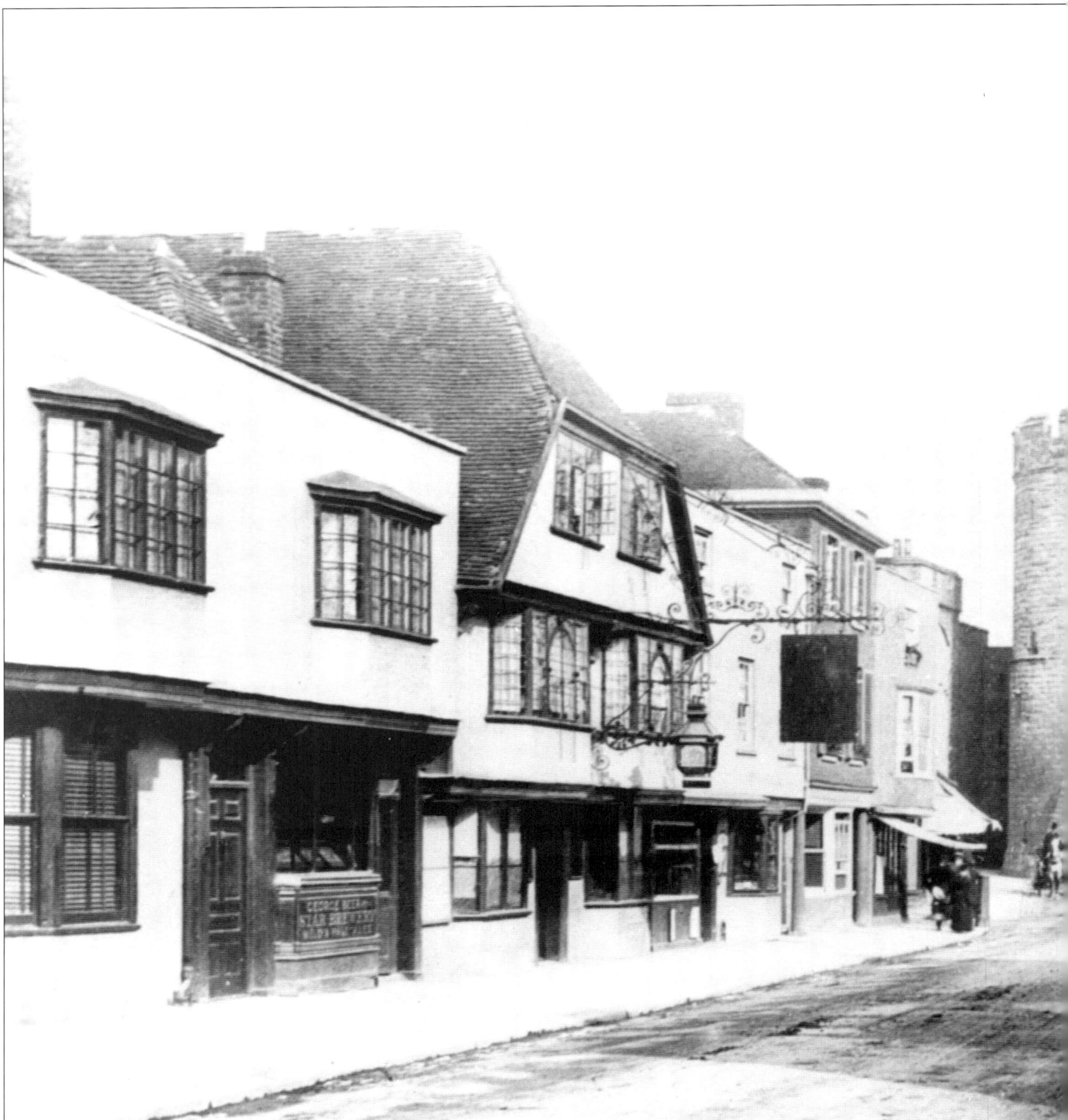

25695
A view of the West Gate of the city taken in 1890. The massive proportions of the West Gate emphasise the wall that once guarded the town. Three boys pose for the camera.

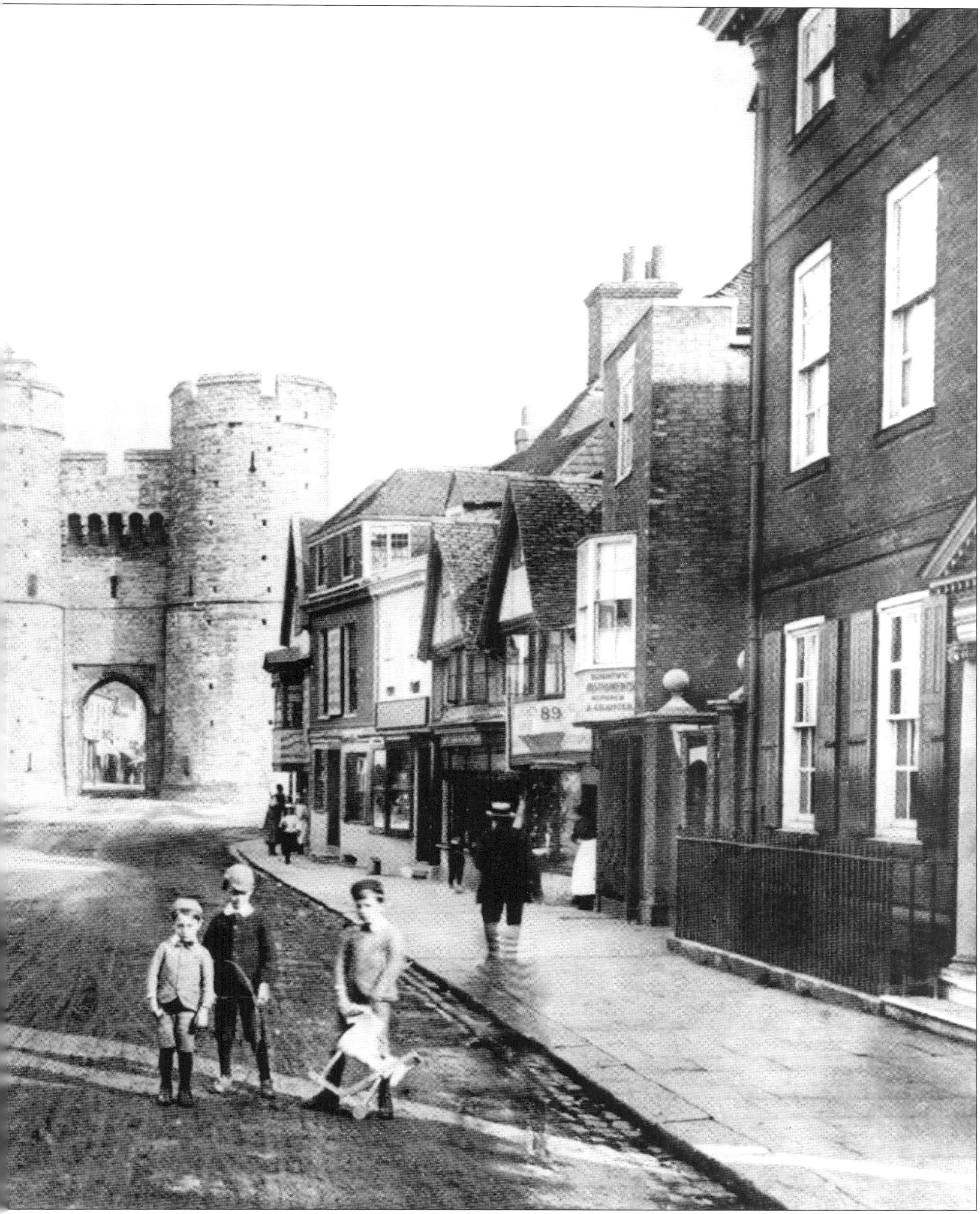
89

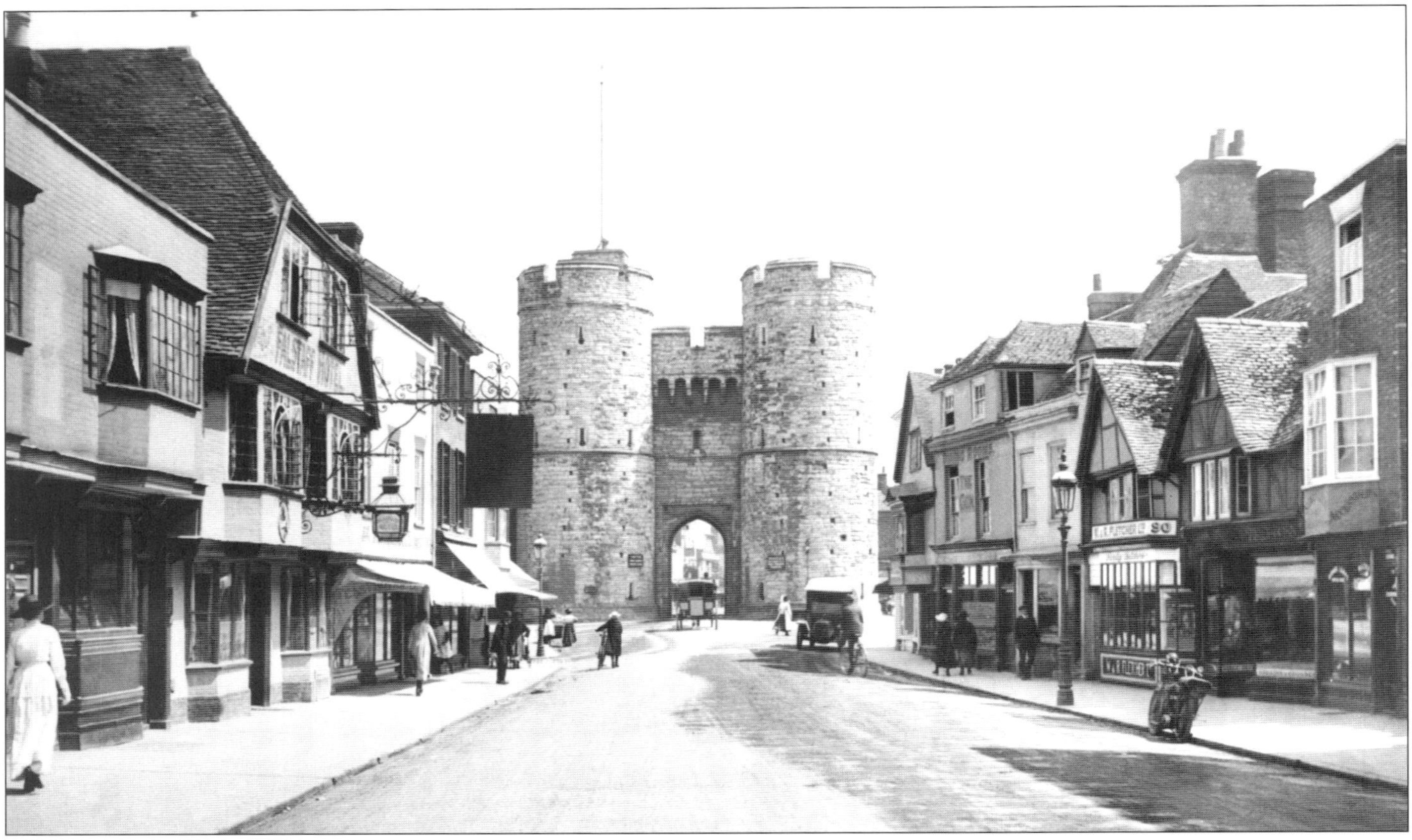

70330
The photographers returned just over thirty years later to take a further picture of the West Gate. A car and motorcycle are now in evidence, but little else has changed.

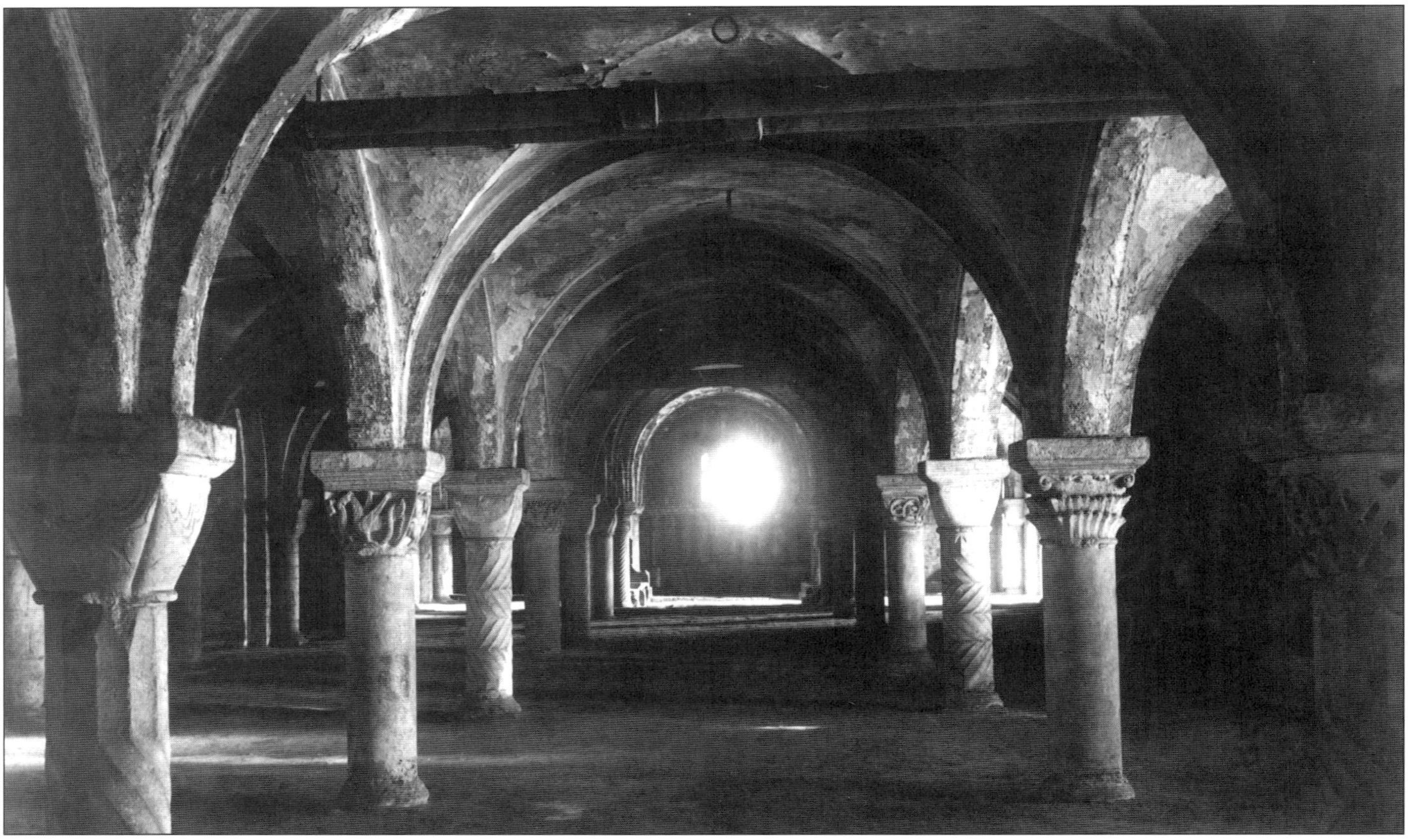

21396
The crypt at Canterbury dates from Norman times and is one of the cathedral's many treasures. This excellent study was taken in 1888, and is a rare and wonderful picture, symbolising the awe of Christianity.

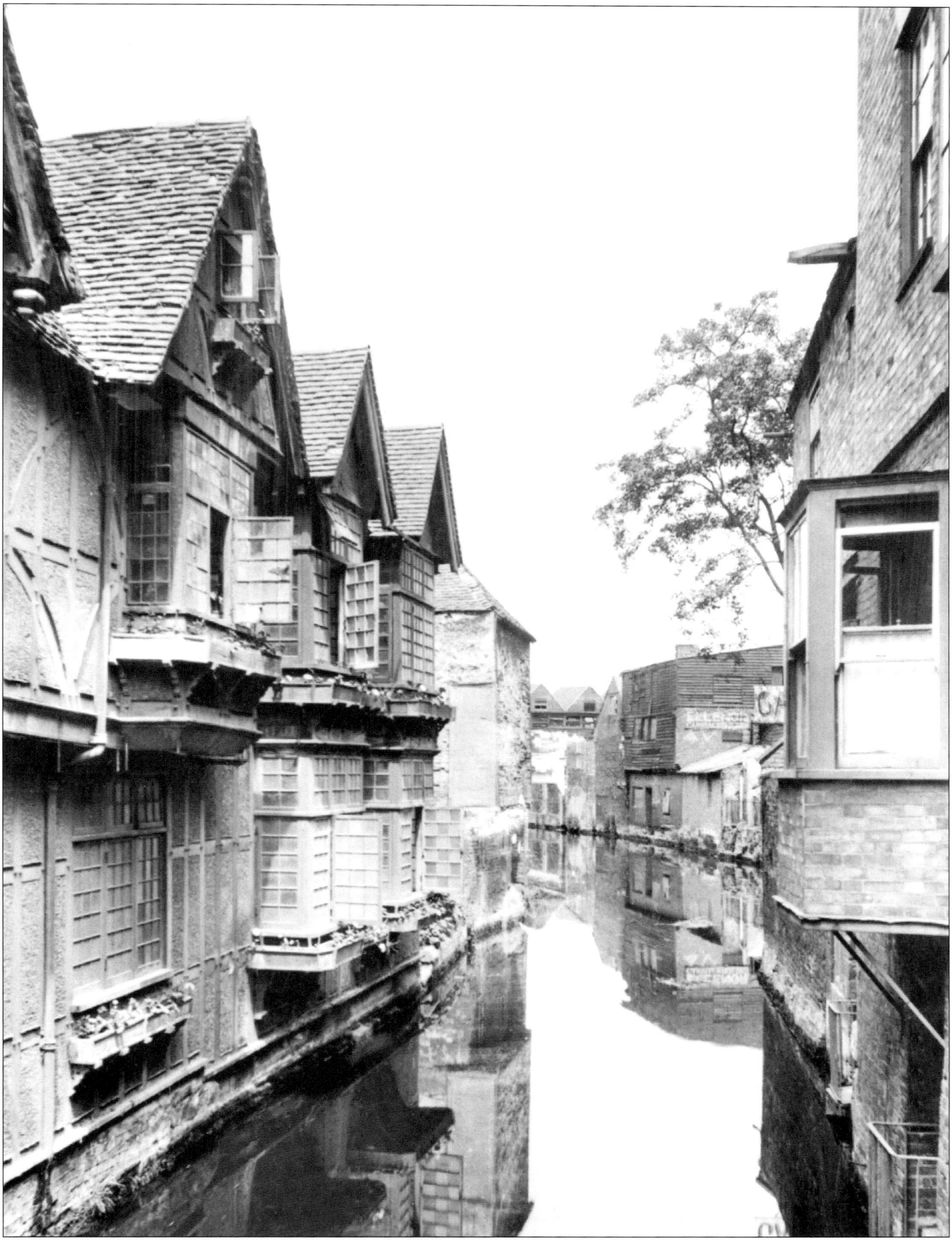

70331a

A fine 1921 study of the Weavers, the back street cottages on the river, where the Huguenot weavers once worked on the Kentish cloth. This scene is just off the High Street - the river is the Stour.

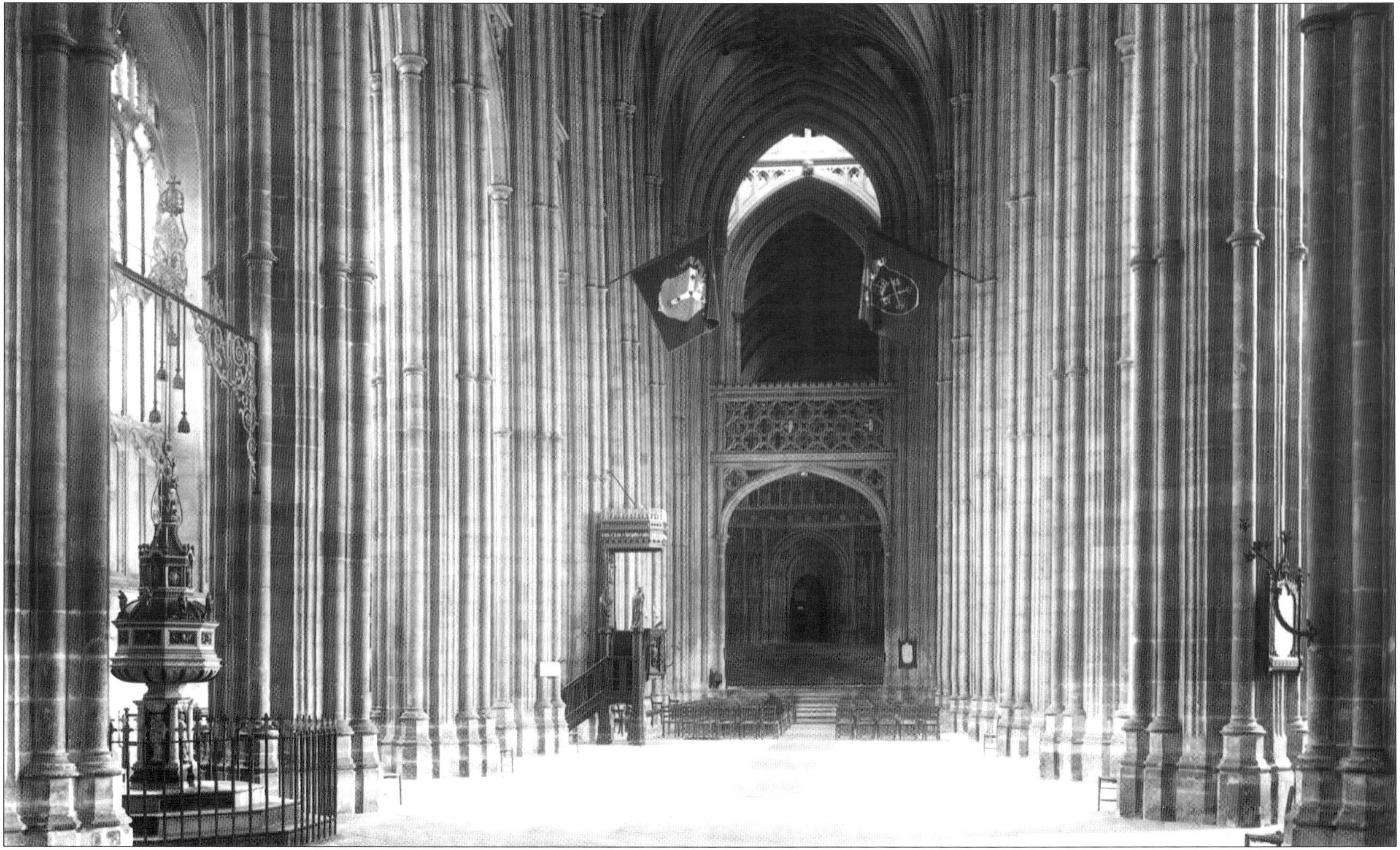

40840
This view of the east nave was taken in 1898. The nave took 28 years to build, and was completed in 1405. The huge proportions and the nobility of the architecture are still breathtaking, almost 600 years later.

# CHATHAM

Chatham is famous in the annals of English seafaring history. It was first developed as a safe anchorage in Tudor days, and later a large dockyard and arsenal were established. In recent years, it has become, with Rochester, a major tourist attraction.

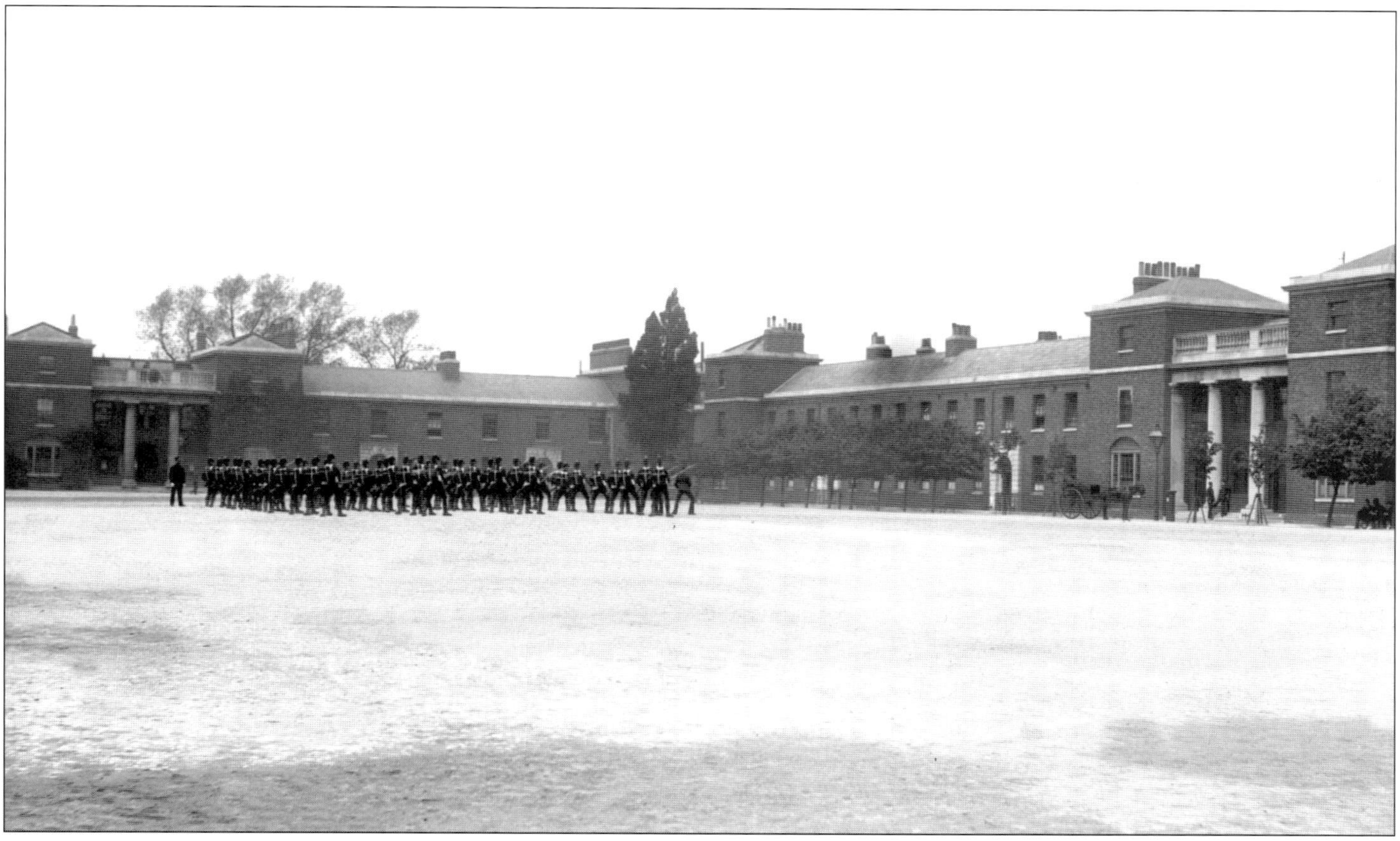

34041
This 1894 view shows the Royal Engineers on parade at their barracks on the hilltop, and emphasises Chatham's long association with the military. Note the spectators sitting under the trees on the right.

# CHILHAM

A delightful village, set high on the downs. Its pretty houses grouped around a square by the castle gates lend it a timeless air. The ancient castle was replaced in the seventeenth century by the present mansion, with spacious gardens set out by Tredescant. The fifteenth century church is rich in monuments.

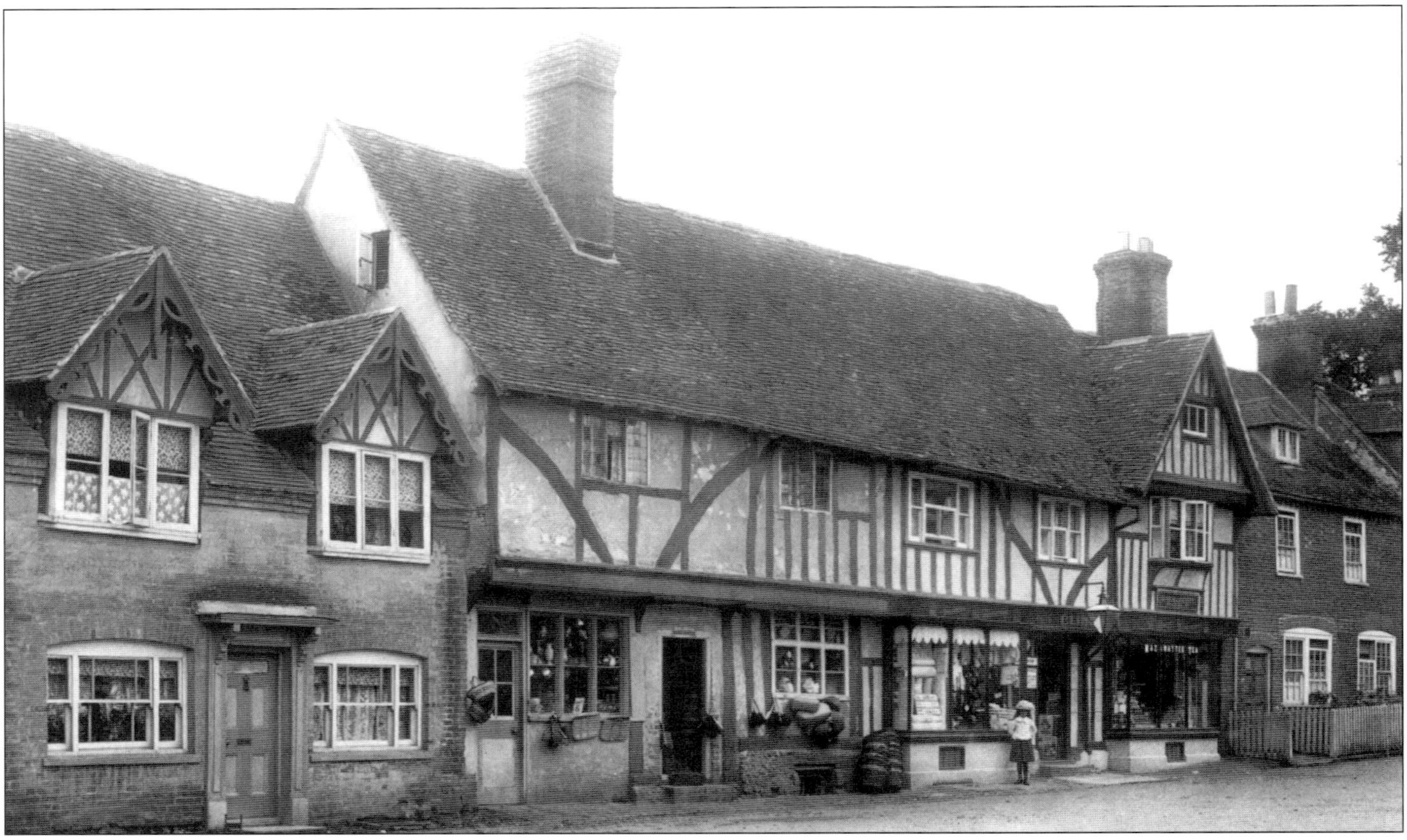

50344
An early twentieth century view of that bastion of English life, the Post Office. Here is a lovely half-timbered building in the picturesque little village on the Canterbury road. A little girl stands proudly in front, whilst next door baskets are for sale.

# Cranbrook

A perfect little town, the capital of the Kentish Weald, formerly a centre of cloth weaving. Its typical Kentish architecture of weatherboarded houses is complemented by the Union Mill, the largest working windmill in England. The view from Stone Street is perhaps one of the most famous of all Kentish scenes. The ancient church has many treasures, and there are many other interesting buildings.

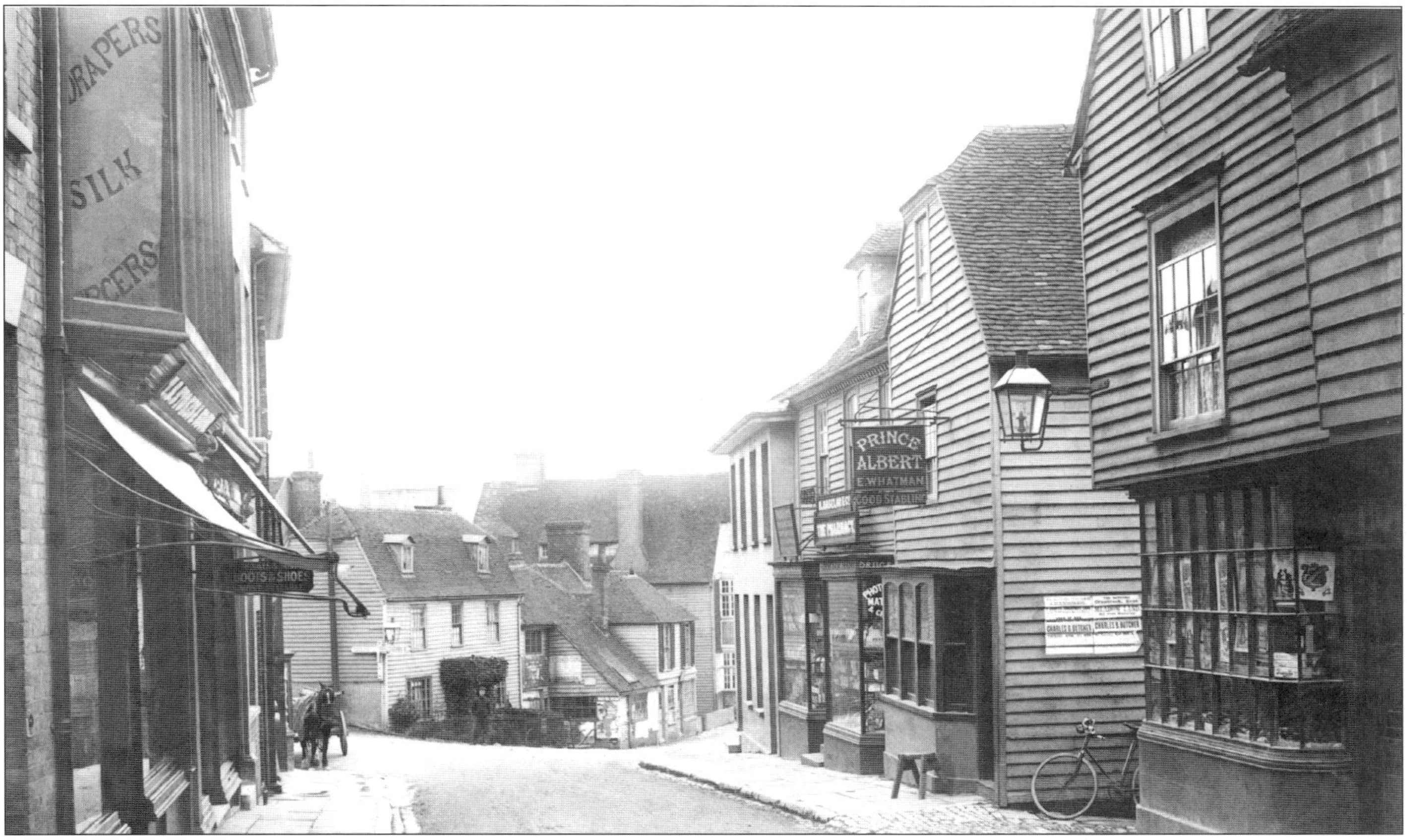


51010
This is the classic view of Cranbrook, taken in 1903. It looks down Stone Street, and the Kentish weatherboarding is much in evidence. The white painted Union Mill merges into the grey of the skies.

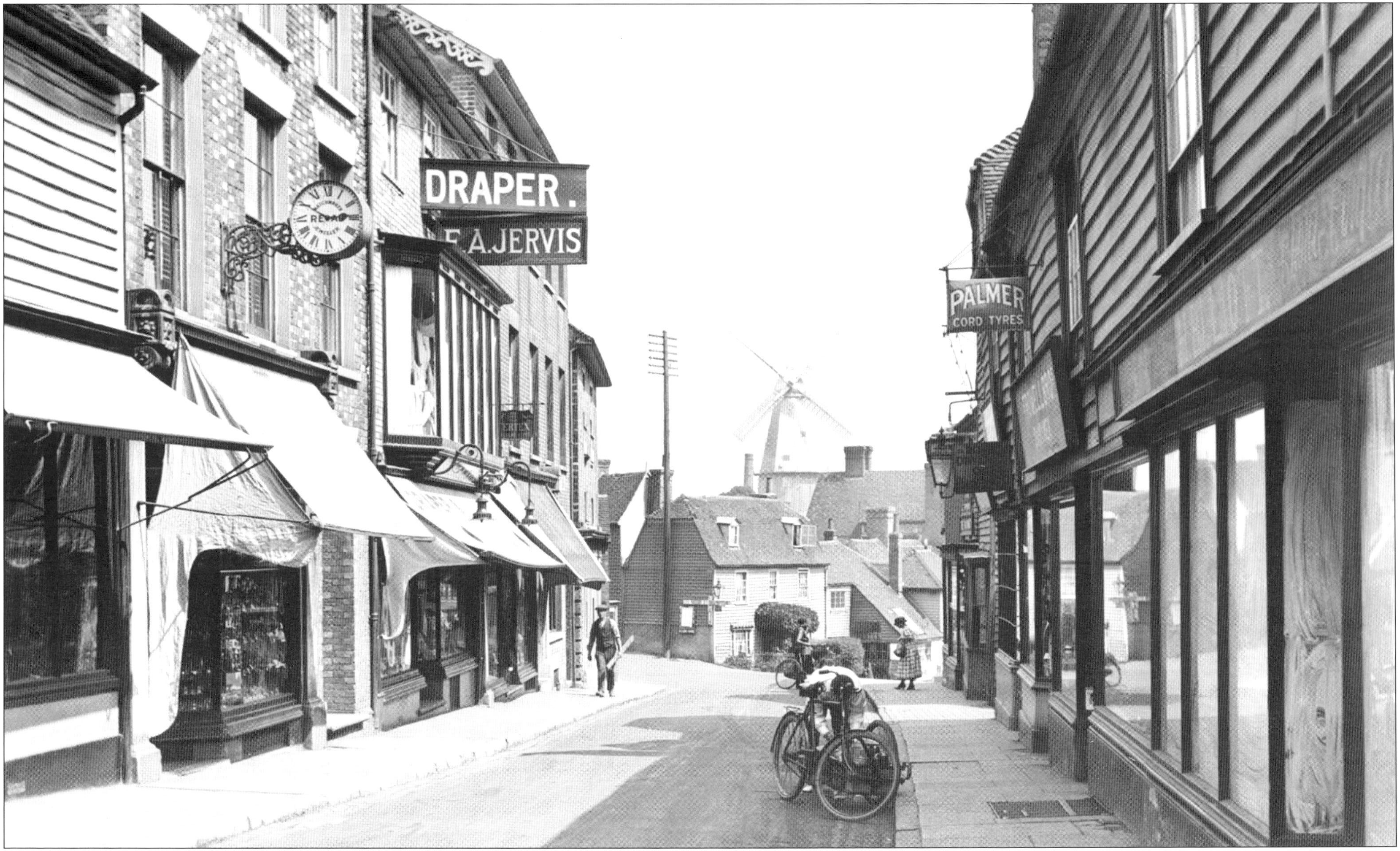


77023
A fine study of Stone Street, this time taken on a sunny day in 1925. In this view, the famous Union Mill stands proudly on the hill, whilst bikes are parked along the kerb.

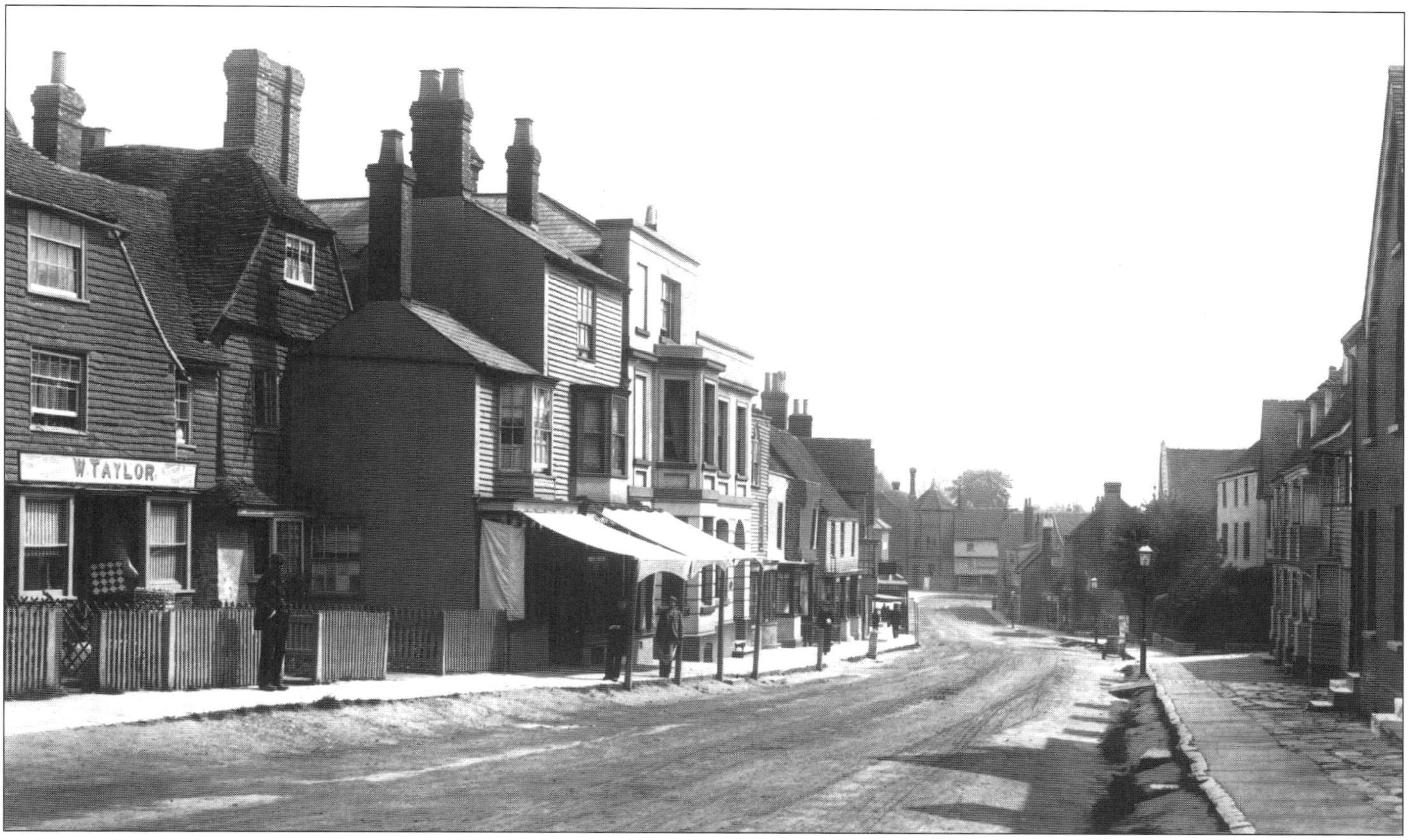


46430

Looking down Cranbrook's High Street in 1901. Note the width of the street where the market used to be held, the pleasing variety of architecture and the raised pavements.

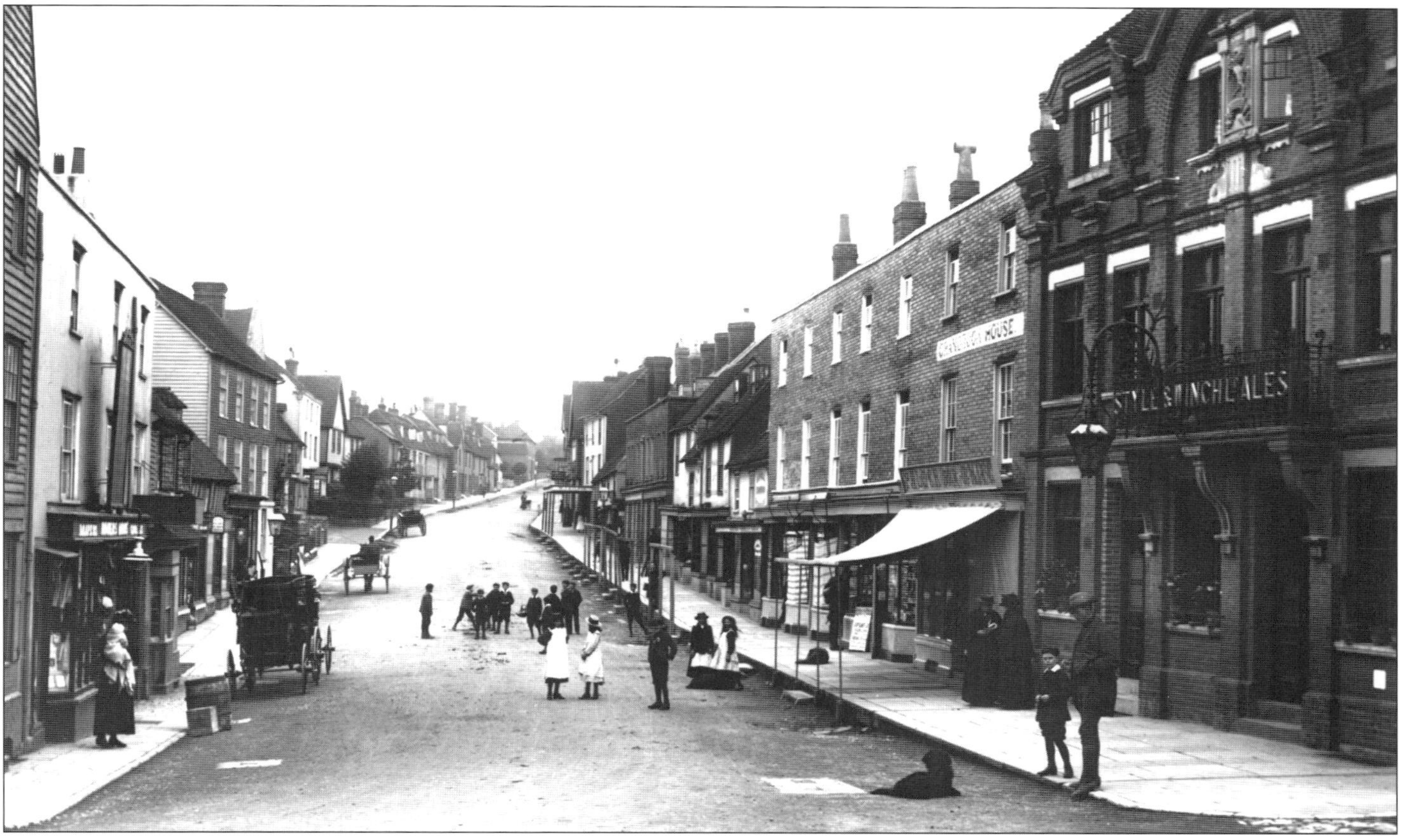

51009

A further view of the High Street, this time taken in 1903 from the junction with Stone Street looking up from where the previous picture was taken. This shows much more activity, with horse-drawn carriages and children playing in the wide road.

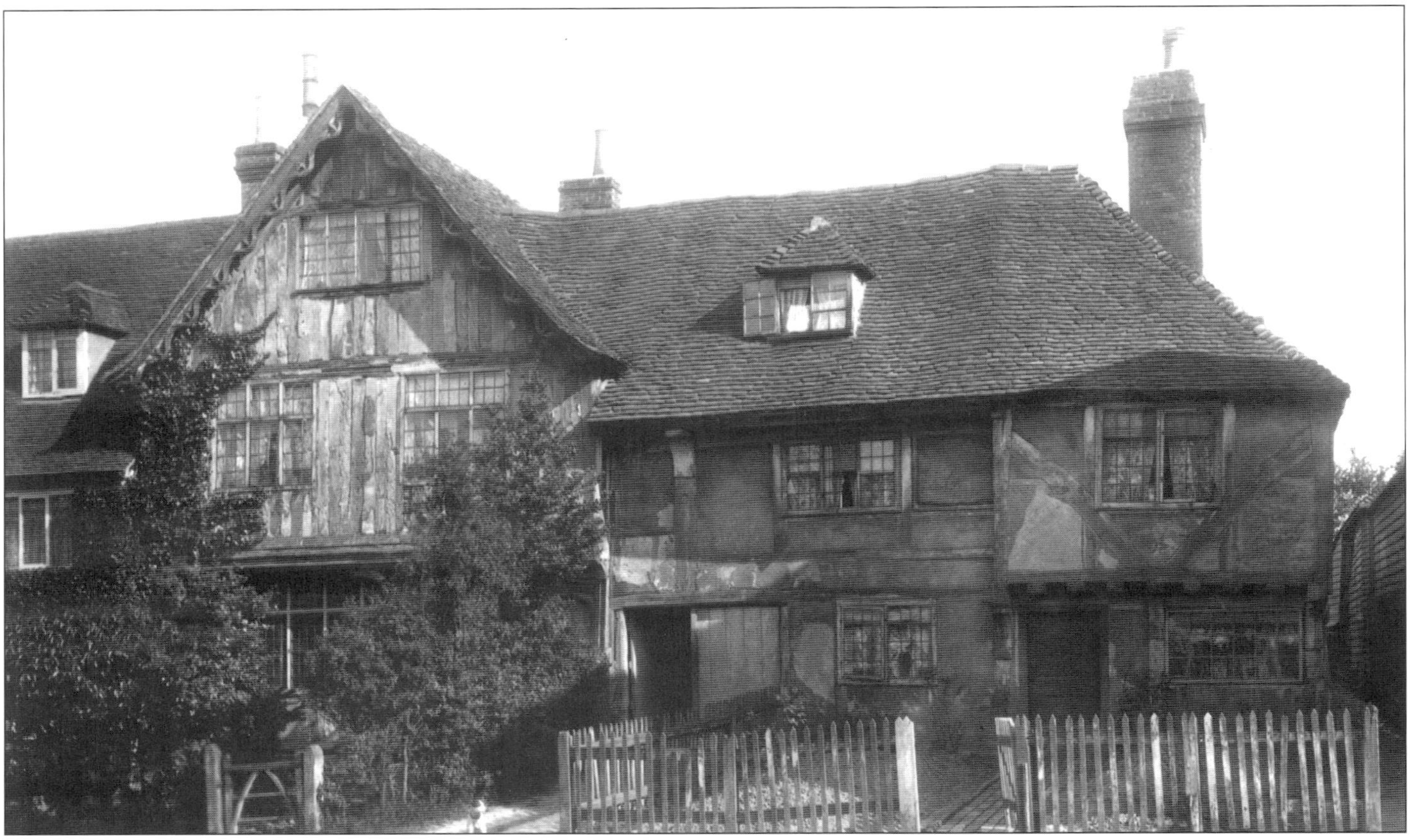

46432
Situated on the High Street is The Studio, a Wealden Hall House, with a later gable on the left-hand side. This picture was taken in 1901, before restoration. Note that it is divided into several houses.

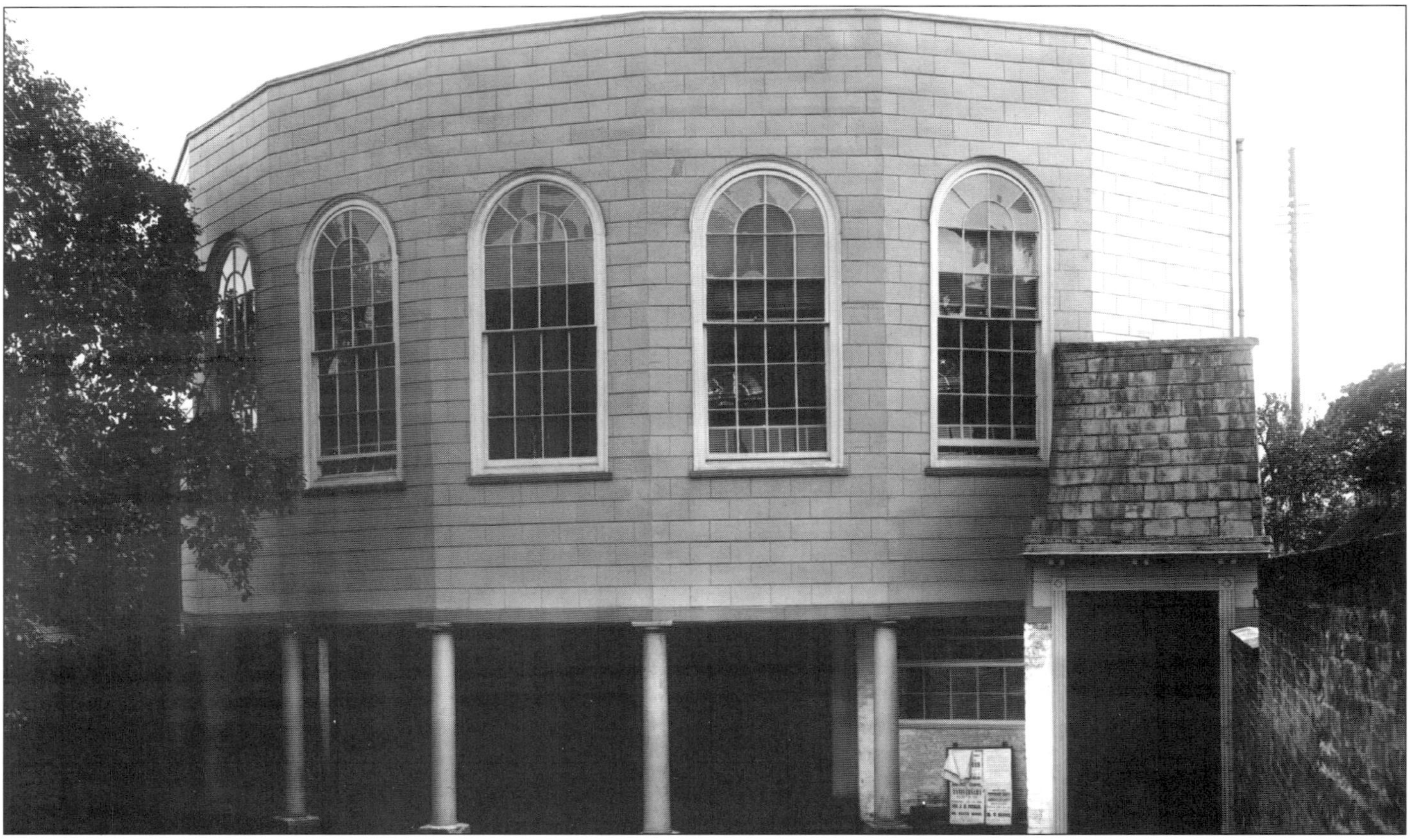

60297
The Providence Chapel was built in 1828, and was 80 years old when this picture was taken. It is one of Cranbrook's most memorable buildings, a seven-sided front made of timber, but grooved to look like stone.

# Dartford

Although Dartford, the crossing place over the River Darent, is now an industrial town, it has a long history that stretches back to Roman times and earlier. The church has Norman foundations, and there was once a priory. In later years Dartford became a shipbuilding centre. Famous for the Dartford Tunnel, it is overshadowed by the new Queen Elizabeth Bridge, carrying the M25 over the River Thames.

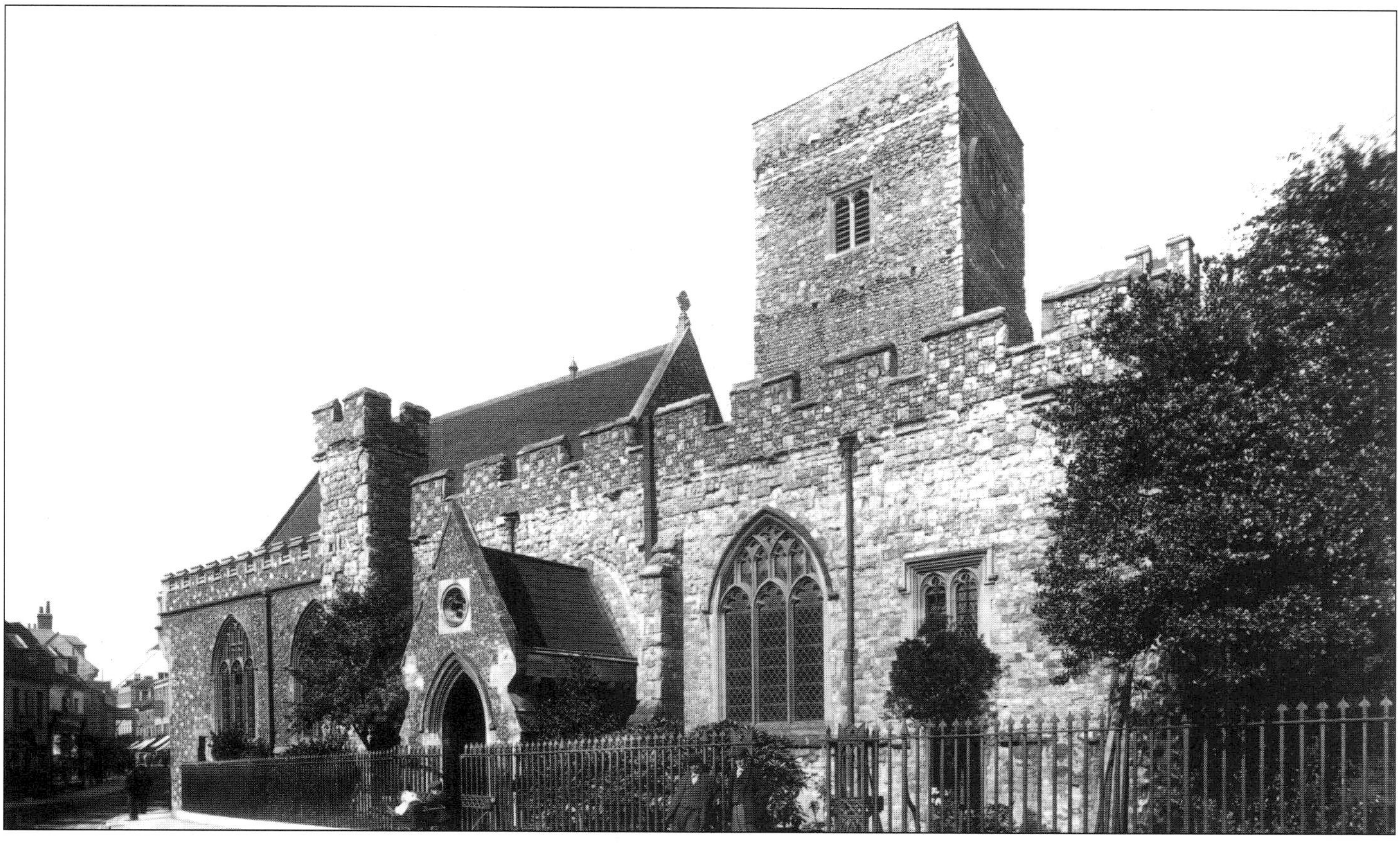

49020
A fine view of Dartford's Holy Trinity Church, taken in 1901 showing the Norman tower. Note the baby in the pram by the church door, and bystanders posing for the camera.

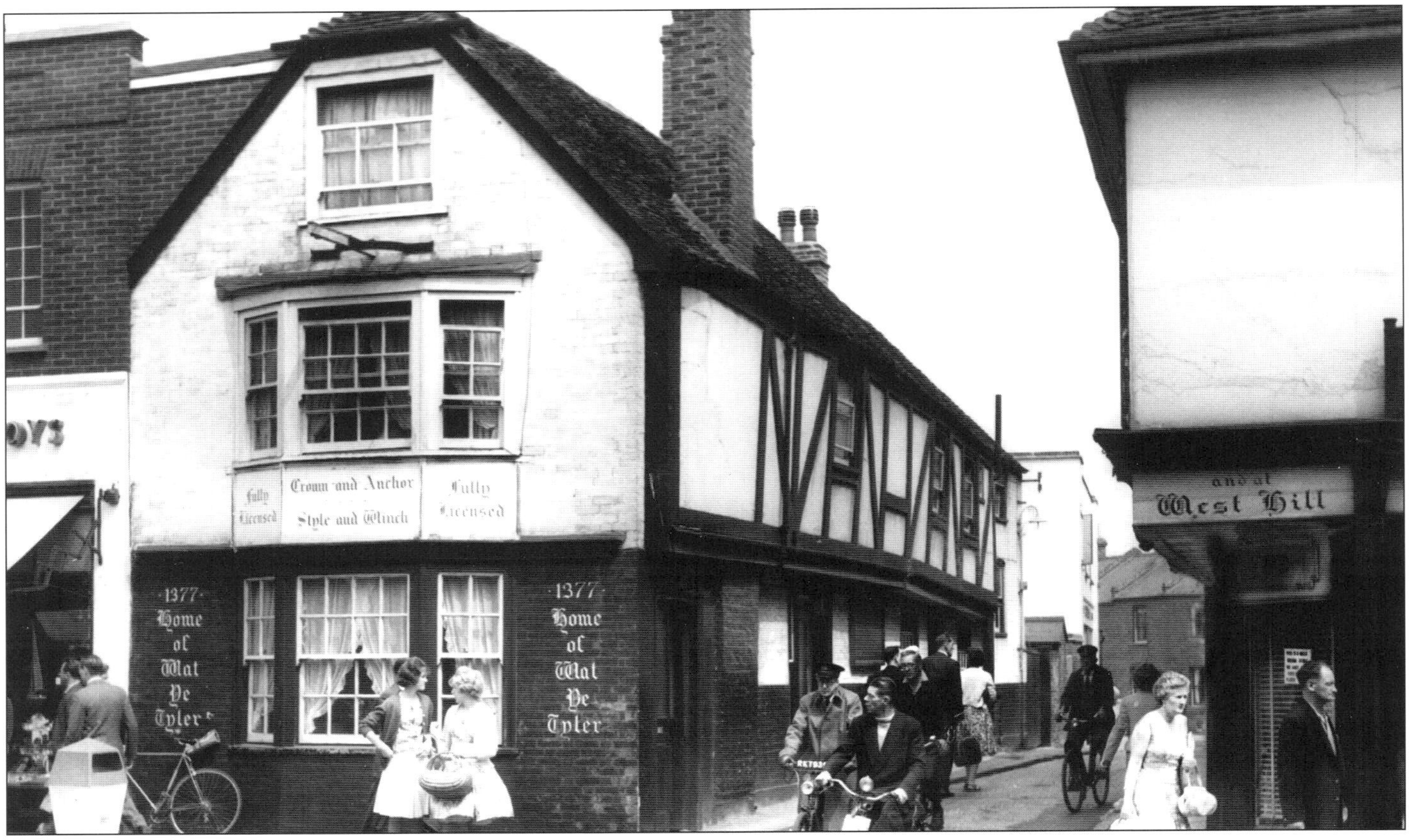


D3069

A mid-1950s view of the Crown & Anchor, showing Dartford's narrow streets. The Crown is paying homage to Dartford's celebrated rebel, Wat Tyler, who was born here in the fourteenth century. His name has now been appropriated by the pub.

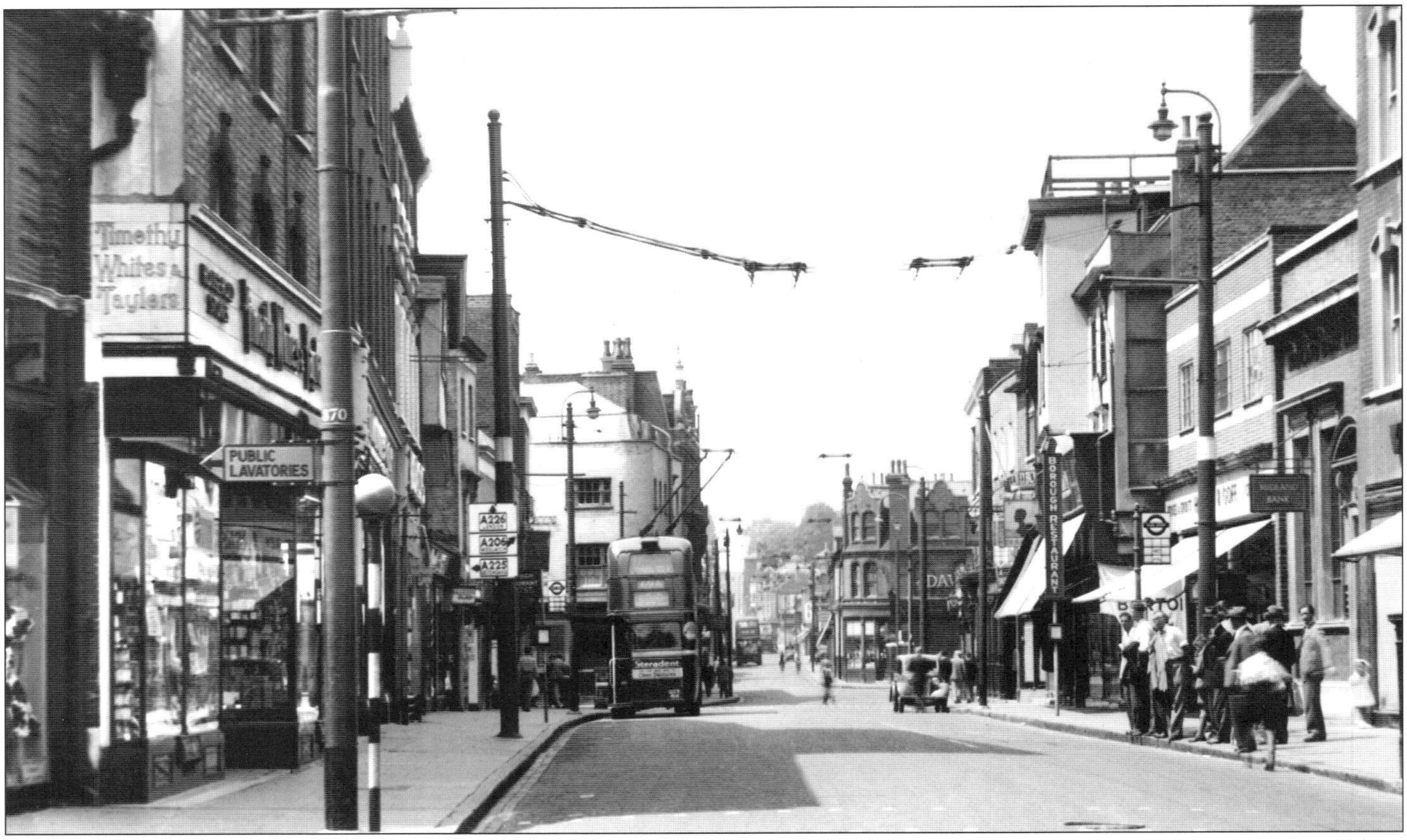


D3031

A fine view of Dartford's pleasing High Street taken in the 1950s. The lack of traffic strikes us today as remarkable, and the trolleybus emphasises that this picture was taken in an era now vanished

# Deal

Deal is a delightful small resort which became very popular Victorian times, but it is an historic place. There are attractive eighteenth and ninteenth century houses tucked away in the lanes of the Old Town. However, Deal is best known today for its attractive seafront, including a promenade and pier. The castle was built in Tudor times as part of the coastal fortifications.

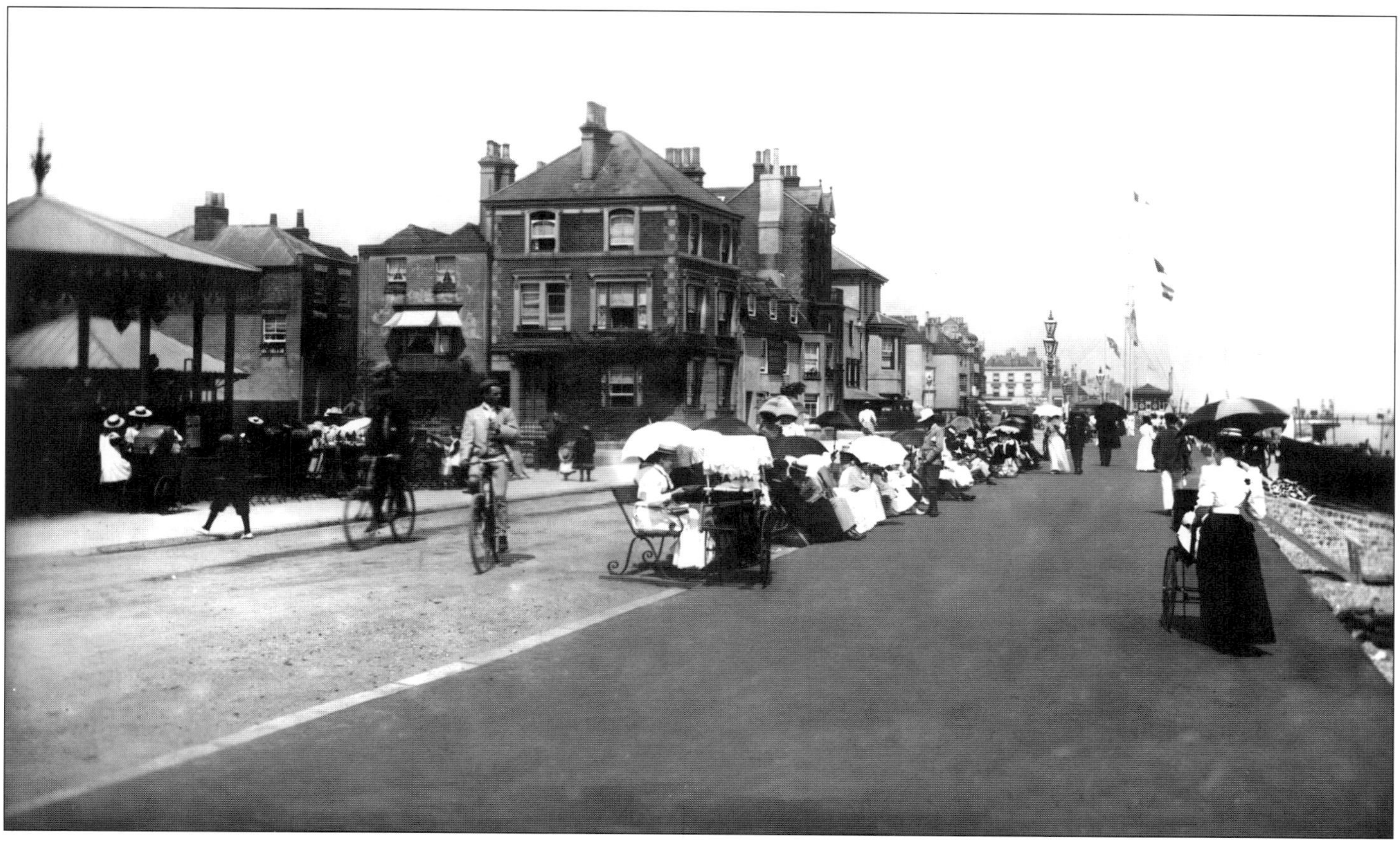

44206
A windy day on the Esplanade in 1899, epitomises the closing days of the Victorian era at a refined seaside resort. Parasols, prams and bicycles are much in evidence.

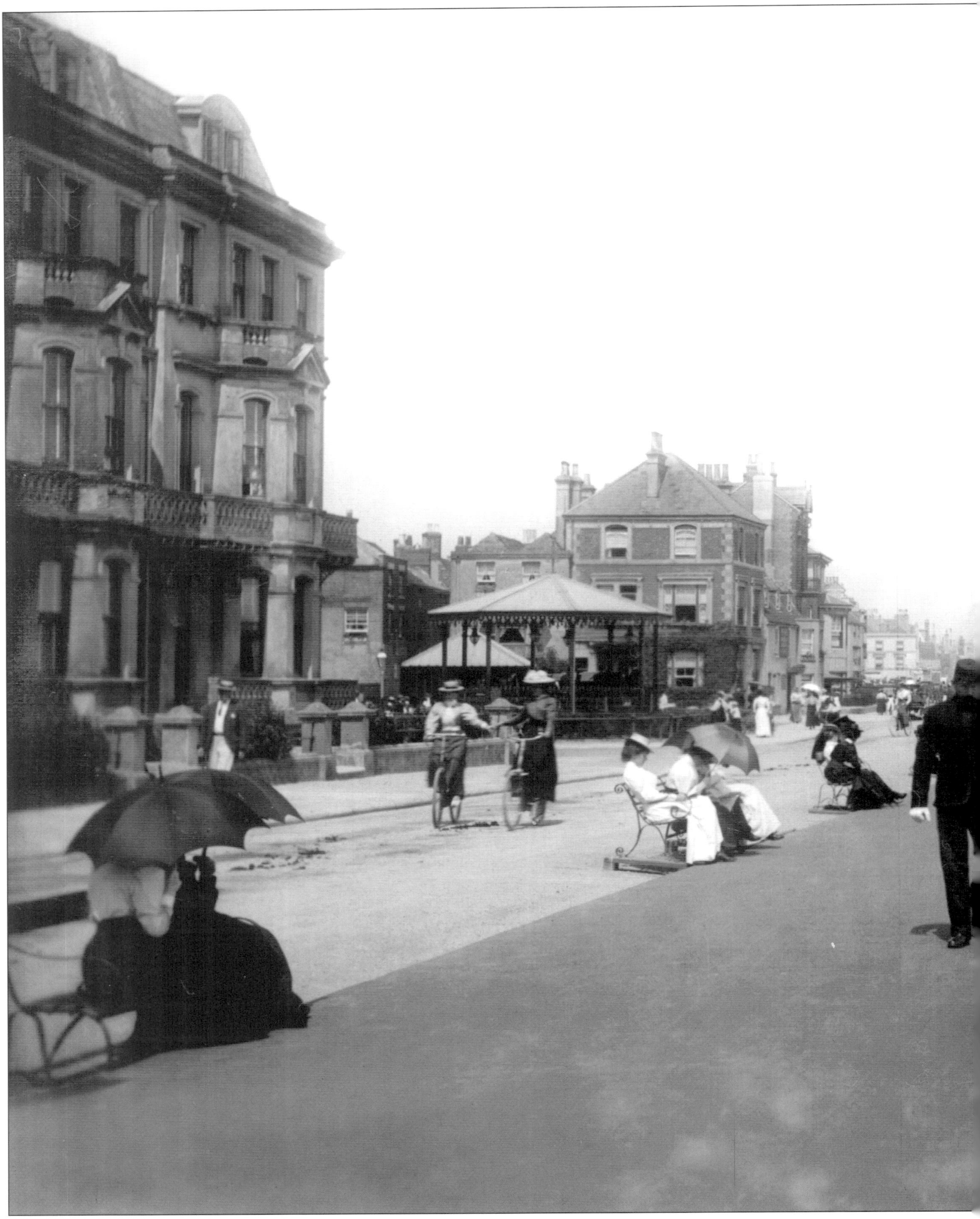

44208

This view, also of 1899, is taken from slightly further along the Esplanade. It shows clearly the steps down onto the shingle beach, together with the boats drawn up in time honoured fashion. Part of the pier can be seen.

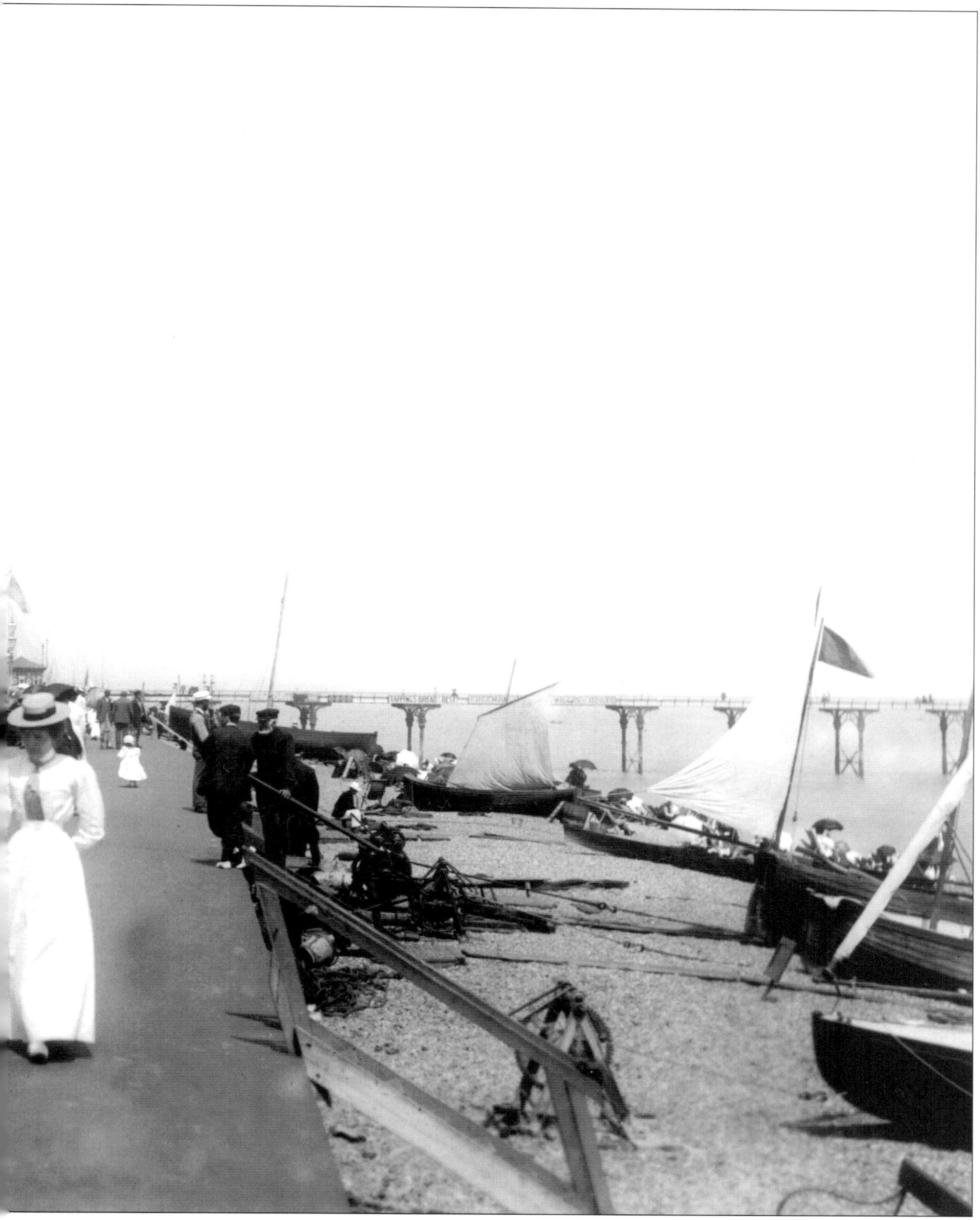

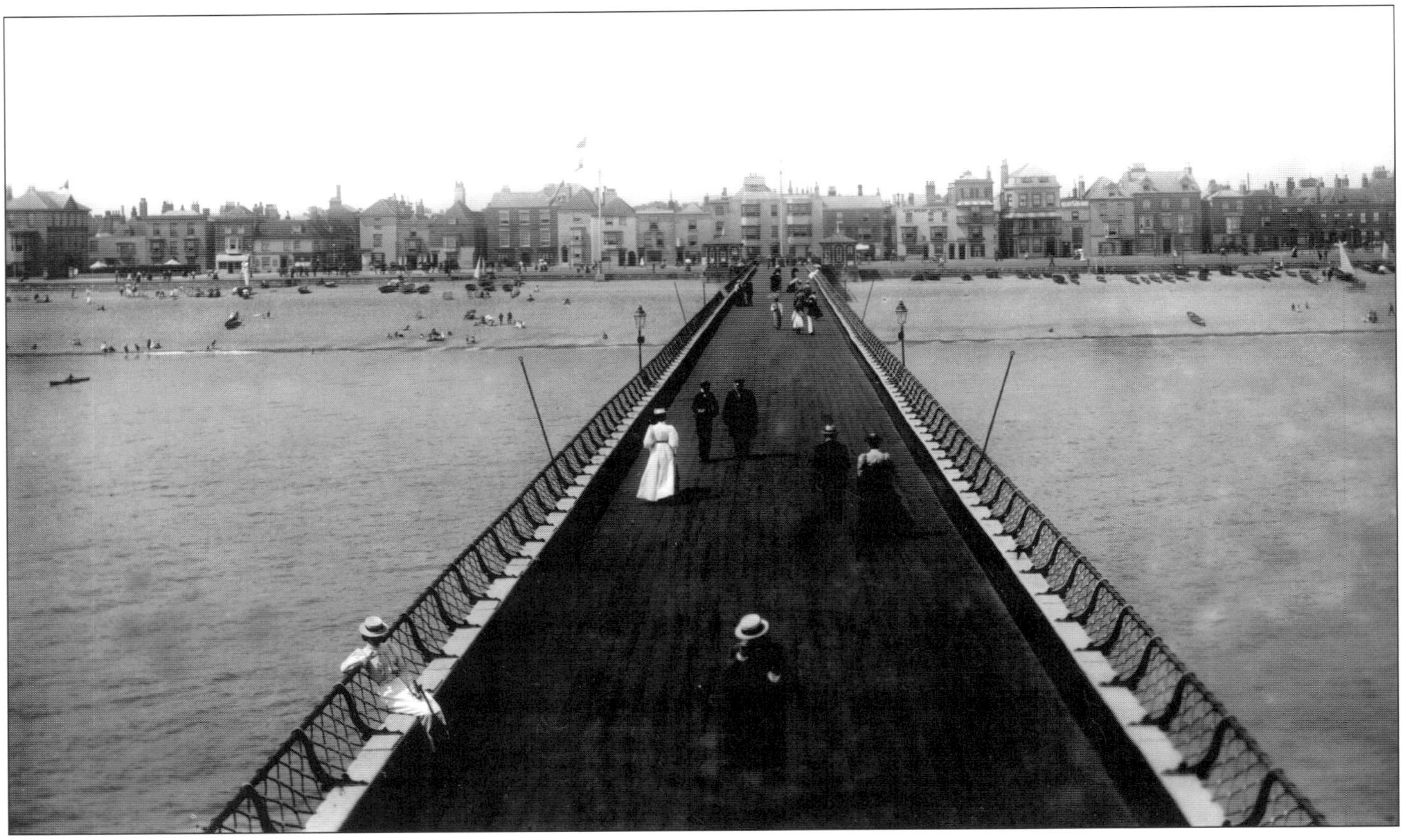

44203
Deal is an elegant town, and nowhere is this clearer than in this 1899 view, taken from the Pier pavilion looking back to the town. The grace of the pier is matched by the best dresses and suits of the promenaders. The pier has now been replaced with one built in the 1950s.

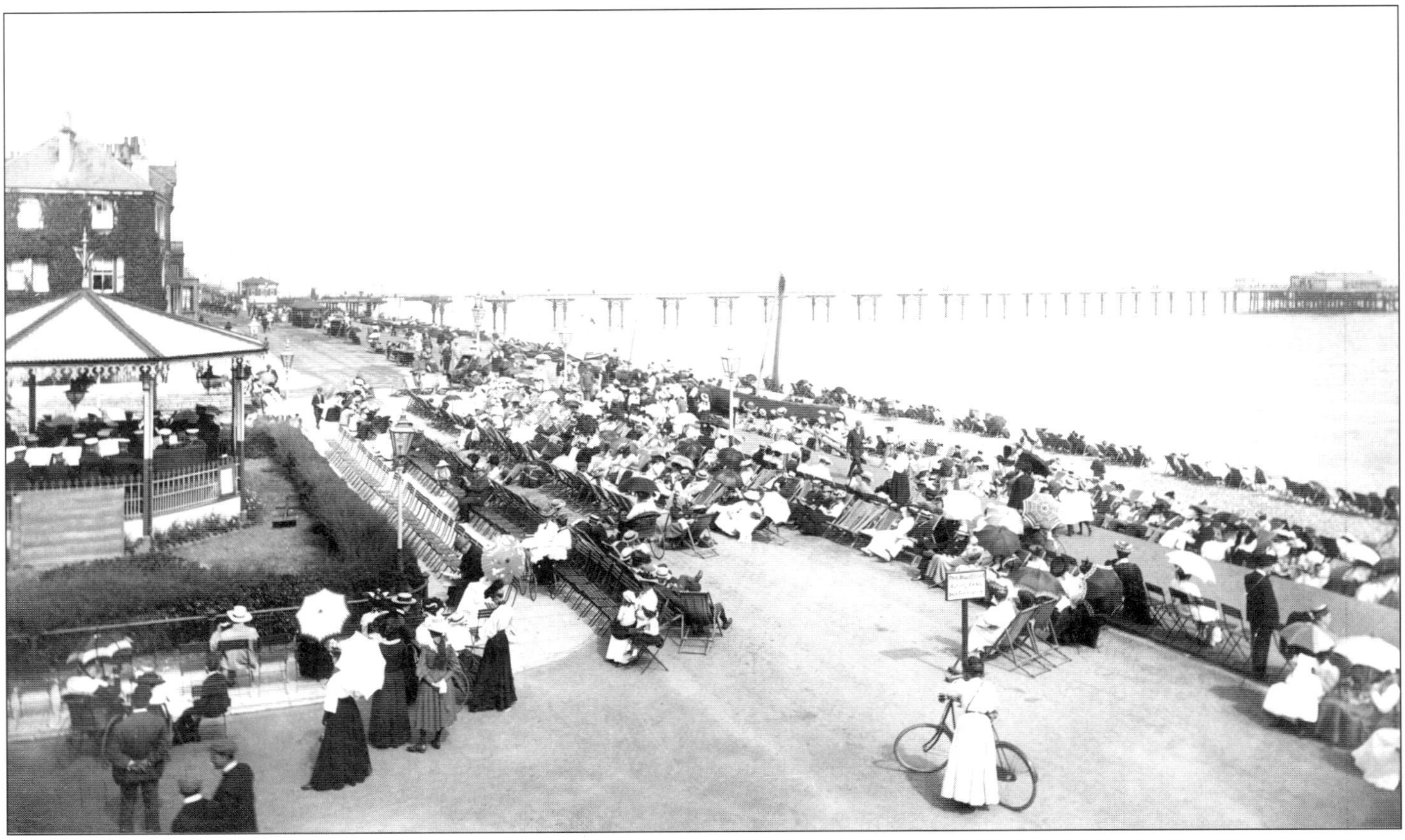

56911
This view, taken in 1906, shows the bandstand and the graceful pier and pavilion. The beach is now full of deckchairs, and a band is busy entertaining the summer visitors.

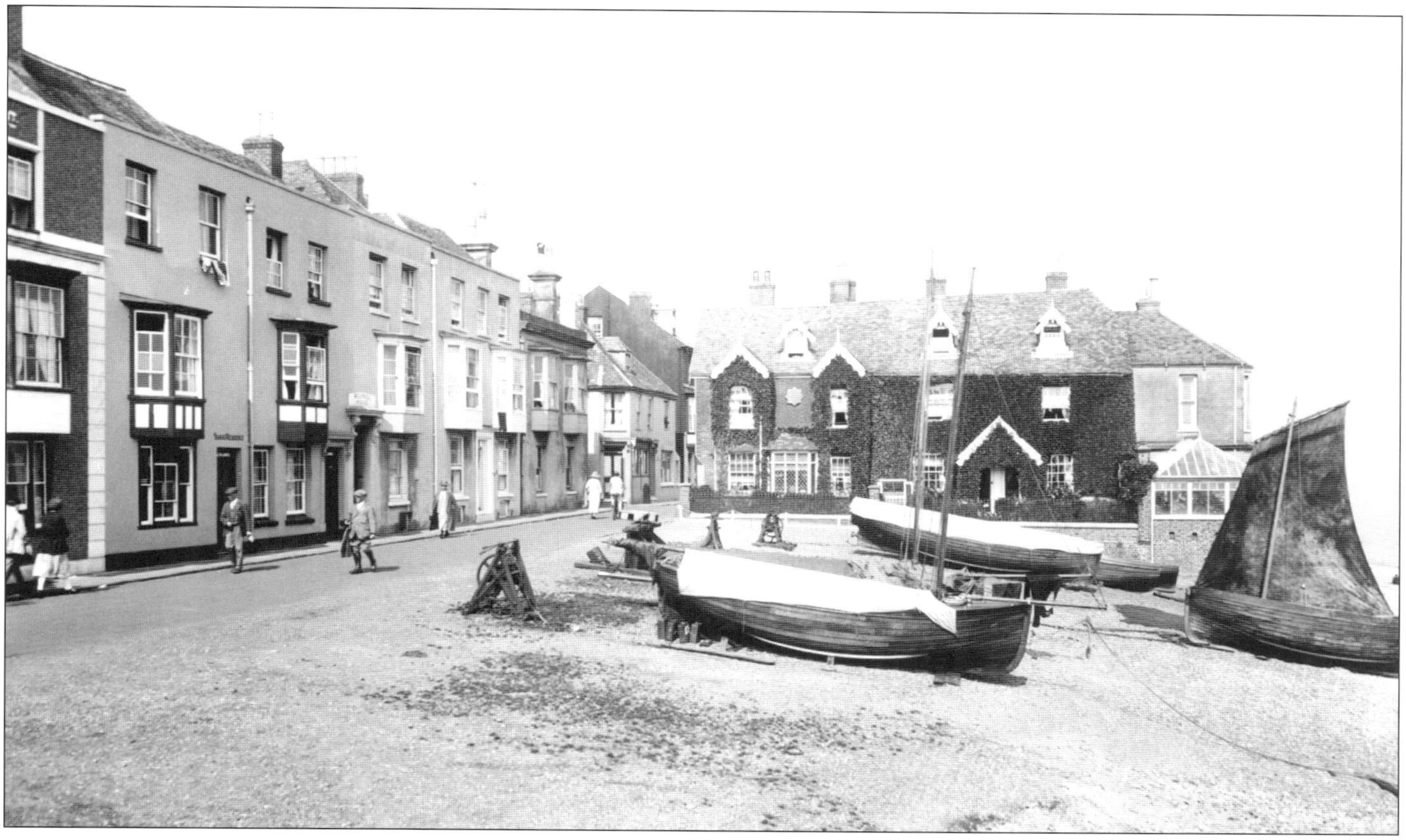

76068
This interesting view of Beach Street was taken in 1924. The fishing boats are drawn up onto the shingle beach, and in the foreground can be seen the capstans used to haul the boats up the beach.

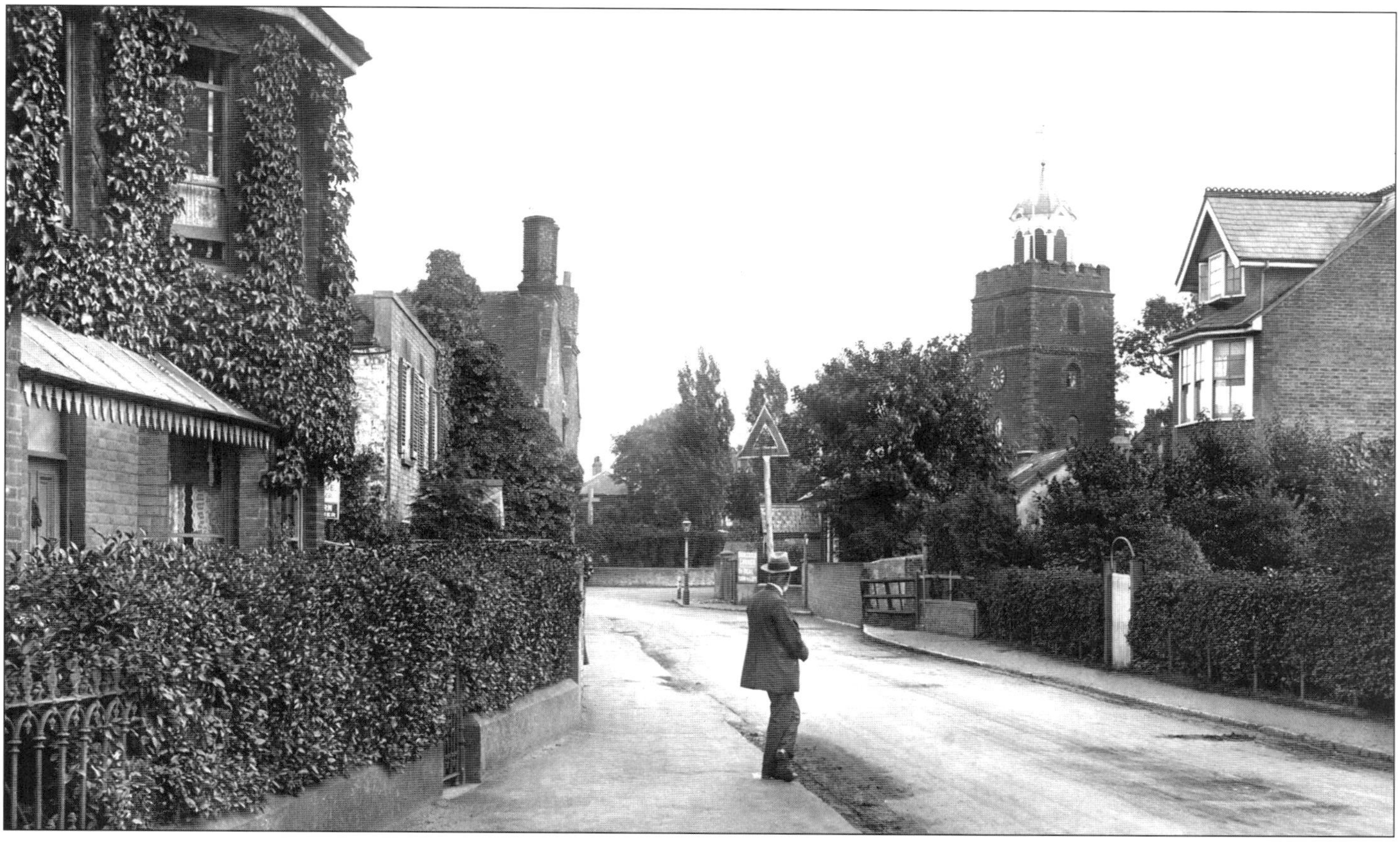

68501
The old village of Deal, now known as Upper Deal, as it looked in 1918. The parish church is St Leonard's, basically medieval but much rebuilt in 1684 and sporting a cupola, is a landmark for shipping.

# Dover

One of England's most important seaports, and still very busy today. The castle dates from Norman and medieval times, but was remodelled greatly in the Napoleonic era. The site was first developed by the Romans, and the Roman lighthouse stands within the modern castle walls. The old harbour lies under the modern town, which was hit by bombing in the Second World War.

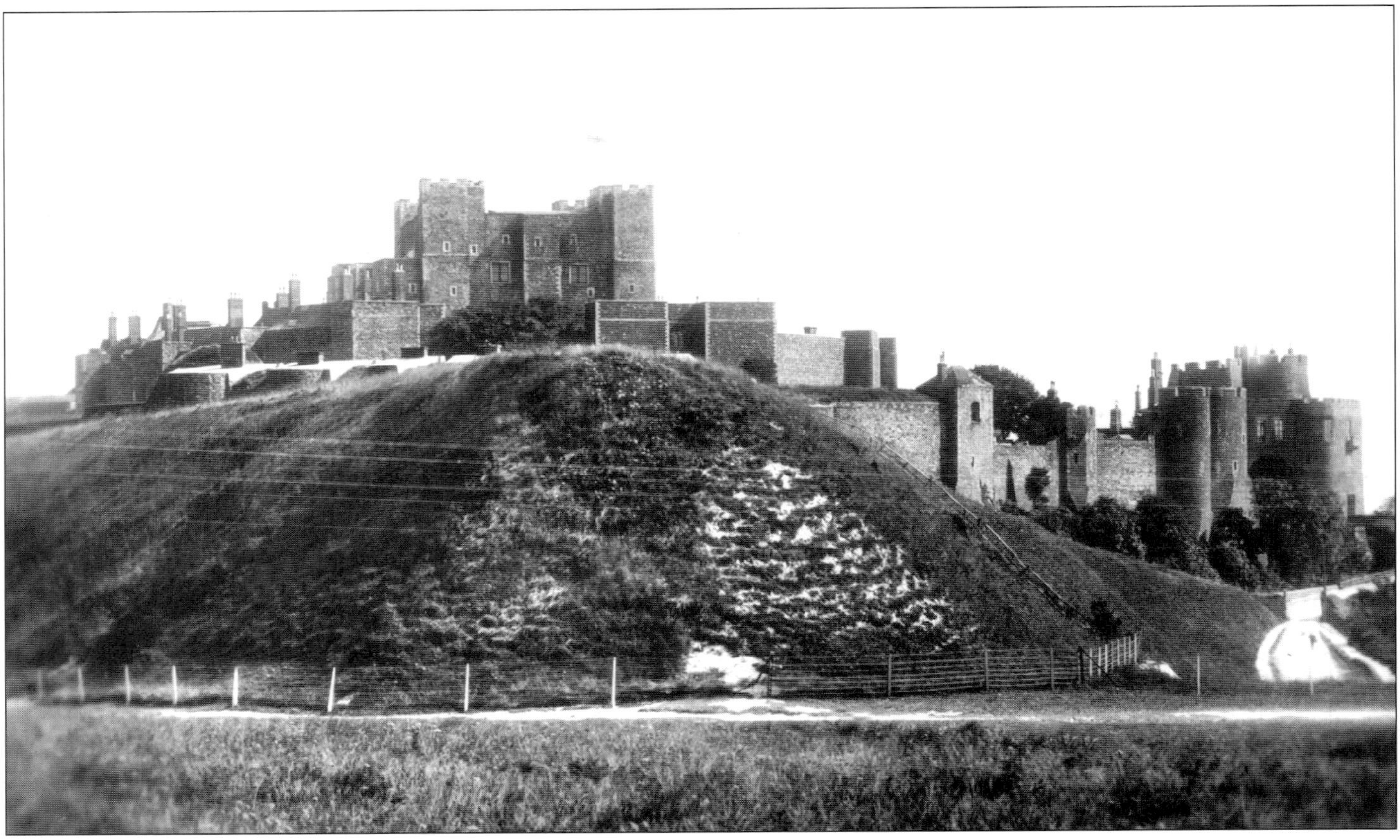

25703
A rather menacing view of the famous castle, taken in 1890. It is a magnificent building, which dominates the town and the harbour. It was always a vital fortification, and was still used by the Army up until the late 1950s.

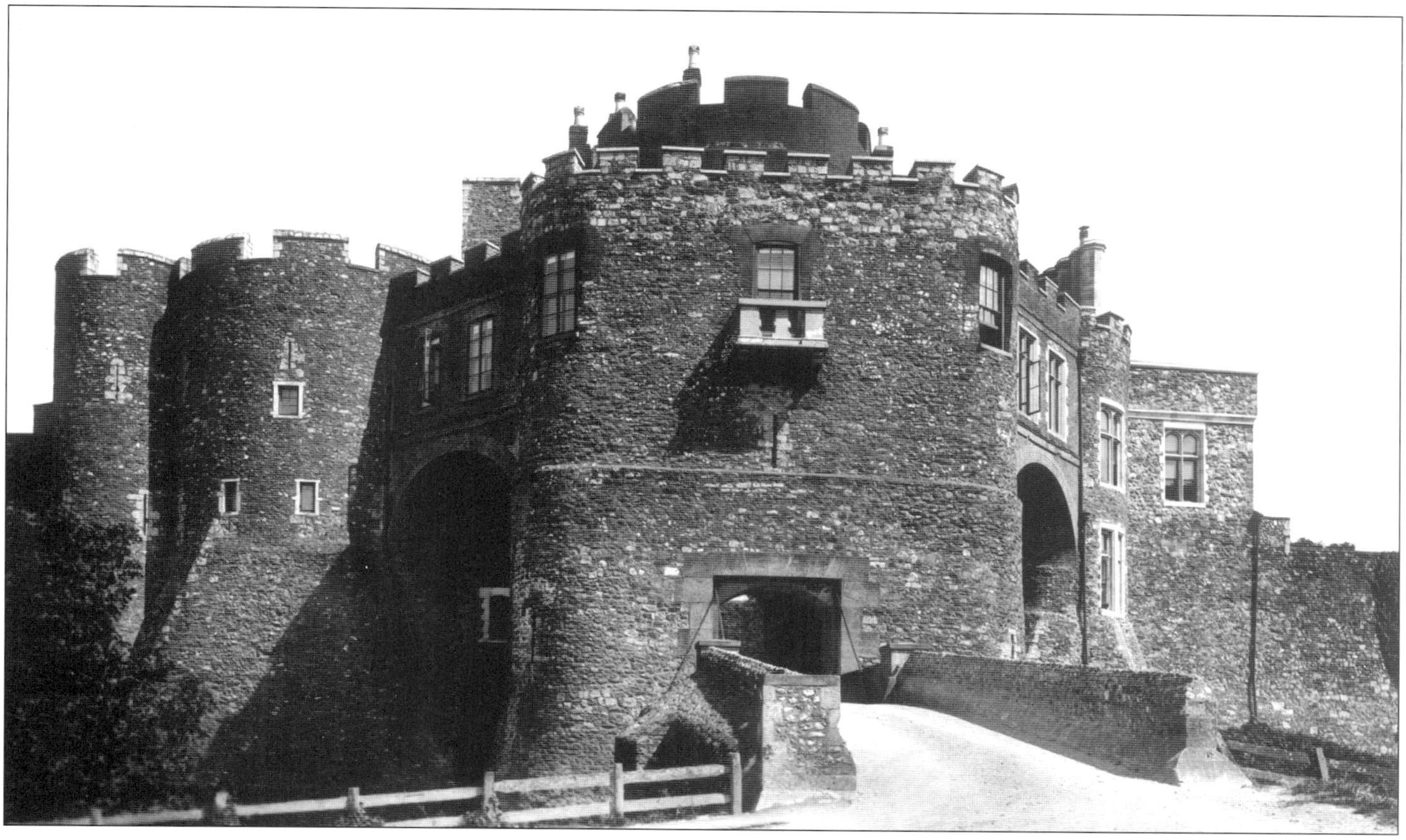

25707
The enormous proportions of the castle can be seen in this view of one of the three entrances to the castle, Constable's Tower. Today, the castle is in the care of English Heritage.

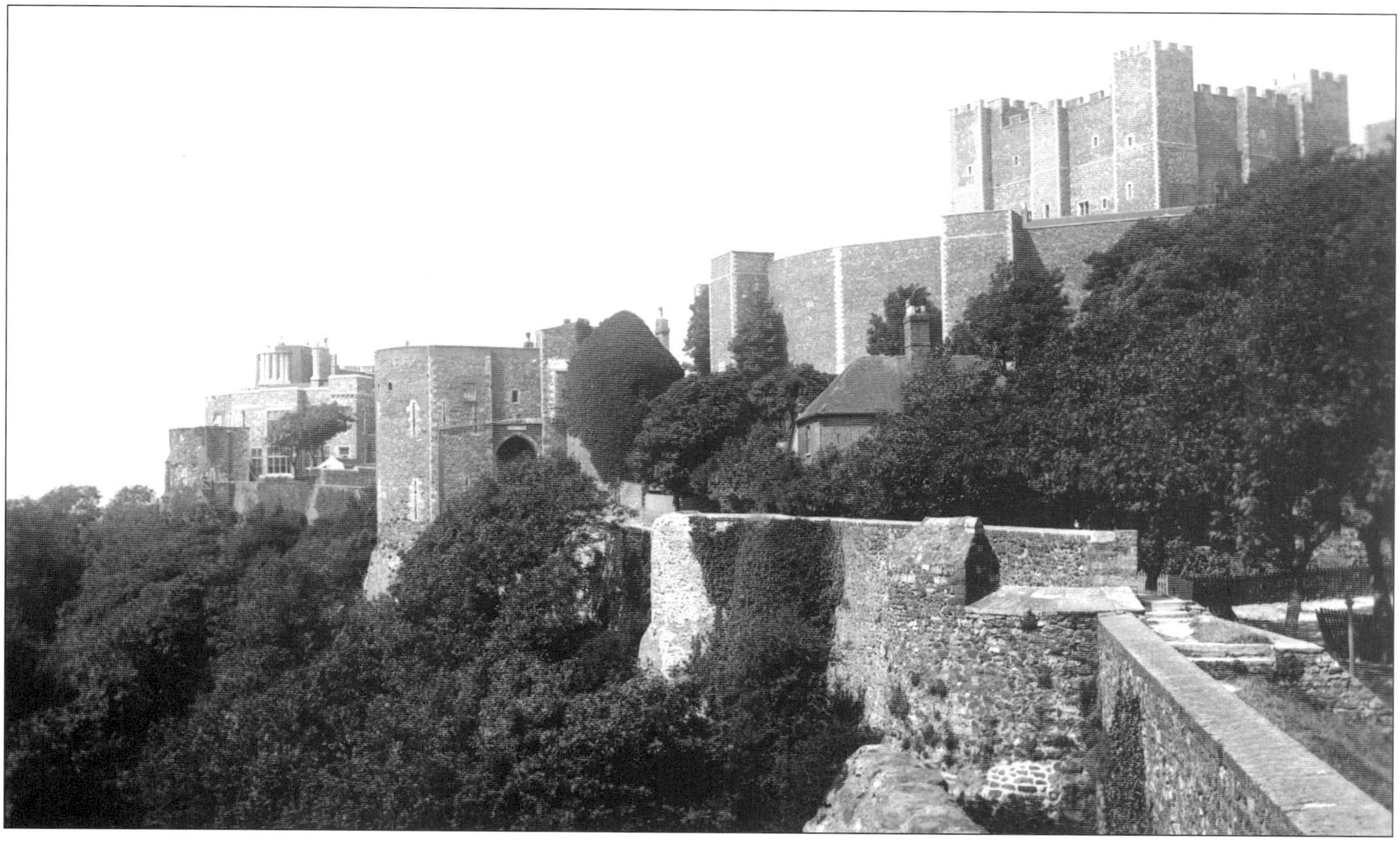

25705
A fine 1890 study of the castle, showing the vast curtain wall and the medieval Castle Keep. It was built by Henry II and is the main residential building.

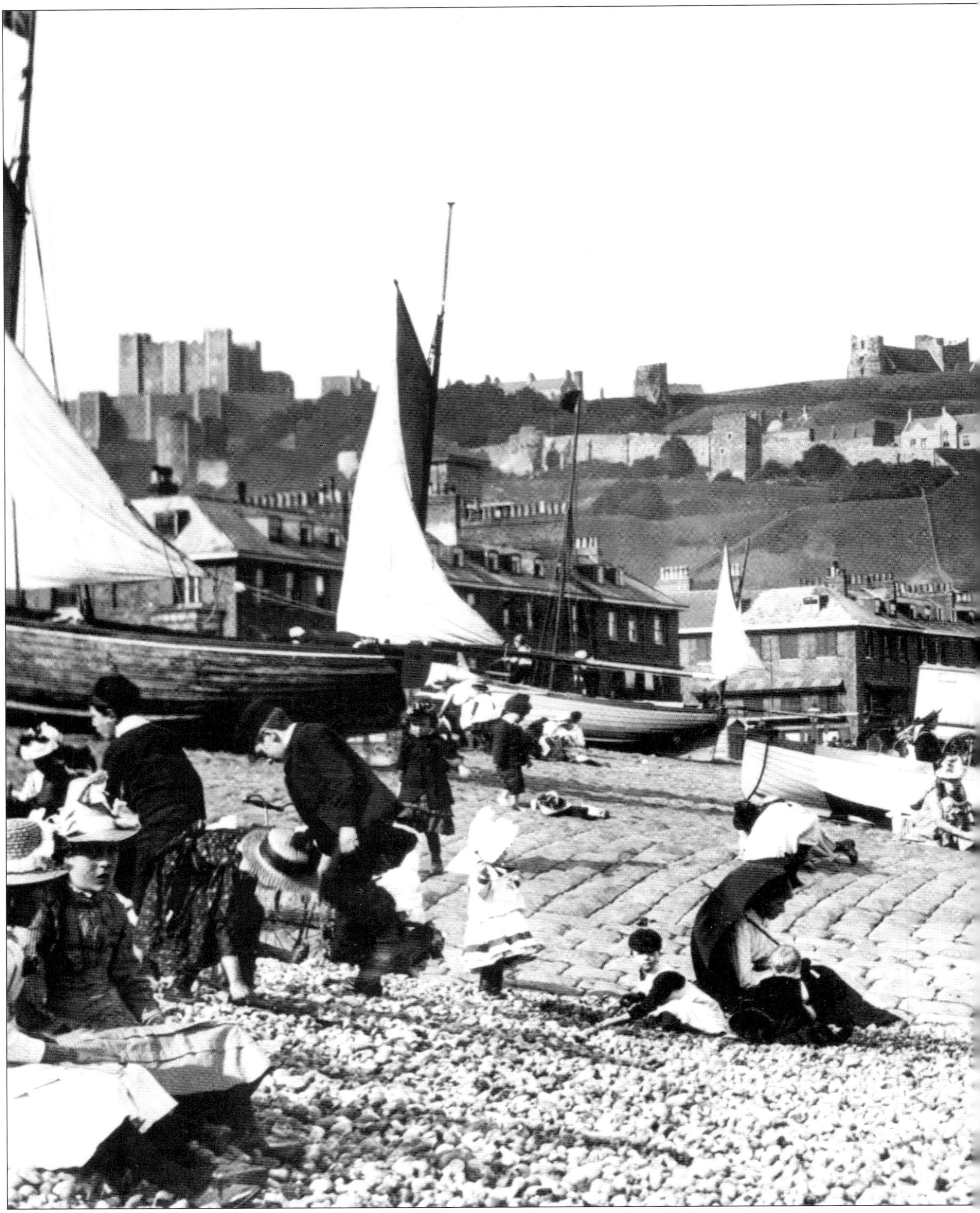

25699
This picture, also taken in 1890, shows a shift in scene down to the beach, looking east to the castle and the chalk cliffs. Boats and holidaymakers are clearly enjoying a day in the Victorian sunshine.

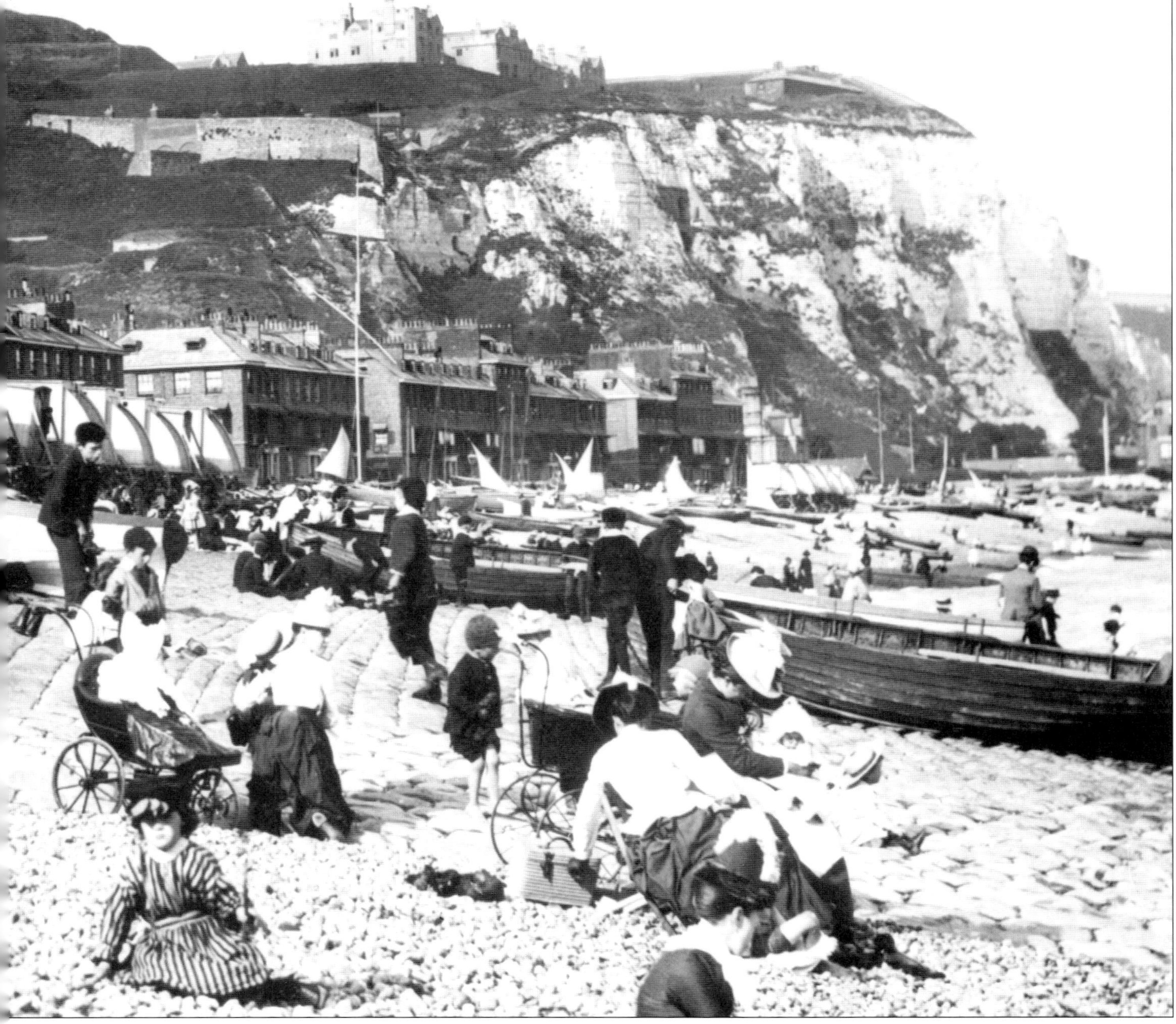

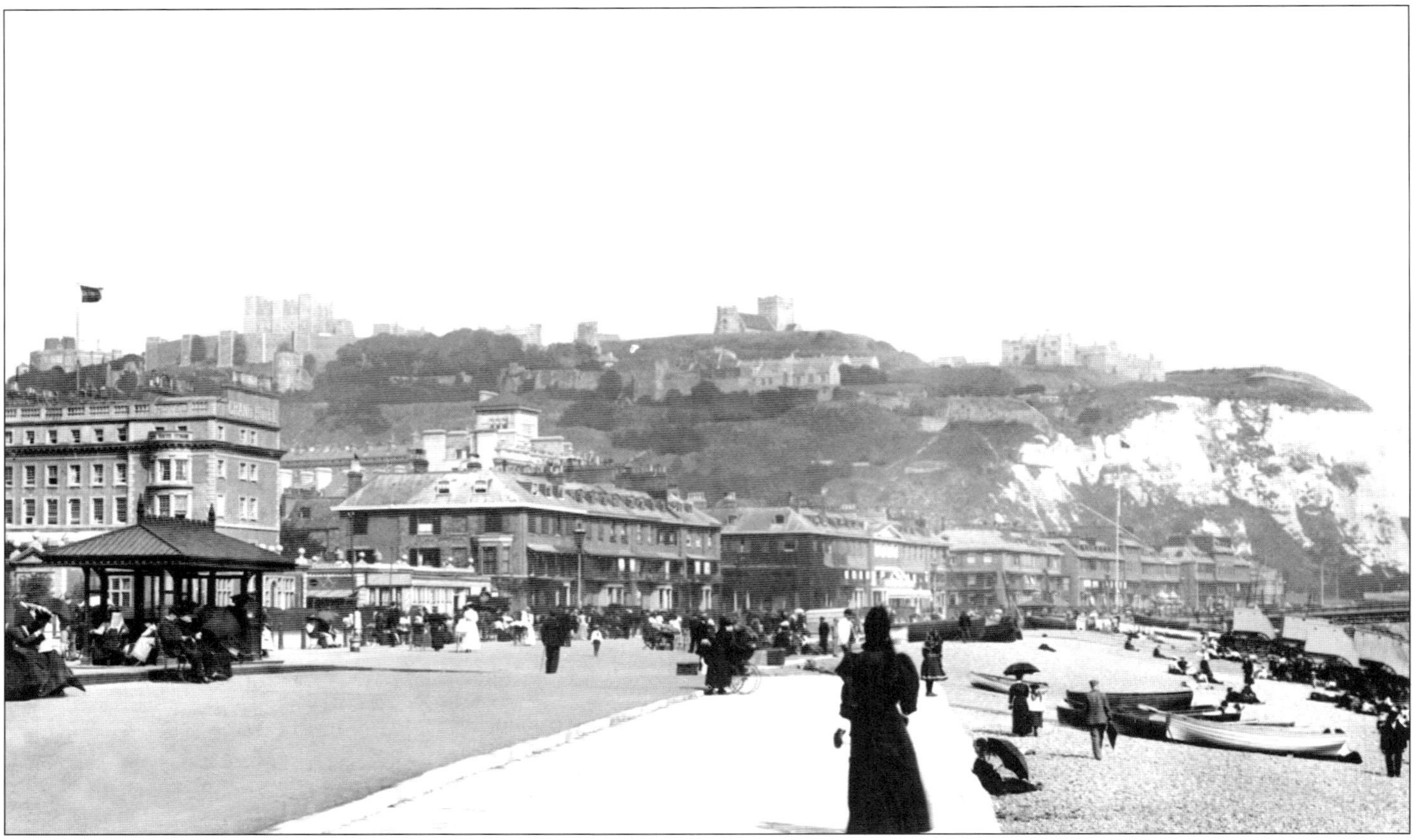

44794

A fine view of Dover's sweeping Esplanade, taken in 1899, showing bathing machines pulled down near the water. Dominating the scene is the castle, with the Saxon St Mary's Church, together with the Roman lighthouse, in the centre.

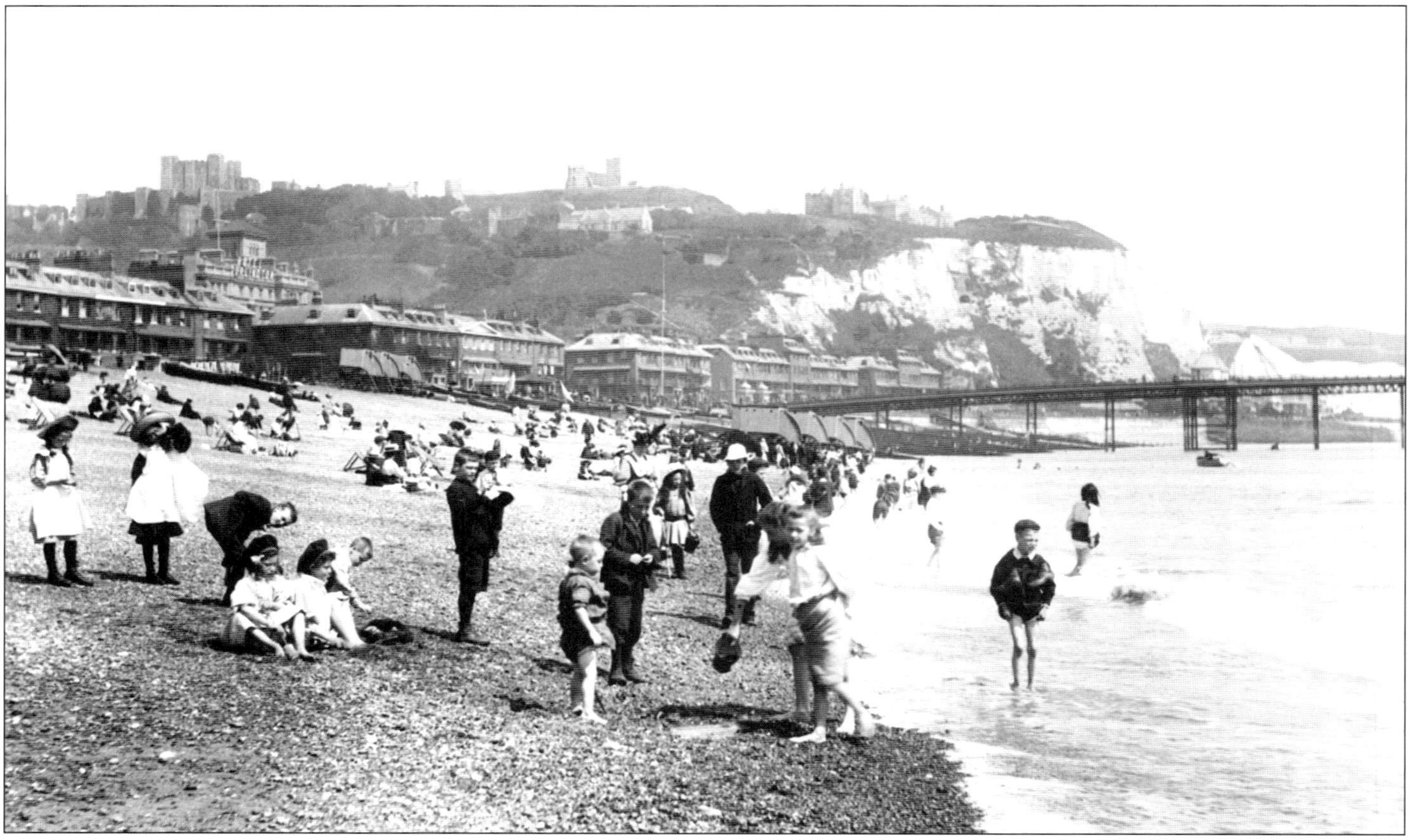

60402

A 1908 view of Dover Beach, showing a delightful grouping of children enjoying a paddle in the sea. In this timeless scene, the guardian white cliffs can be seen in the background.

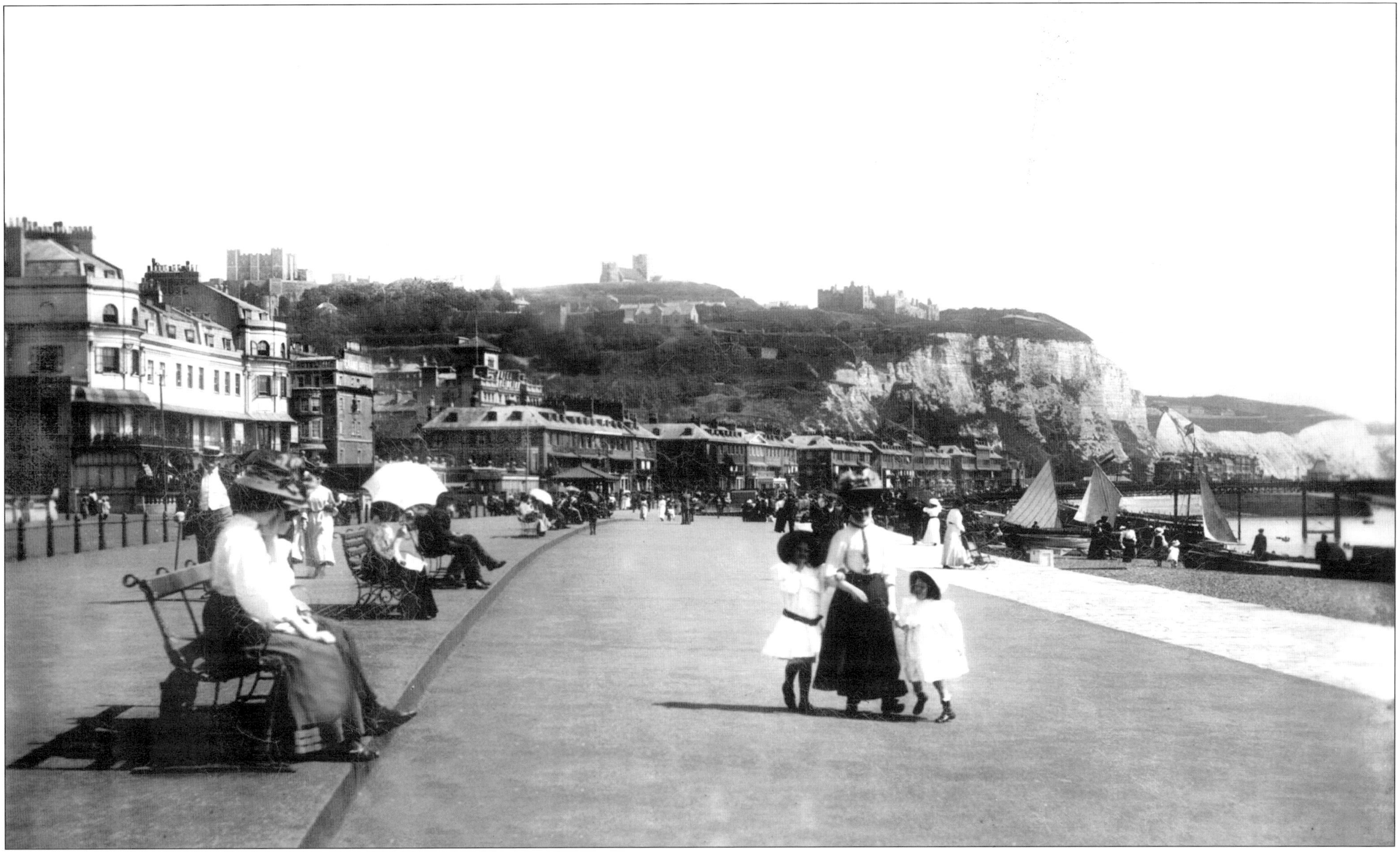

60393
Another 1908 view, this time taken from up on the promenade. Parasols and hats are much in evidence on this sunny summer day, as a woman and two girls pose for the photographer.

# Faversham

There has been a settlement at Faversham since Roman times, and this little town at the head of a tidal creek still has a commercial quay. Although the centre of an industrial area, notably brewing, the town retains an ancient peace. It was granted a charter in Saxon times.

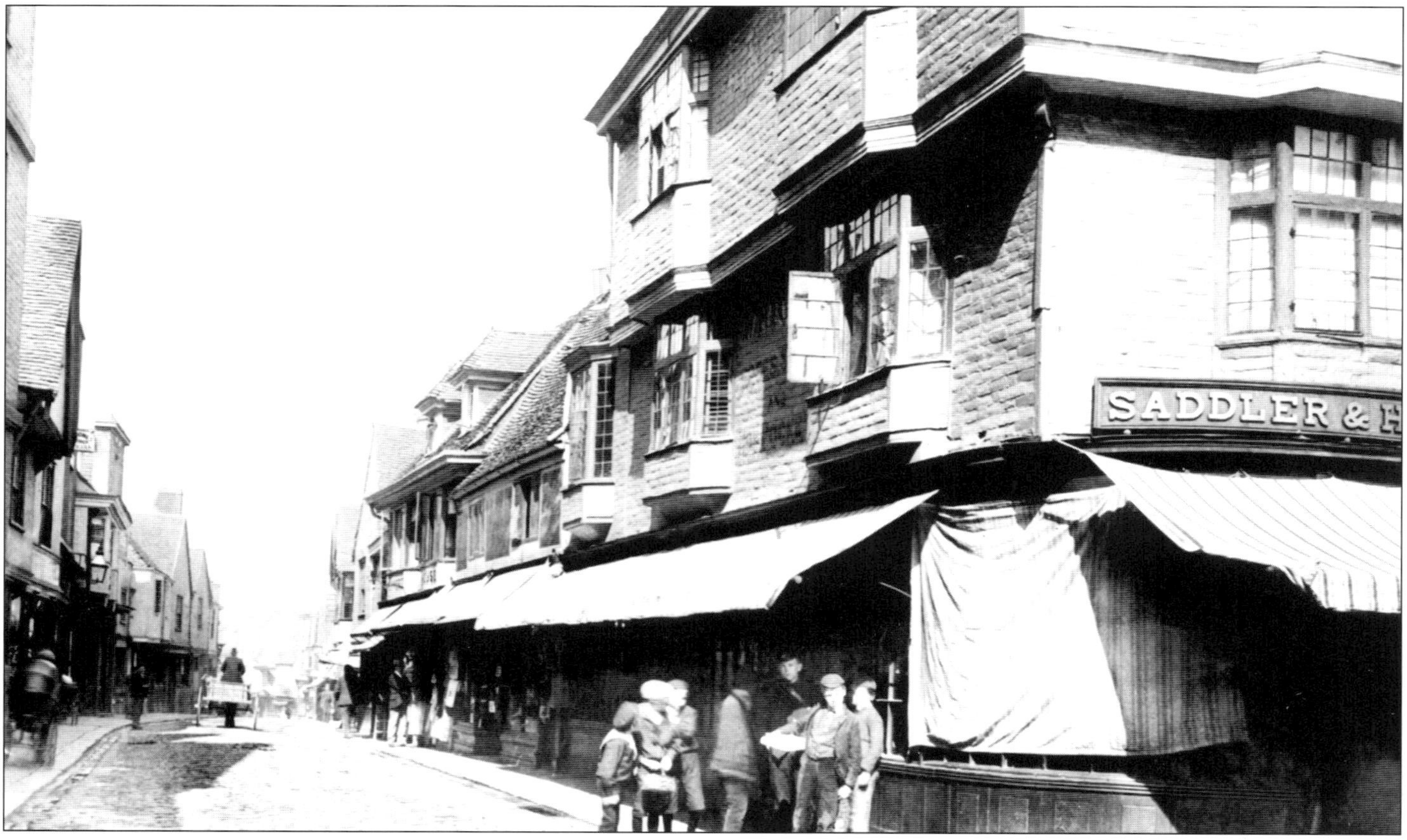


31470
A 1892 view of West Street, Faversham's most famous street. It is lined with many historic buildings, and connects the historic town with Faversham Creek. When this picture was taken, the street was cobbled.

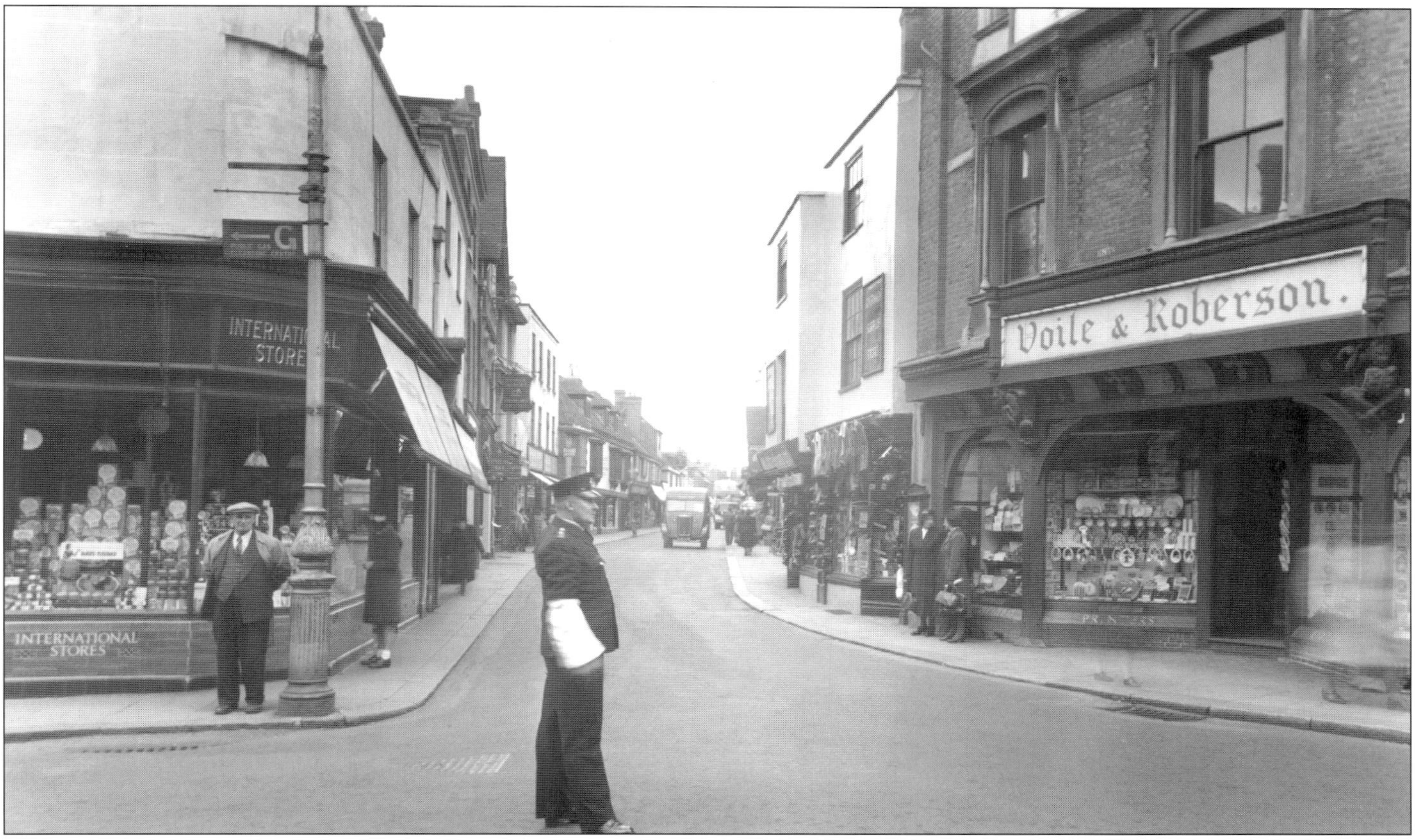


F13019

A 1950s view of Preston Street, which links the station with the market town centre. A policeman stands on points duty, but once again, one is struck by the lack of heavy traffic.

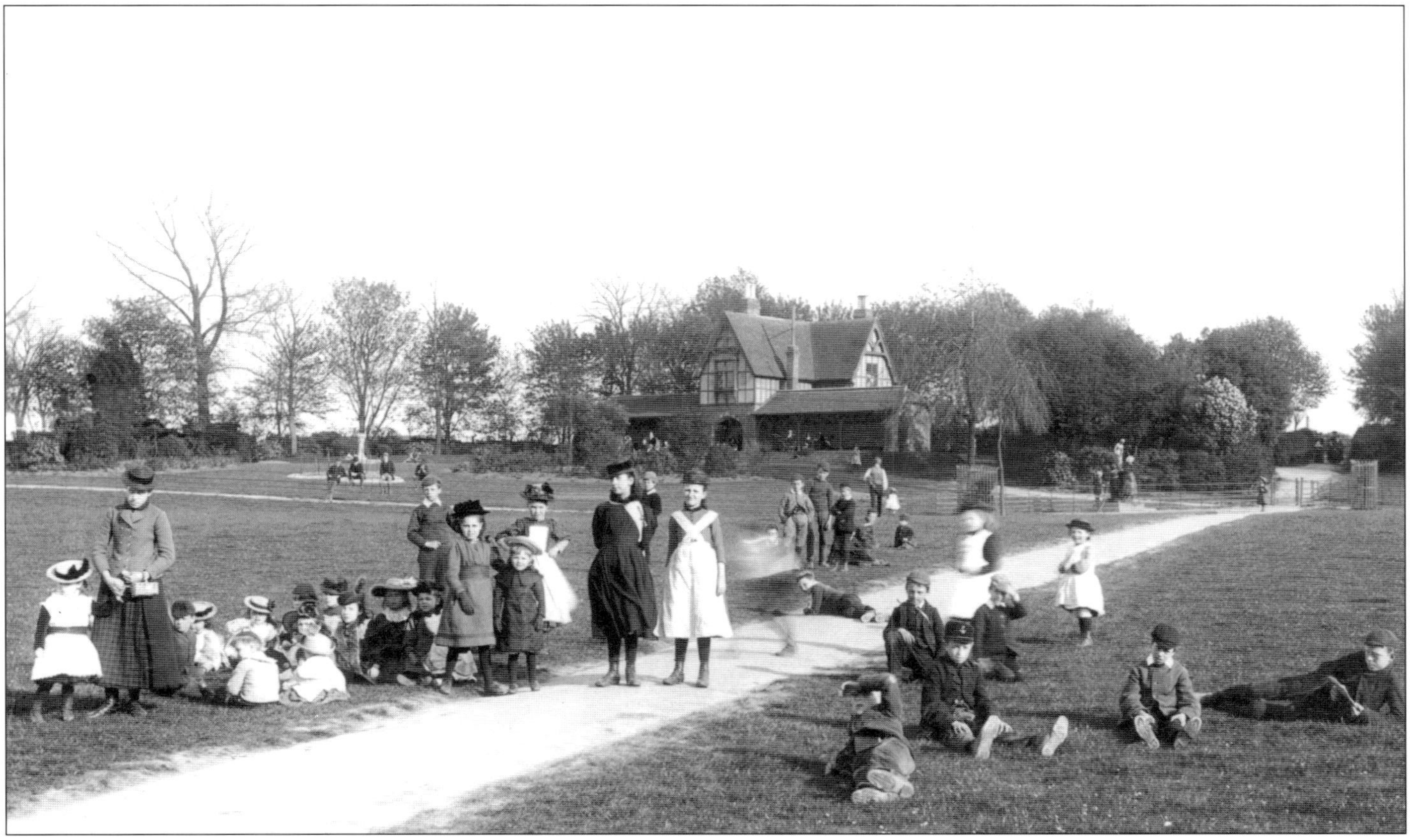

31474

Faversham Recreation Ground in 1892 showing a group of children posing for the photographer. They have managed, with one notable exception in the middle, to keep still for the length of time exposures needed in those days.

# FOLKESTONE

Folkestone has been a channel port since Saxon times, and France is visible on clear days. The Old Town is based around the steep narrow streets of the fishing harbour. The extensive seaside resort was developed in Victorian days, after the arrival of the railway. The docks are still busy, but the pier has now gone.

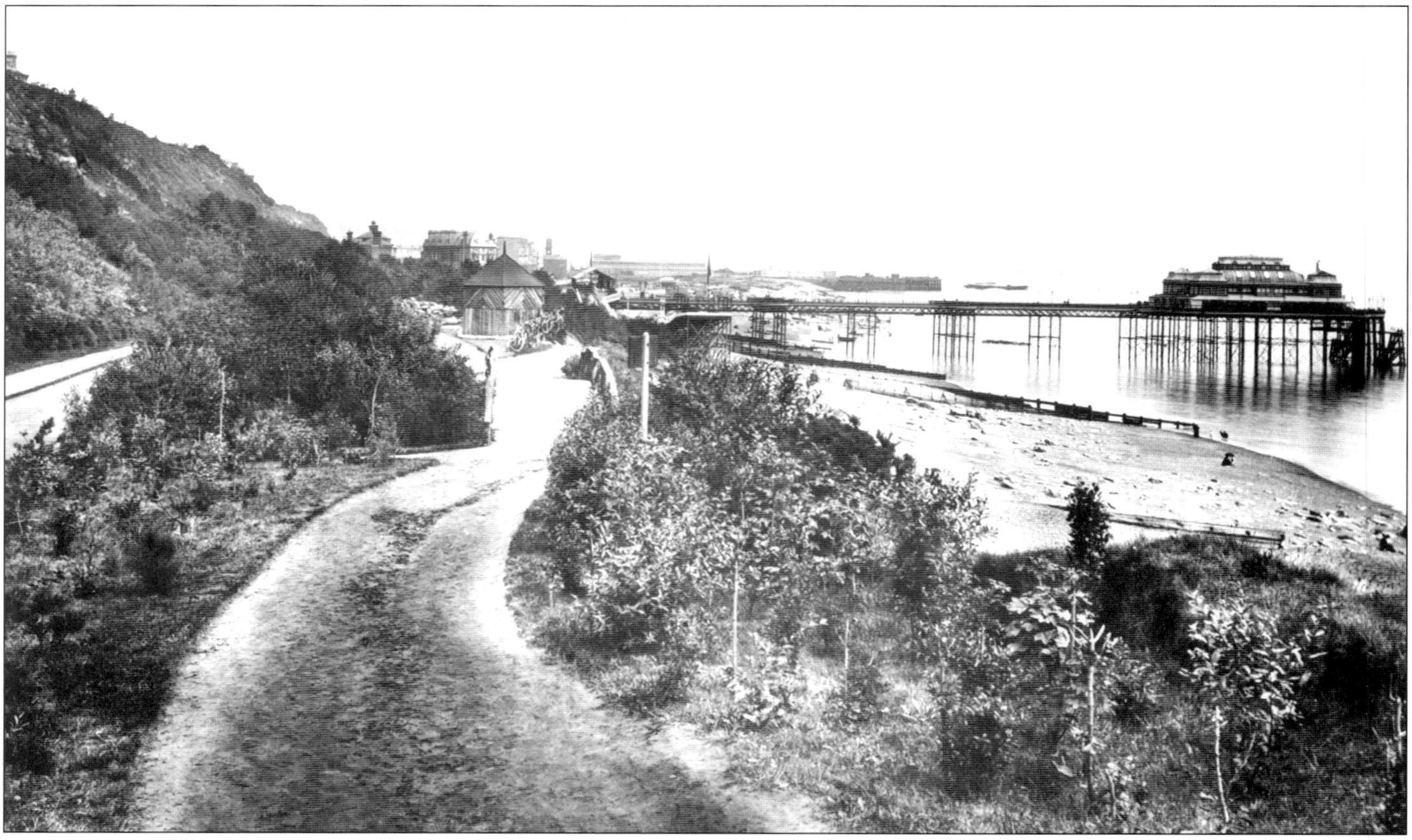

29939
A fine view taken in 1892 of the 680 ft long Victoria Pier. The handsome pavilion could accommodate 800 people and in the summer concerts were given daily.

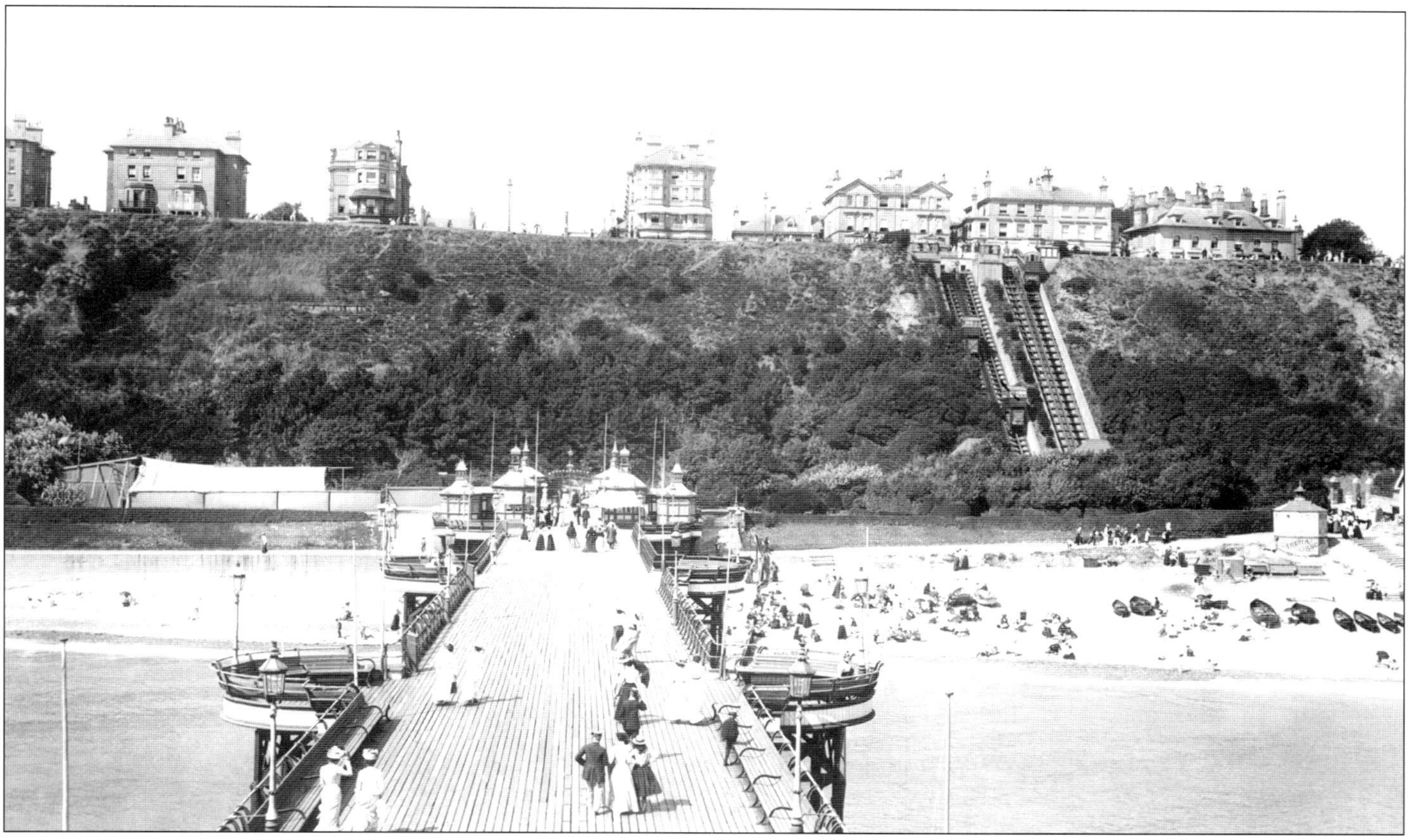

48054
A 1901 photograph of the Leas taken from the pier. This promenade is about one and a half miles long, with gardens and a pavilion. To the right can be seen the water-balanced lift, which still saves holidaymakers the bother of climbing to the top.

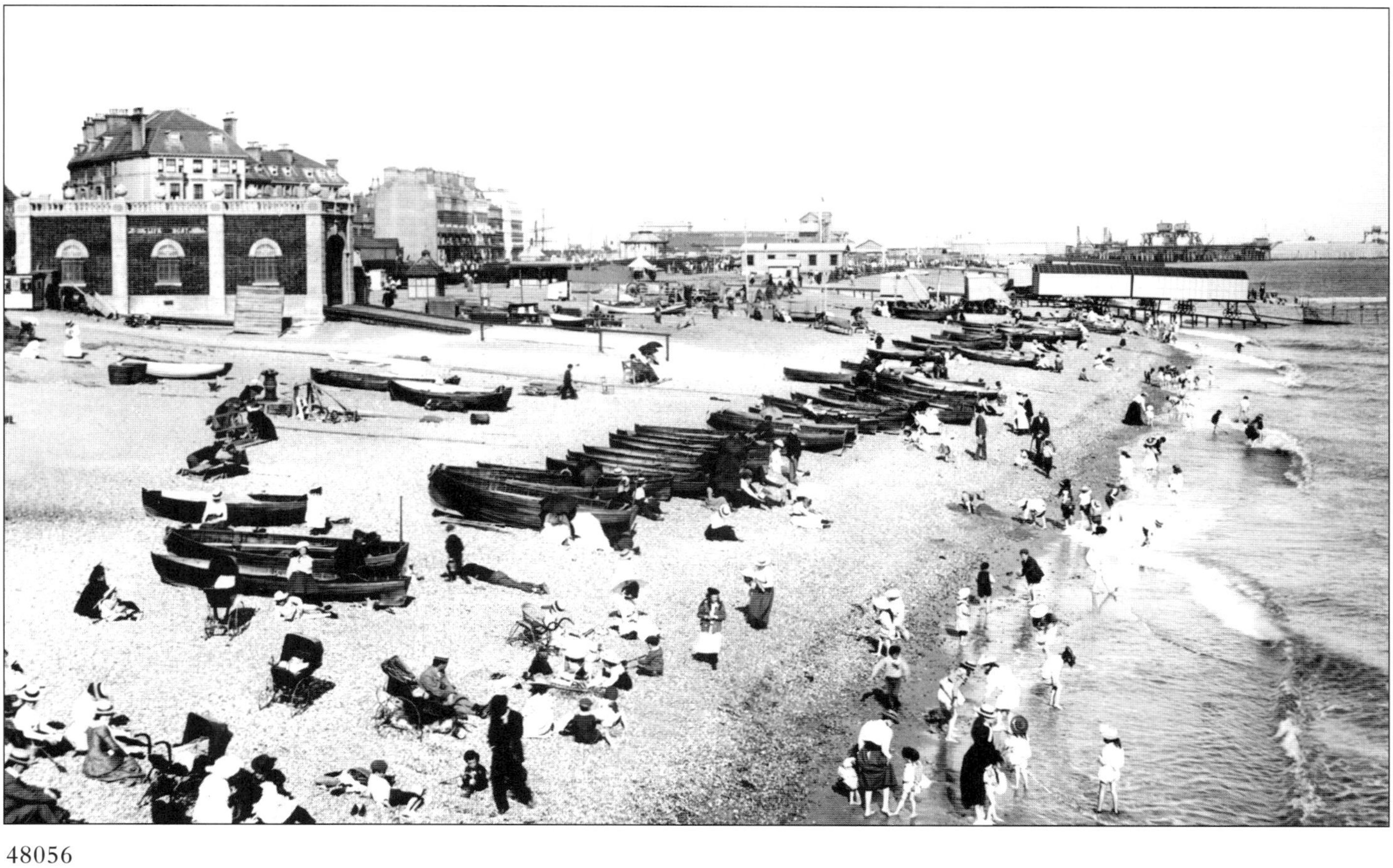

48056
A view of the beach taken in 1901. Rowing boats are drawn up, and mothers and children are enjoying a paddle in the sea. The harbour is in the background.

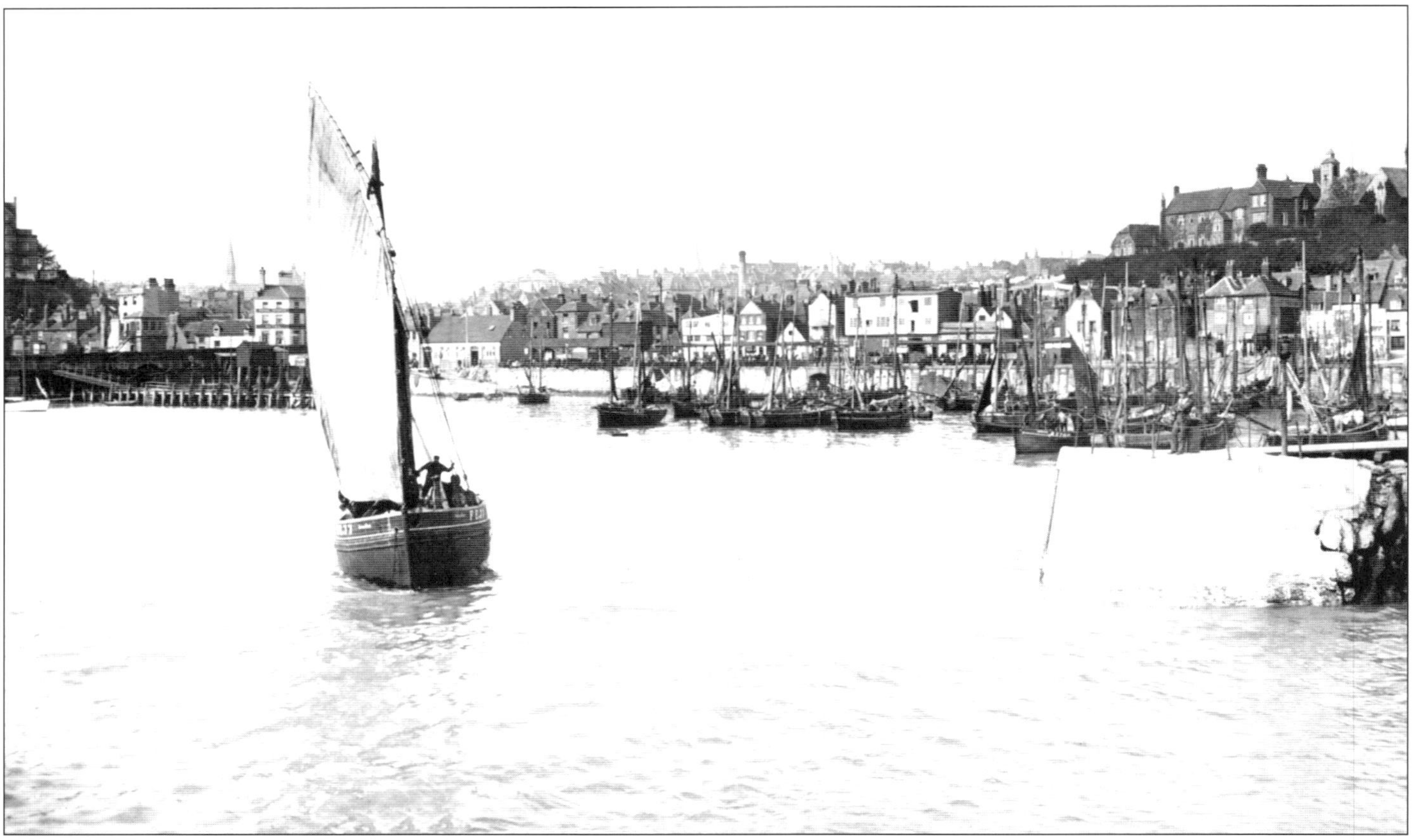

65003
Setting out on a fishing trip - one of Folkestone's fleet leaves the inner harbour in this picture, taken in 1912. Folkestone is now known as a cross channel port which developed in early Victorian days, and a steeply graded branch was built from the main line to the harbour.

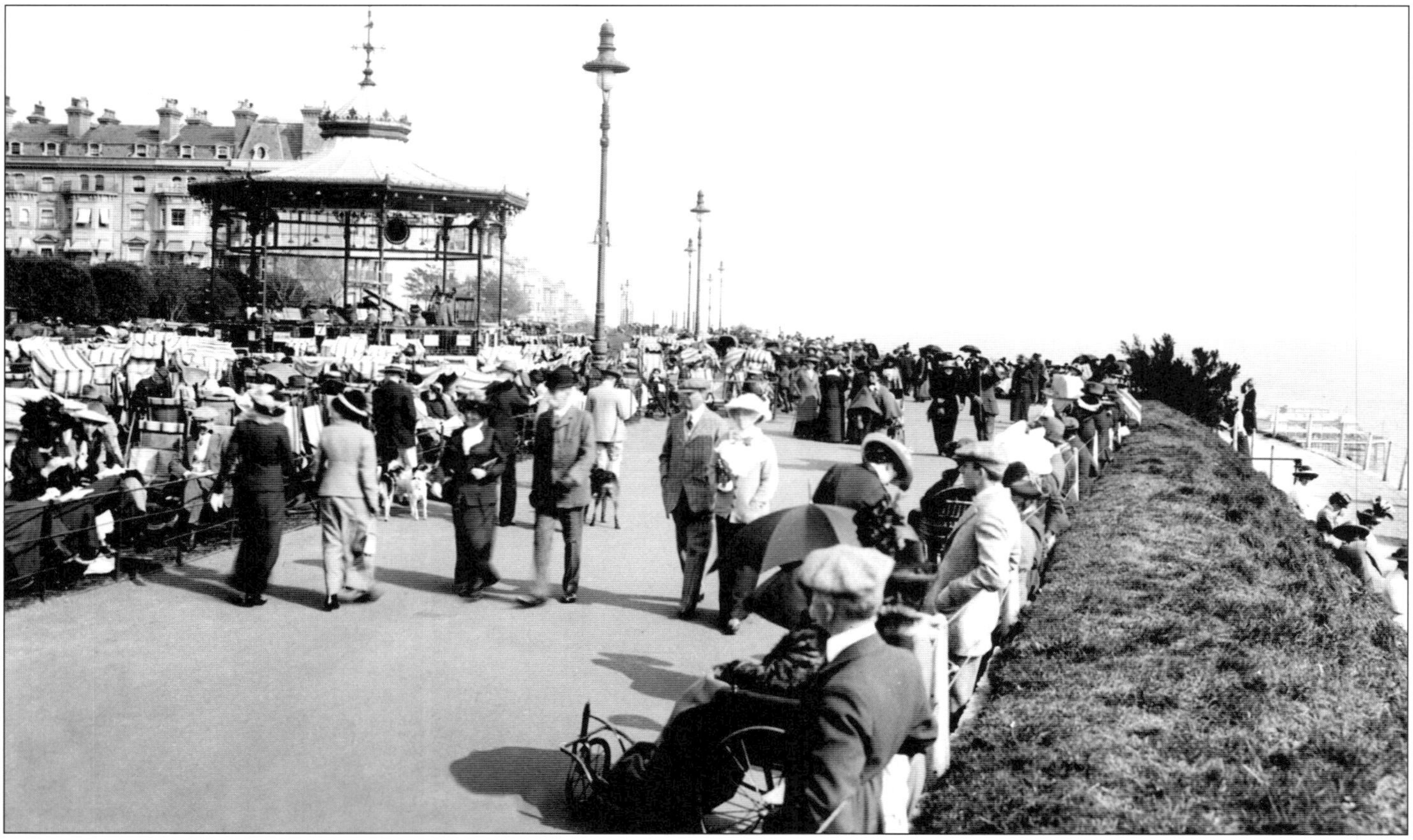

64993
A happy summer scene of Folkestone promenaders taken in 1912 from near the bandstand. Folkestone was proud of its bandstands. It had three at one time, and only bands of the highest standing were engaged.

# Gravesend

A busy industrial town on the river Thames, where it narrows to become a London river and coastal pilots hand over to the river men. It has a long history of seafaring, and fleets were assembled here in Tudor times. Its grimy façade hides buildings and churches of much interest. The view from nearby Windmill Hill is spectacular.

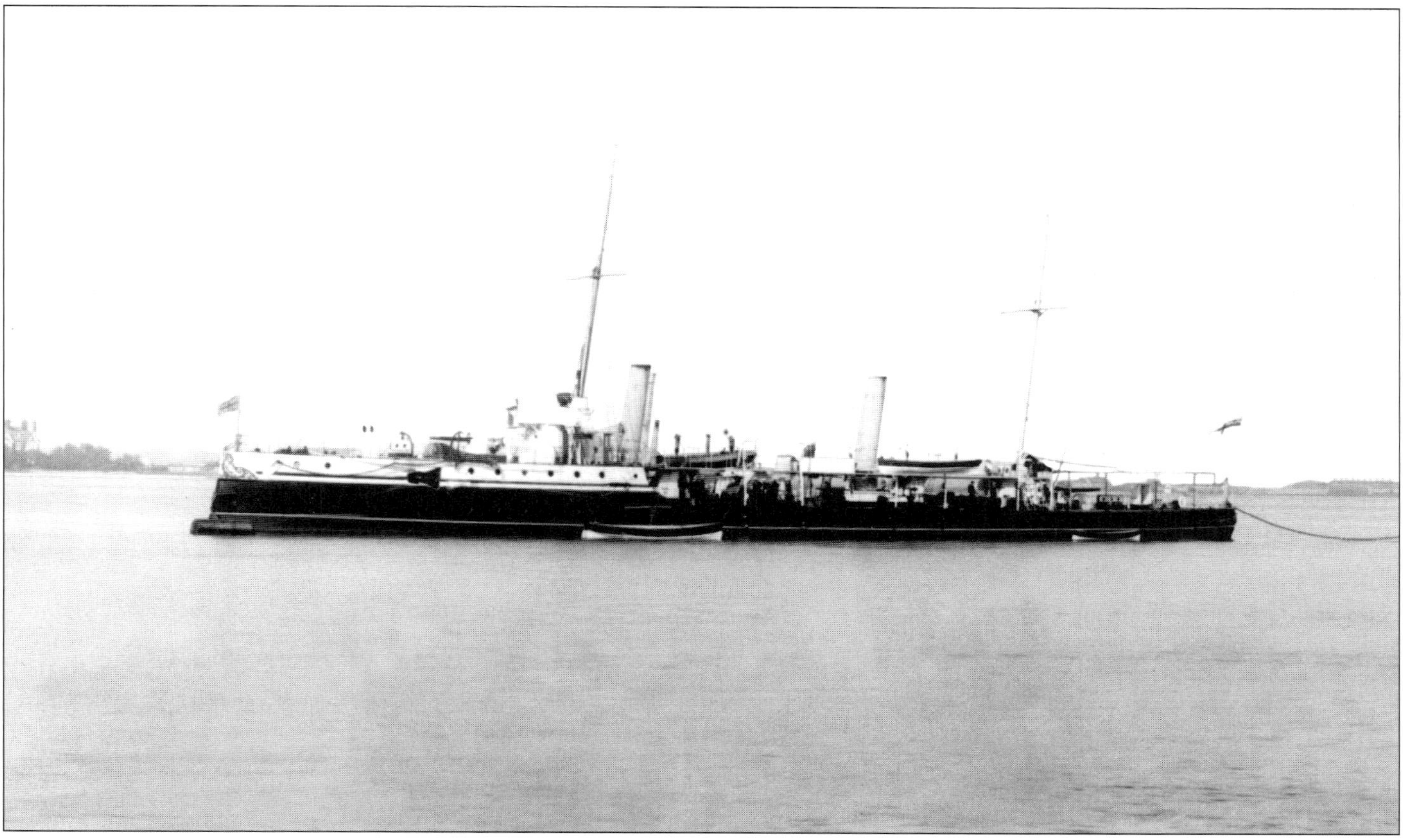

49043
The destroyer, HMS *Gleaner*, 1902, anchored out in the London river where it becomes the Thames estuary. Gravesend was the place where those who had died at sea would be offloaded for burial in the town cemetery.

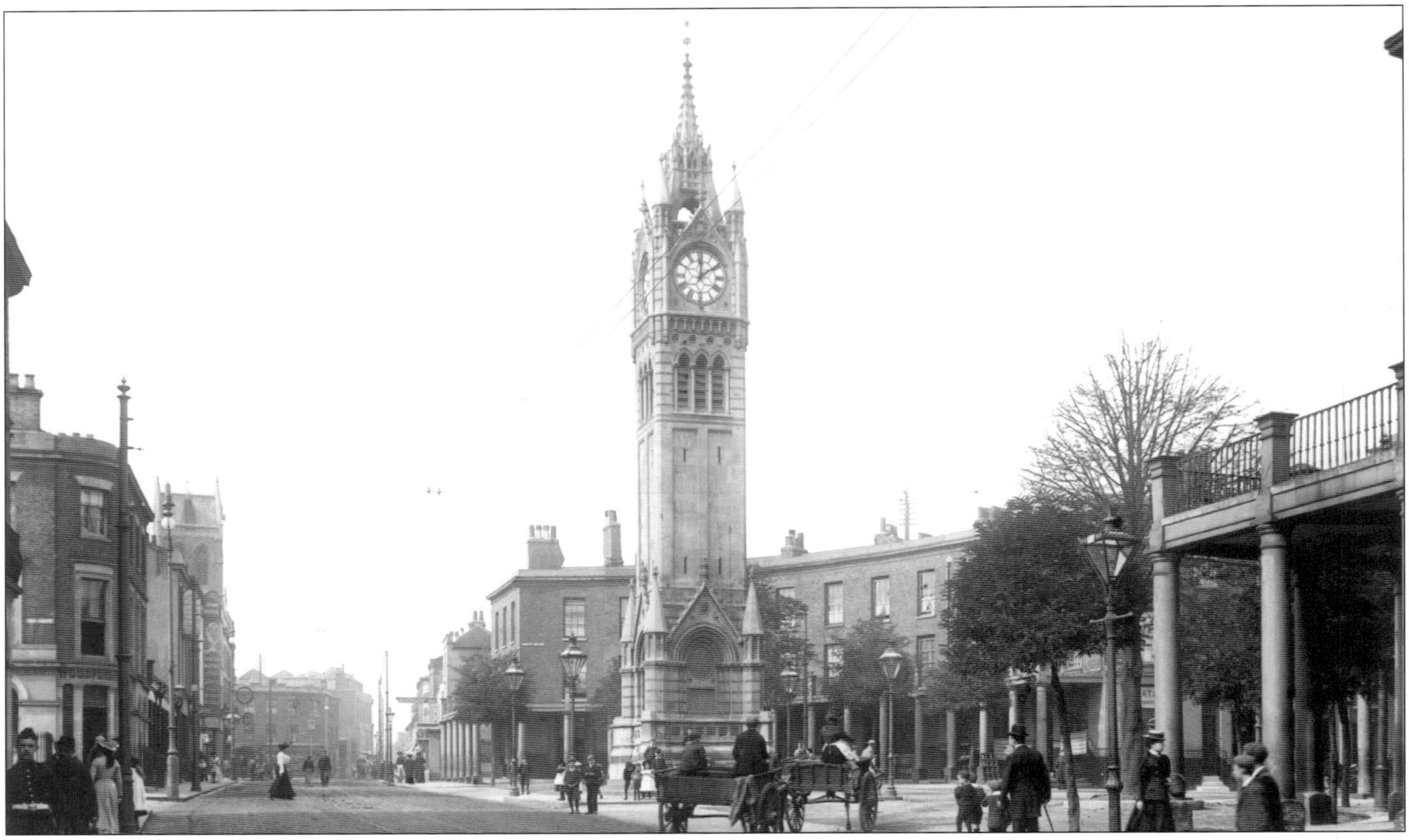

49026
The handsome clock tower was built in 1887, and was only 15 years old when this photograph was taken. The overhead wires for the trams clutter the scene.

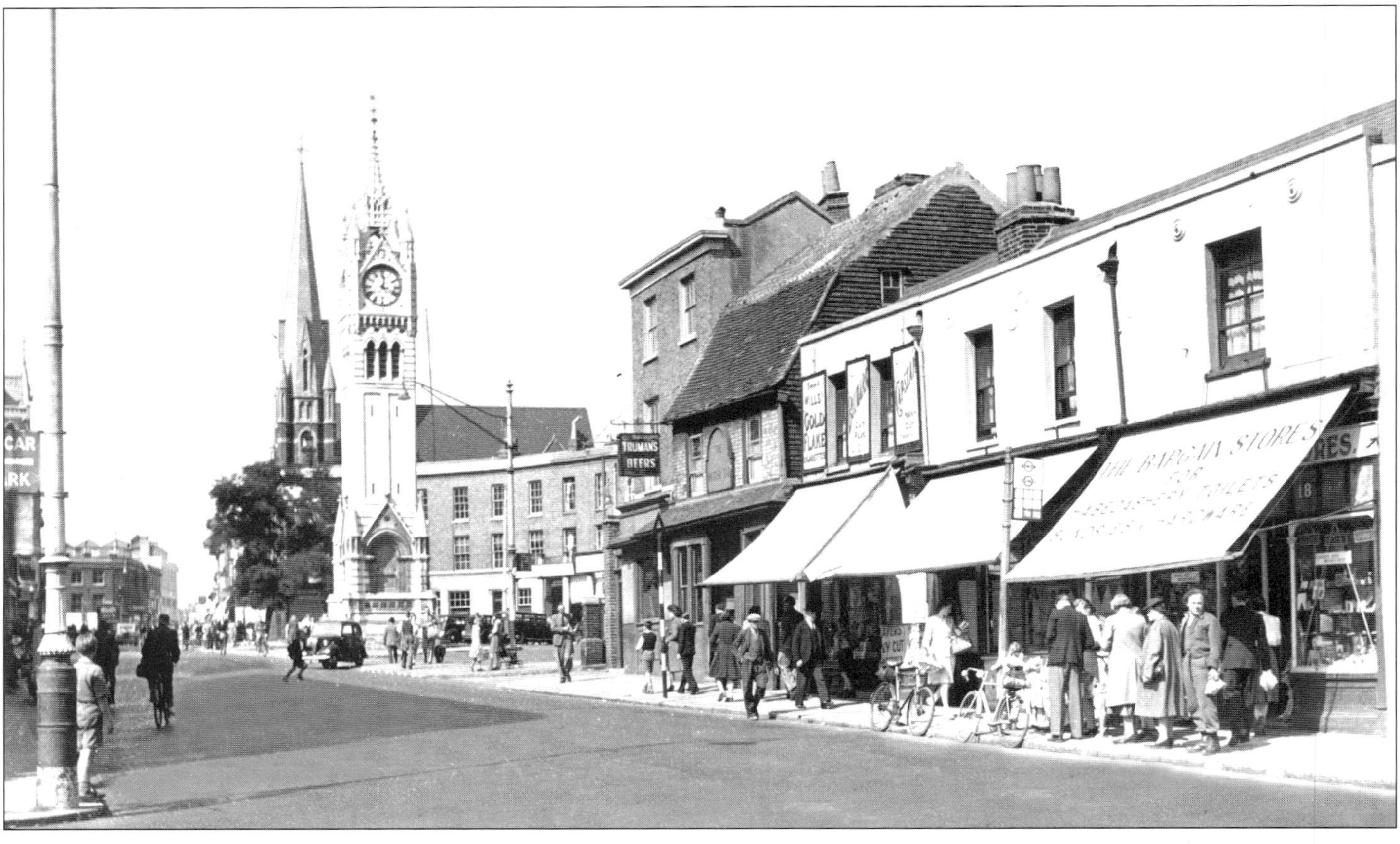


G47009
A further picture with the clock tower as the centrepiece, this time taken in the 1950s. Behind the clock tower has appeared the Methodist church, built in 1906. The tramlines have disappeared.

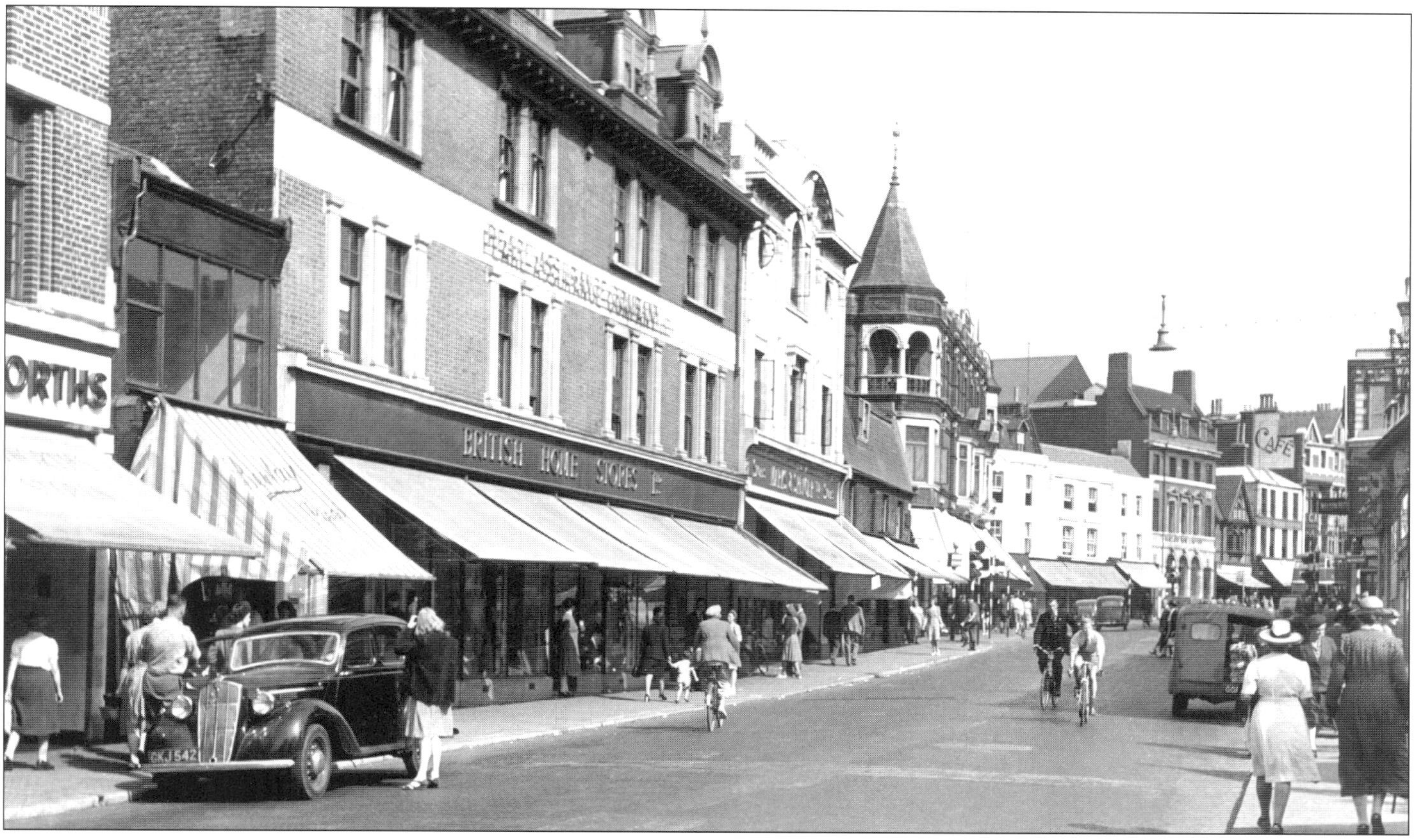


G47003
A 1950s view of New Road, one of the main shopping streets of the town. The roads seem empty by today's standards. In the foreground is British Home Stores, and Hepworths - men's clothing store on the extreme left.

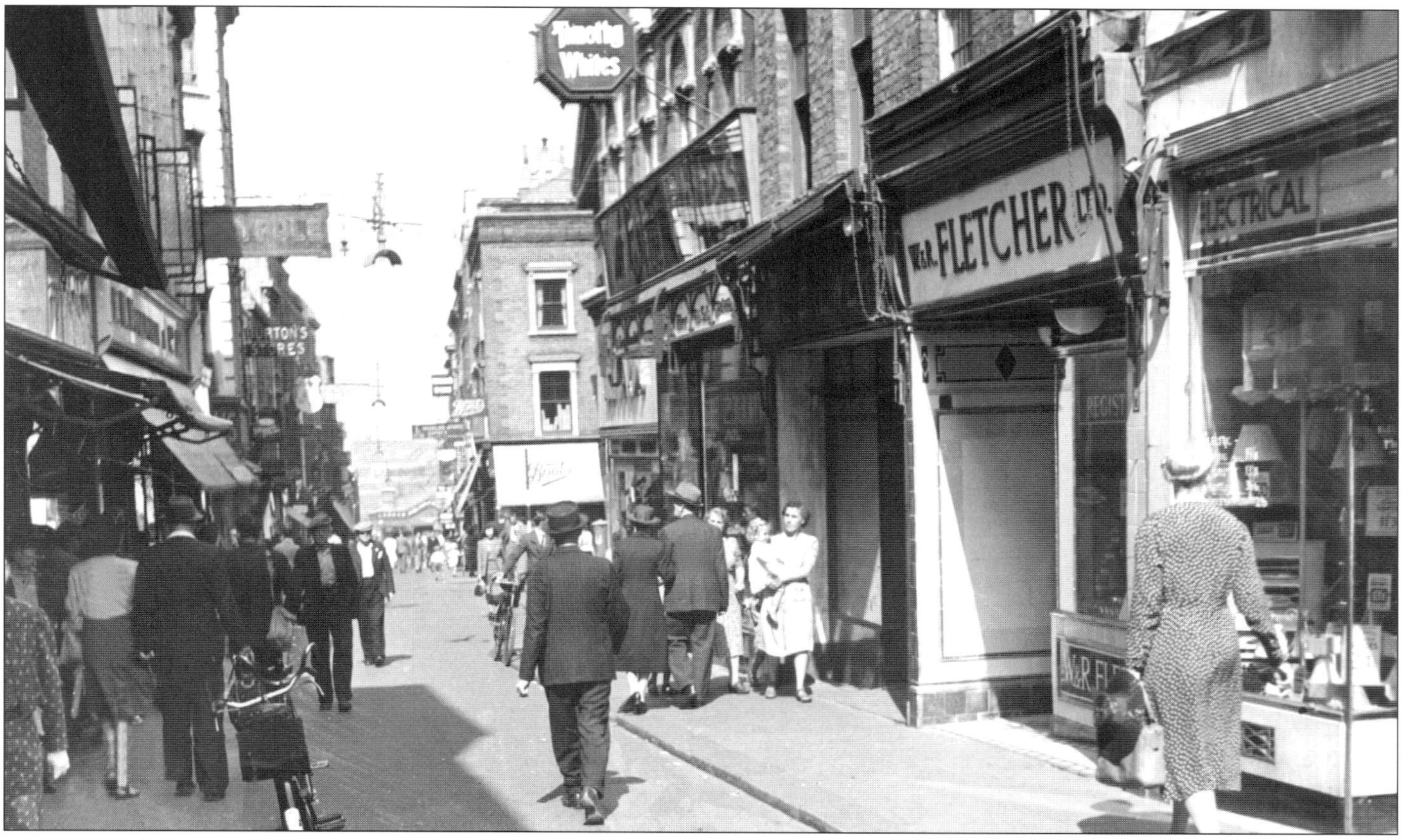


G47010
A final view of Gravesend, this time showing the narrow High Street in the 1950s. No cars can be seen. The sign in the top middle of the picture shows Timothy Whites, which was bought out by Boots and closed down in the late 1970s. F.W.Woolworth can be seen on the left of this photograph.

# Goudhurst

A beautiful village set up on a hilltop of the High Street, surrounded by orchards and hopfields. High Street has attractive tile-hung and weatherboarded cottages, tumbling down the hill. From the church it is possible to see Rochester and Hastings. The fourteenth century church has many monuments to the Culpepers. Near the village is Twissenden Manor, a fine Jacobean house.

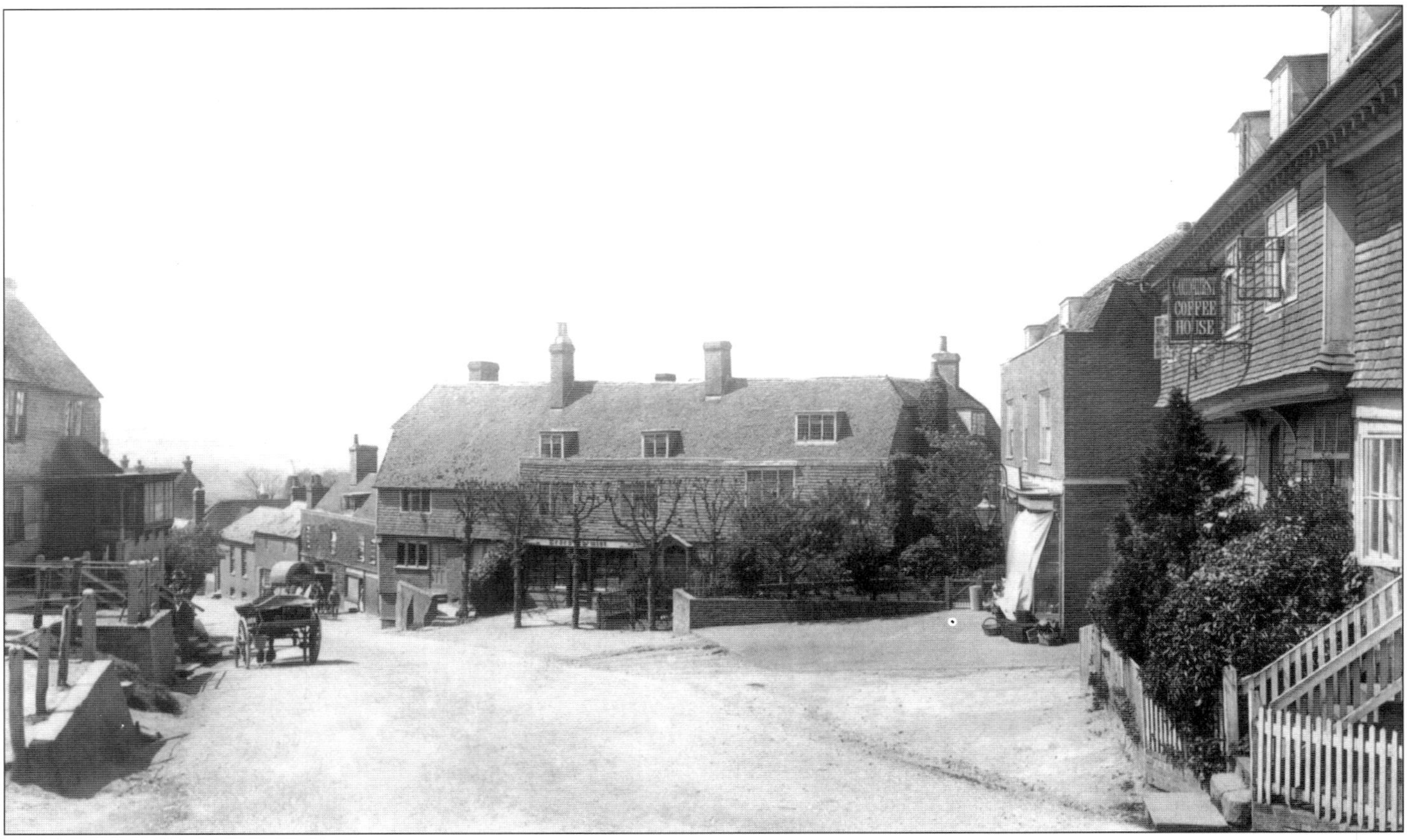


46377
The village of Goudhurst has always ranked as one of the most graceful of the Kentish Weald. This view, taken in 1901, shows the hilly nature of the place, perched over 400 ft up.

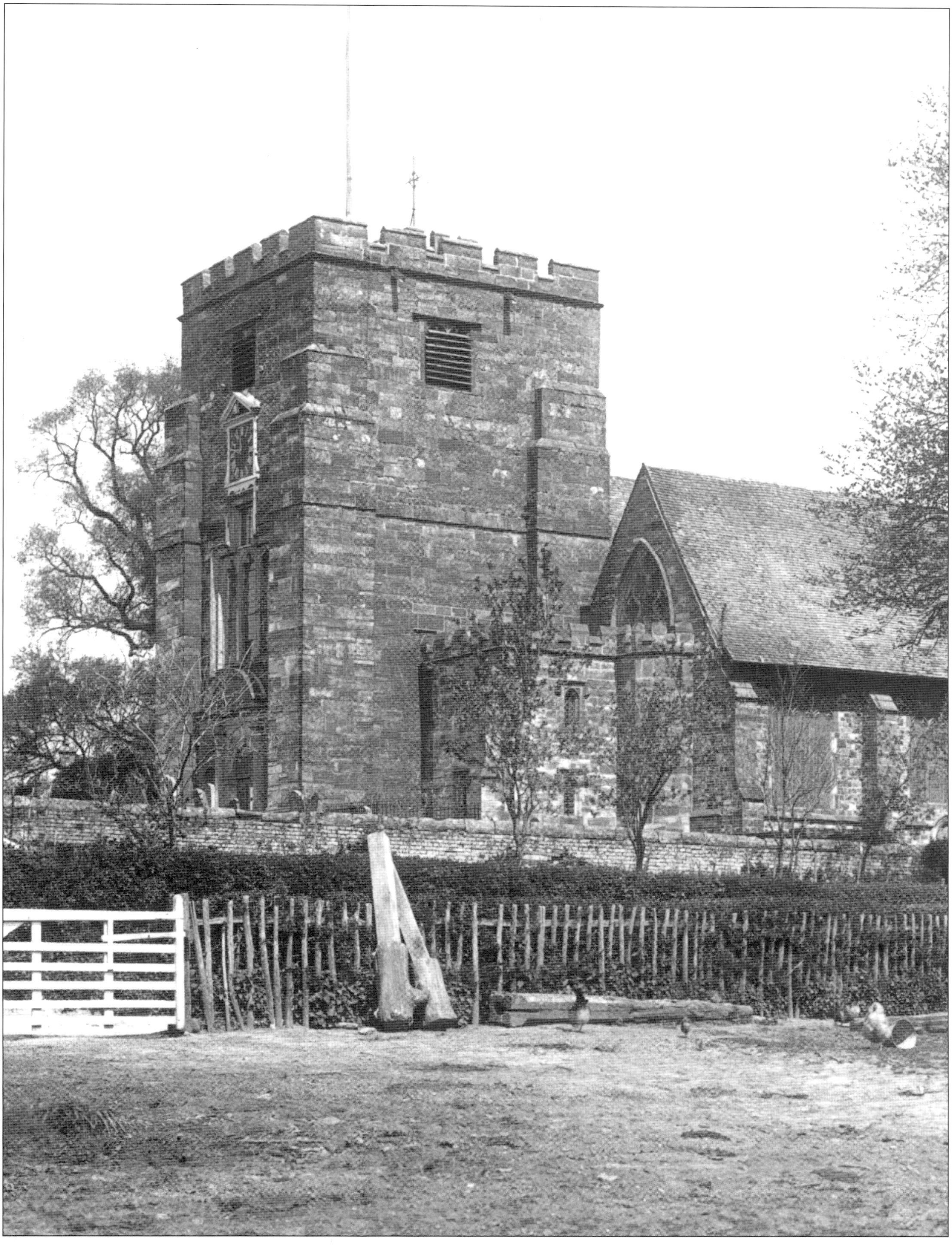

46379

A 1901 view of St Marys, the Goudhurst's church founded in the fourteenth century, with its tower built in 1640. It crowns the hill, and has many monuments to the Culpeper family.

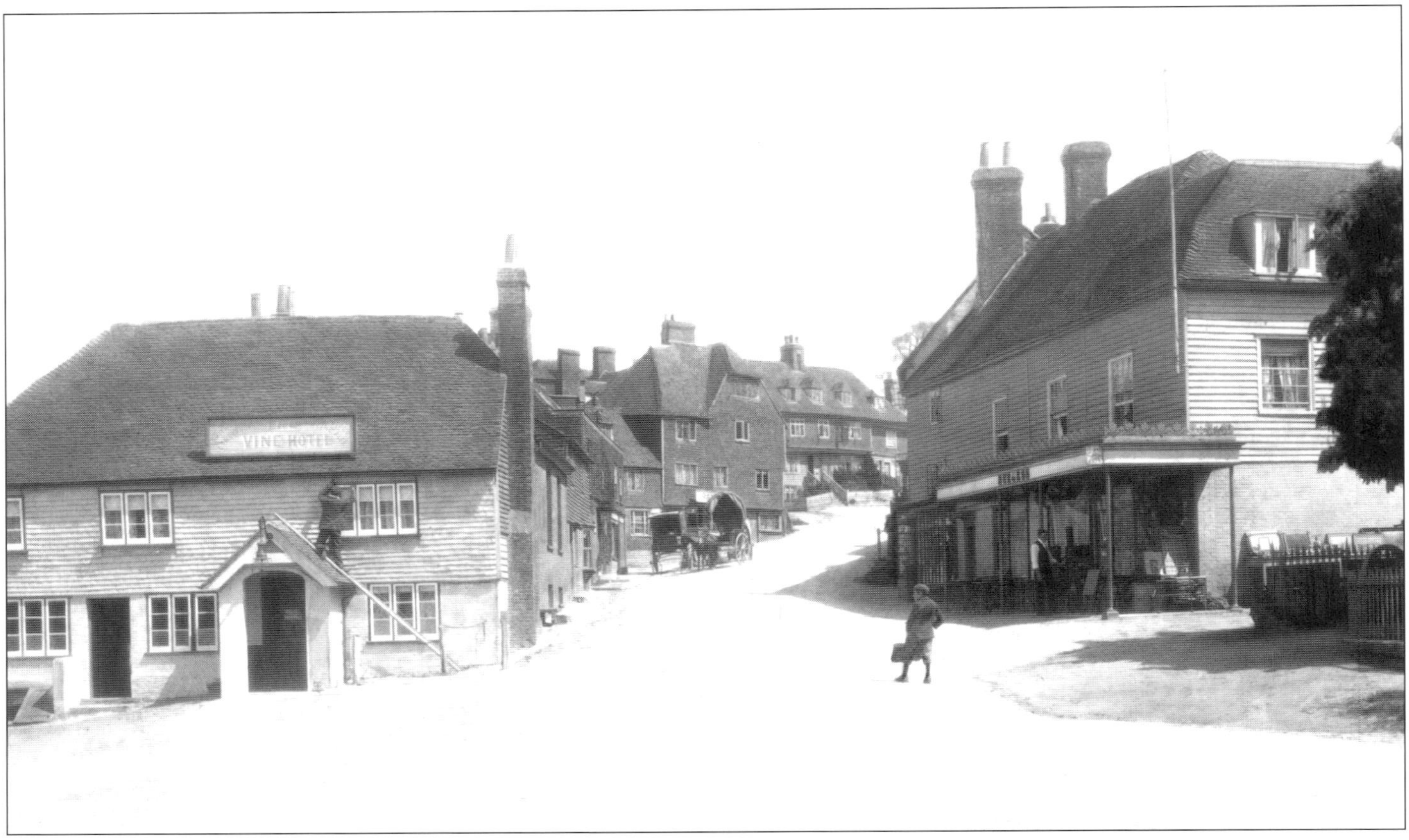


46376
A fine study of Goudhurst also taken in 1901, but this time looking up the High Street. The Vine Hotel stands on the left, whilst halfway up the hill is a horse-drawn wagon.

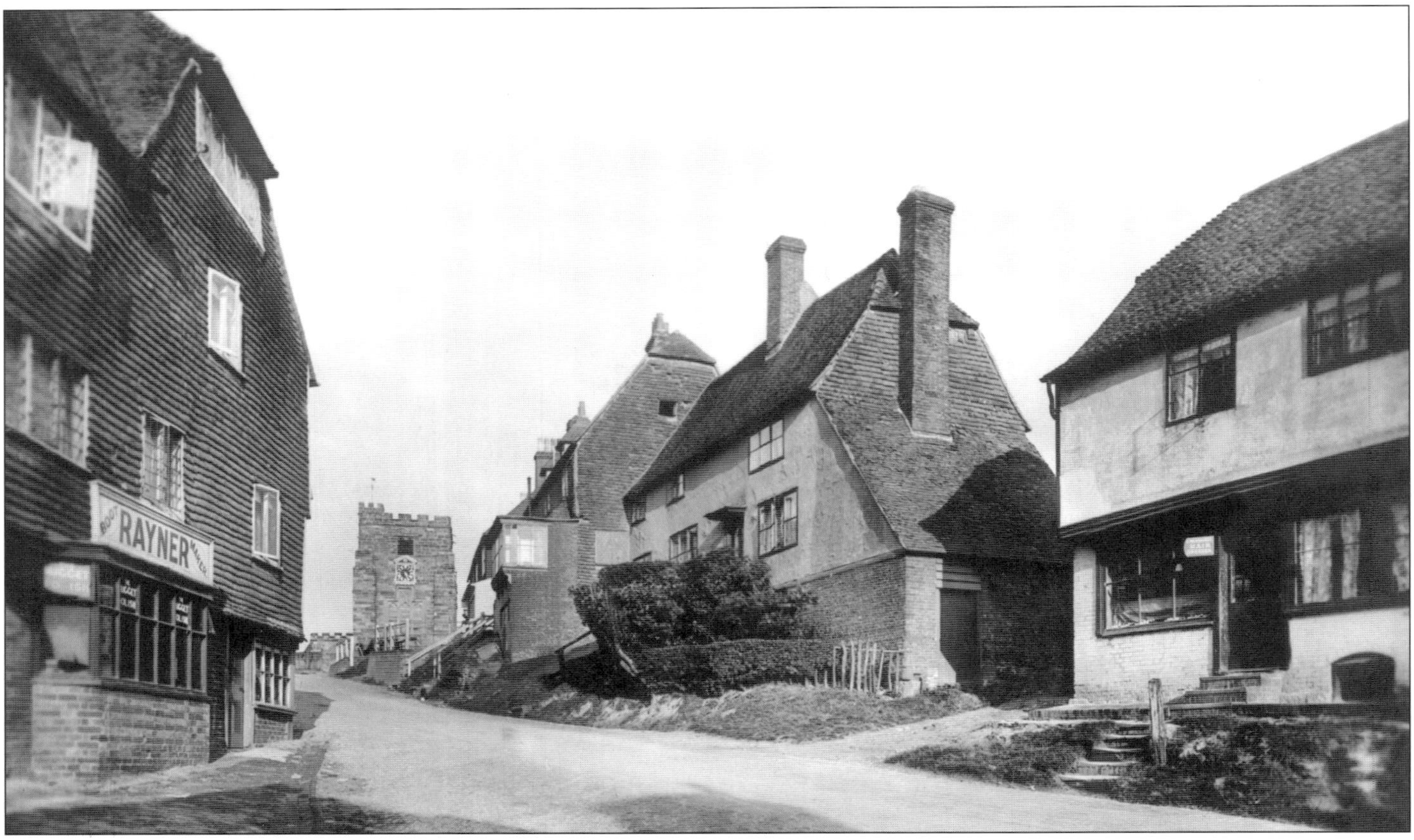


52537
A picture postcard view of Goudhurst, looking up the hill to the church peeping out at the top. This view in 1904 is little changed today. Note the typically Kentish hipped roofs and hung tiles.

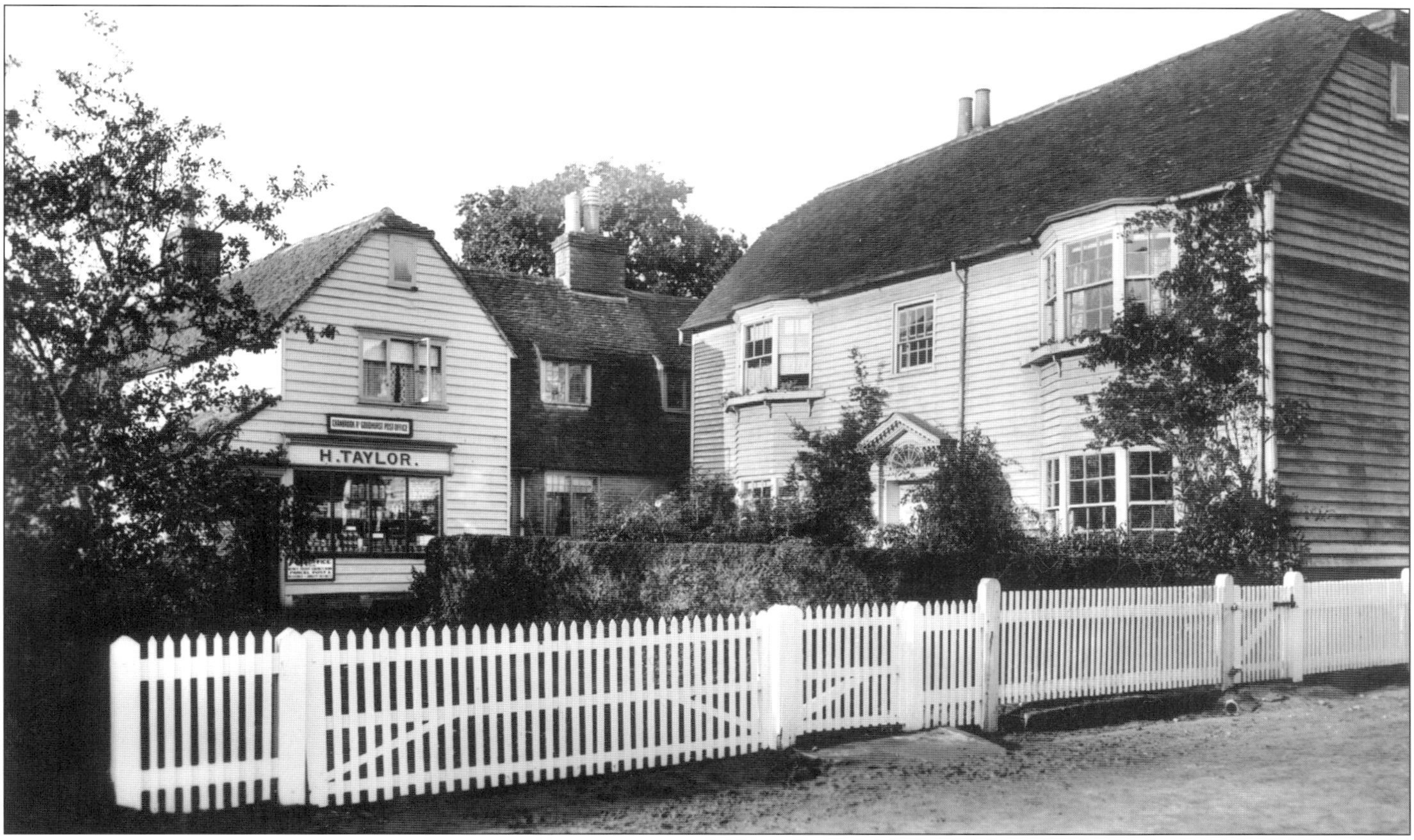


52546
A further view of Goudhurst, this time showing the Kentish weatherboarded houses and shops on the Cranbrook Road on a summer's day in 1904. Note the white painted fence - another Kentish speciality.

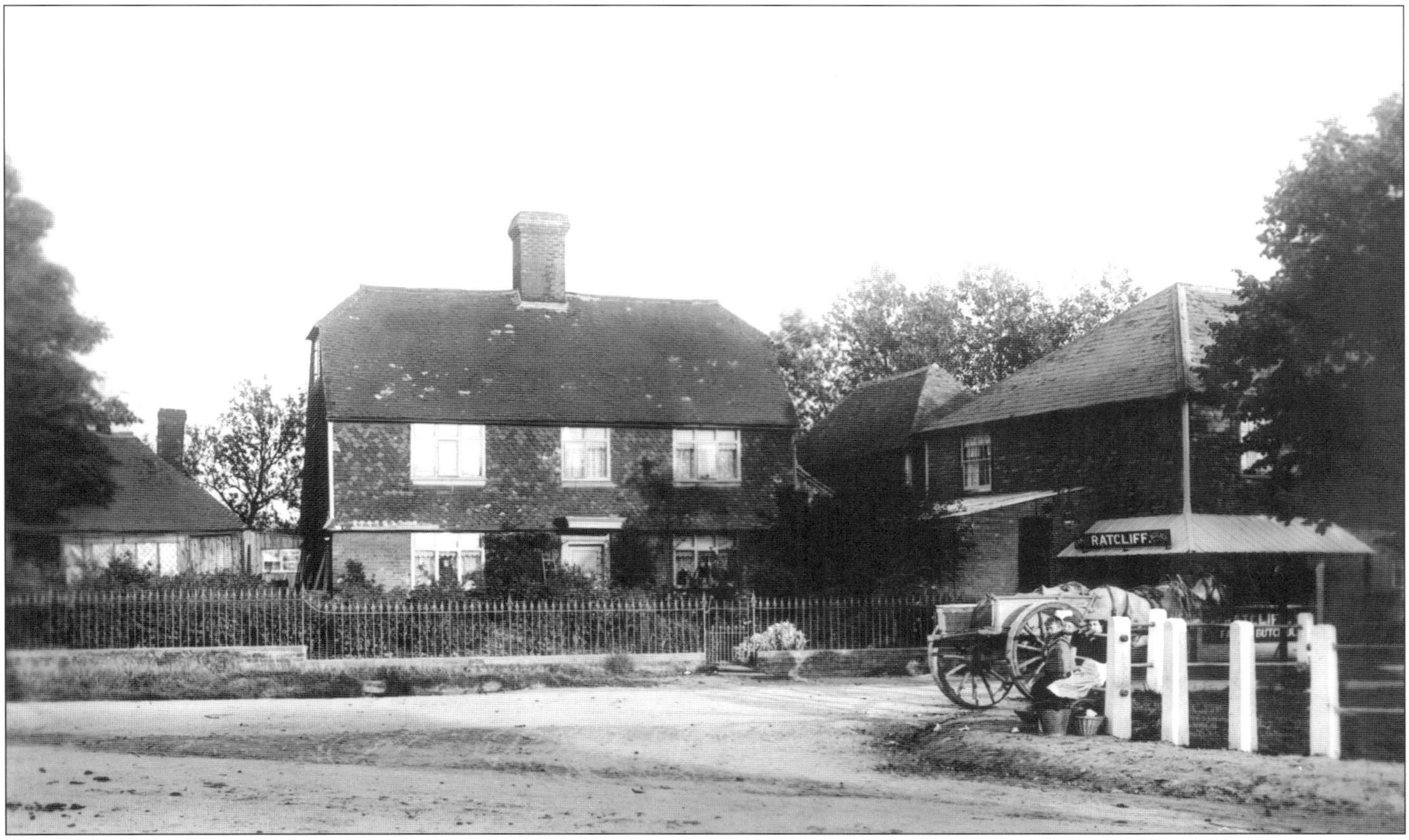


52538
The Plain, also taken in 1904. On the right, beside the village pond, a horse-drawn wagon and a group of people wait in the shade.

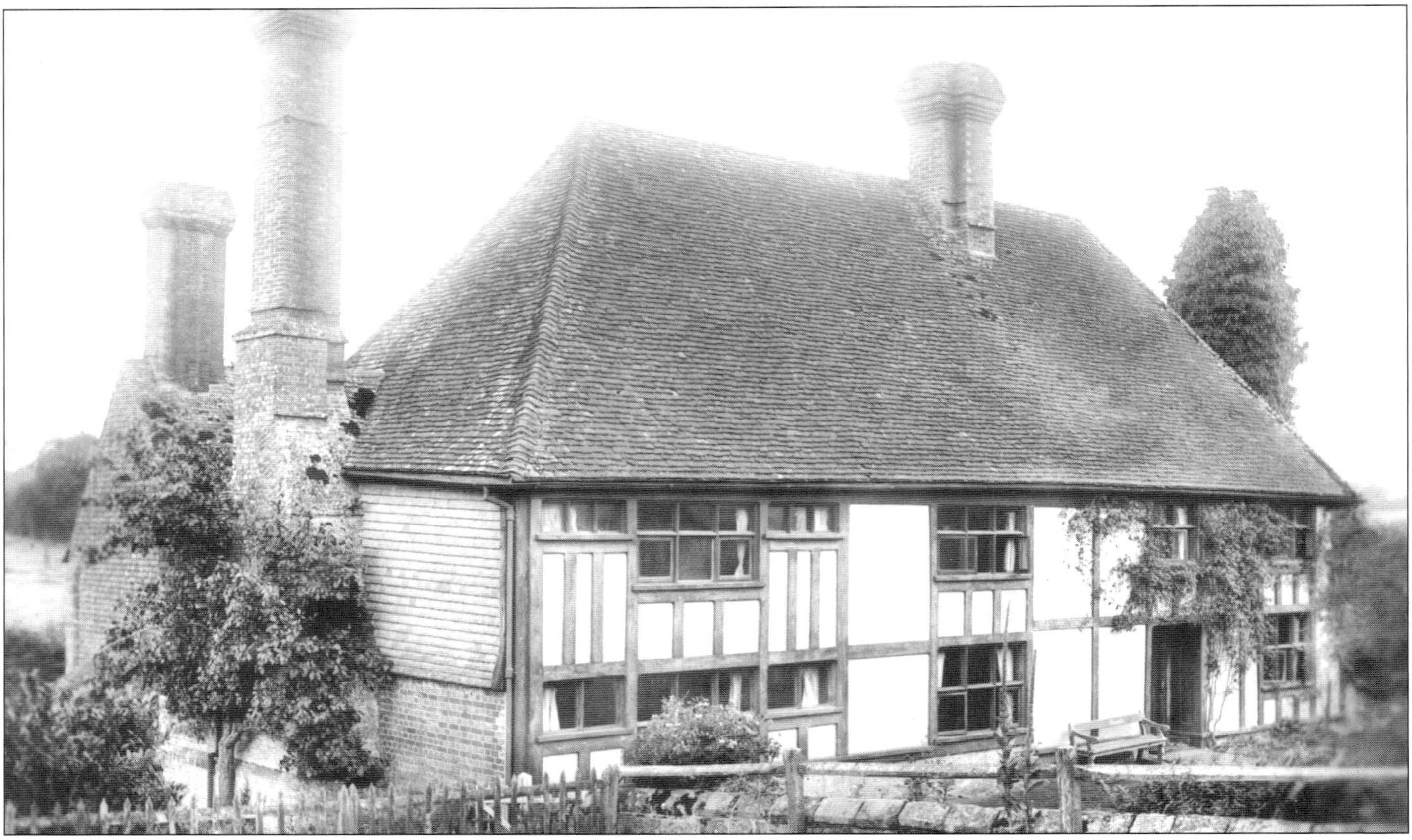

52562
A few miles to the south of Goudhurst is Twissenden manor, now a youth hostel. This half-timbered Wealden Hall House has a late sixteenth century sandstone façade at the back. This view was taken in 1904.

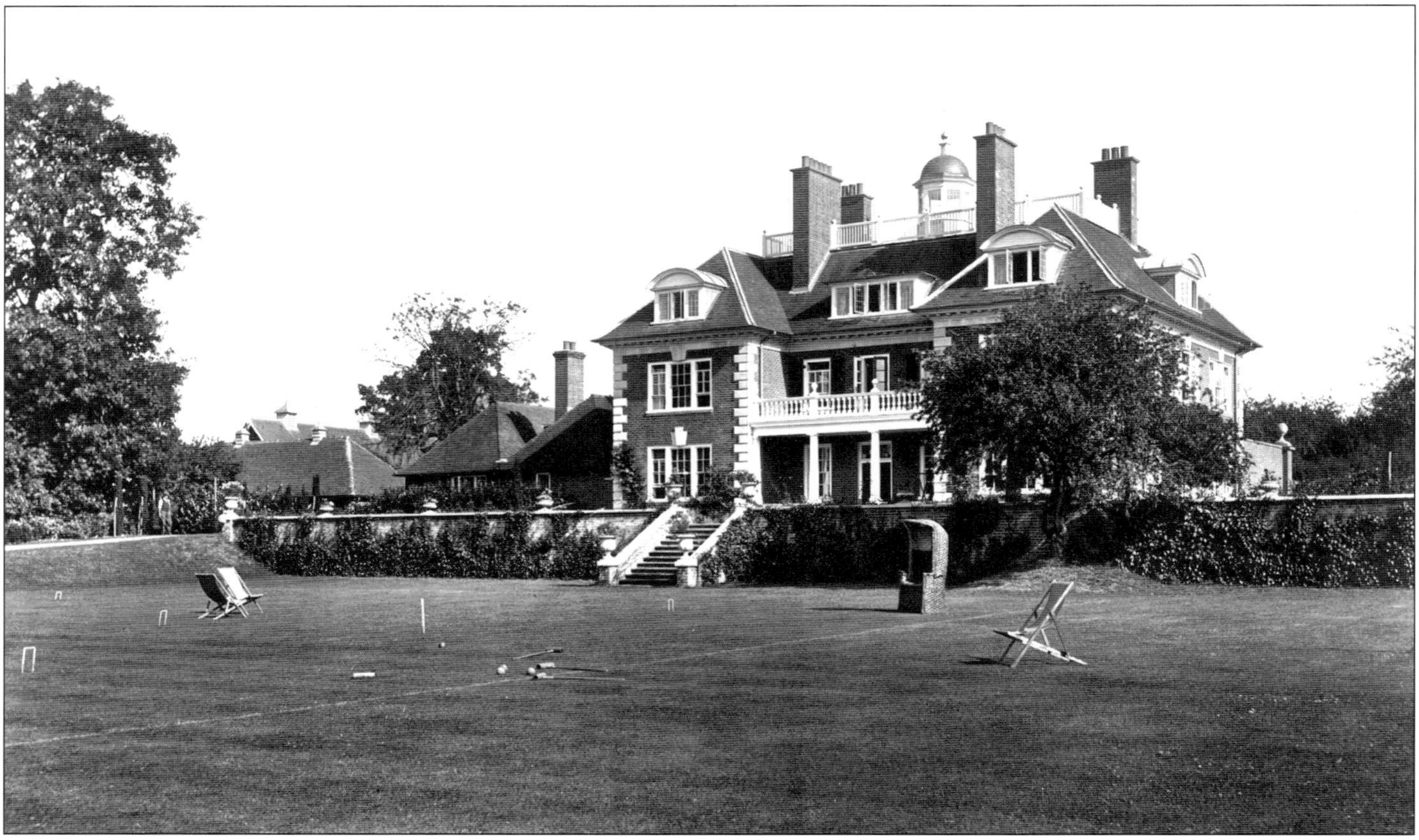

52557
Croquet on the lawn at Ballards in 1904 - visions of a vanished English summer whose complacency would be shattered in ten years time.

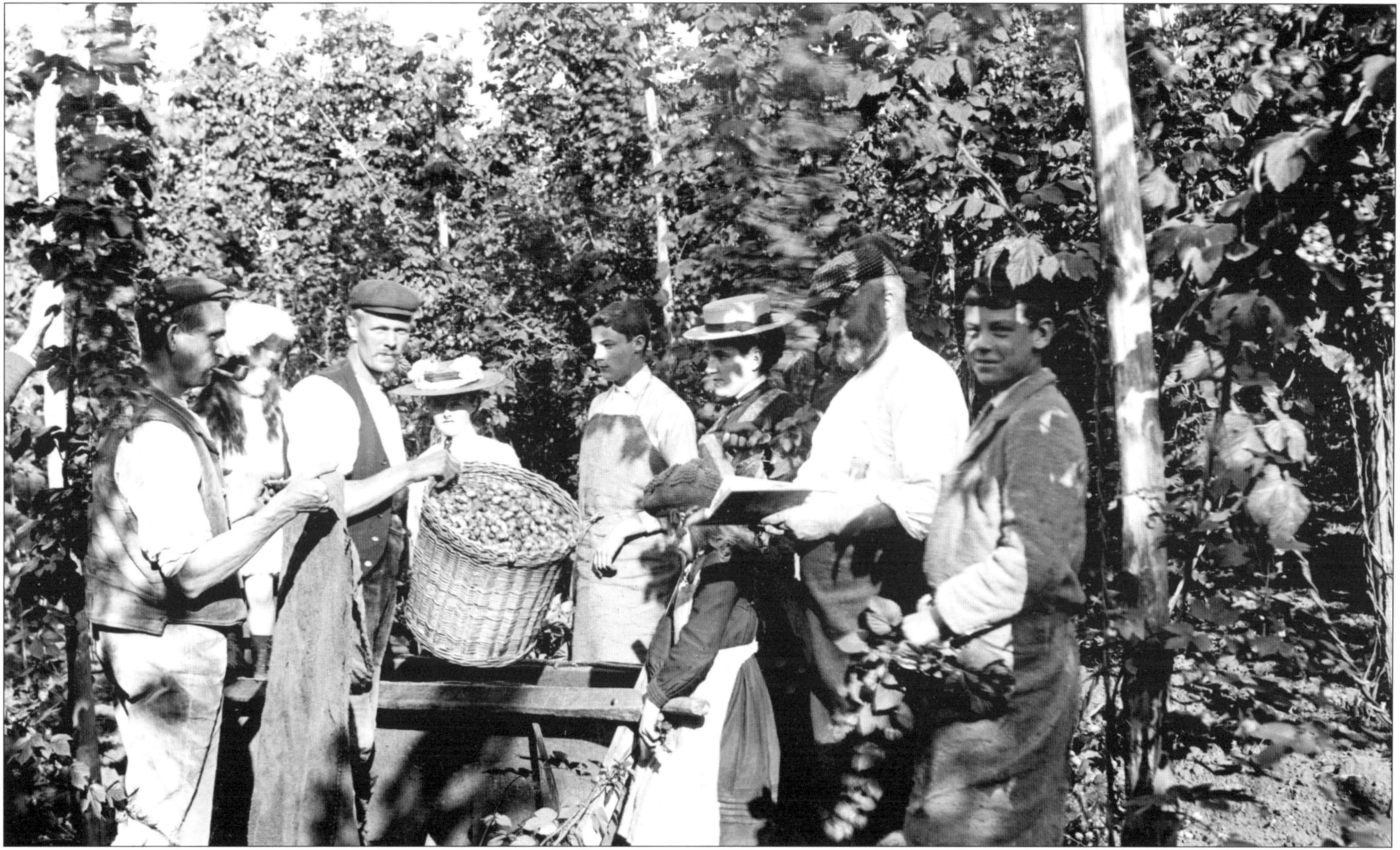

52571D
Kent is synonymous with the growing of hops. This labour intensive work was done by poor London families coming down for their annual paid holiday. Here, the hops are being measured before being loaded into a poke - the tallyman is second on the right.

# Hawkhurst

A scattered village situated in the heart of the Weald. It is an old centre with a fifteenth century church, which has many fine treasures. Its weatherboarded cottages surround its tree lined green. There is also an elegant Regency parade of shops, the Colonnade, situated at the crossroads.

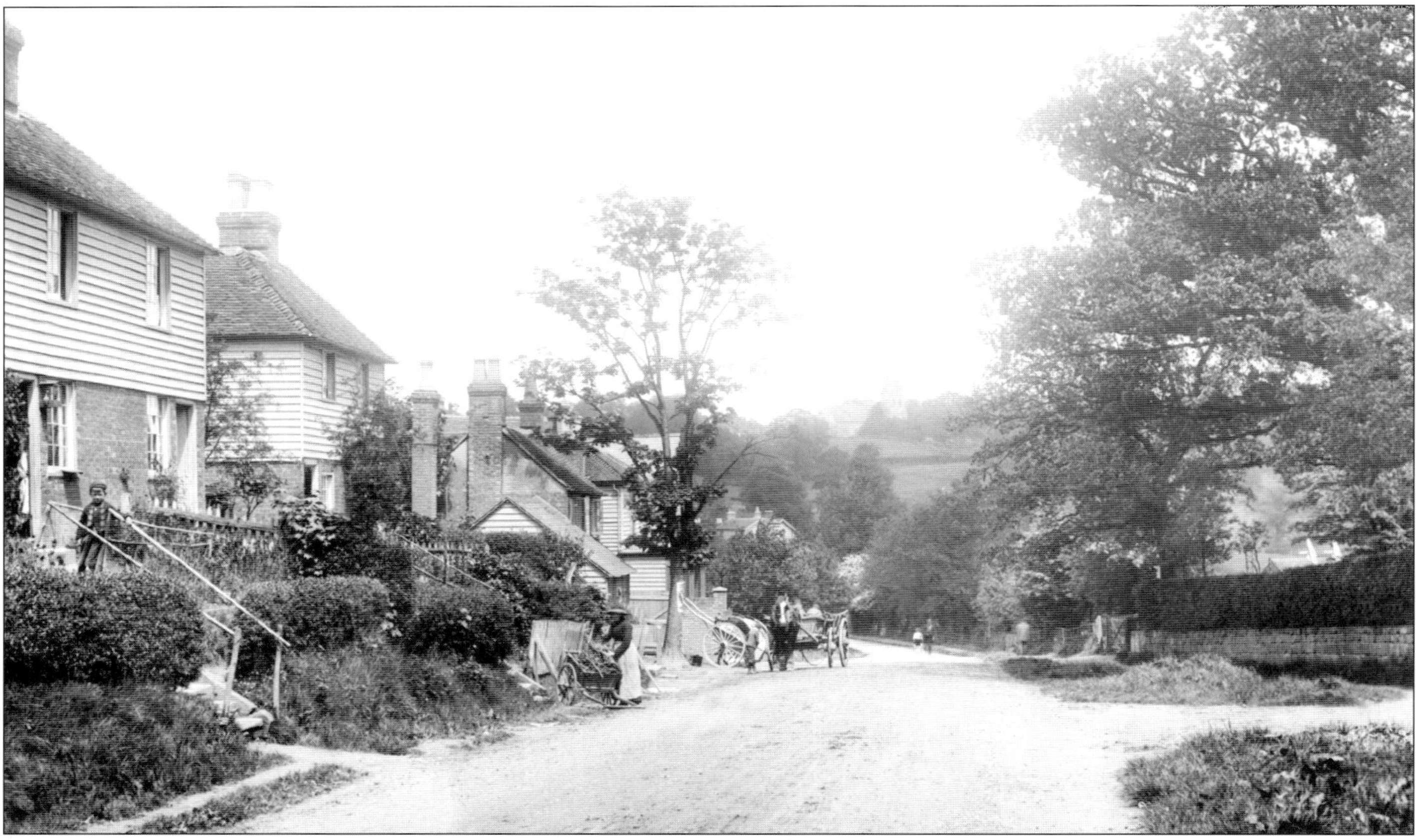

48255
This view, taken in 1902, looks towards the spire of the church across the valley. It shows a cart ascending Moor Hill, past typically Kentish half-weatherboarded cottages.

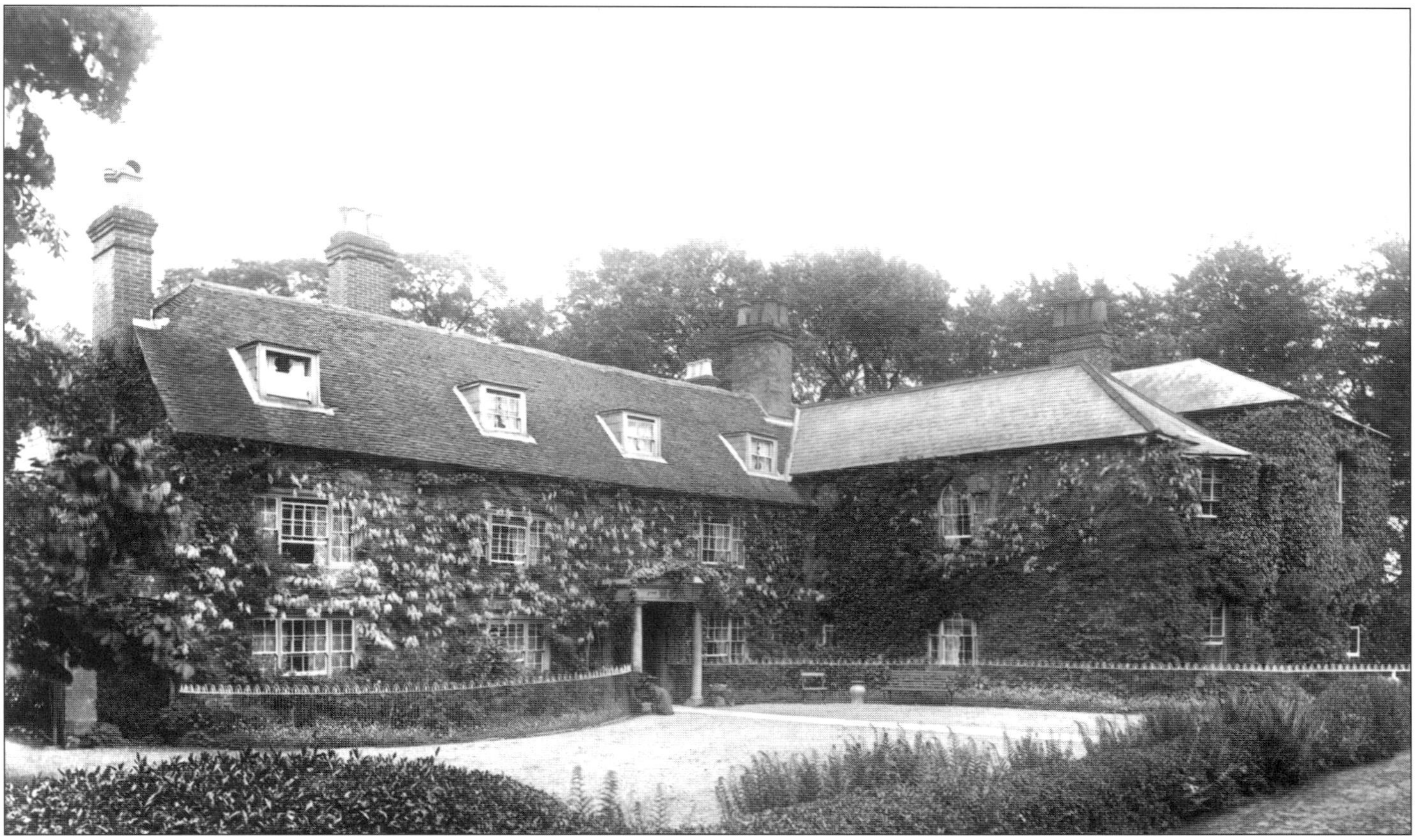

48248
A fine study of the Queen's Hotel, taken in 1902, possibly as a picture postcard or promotional picture. This old coaching inn was built to serve travellers on the Flimwell-Rye turnpike road - set up in 1762 - now the A268.

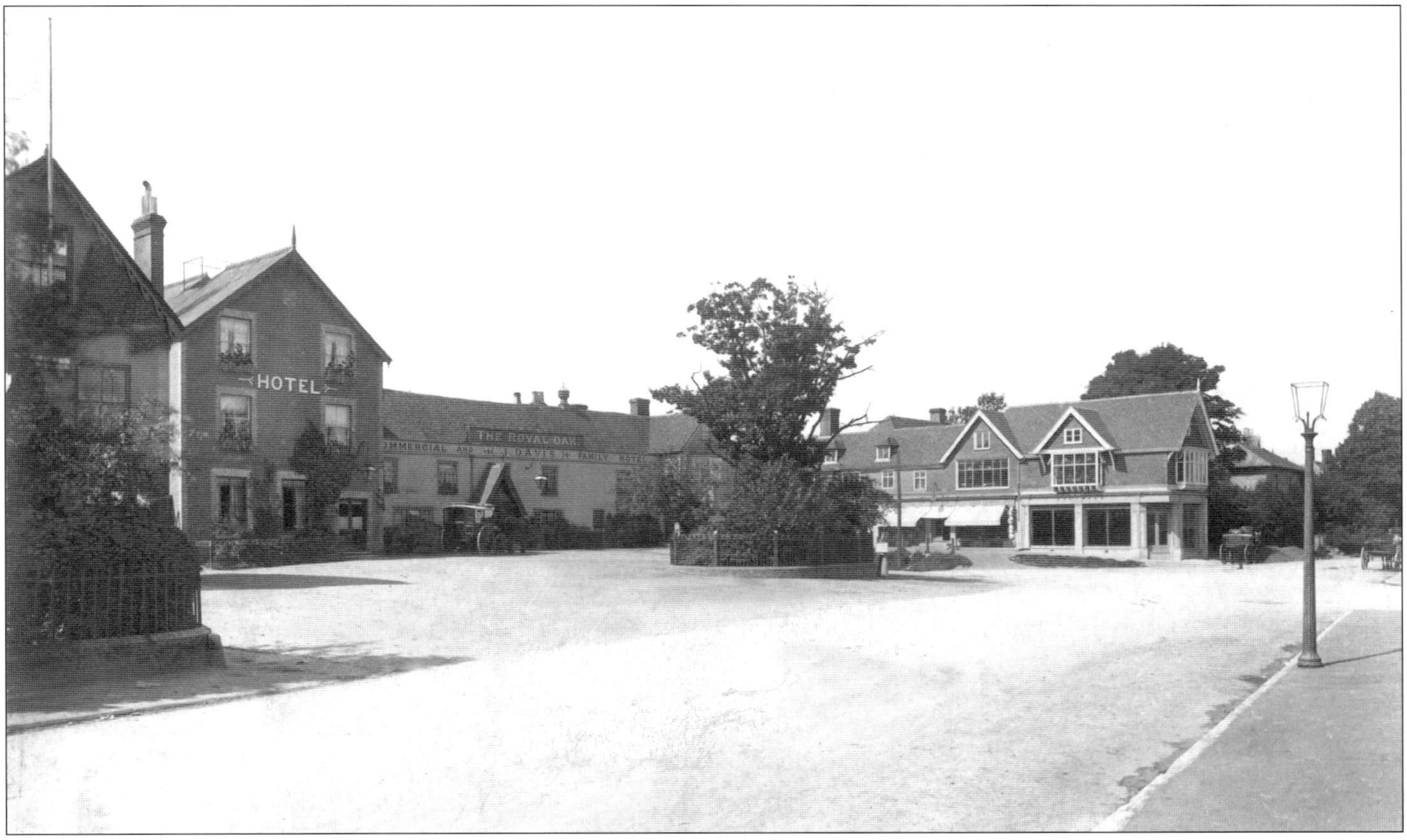


52118
Highgate is the modern Hawkhurst, which has grown up along the A268. This 1904 view shows the square, with a few carts to be seen, but otherwise a quiet afternoon scene.

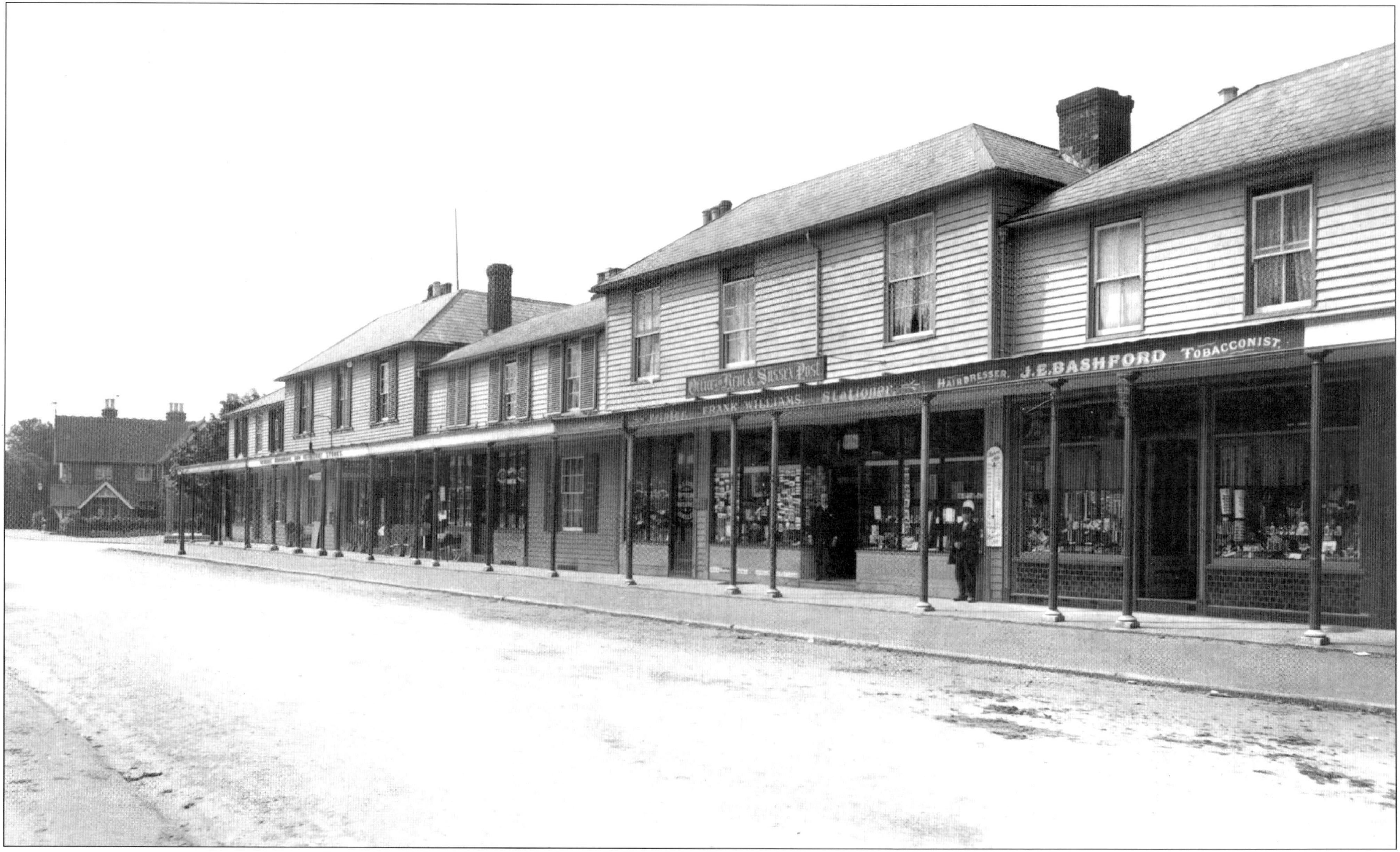


52119
The photographer moved back down the road and caught the colonnade of shops, one of Hawkhurst's best known features, an early ninteenth century shopping arcade with weatherboarded houses and cast-iron columns.

# Herne Bay

A popular resort on the north Kent Coast, founded in the 1830s, and popular ever since. The town has a seven mile beach, stretching from Warden Point to Reculver. The seafront is dominated by a Victorian clock tower. The pier was burned down in 1970, and the spot is now marked by a leisure centre.

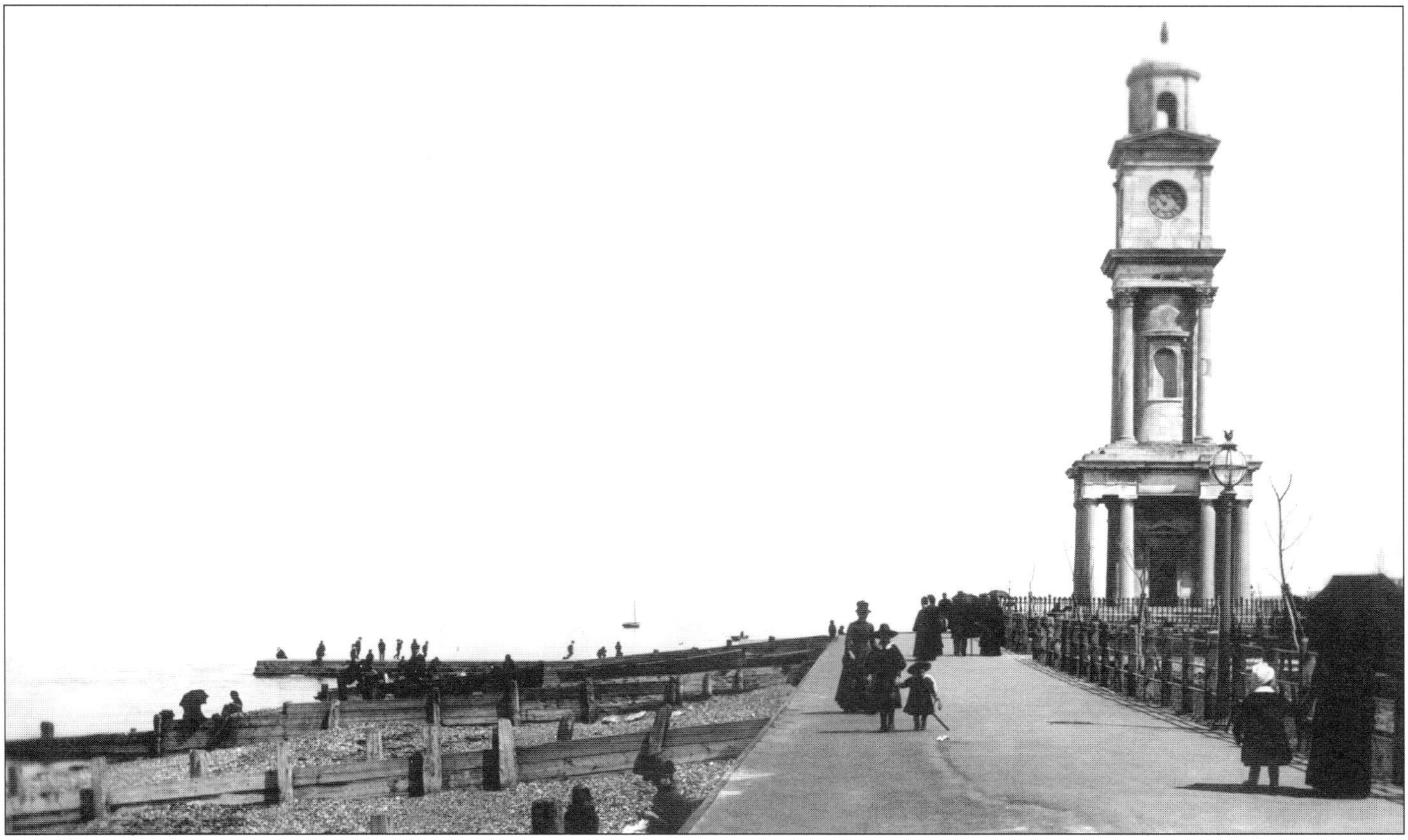

22313
The 85 ft high clock tower dominates this view of the parade in 1889. The clock tower was built in 1837, the tallest in the world at the time.

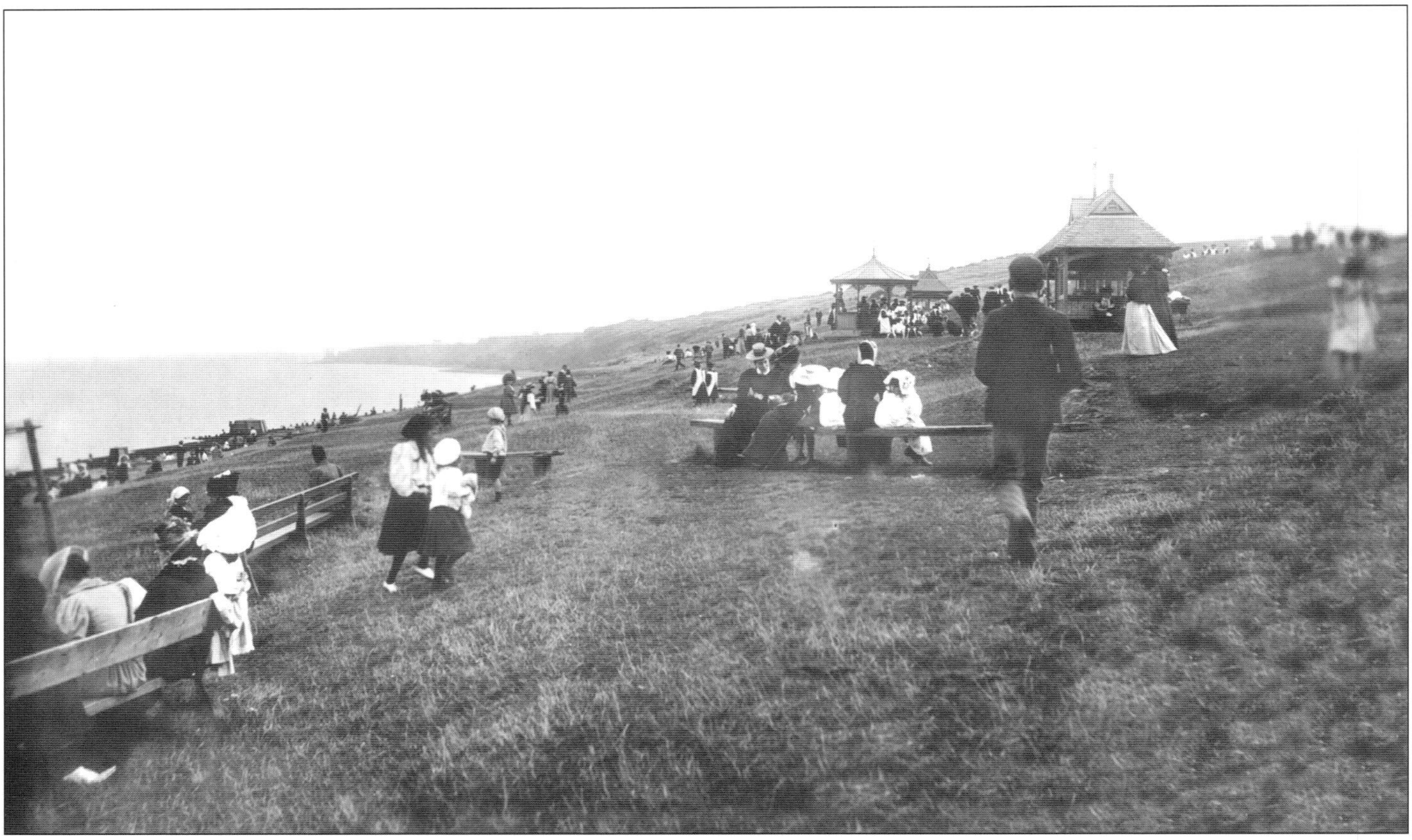

40162
A view of East Cliff in 1894. A popular spot of rough grassland where the downs meet the sea. The beach could be reached by a series of steps known as 'The Hundred Steps'.

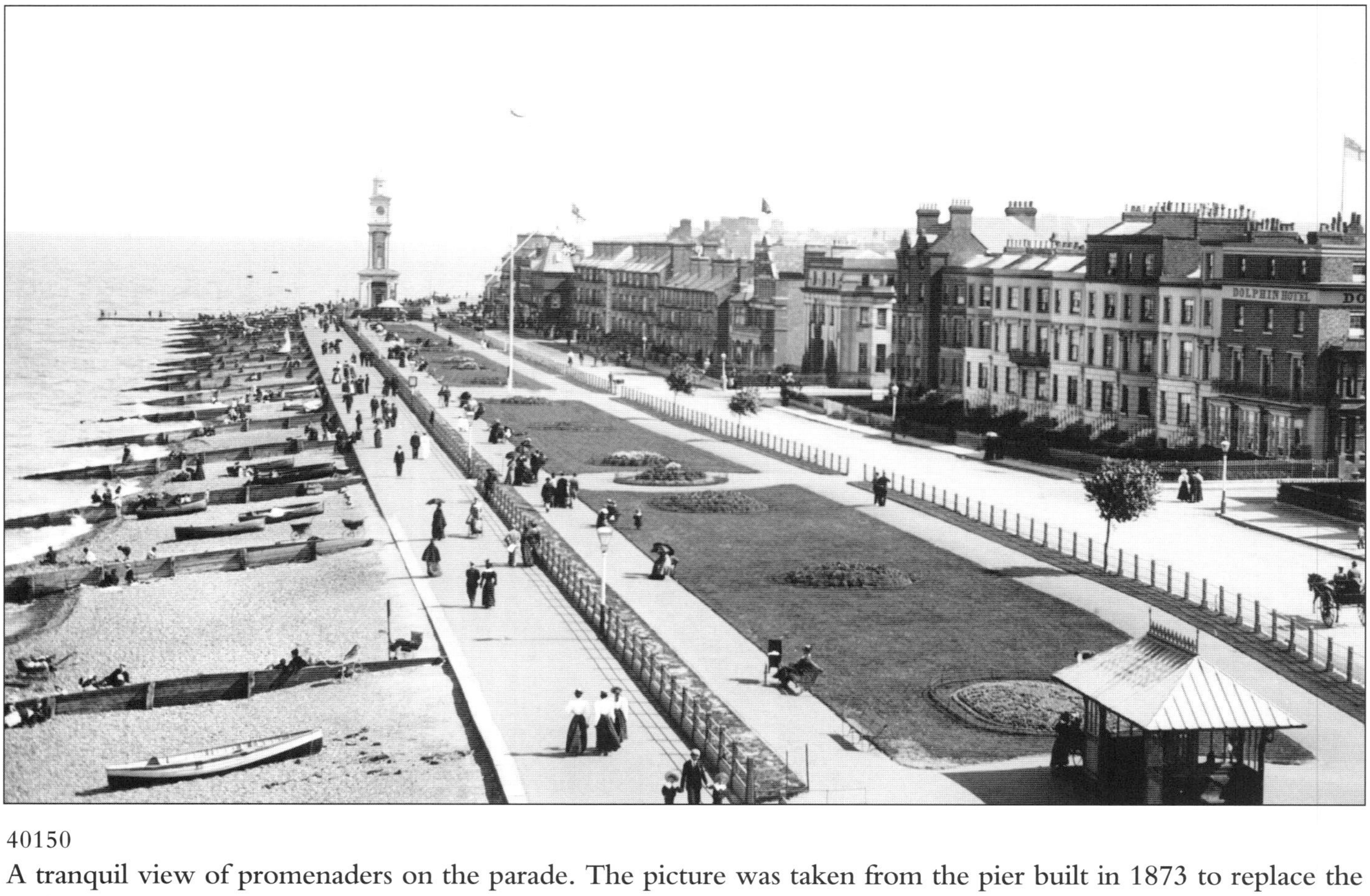


40150
A tranquil view of promenaders on the parade. The picture was taken from the pier built in 1873 to replace the earlier and more ambitious pier designed by Telford. Herne Bay was always a popular family resort.

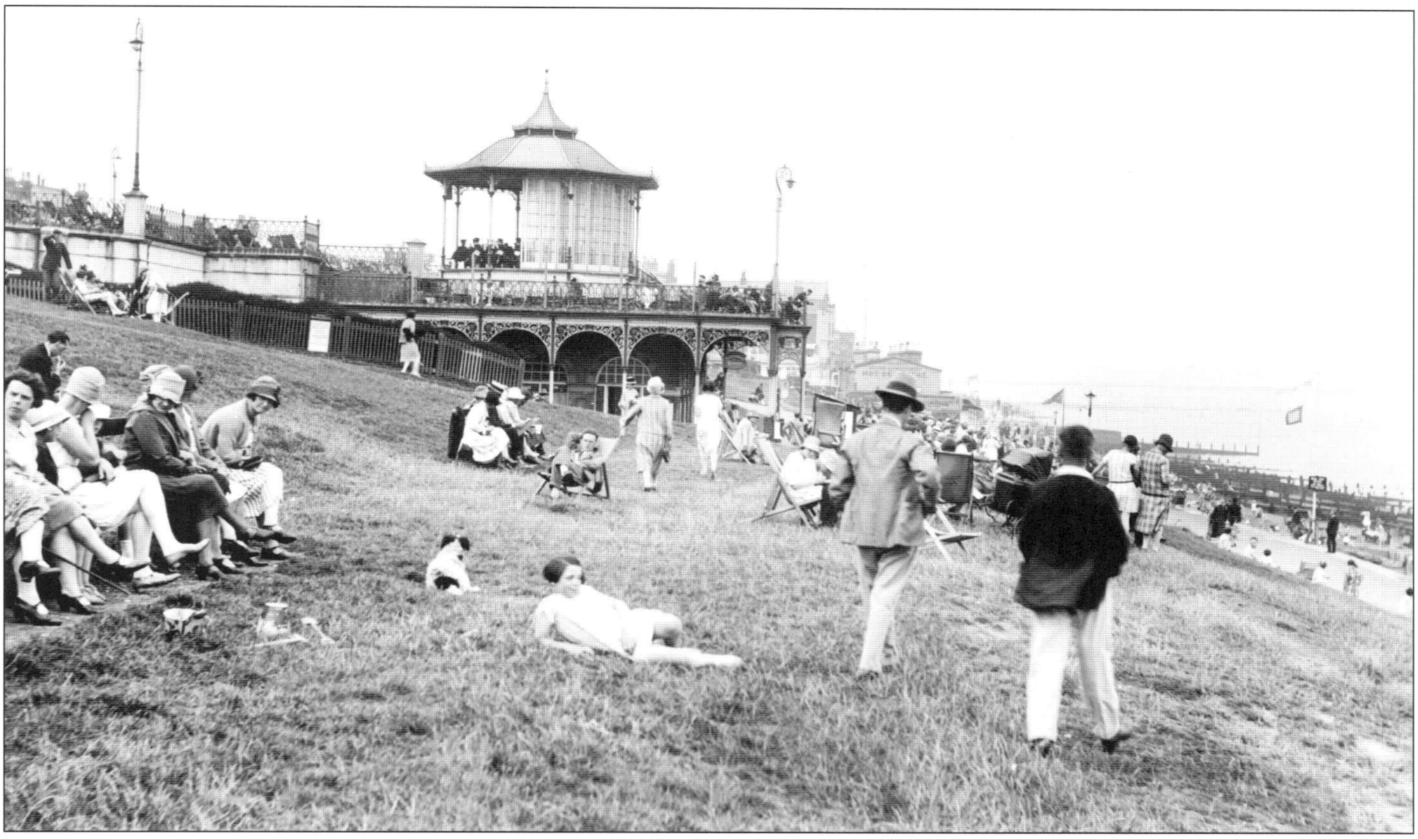

80119
A generation later, and fashions have changed among holiday makers on East Cliff, as this 1927 picture shows, although nearly everyone is still wearing a hat. Deckchairs are much in evidence.

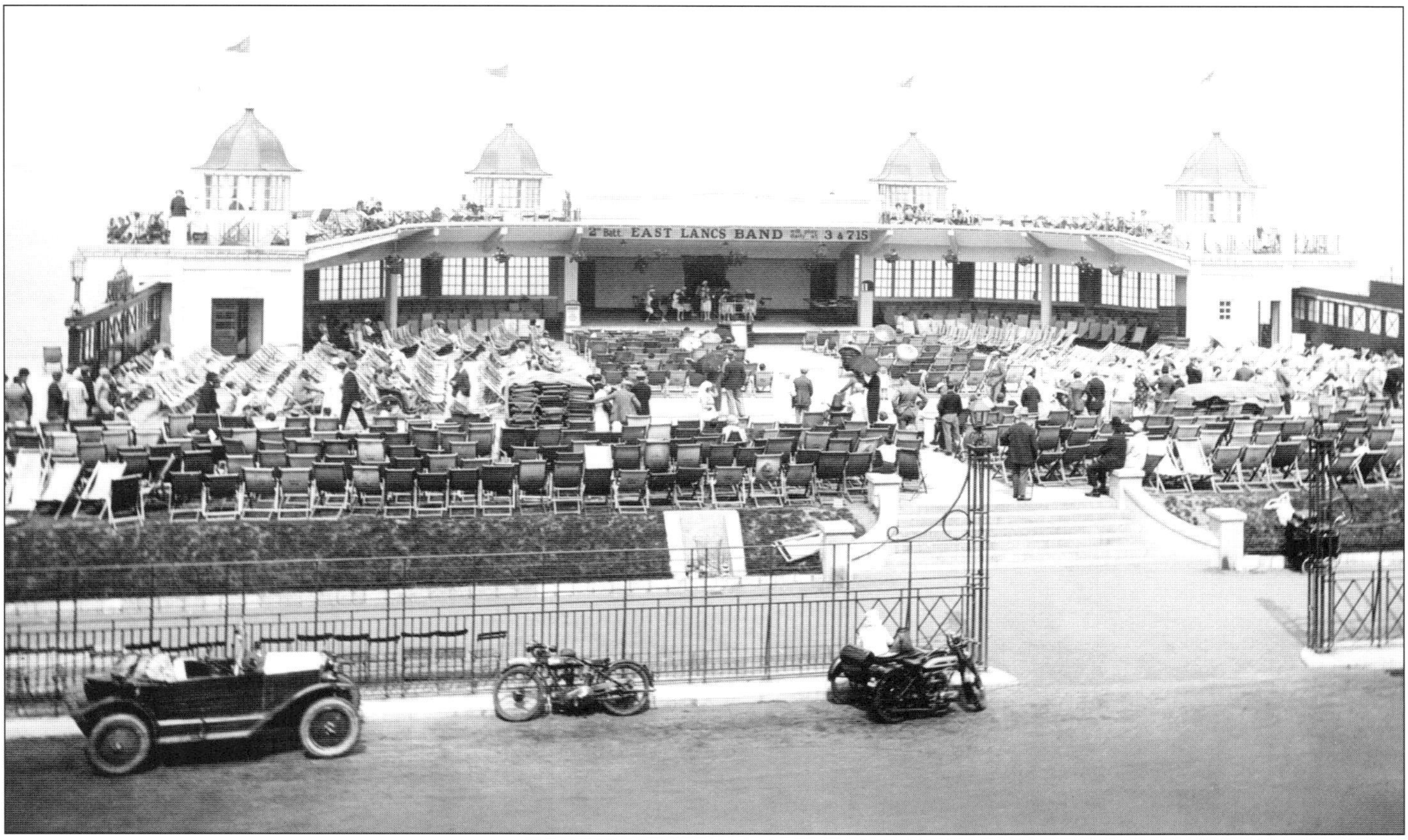


80116
The central bandstand on the seaward side of the parade in 1927. Here the audience are assembling for what looks like a Sunday Concert. An open-topped tourer and motor-cycles are parked by the entrance railings.

# HEVER

A castle, church, inn and houses huddled closely together near the Sussex border. The church is fourteenth century, with a charming shingled spire. Today, it is best known for the moated Hever Castle, restored at the beginning of the twentieth century. The gardens are magnificent, and the house contains a marvellous collection of paintings and furniture.

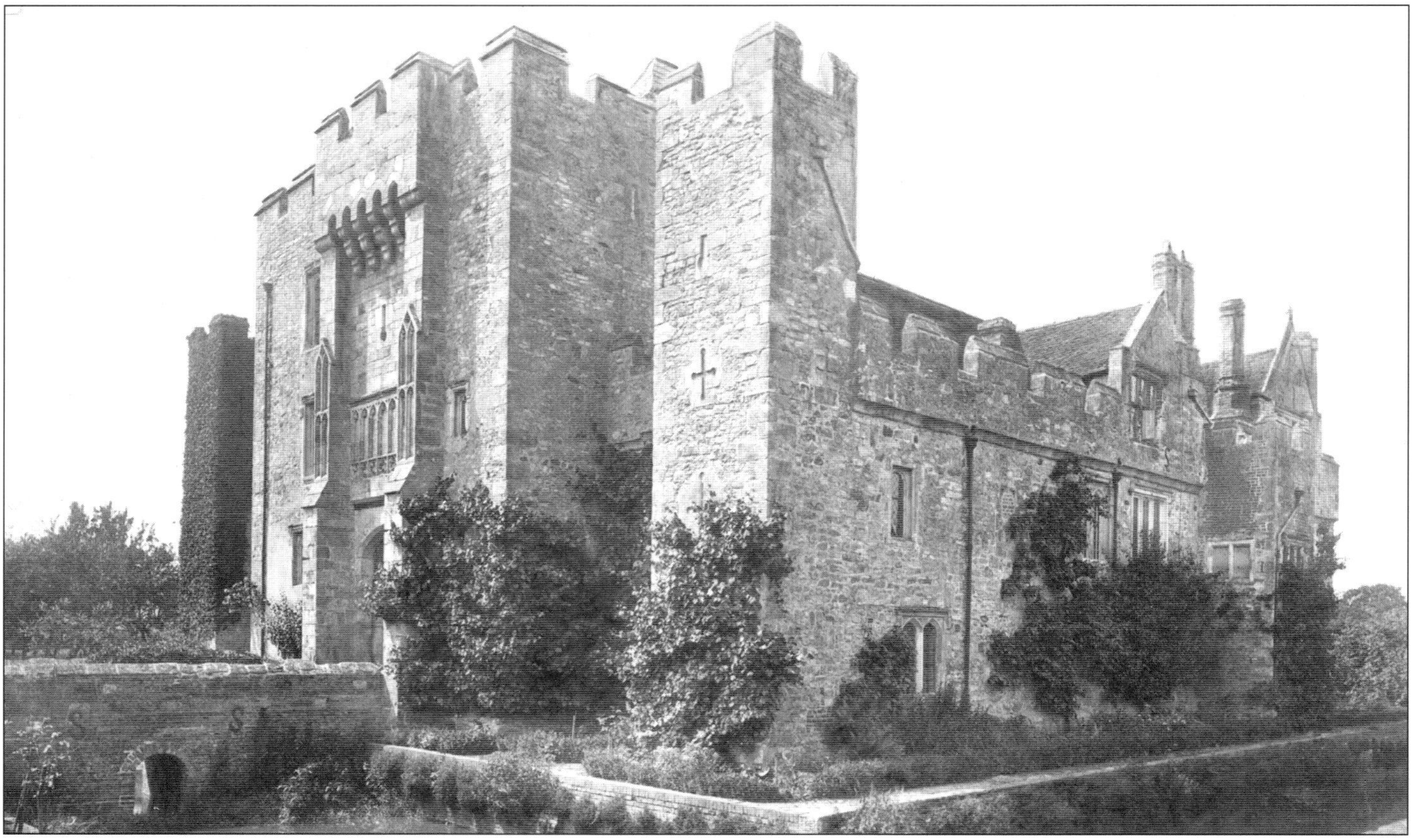

29396
Hever Castle in 1891, twelve years before the start of its restoration by Lord Astor, when its associations were solely with the romantic attachment of Henry VIII and Anne Boleyn. The square sandstone house is of 1384.

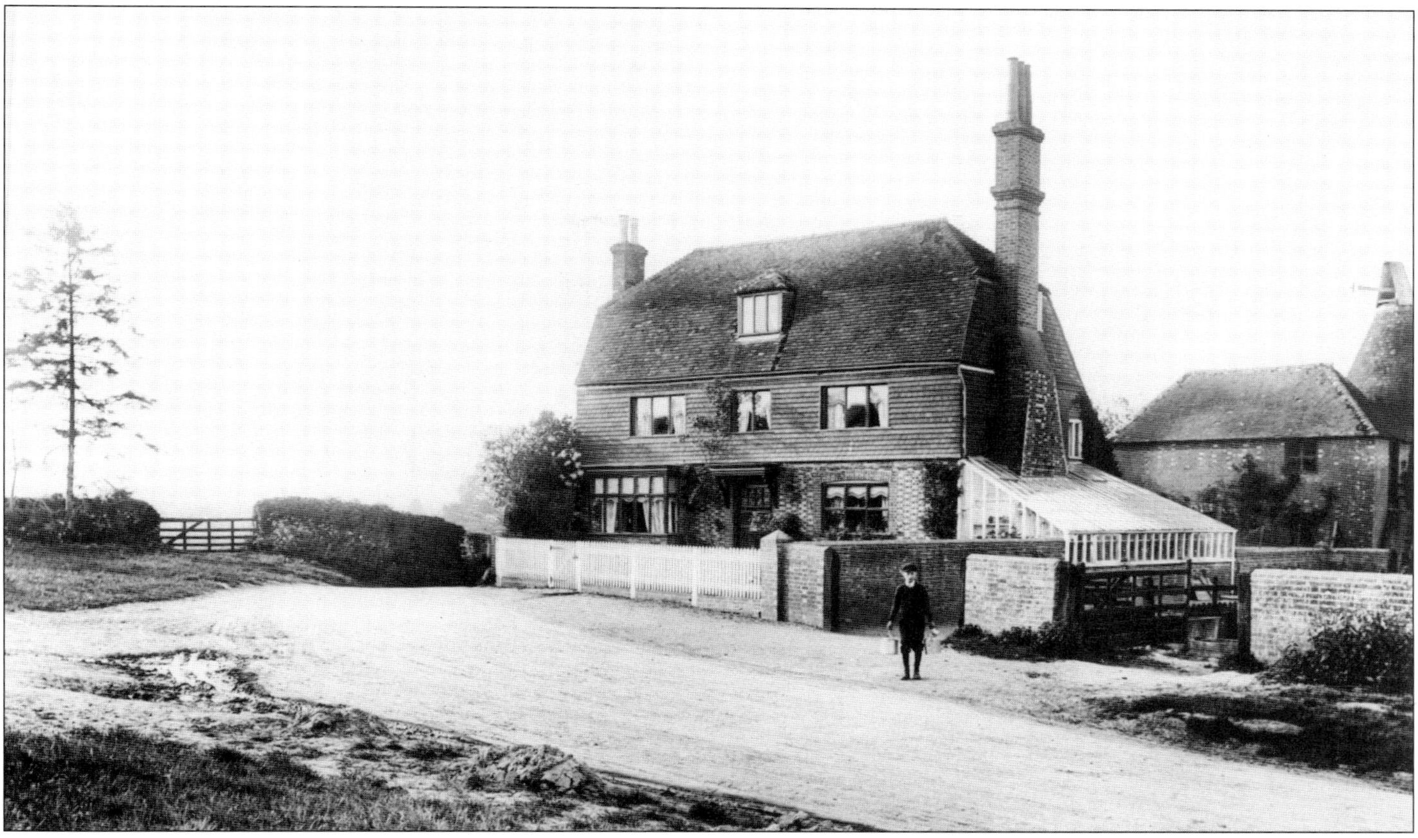

53557

A charming piece of old Kent, the Bower in 1906. Note the architecture with hung tiles and hipped roof, with the big conservatory and the round oast house to the right.

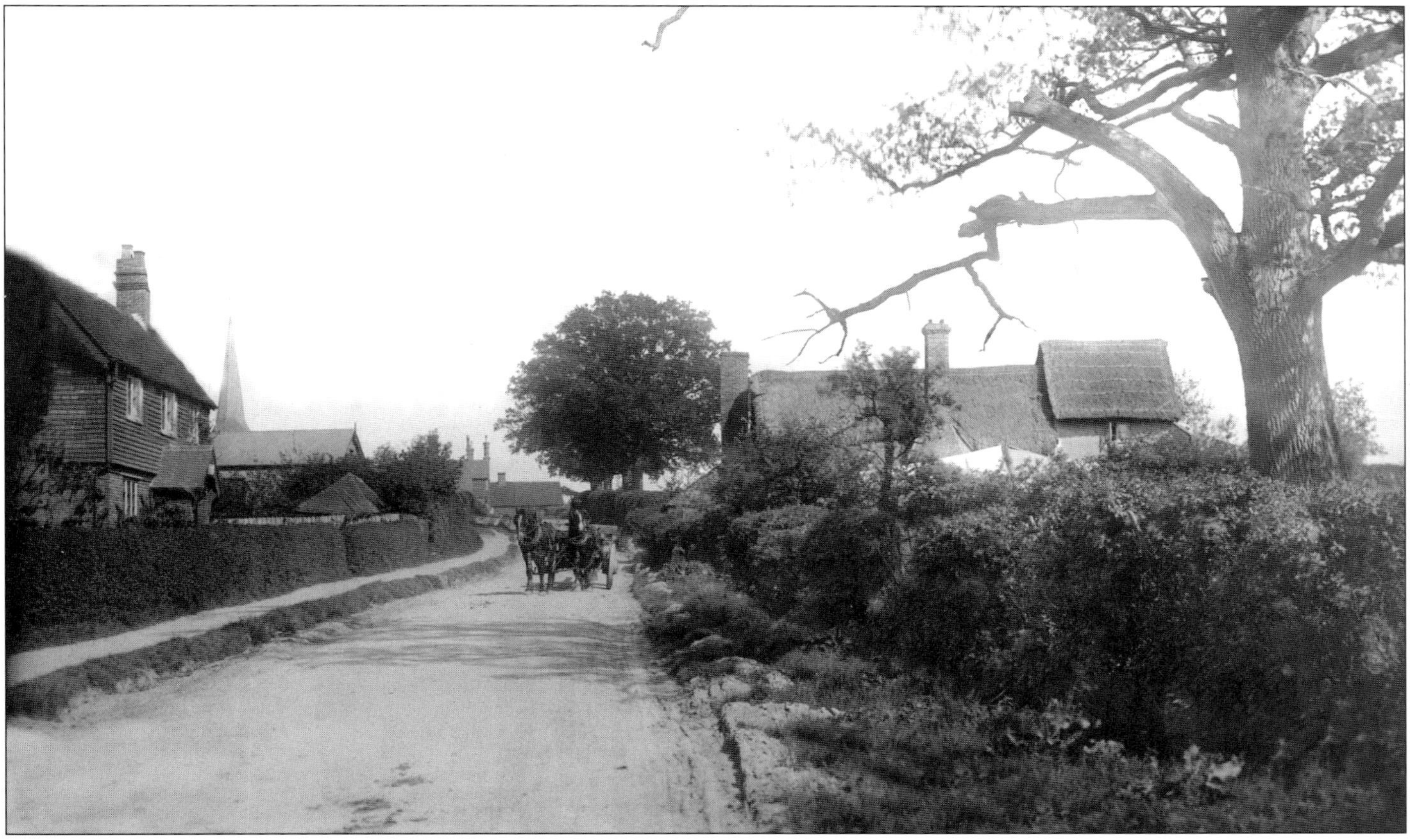

53550

Hever village in 1905, prior to Lord Astor's creation of a Tudor-style village adjacent to the castle. A horse-drawn wagon comes down the lane, and to the left is the spire of St Peter's Church.

# Hythe

An old town, one of the Cinque Ports, is now very much a seaside resort close to Romney Marsh. The Royal Military Canal divides the resort from the old town, with its narrow twisting streets leading up to the medieval church. Today, it is the terminus of the Romney, Hythe and Dymchurch Railway.

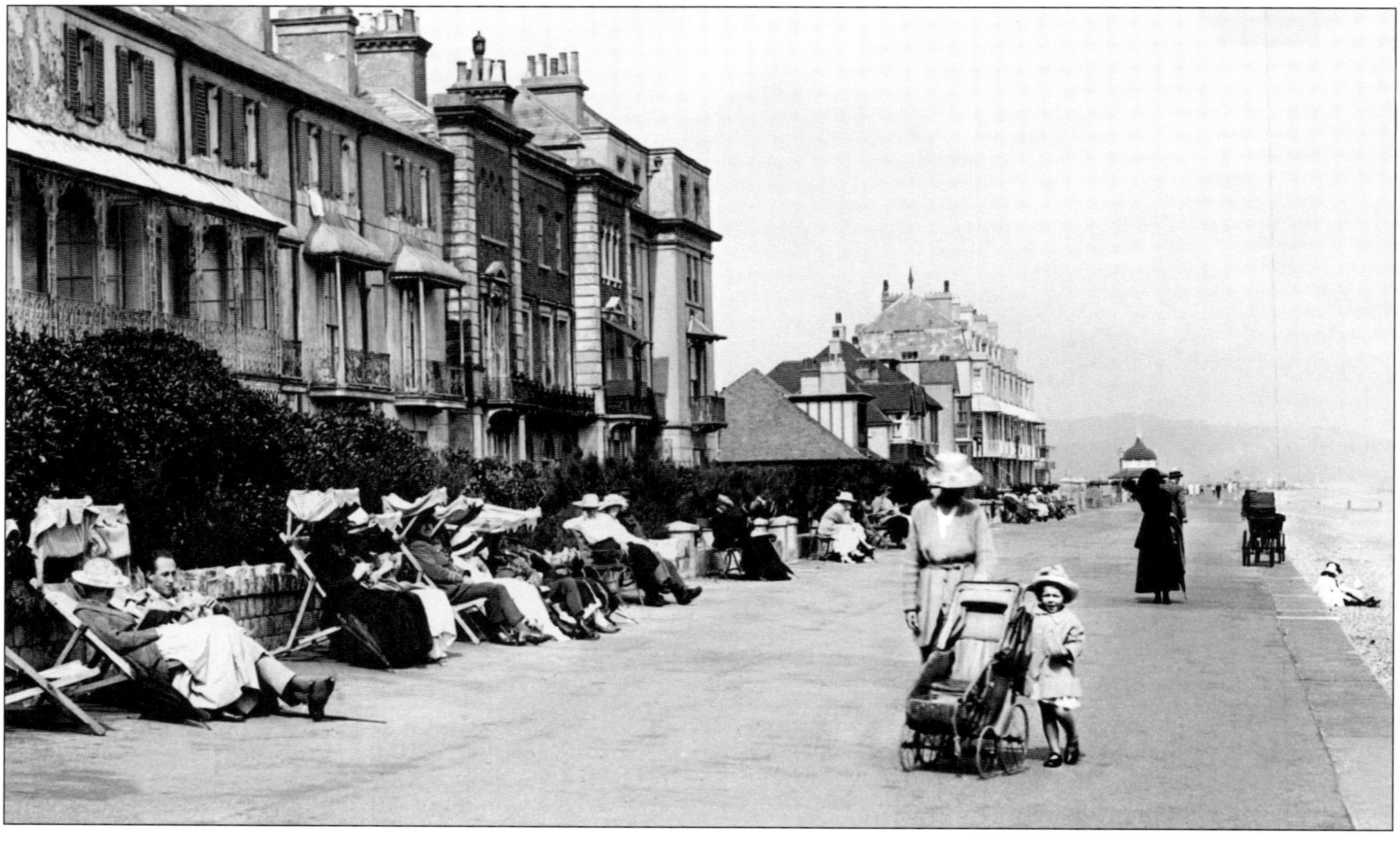

68149

A wonderful study of the canopied deckchair on Hythe Parade dated 1918. It is curious to realise that this gentle holiday scene was probably taken during the closing months of the First World War.

# Ightam

A lovely old village of half-timbered cottages and houses, with fourteenth century church. Nearby is Ightam Mote, a famous secluded manor house, which can trace its history back to medieval times. Among its many splendours, the mote has a fifteenth century great hall, an old chapel and a crypt.

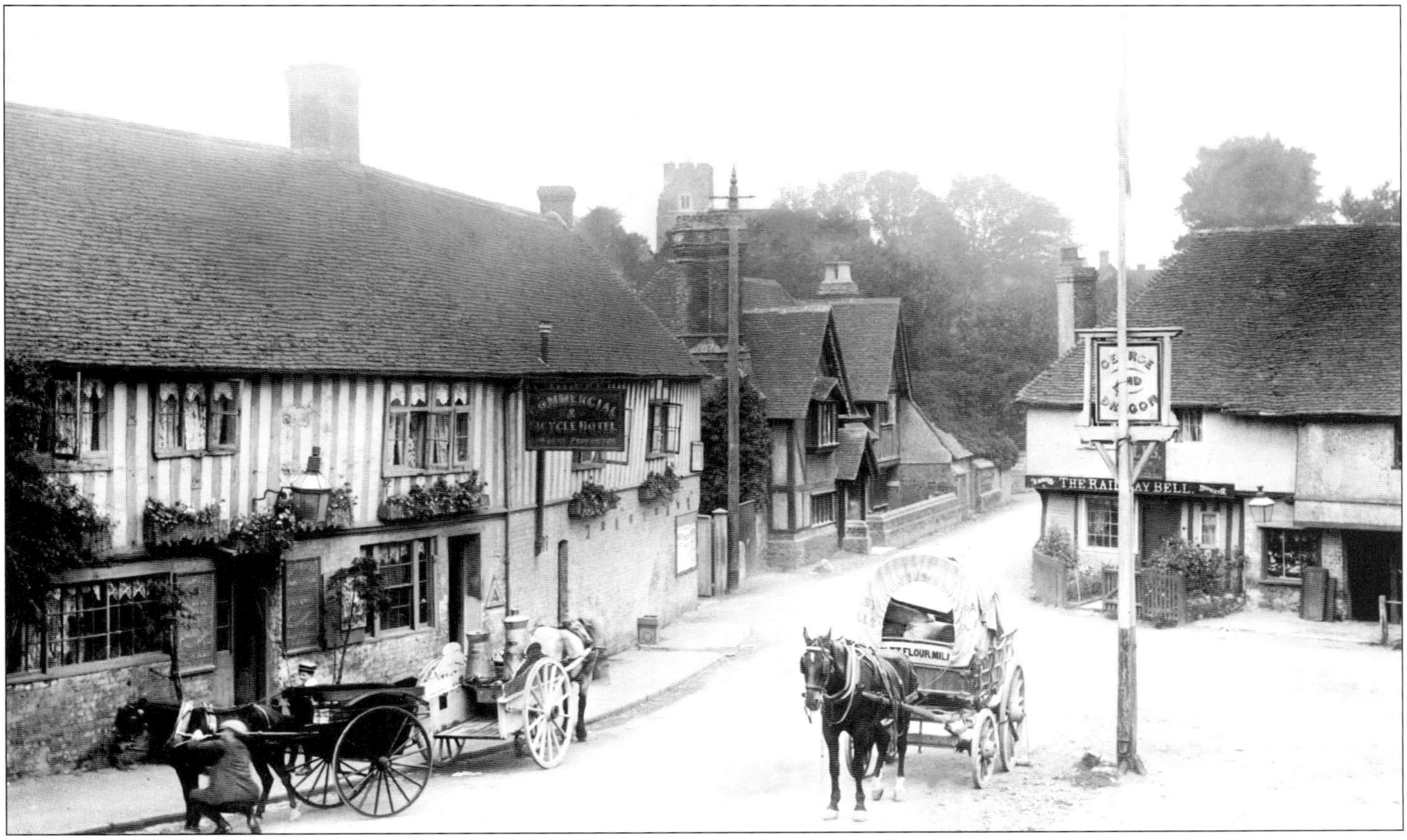

47623
Ightham Square pictured early one morning in 1901 with delivery men making their rounds - note the churns on the milk cart in the centre. The George and Dragon Inn, on the left was built in 1515.

# Kingsdown

Situated to the south of Deal, modern housing on the cliffs lies the older fishing village beneath the cliffs by the beach. It is reputed that Julius Caesar landed here on the steep shingle beach in 55 BC. The church, built in florid Gothic, is Victorian.

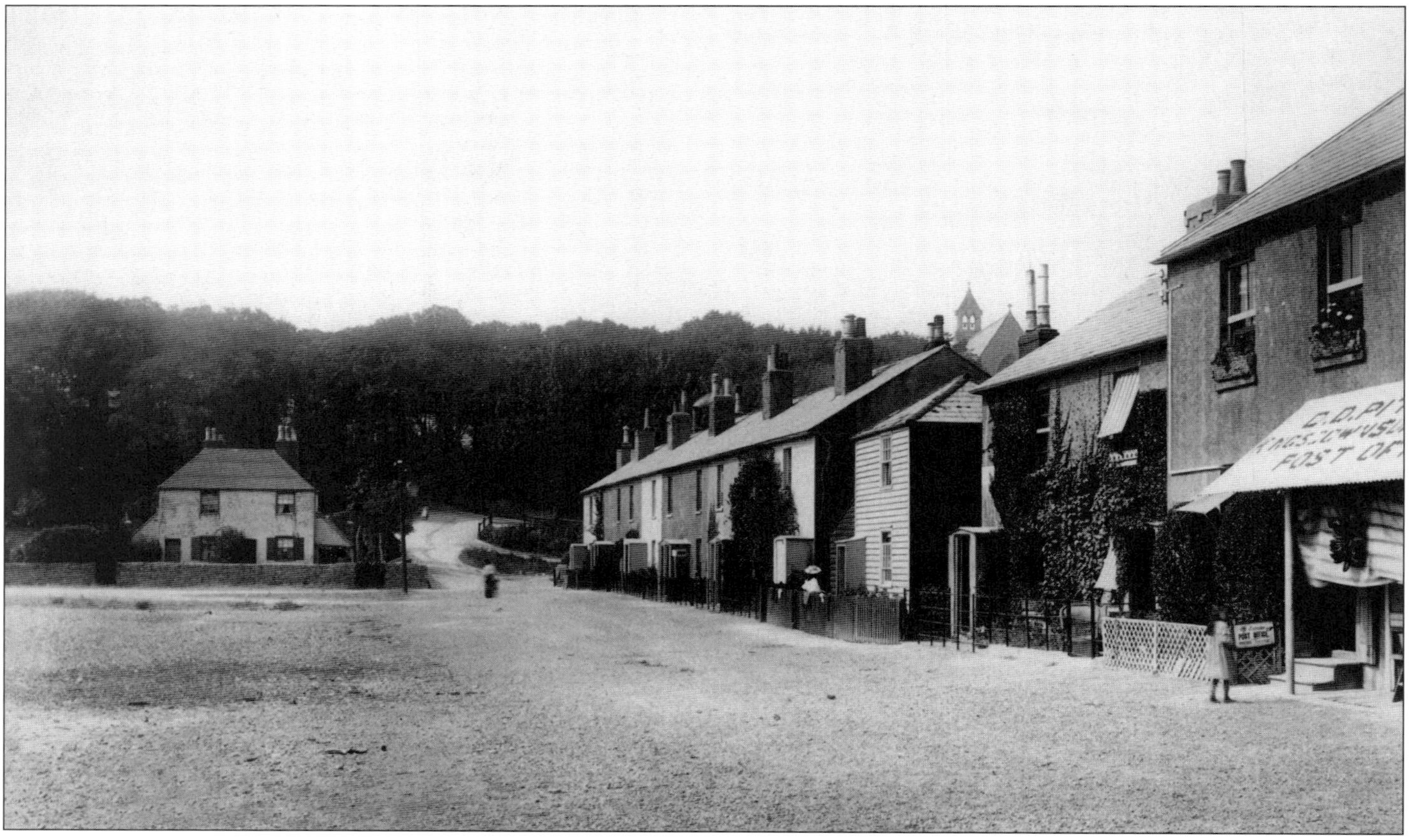

56926
The old fishing village in the summer of 1906. The post office is on the extreme right of the photograph, while the church roof is visible to the right of centre. The wooded cliff behind is now largely developed.

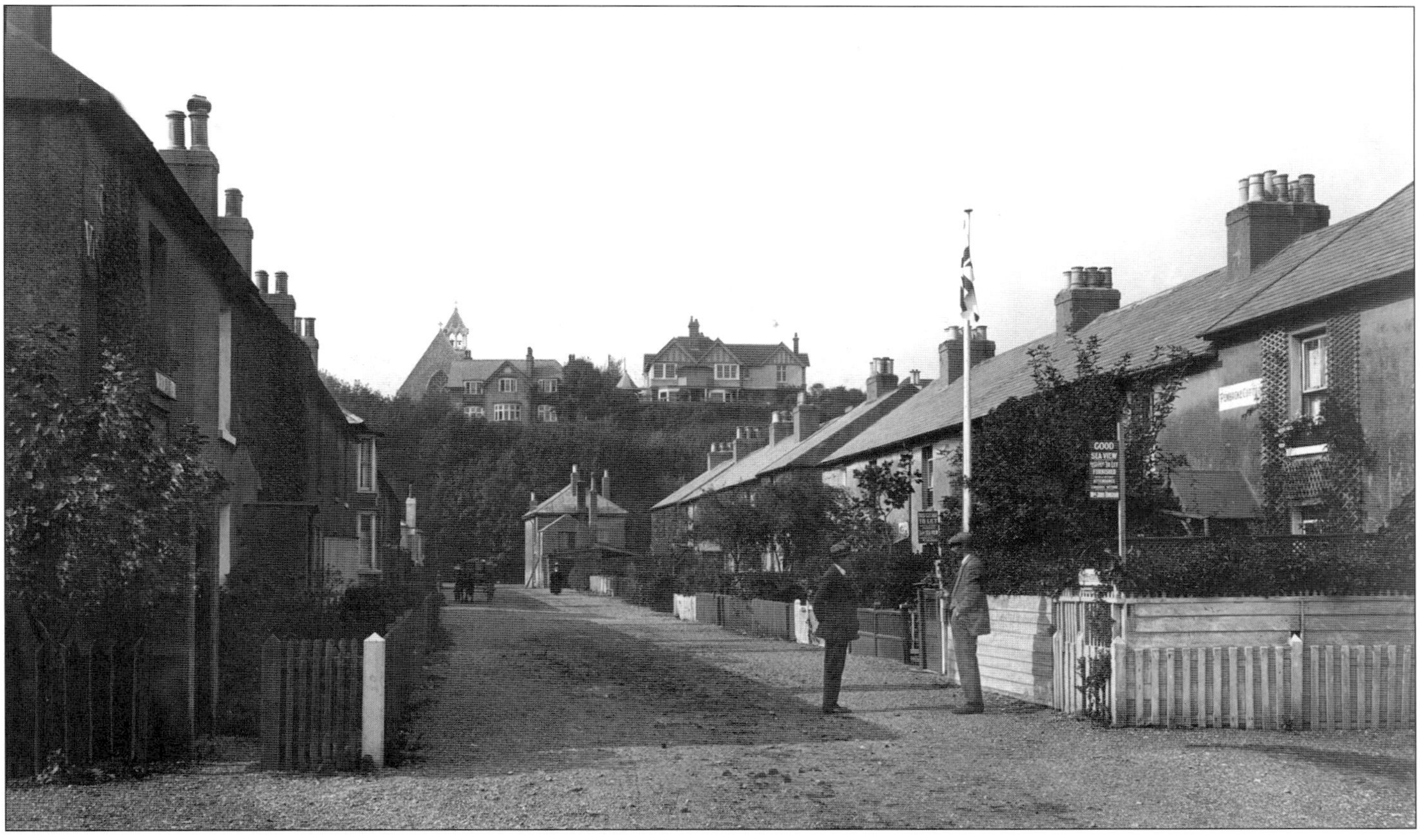

68506
Conversation piece in Kingsdown village dated 1918. With the First World War still rumbling on the Union flag has been hoisted on its white flagpole, but hardly stirs in the summer breeze.

## LITTLEBOURNE

A pleasant village at a crossing of the Little Stour River on the old Roman road east of Canterbury, with a green and pretty cottages. The old water mill still stands by the river. The flint-built church dates from the fifteenth century, and the churchyard is bounded by a remarkably long thatched barn.

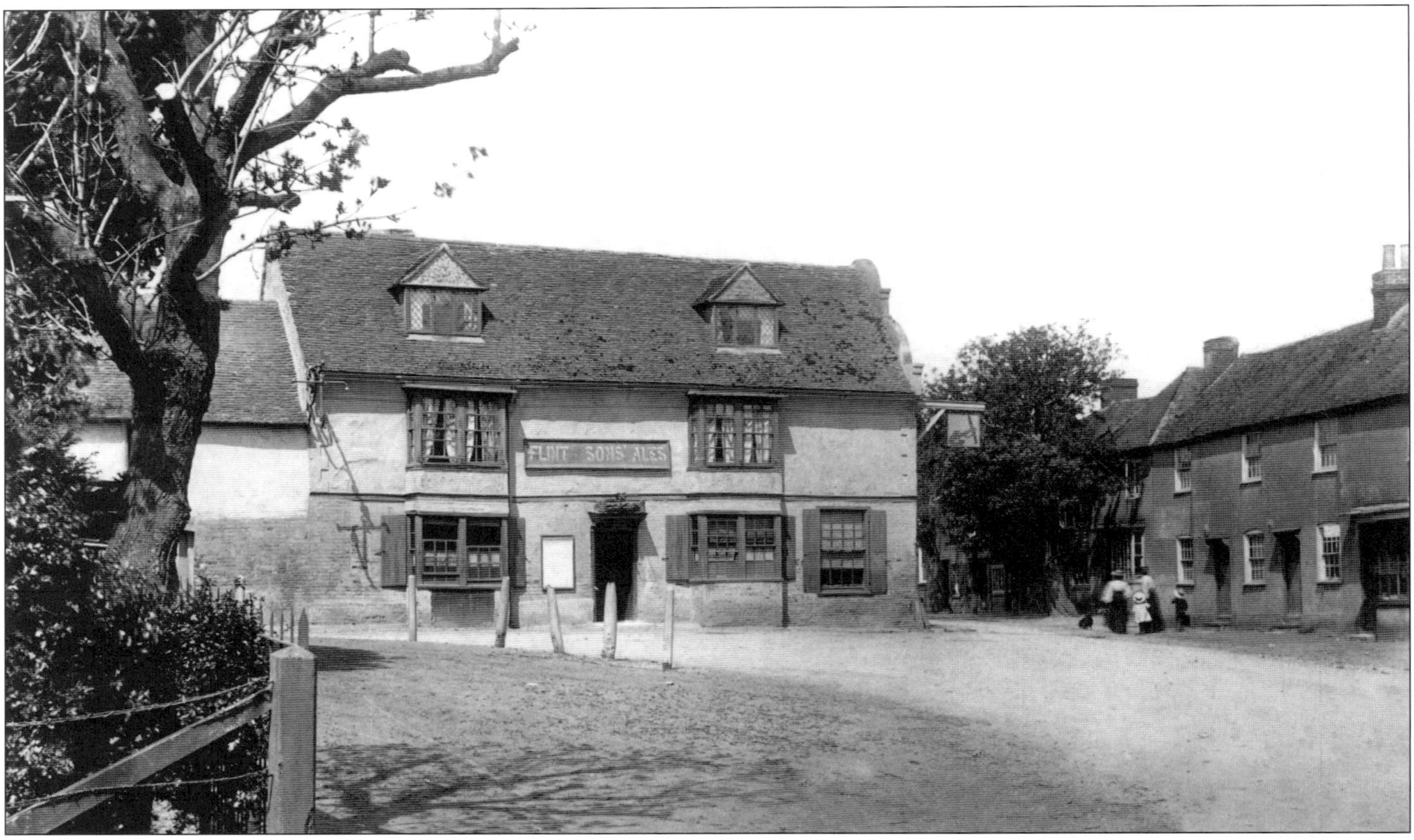


51052
The sleepy summertime picture of the village square in 1903, deserted save for the little group on the left. The old established Anchor Inn advertises Flint Son's Ales, a local brew.

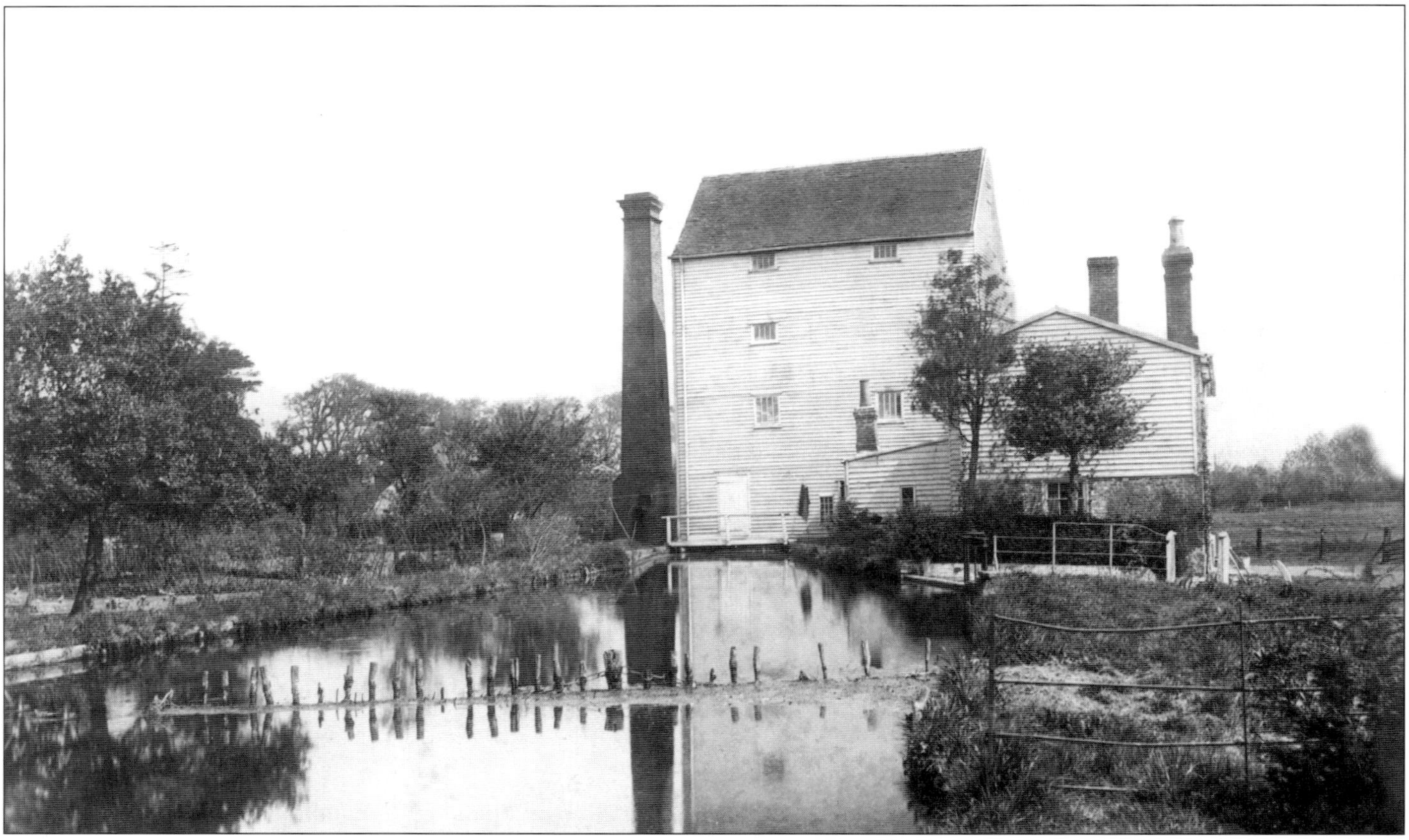

49432
The tall weatherboarded mill on the Little Stour River, pictured on the same quiet summer's day in 1903, its reflection plunging deep into the mill pool.

# Leeds Castle

The small village of Leeds is dominated by the presence of its large romantic castle. The castle is Norman, but there was an earlier Saxon castle on the site. The castle remained a royal palace for centuries afterwards, and was left to the nation in 1974. Since then it has become a full blooded tourist attraction, set in its 500 acre park.

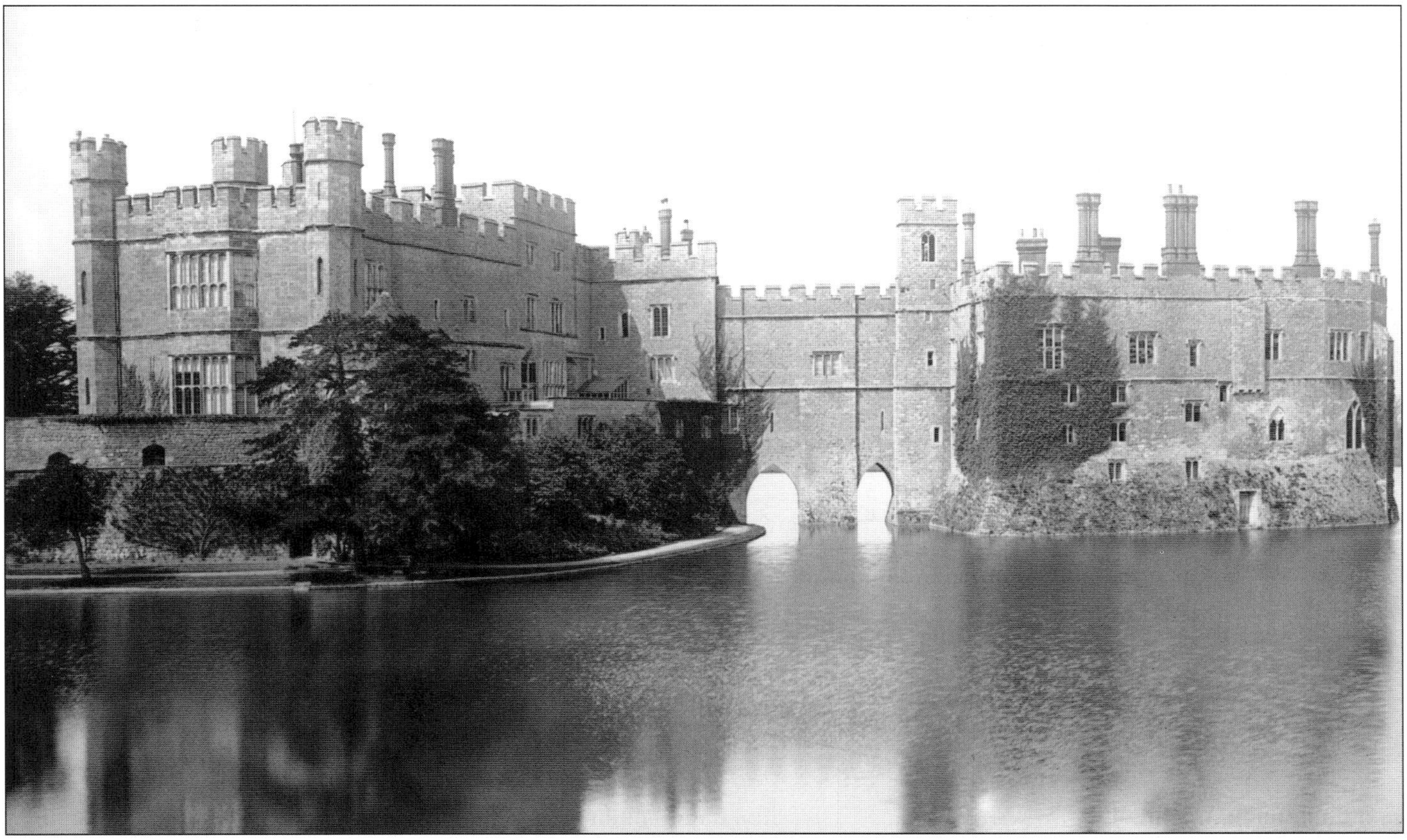

31500
Leeds Castle pictured in 1892, rising serenely from its two islands in a lake on the River Len. At that time it was still a private residence, half forgetting its past as a 'queen's castle' and a prison for 'persons of consequence'.

# Maidstone

The county town of Kent stands on the banks of the River Medway. The oldest building, the Bishop's Palace, fronts the river beside the great medieval church of All Saints. Maidstone has been an important market town since the middle ages, although today it is also an important industrial centre. Much of the medieval heart survives, including buildings such as the museum.

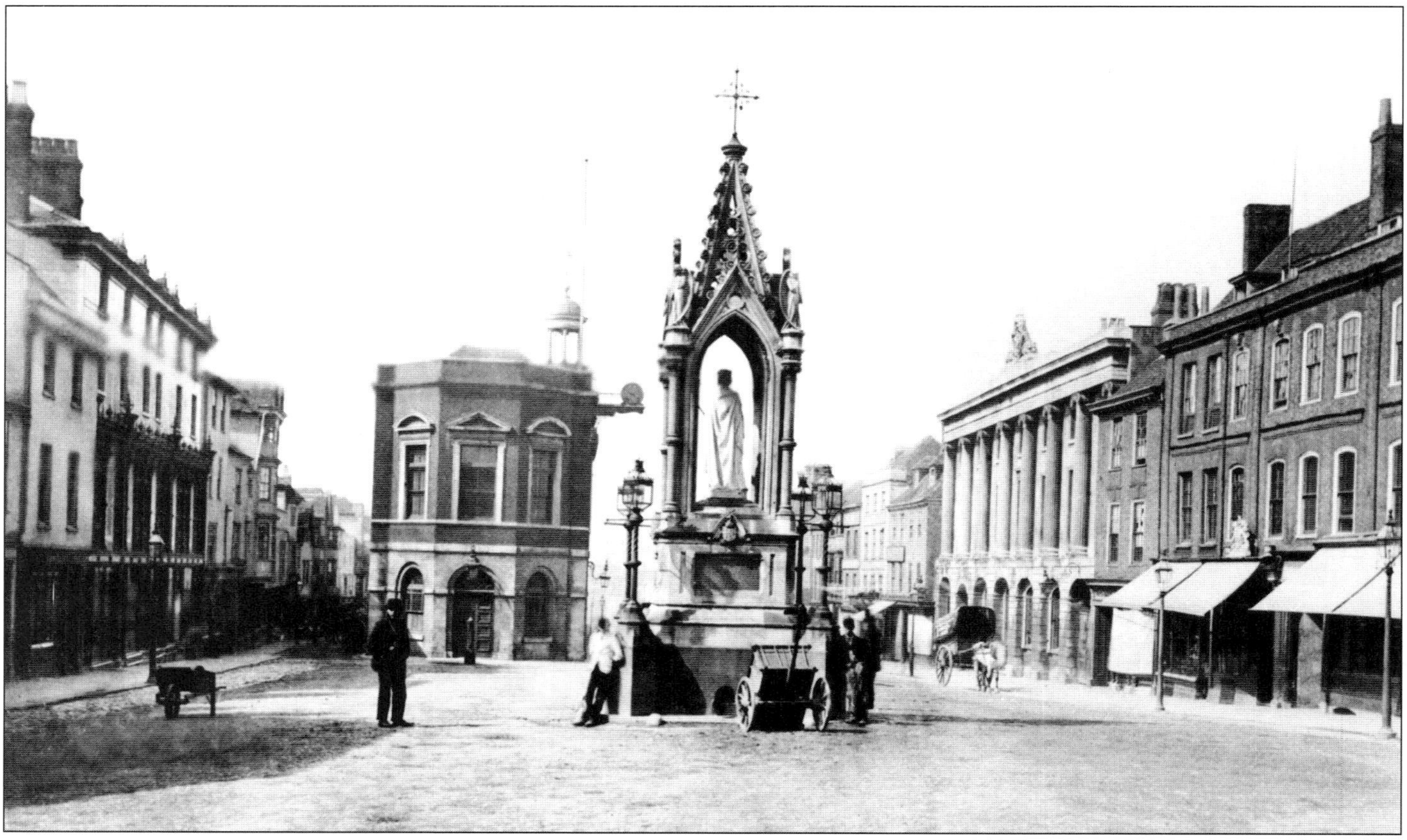

1480
Maidstone High Street in about 1870, showing the drinking fountain and statue of Queen Victoria of 1862. To the left is Bank Street, separated from High Street by a block of buildings which have infilled the formerly very wide High Street.

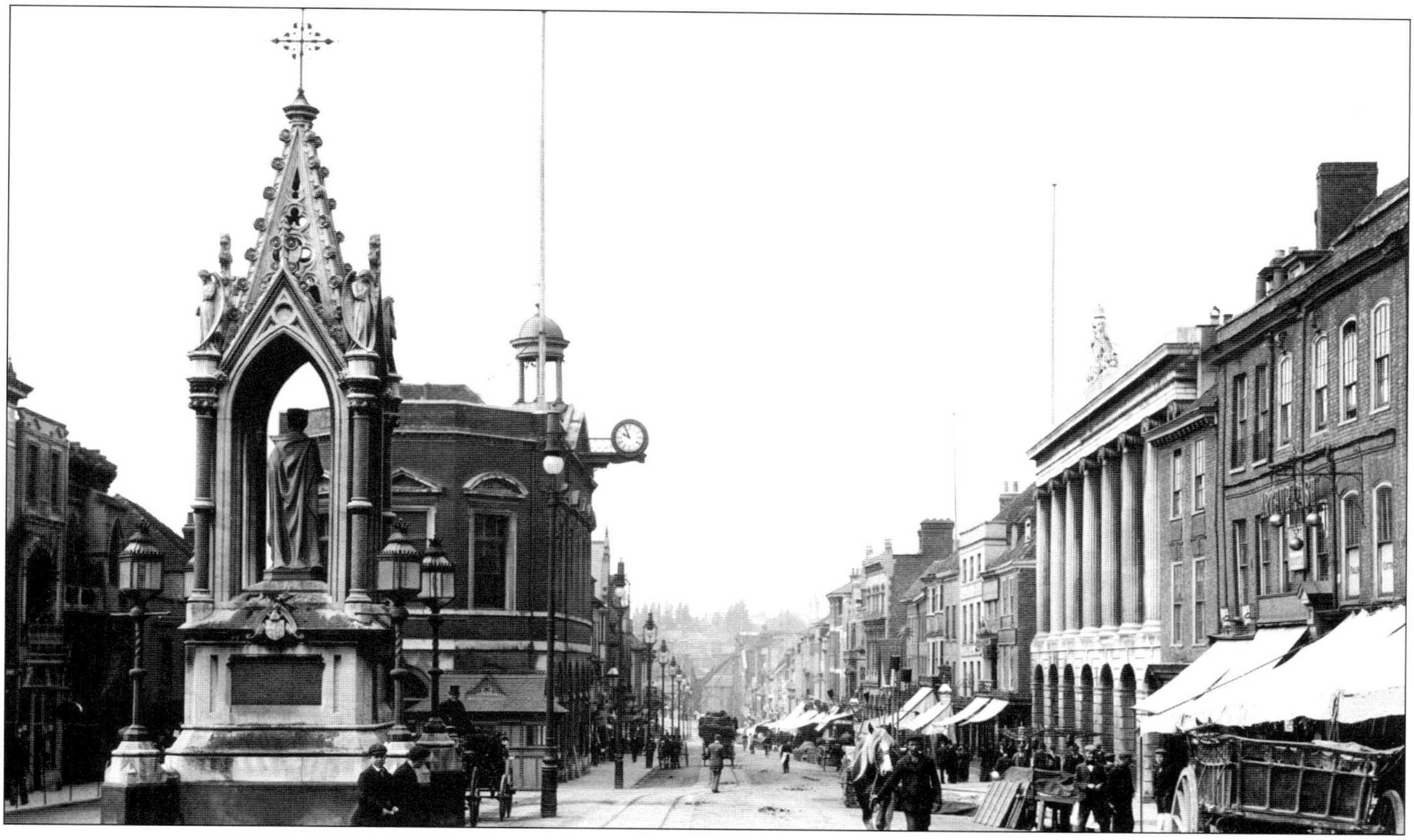

12684
The market in the High Street, 1885. This part of the High Street was Maidstone's market place from early times. The building on the 'island' site with the projecting clock is the Town Hall of 1762-3.

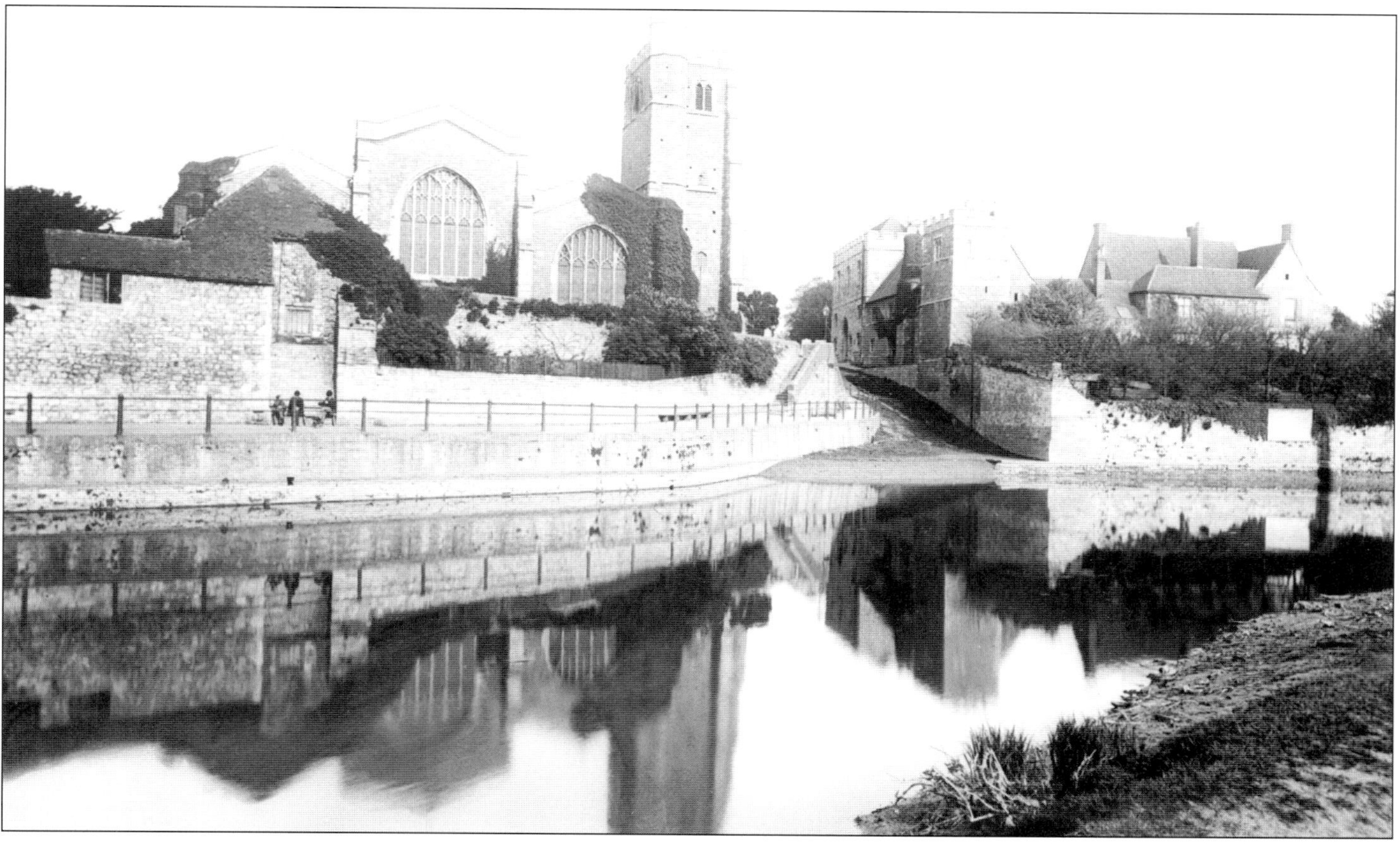

31485
A tranquil scene on the River Medway in 1892, looking towards the magnificent All Saints, Maidstone's parish church, dating from 1395. It was built largely by Archbishop Courtenay, a great-grandson of Edward I.

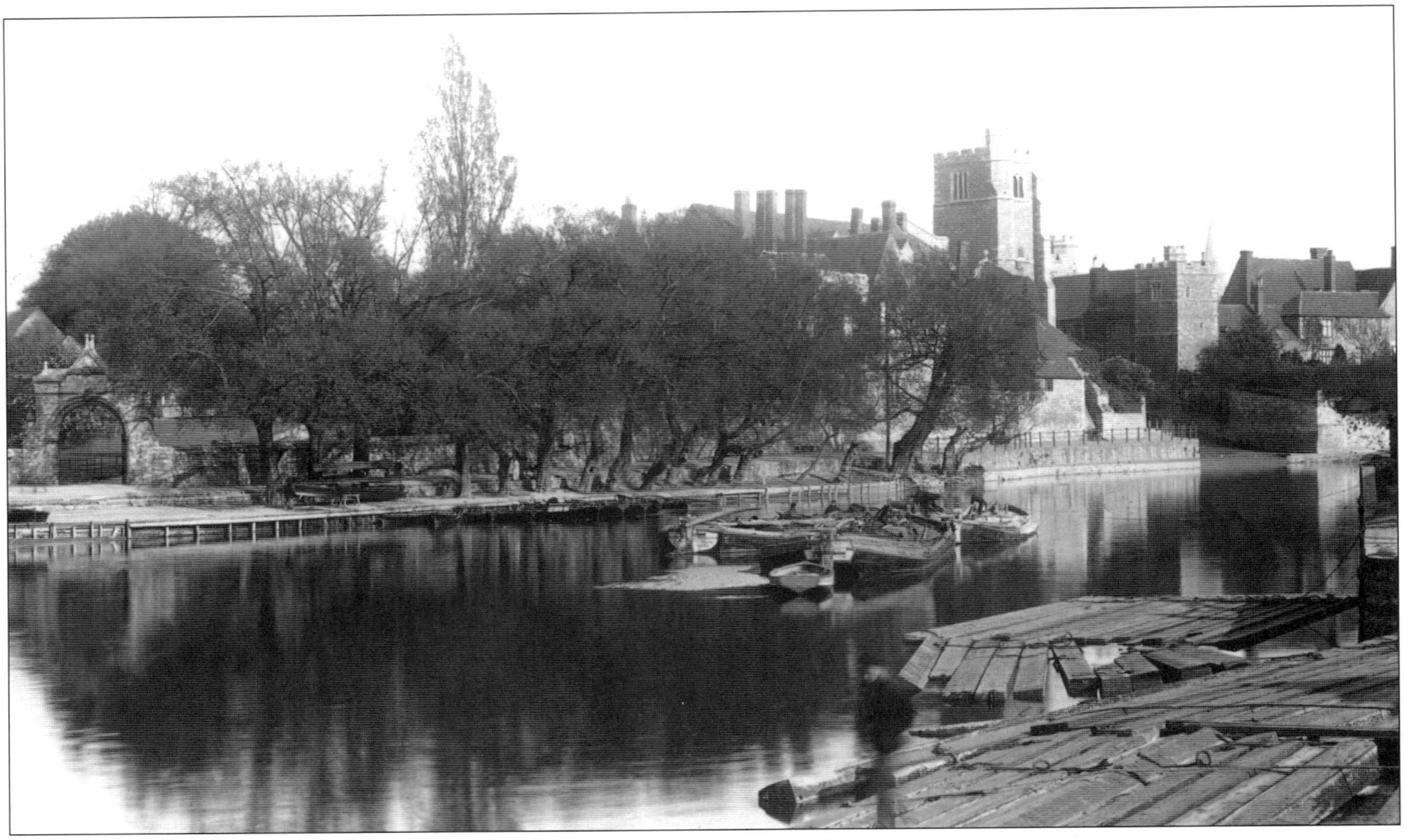

31483
The River Medway as an industrial highway: barges and log rafts going downstream past the Archbishop's Palace and All Saints Church in 1892. Formerly a ferry crossed the Medway at this point.

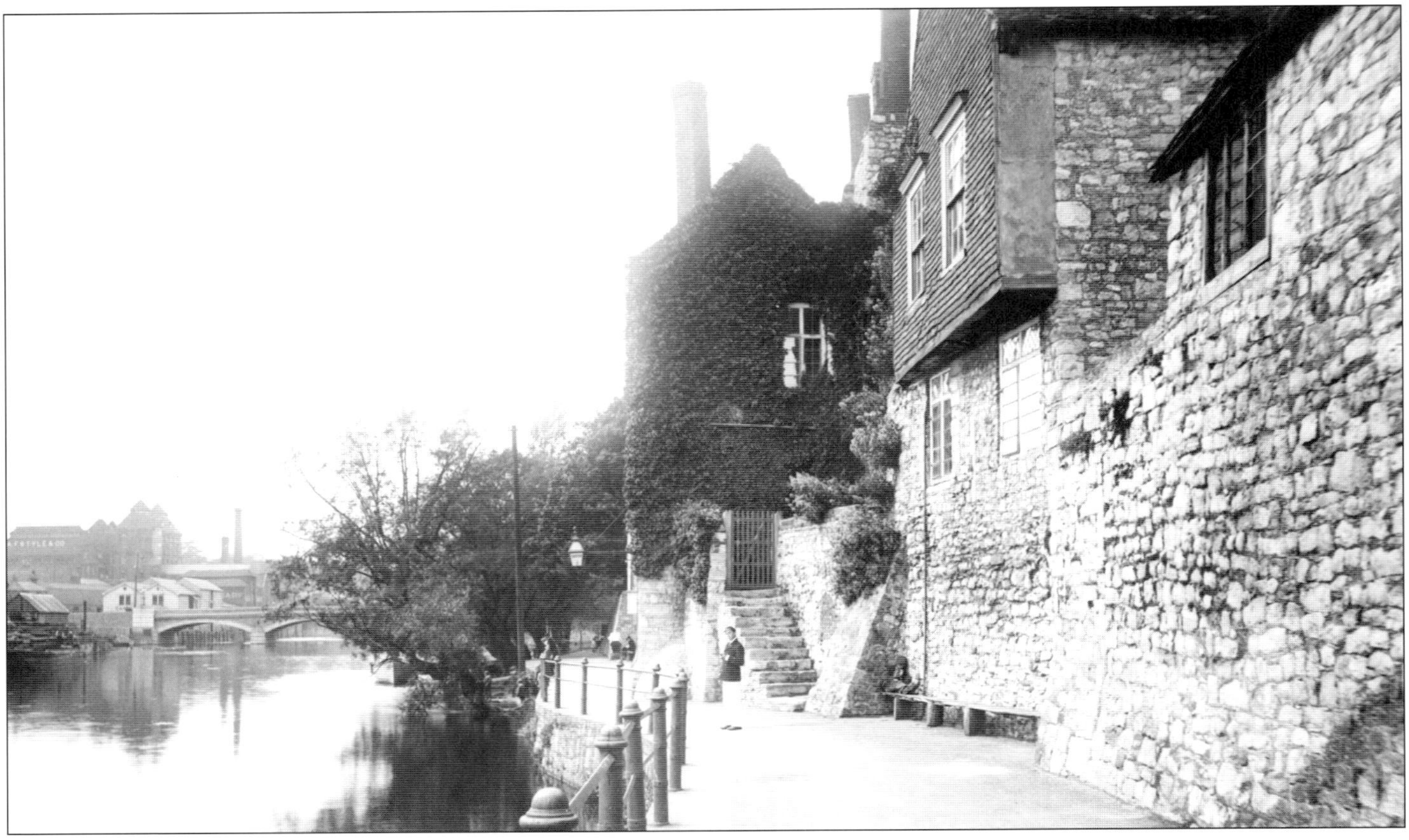

41535
The riverside promenade in 1898, looking past the Archbishop's Palace to Maidstone Bridge and the chimneys of the industrial area beyond. Today St Peter's Bridge (1978) intervenes between the palace and Maidstone Bridge.

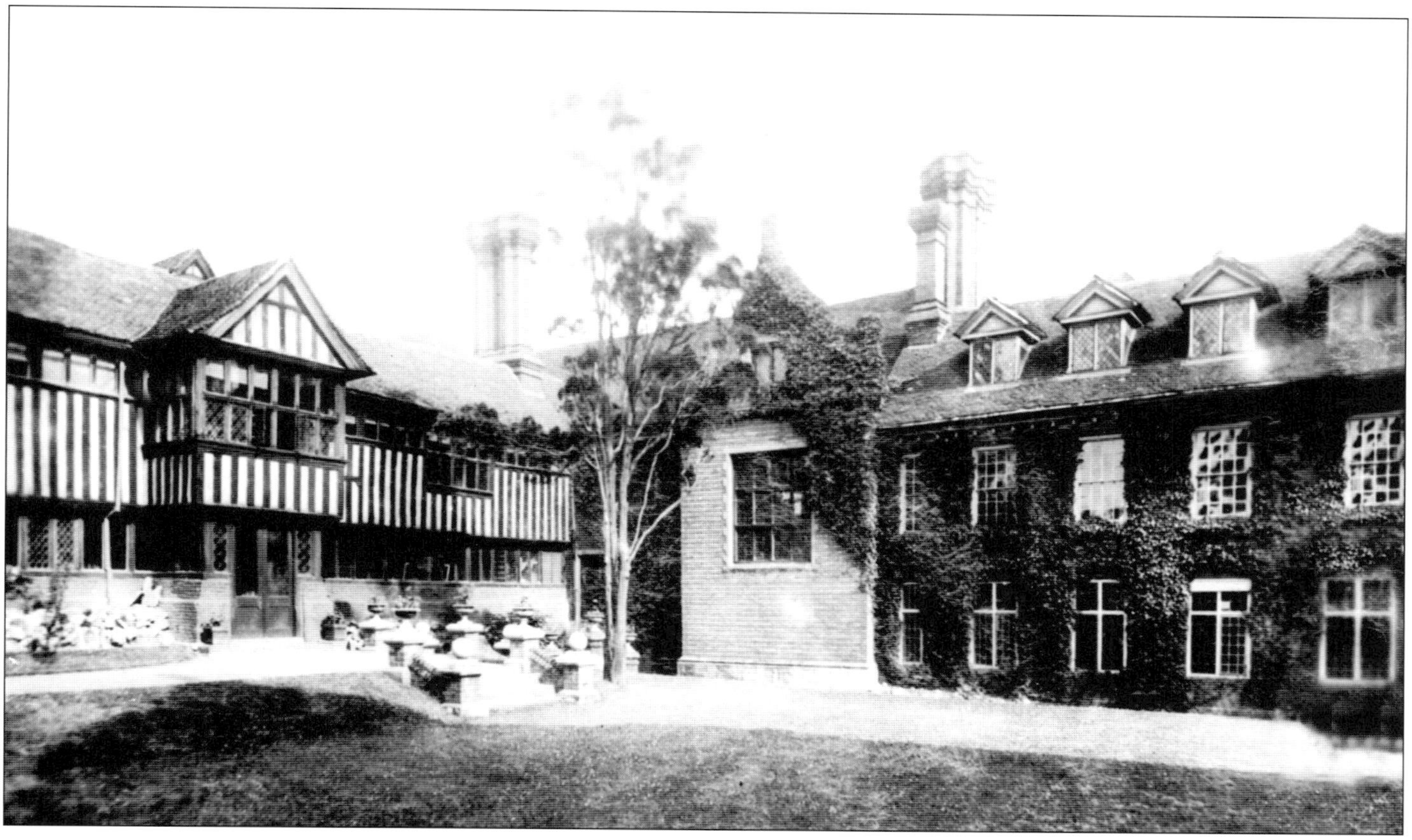

41542
Maidstone Museum in 1898. The splendid red-brick Tudor house was once Chillington Manor, home of the Wyatts, one of whom, Sir Thomas the younger, led the rebellion against Queen Mary's marriage to Philip of Spain.

## Margate

Margate is today a bustling seaside resort on the Isle of Thanet, with many miles of sandy beaches, and typical seaside attractions. Once an old fishing village, it was developed in the mid-1700s as the earliest coastal and seabathing resort. The pier, known as the jetty, has now gone but the wide sweep of the promenade and harbour remains.

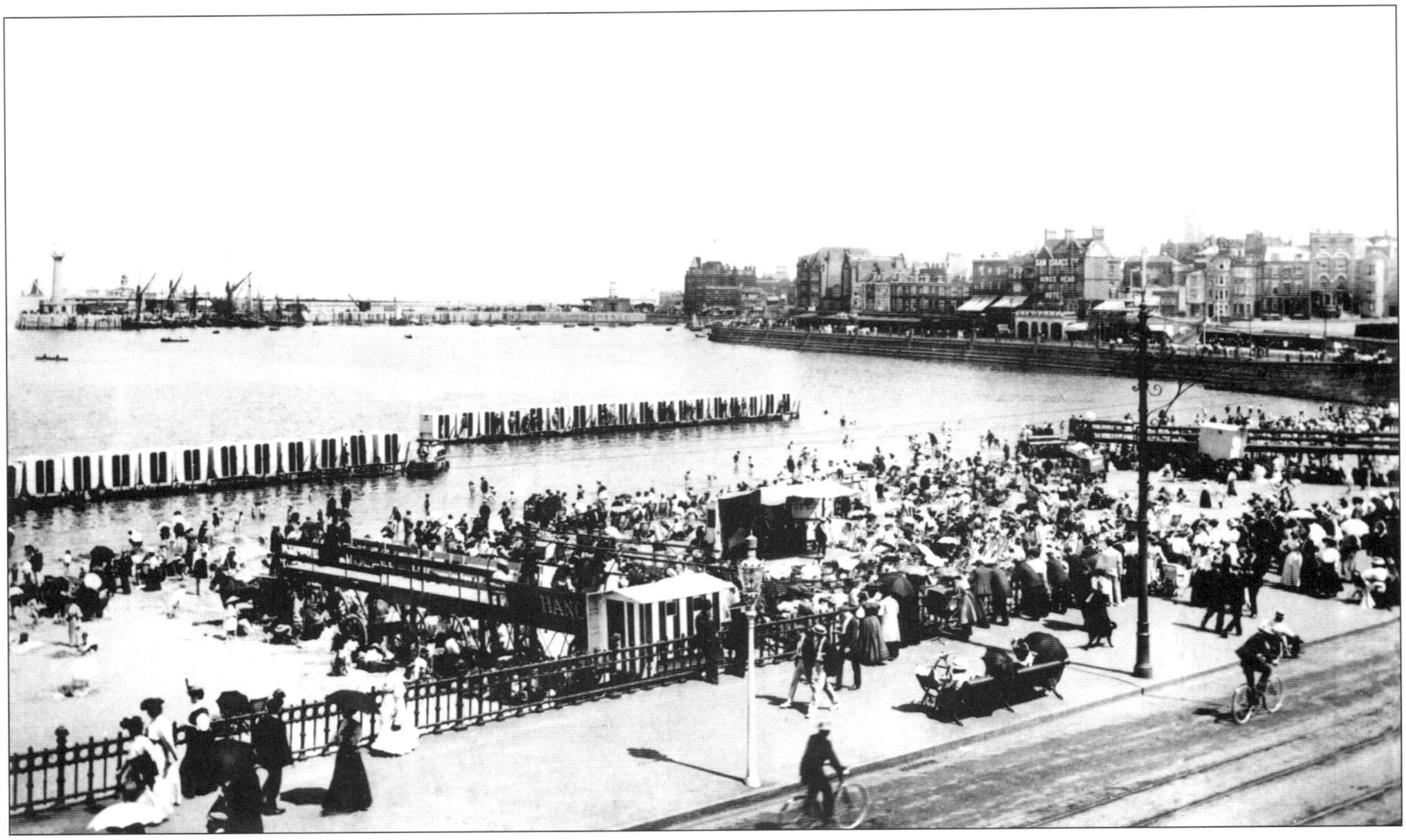

60359
Marine Parade in summer sunshine during 1908, looking across a crowded beach towards the harbour, stone pier and lighthouse. Bathing machines, of which a row can be seen, were invented by Benjamin Beale, a Margate glover in 1753.

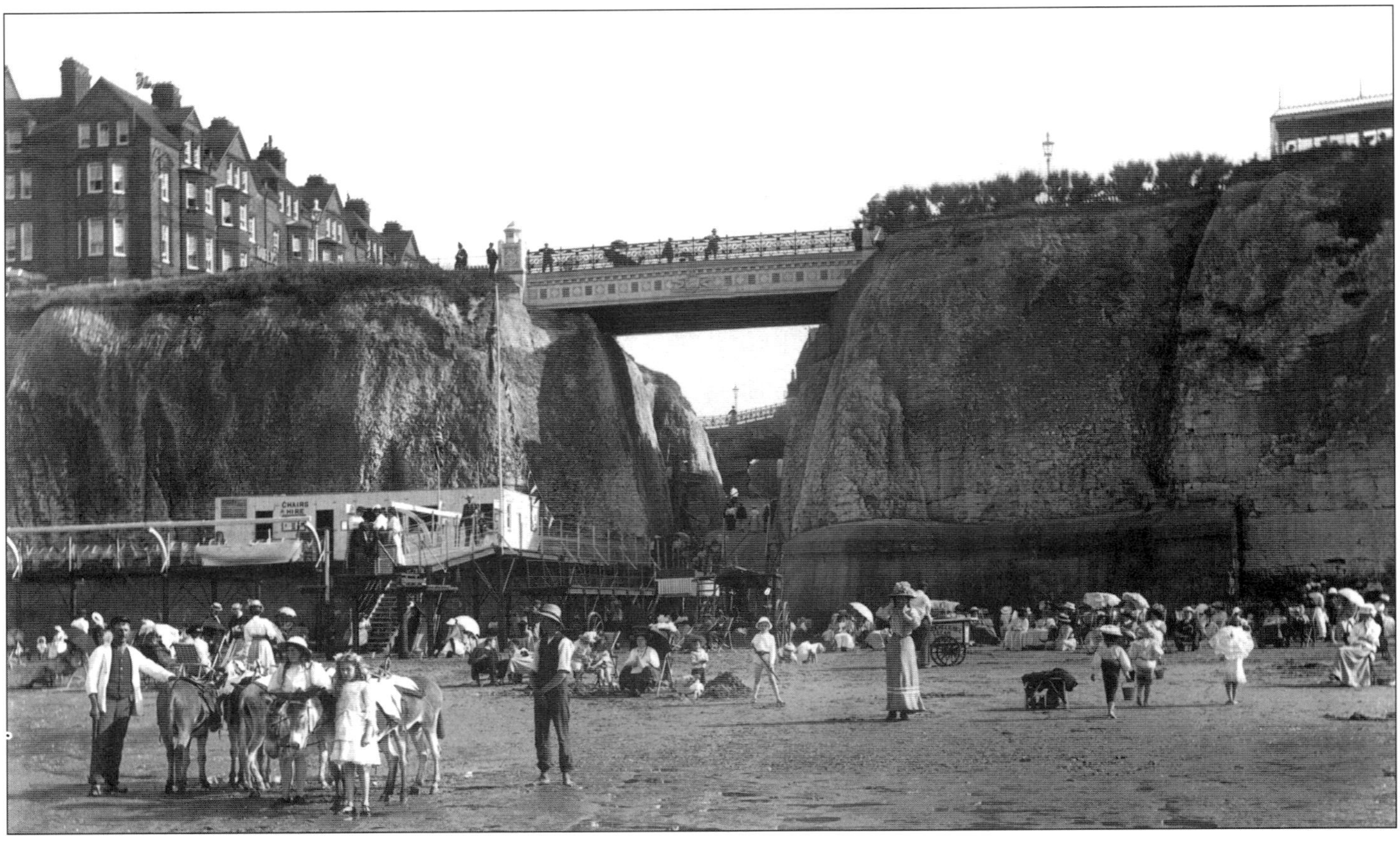

60373
A 1908 picture of the 'new' bridge over Newgate Gap, erected in 1907 to replace the original one of 1861. Below, on the sands of Palm Bay, children build sandcastles and pose with the donkeys.

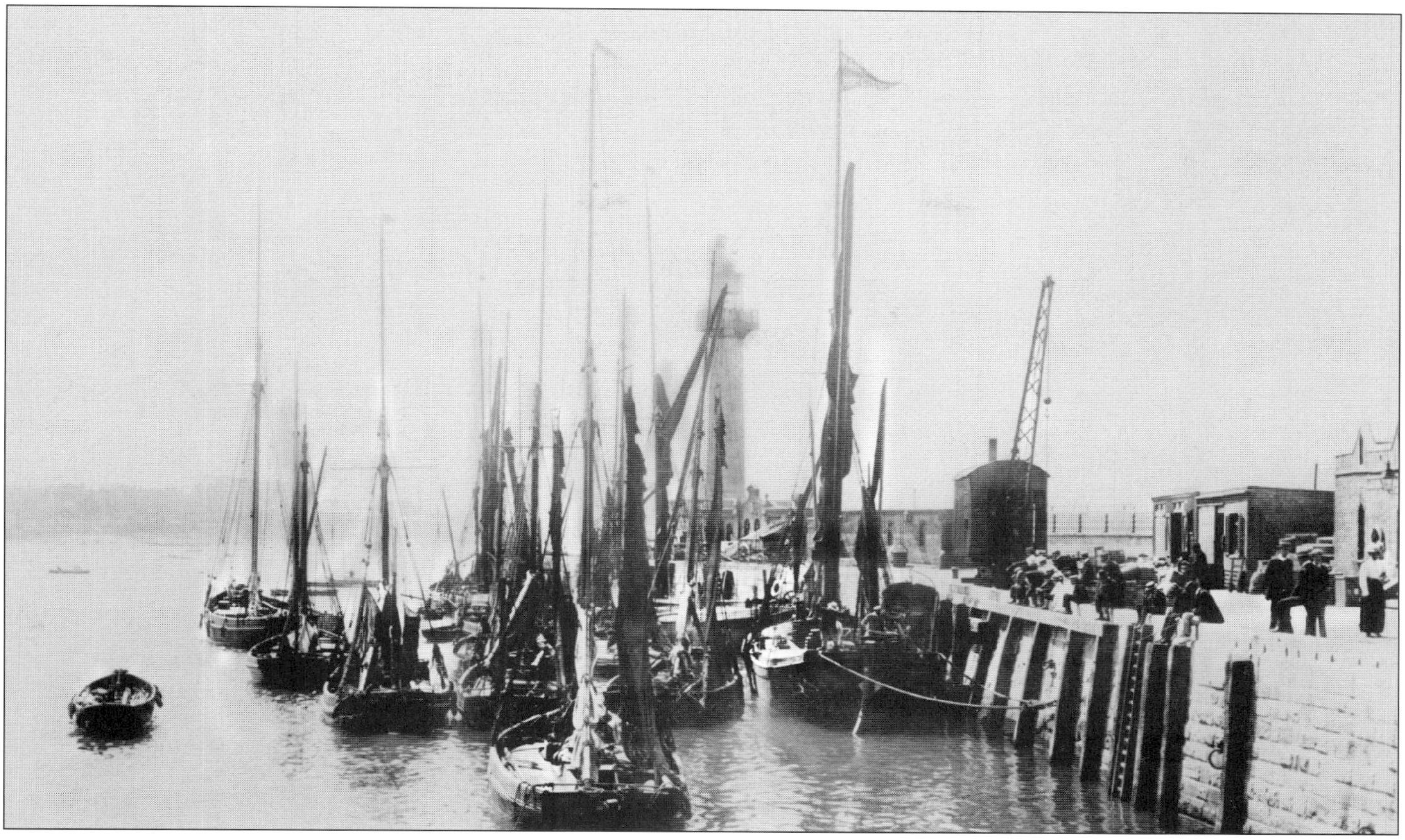

60370
Thames spritsail barges involved in the coasting trade, moored alongside the stone pier of Margate Harbour in 1908. Coasting and river-borne traffic frequented the harbour, mooring alongside the 909 ft long pier built in 1815.

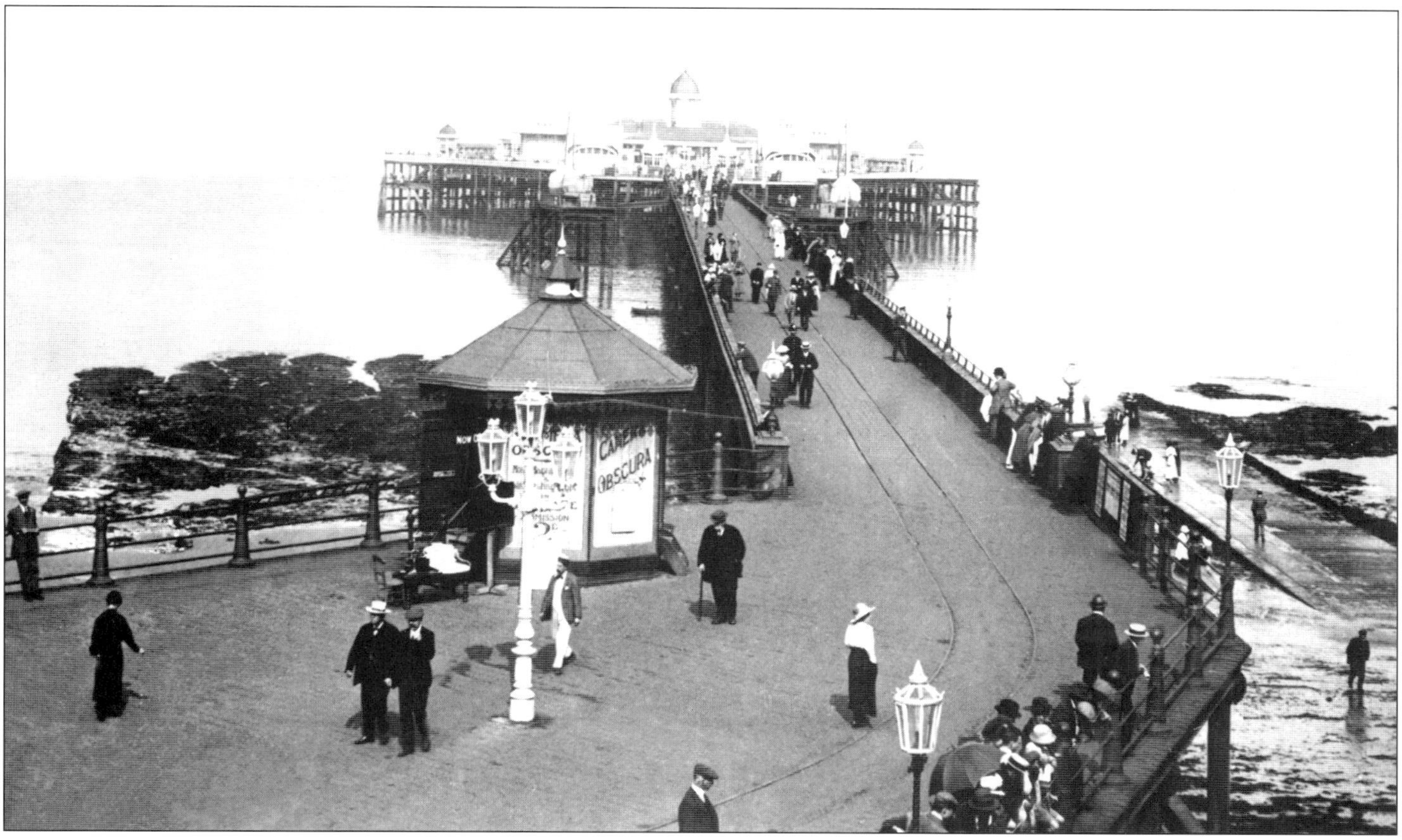


68444
Margate's jetty (pier), built in 1855, was destroyed in a storm in 1978. Here the 1,240 ft long structure can be seen in 1918. The jetty extension at the pierhead was an important landing stage, allowing steamships to come alongside even at low water.

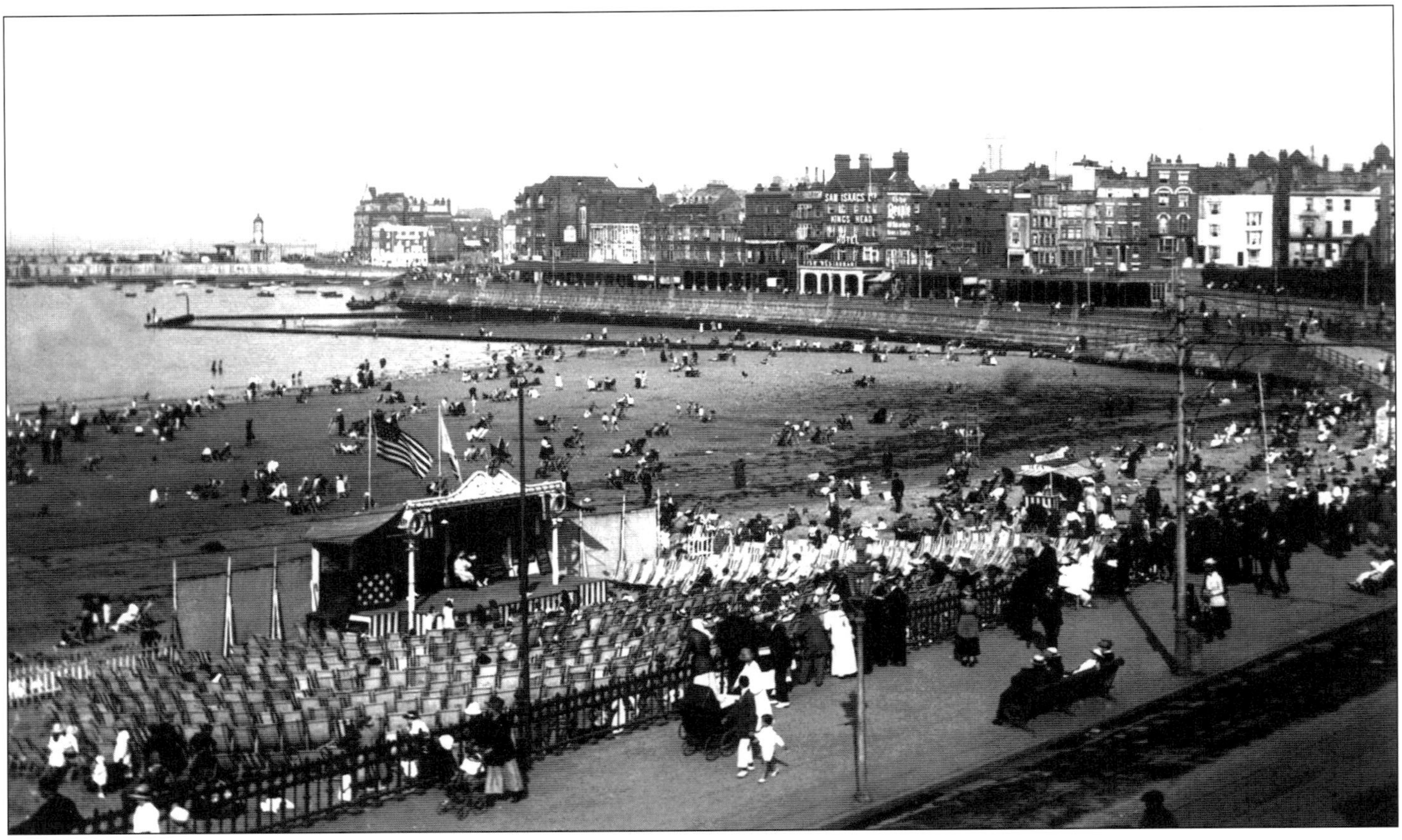

68451
Margate suffered from both bombing and shelling during the First World War and many people left the town. Nonetheless, it was still possible to take holidays there, as this picture of the famous sands dated 1918 goes to show.

## MINSTER

A small village situated in the heart of Thanet, overlooking Minster Marshes. It is well-known for its wonderful old church, which has towers built by the Saxons and Normans. It also has a historic old abbey, now a nunnery, with walls of the old Saxon church.

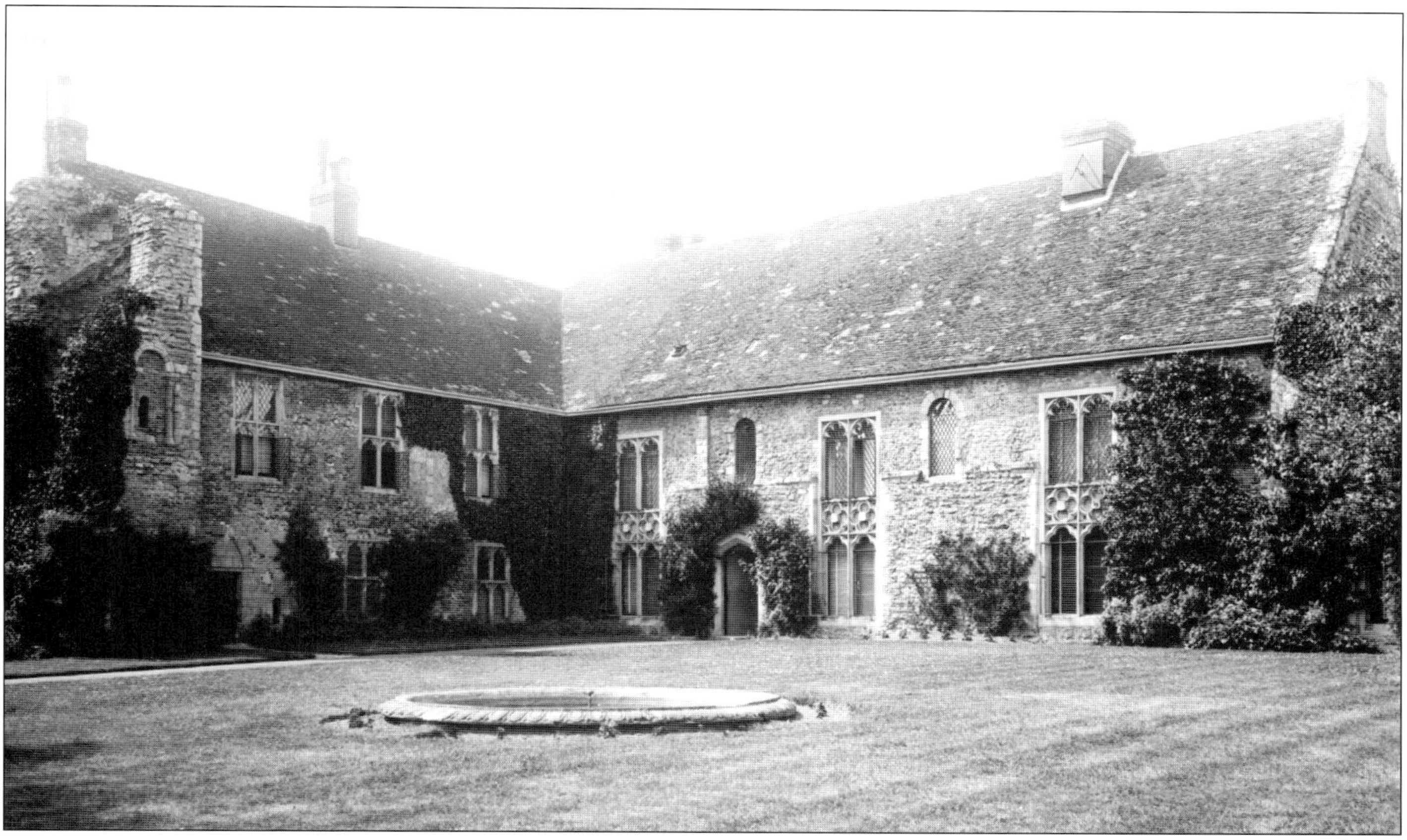

34200

Minster Abbey pictured in 1894. The abbey was founded in AD 670, but the present buildings are Norman - part of a grange of St Augustine's Abbey in Canterbury. It has been a nunnery since 1930.

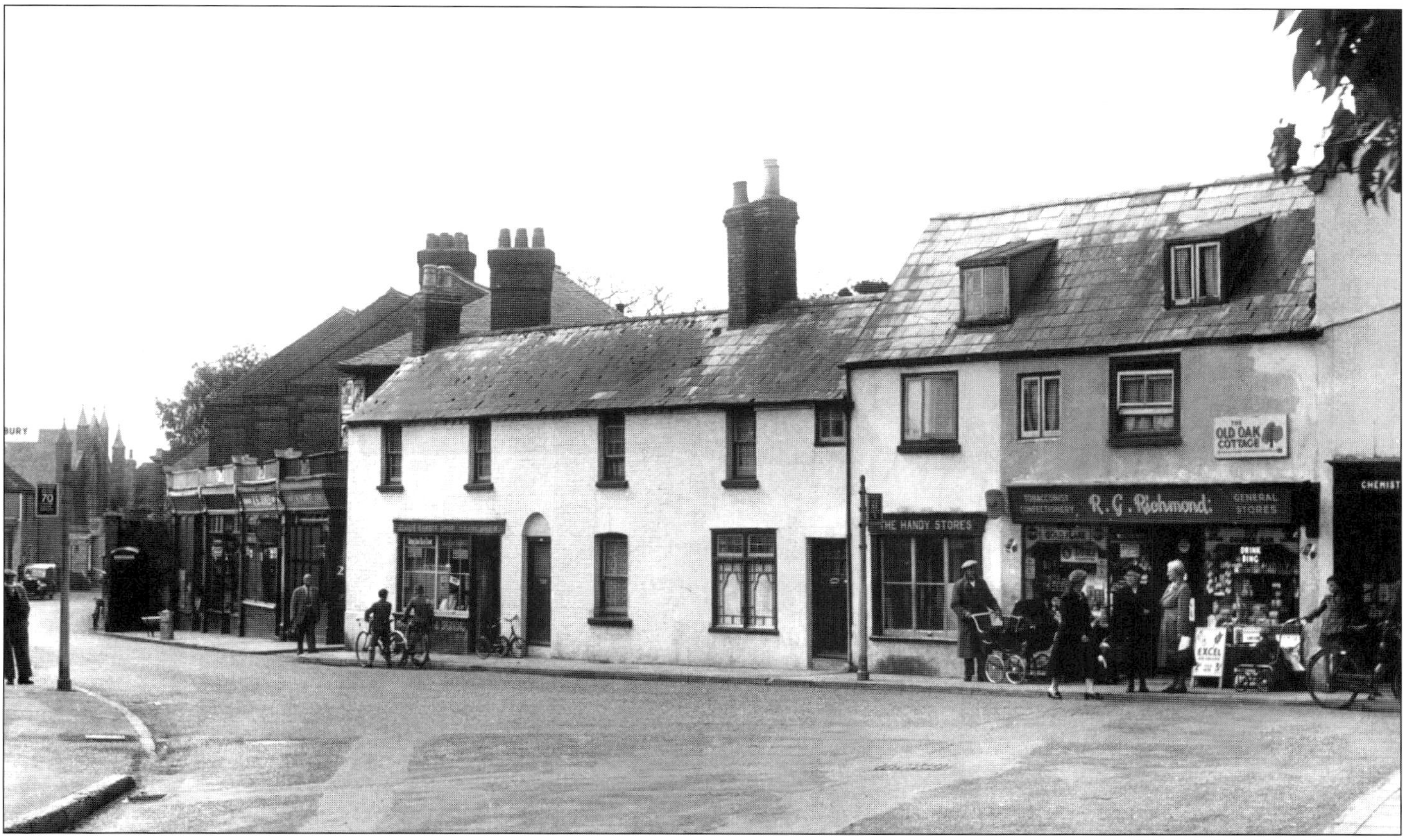


M86020

The Square, remarkably free of traffic, in summer sunshine of about 1955. The famous church is just visible on the extreme left. It is strange to realise that the world's first fatal road accident took place in Minster.

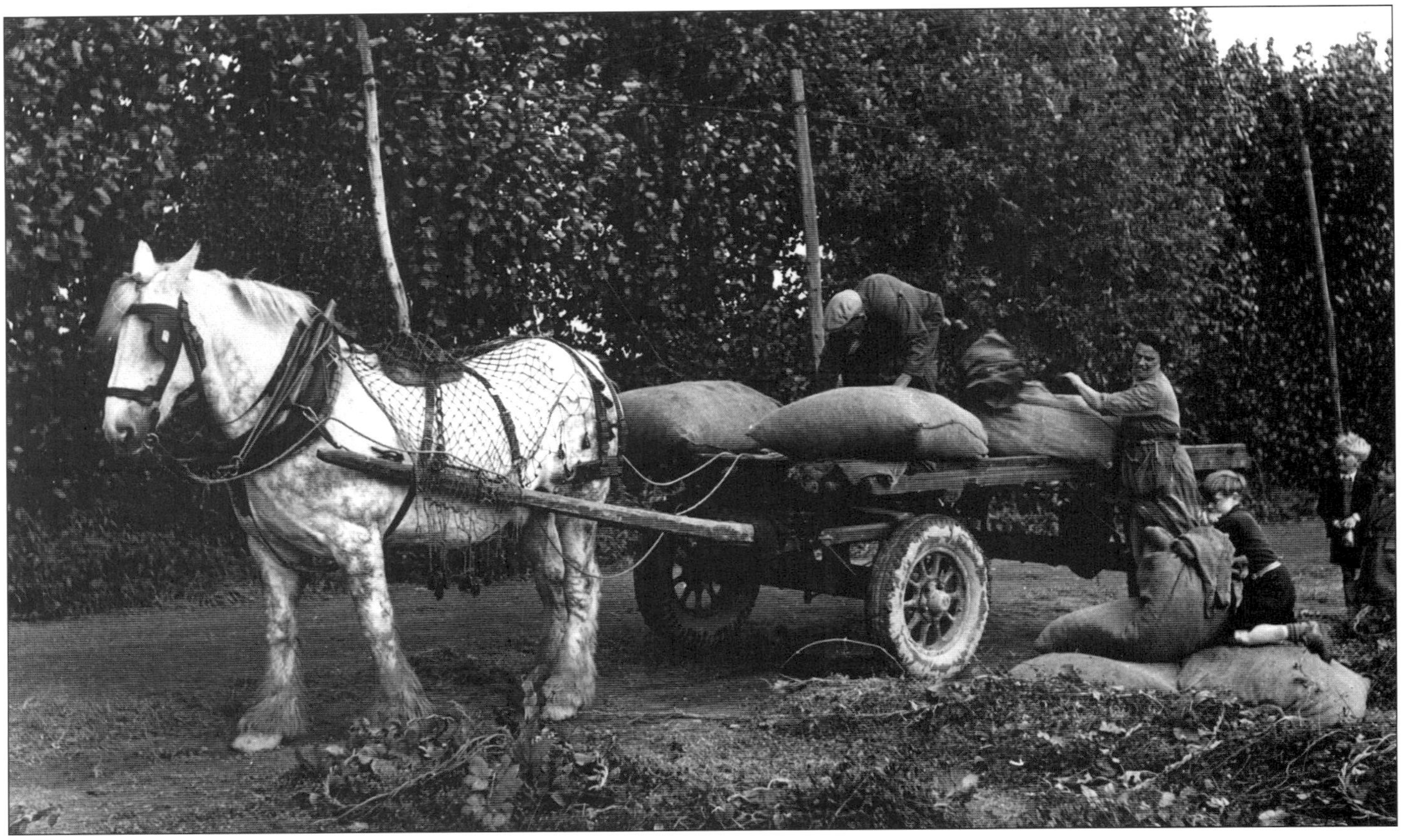

P220018
Pokes being loaded onto a horse-drawn wagon for carting to the oasts. The picture, taken in the 1950s, when the 'hopping' holiday had virtually disappeared, shows how children as well as adults were involved.

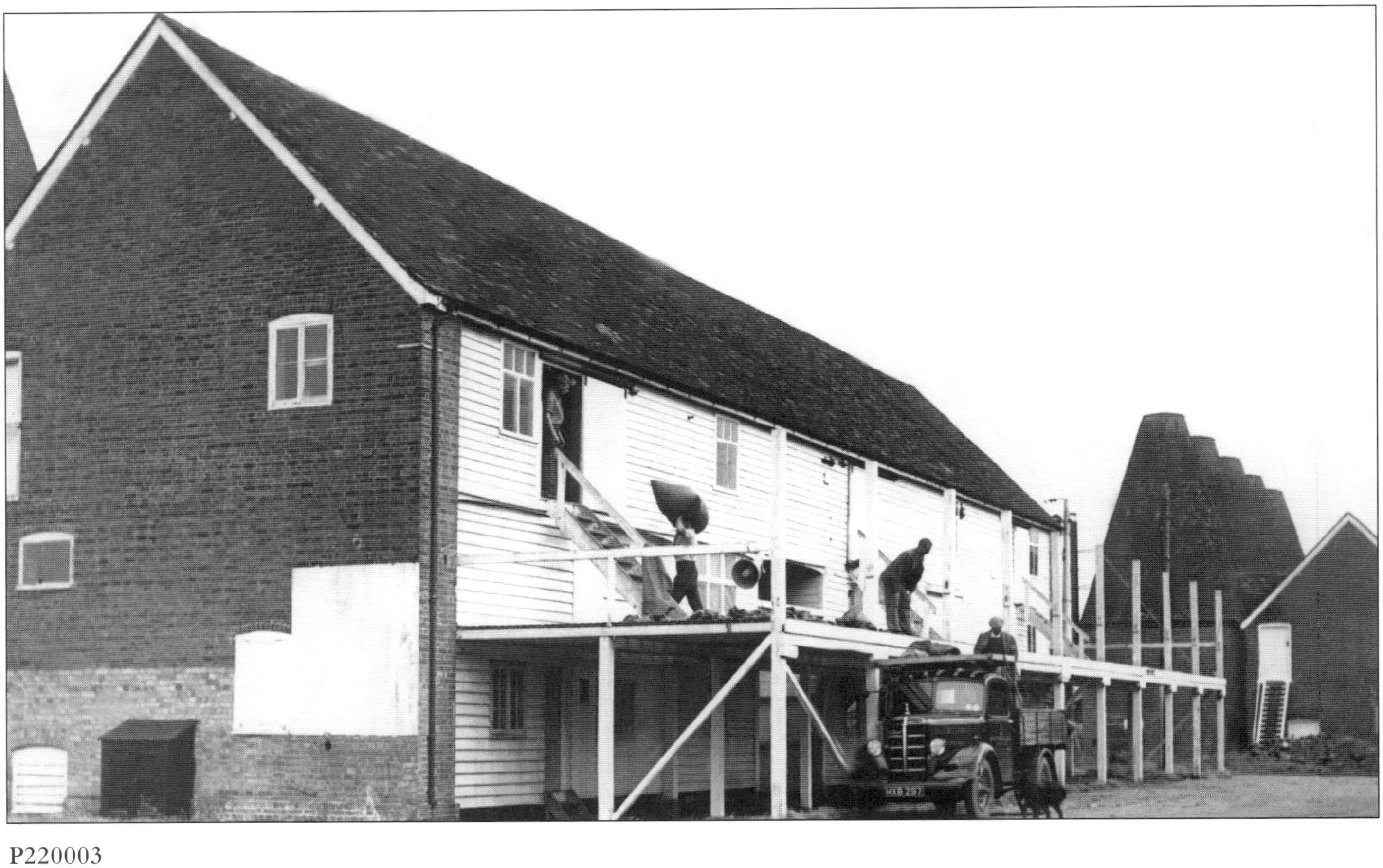

P220003
Pokes being unloaded into the oast house from a truck in about 1955, where the hops will be given some ten hours drying over the furnace. This reduces the weight of the hops by nearly eighty per cent.

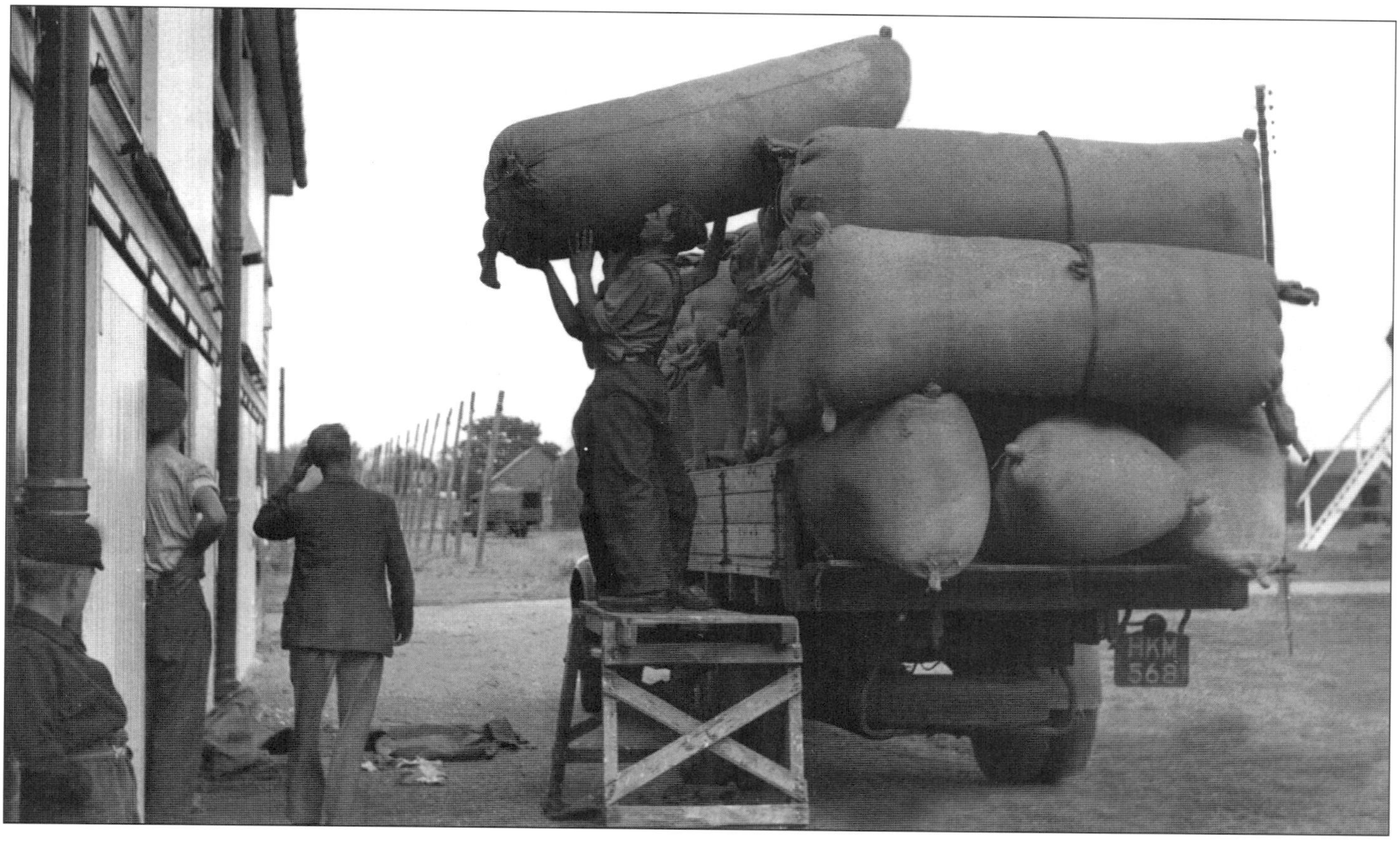


P220011

Dried hops done up in 'pockets' each weighting one and a half hundredweight, being loaded from the oast house onto a lorry to be taken to market.

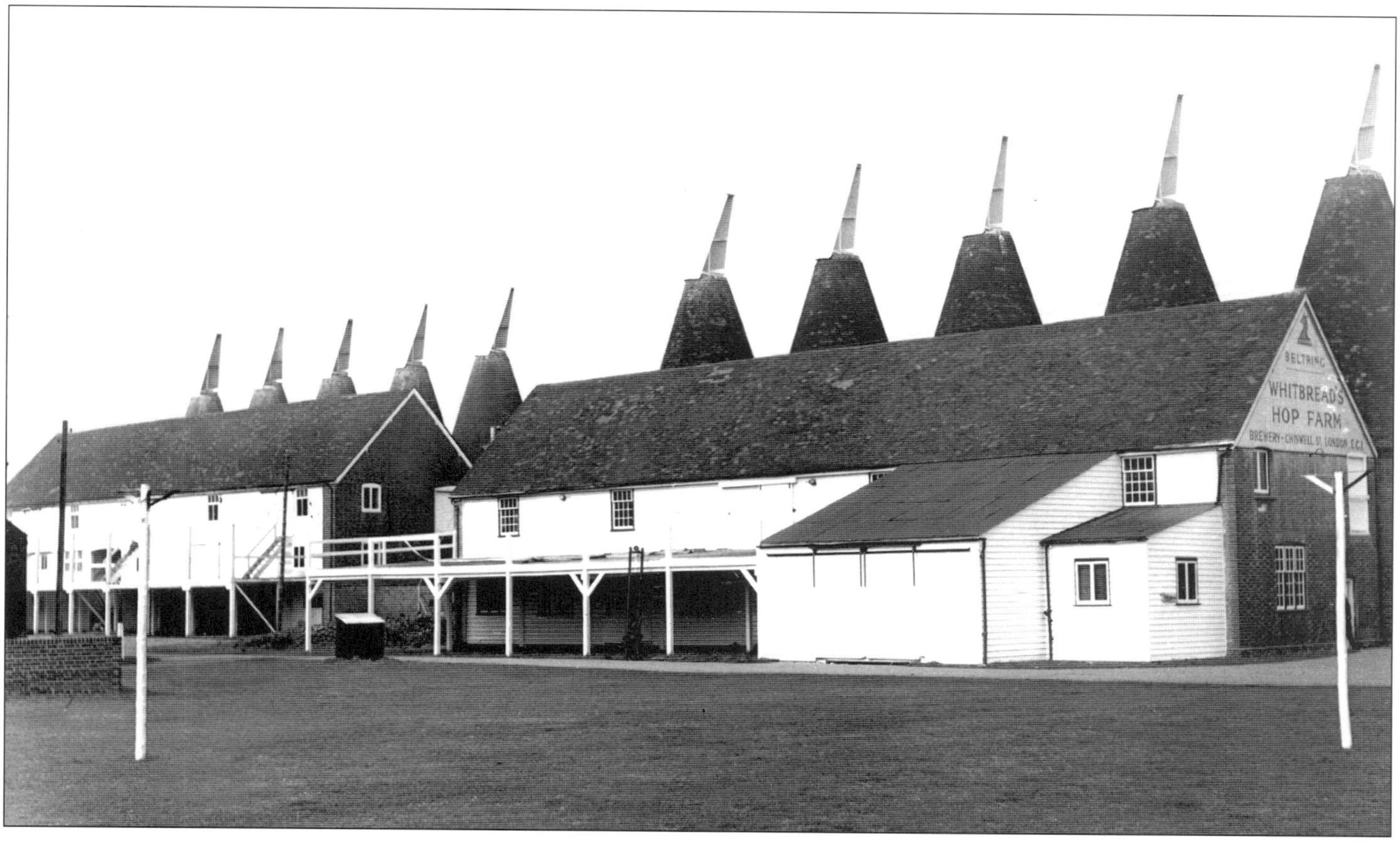


P220005

The famous Whitbread Hop Farm in about 1955. Typically Kentish weatherboarding can be seen on the buildings in the foreground, with the store houses of the oast kilns beyond.

# Pegwell

Situated at the southernmost part of the Isle of Thanet, the bay is bounded by cliffs on the north, and marshes to the south. Tradition has it, that this was the landing place of the Danes and St Augustine.

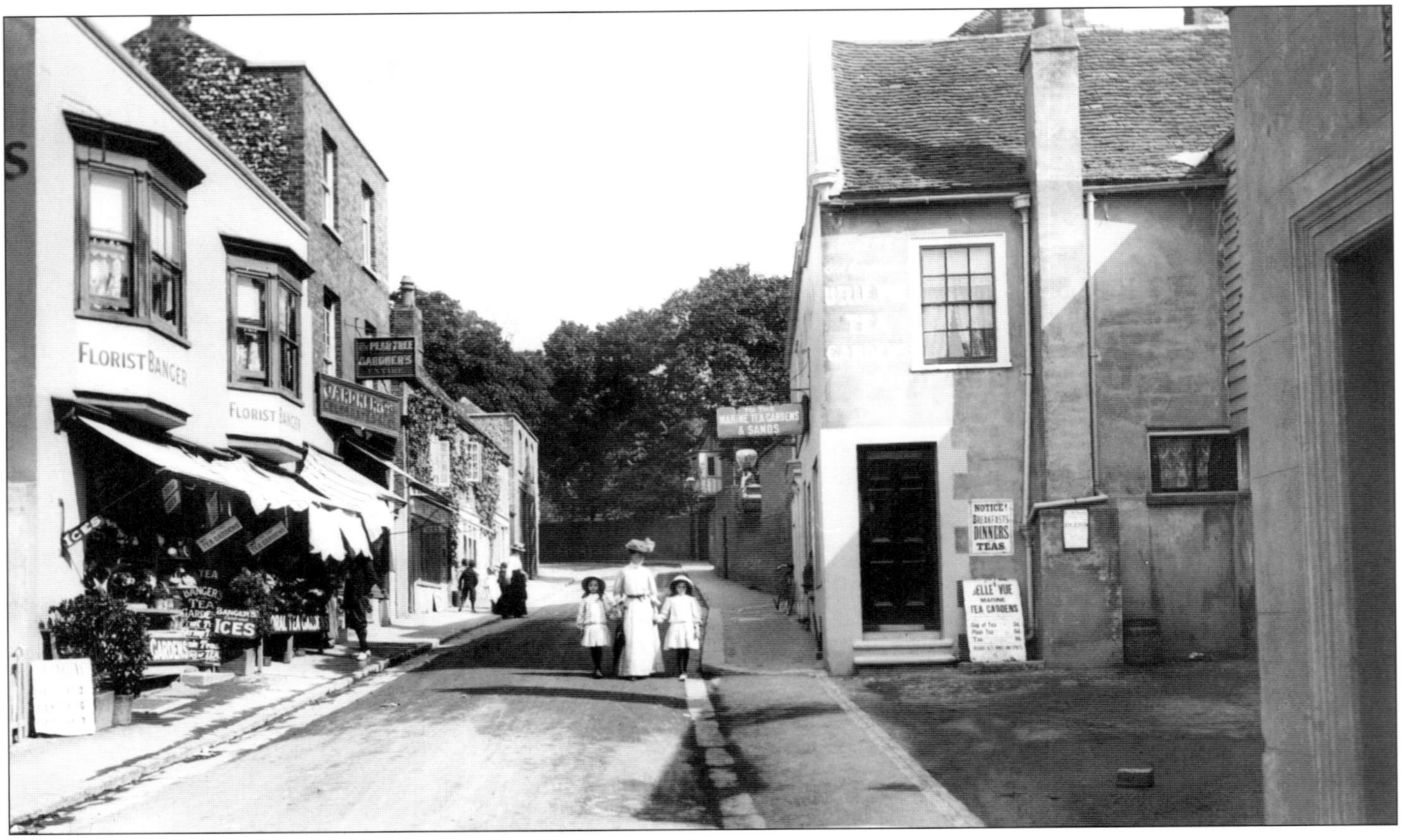


58296
A charming view of Pegwell village in 1907. To the right is the entrance to the Belle Vue Tea Gardens, patronised by the young Princess Victoria when she visited with her mother in 1830.

# Plaxtol

A pleasantly situated hilltop village, with a long main street. There is a lovely group of cottages near the church, which date from the seventeenth century. The church has many riches, including a hammerbeam roof. There is also a working forge, used for making gates, weathervanes and the like.

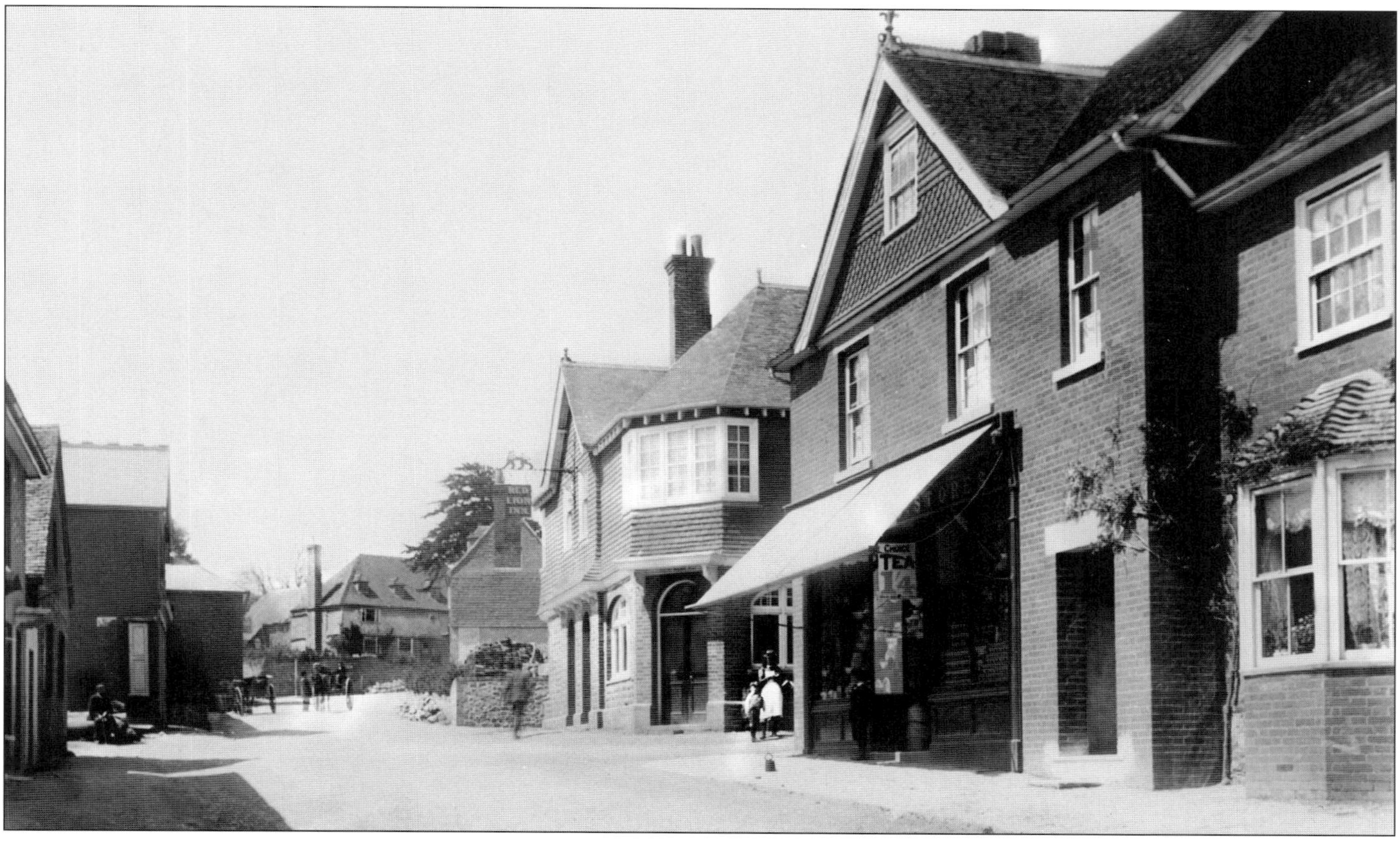

46408

Looking up Plaxtol's village street in 1901. The village store stands on the right, and in the centre, there is a horsedrawn vehicle. The scene looks surprisingly modern.

# Ramsgate

Ramsgate is a fine resort, fishing village and cross channel harbour all rolled into one. The harbour nestles beneath the steep cliff and steep streets. The medieval church stands high above the promenade, and has a Norman tower. The town has pleasant Georgian terraces, with a Victorian development along the promenade.

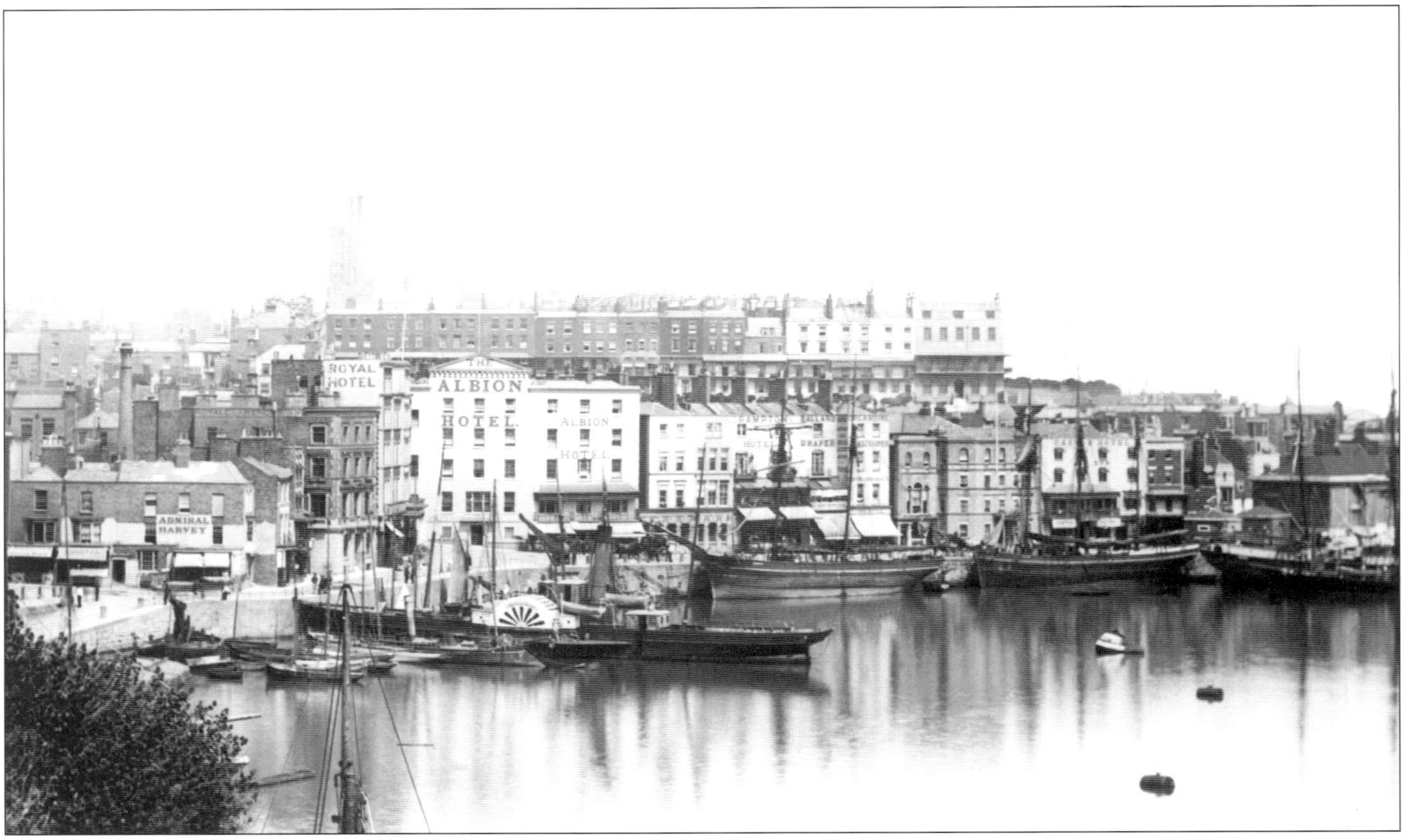


19674A

Looking to the inner harbour - now the Yacht Marina - from West Cliff in 1887. A paddle-steamer and three brigs, probably colliers, are moored. The chimney on the left of the *Admiral Harvey* probably belonged to Ramsgate's first gasworks.

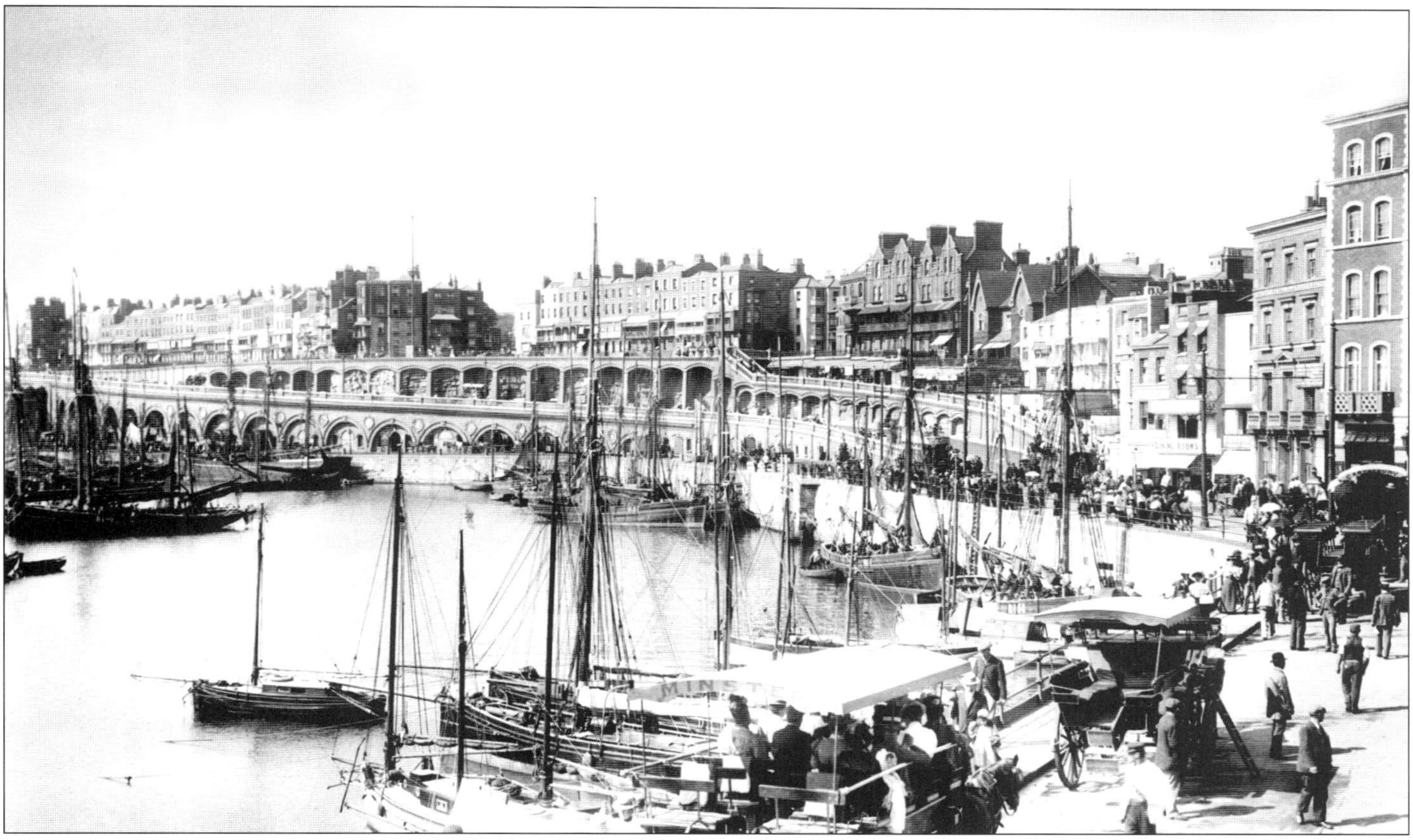

48028
Part of Ramsgate's famous fleet of fishing smacks in the inner harbour, 1901. The horse-drawn 'brakes' in the foreground were used by sightseers - a trip round the harbour was an essential ingredient of a Ramsgate holiday.

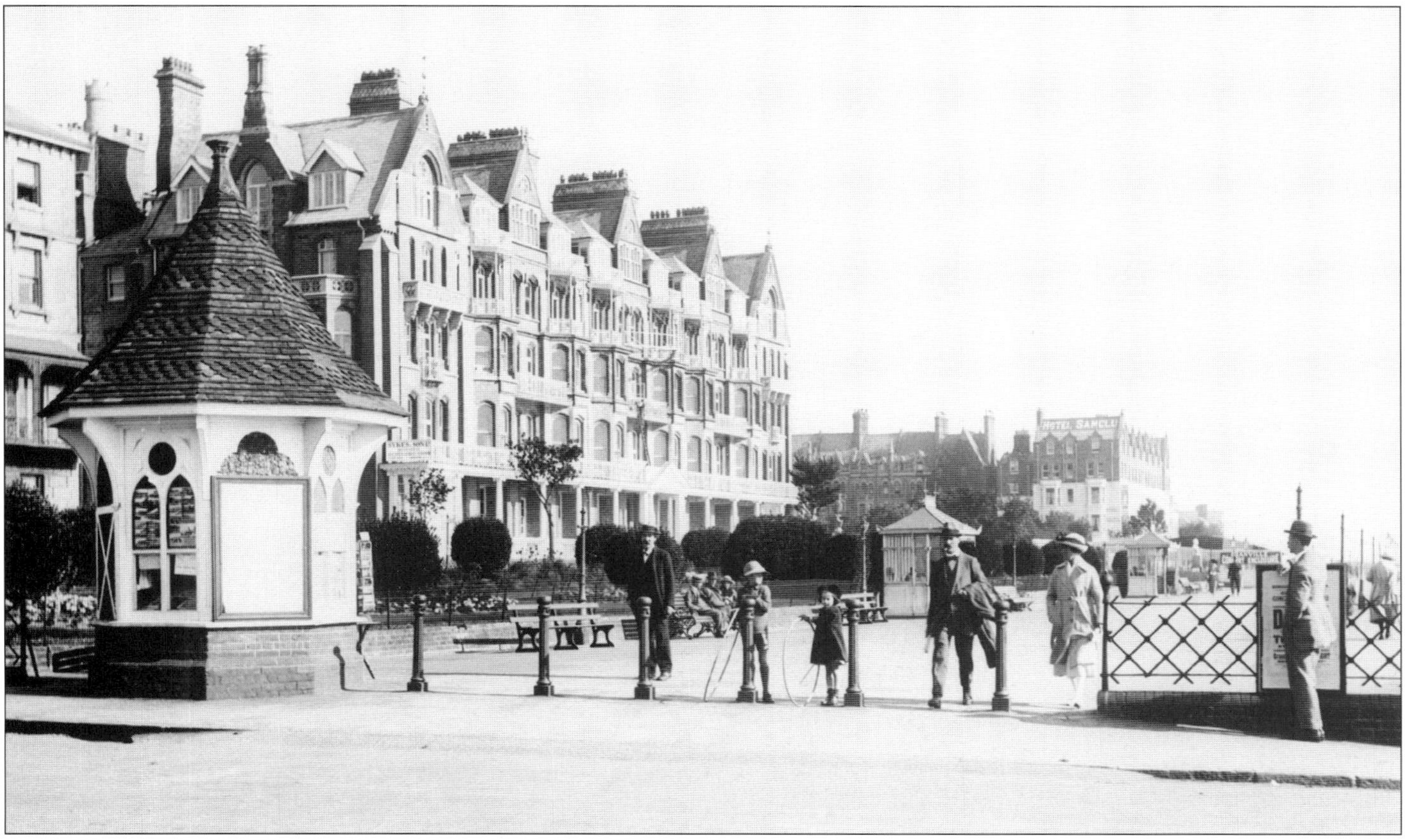

68463
Children with hoops play on the clifftop promenade in 1918, a breezy spot high above the beach. The octagonal building is a newspaper kiosk. Today the east promenade overlooks the new Ramsgate Port.

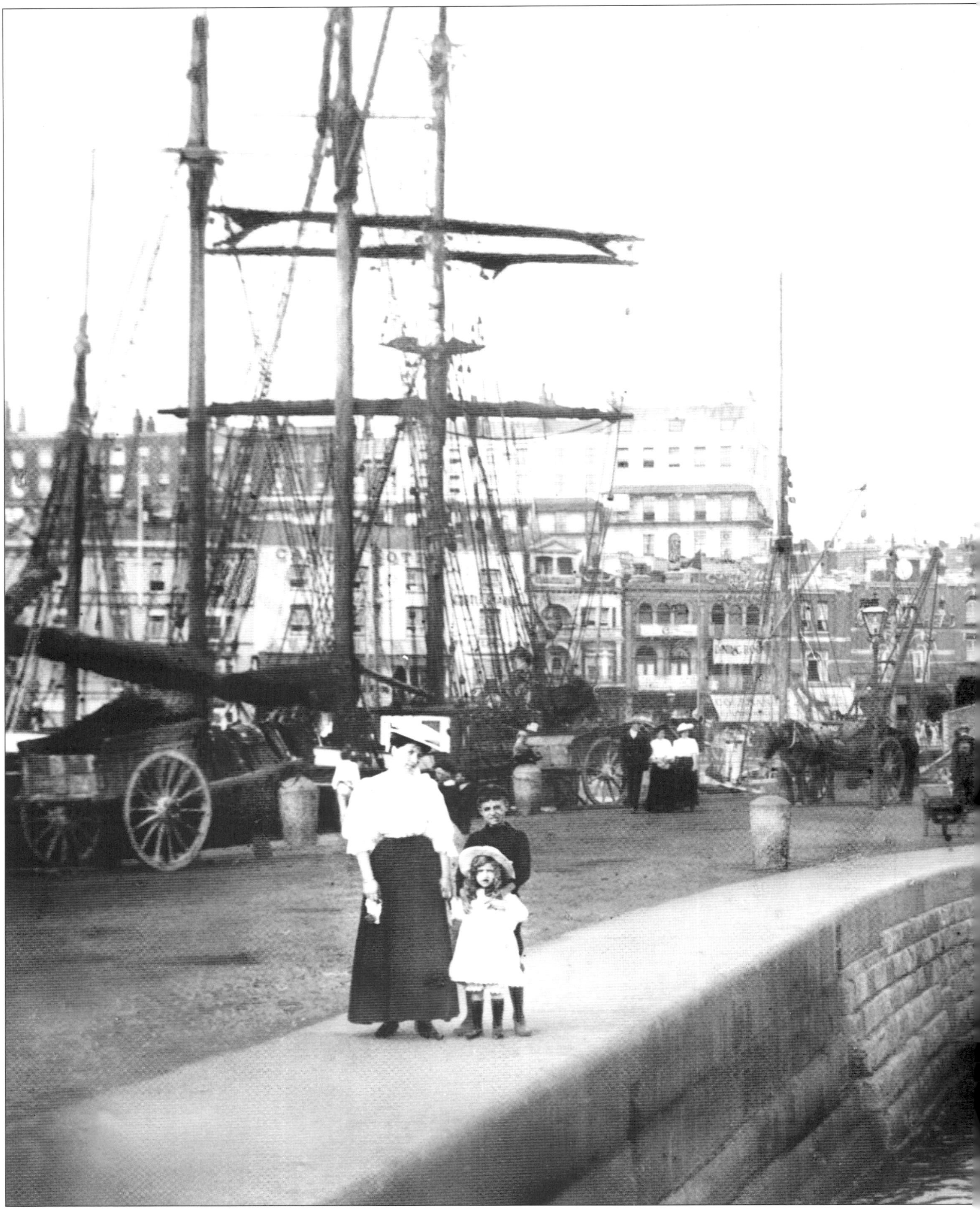

58287
A prettily posed group in 1907. A spritsail barge and her boat are moored on the right. On the left colliers are unloaded. The fishmarket of 1881, demolished in the 1960s, stands in the middle of the picture.

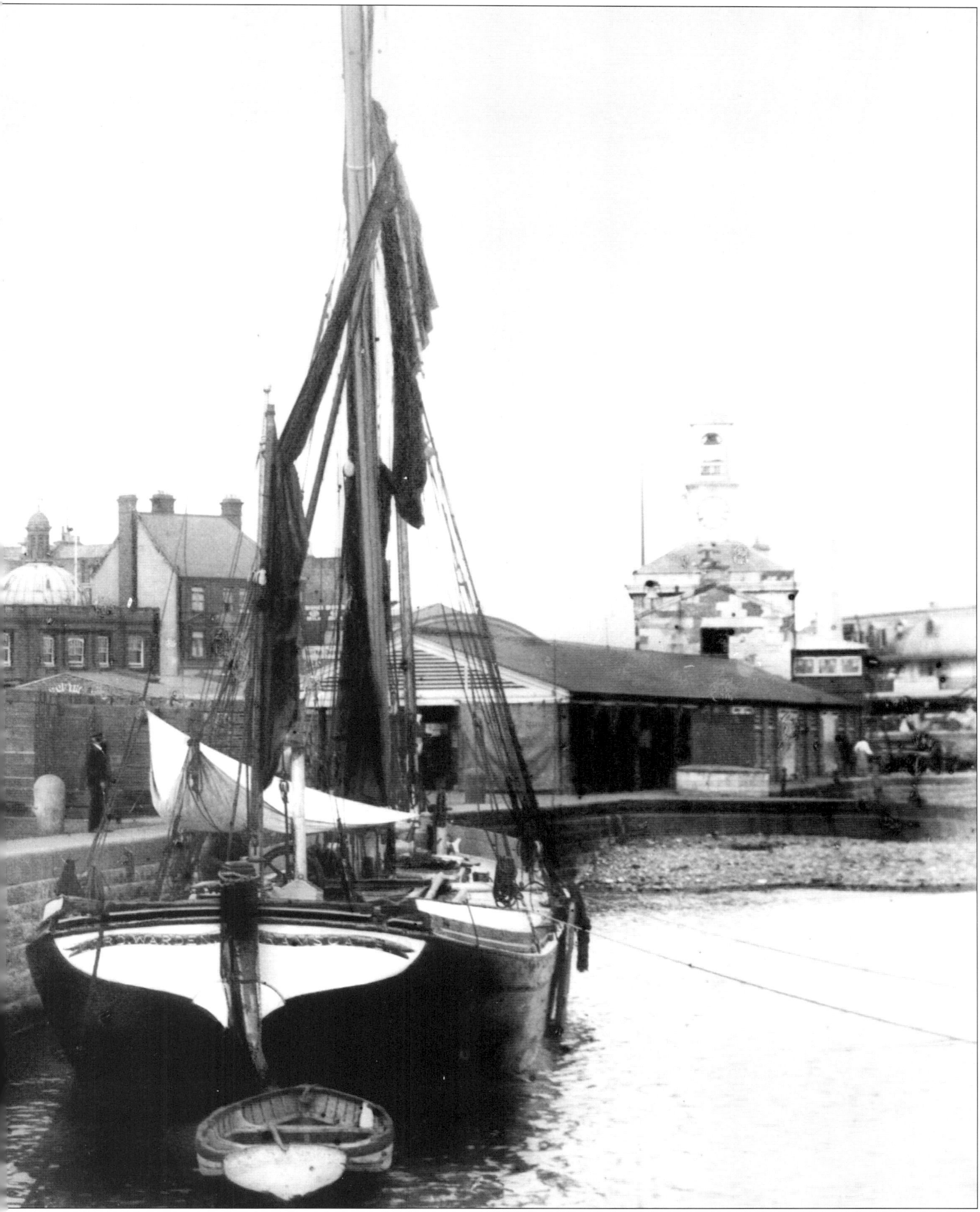

# Rochester

Founded by the Romans, where Watling Street bridged the Medway, Rochester has been important for nearly 2,000 years. The cathedral, founded in AD 604, is second only to Canterbury in age. It was rebuilt by the Normans who also built the castle. The town retains its ancient High Street, with many fine buildings including College Gate. Charles Dickens knew the city well.

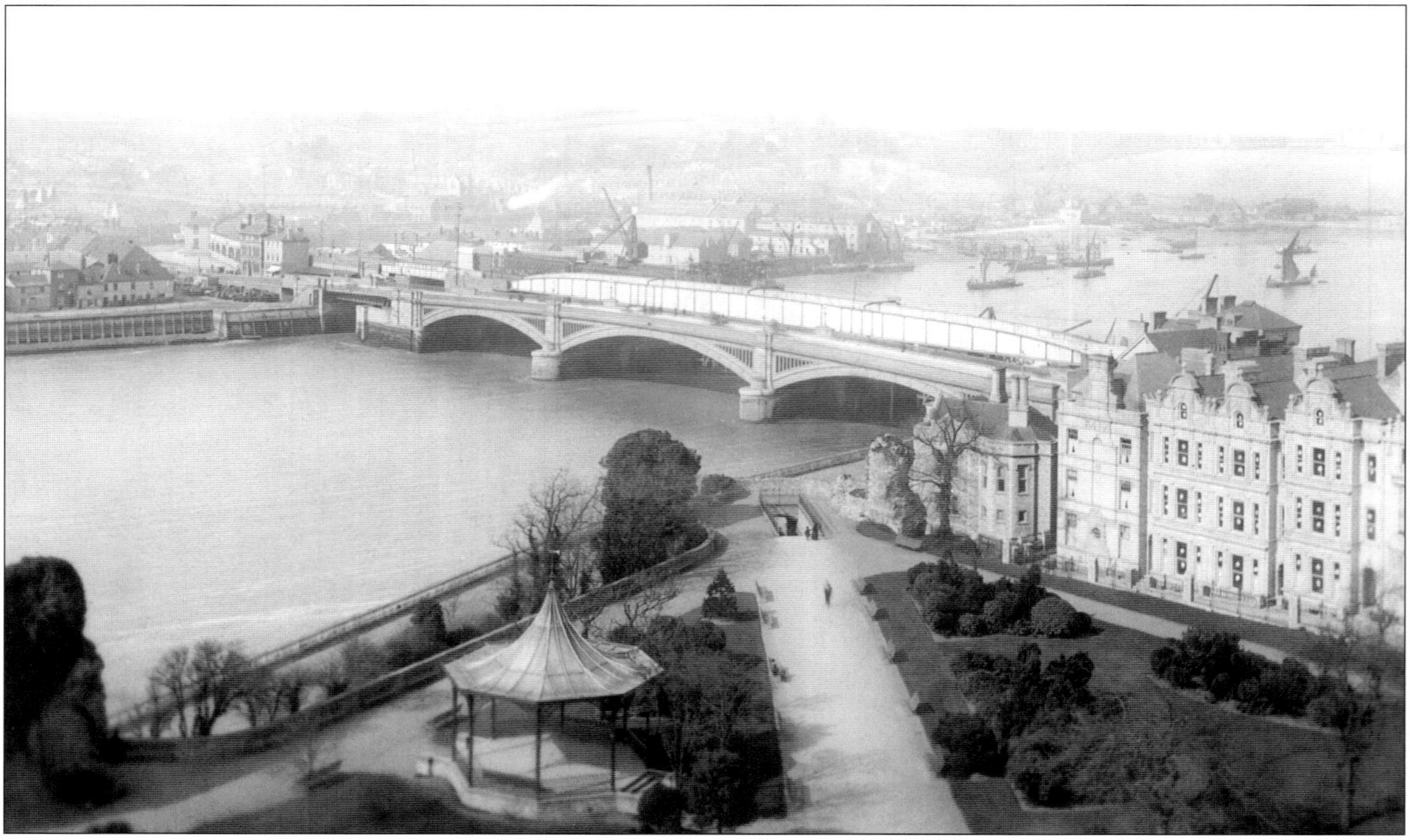

22190
The view from Rochester Castle looking across the River Medway, 1889. The road and rail bridge were built in 1856; today another bridge of 1970 runs alongside it, built with money from the Bridge Trust of 1391.

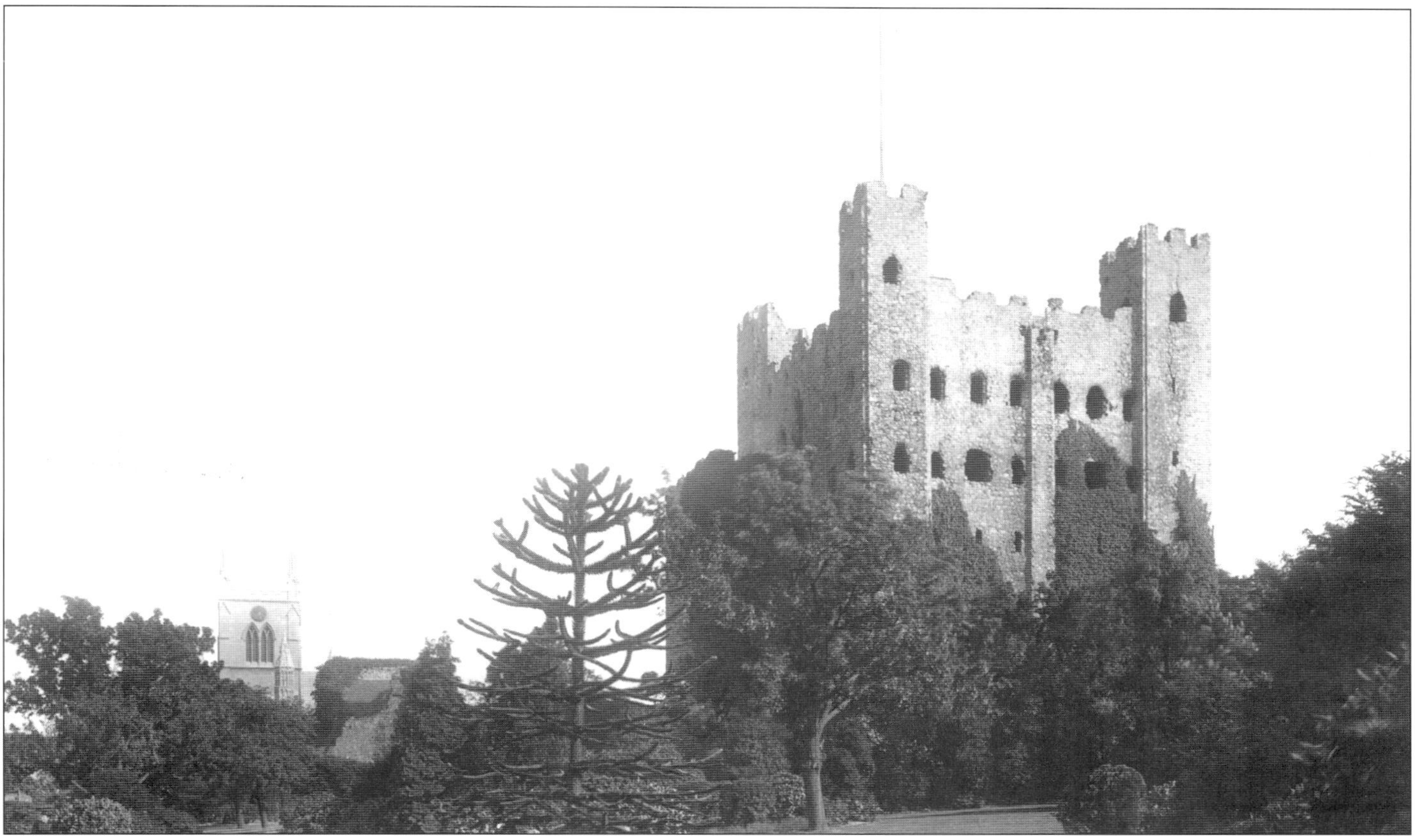

34035
The massive Norman keep of Rochester Castle in 1894. The castle was first raised soon after 1066, and the impressive keep, the tallest in England, went up in about 1127. The tower of the cathedral is on the left.

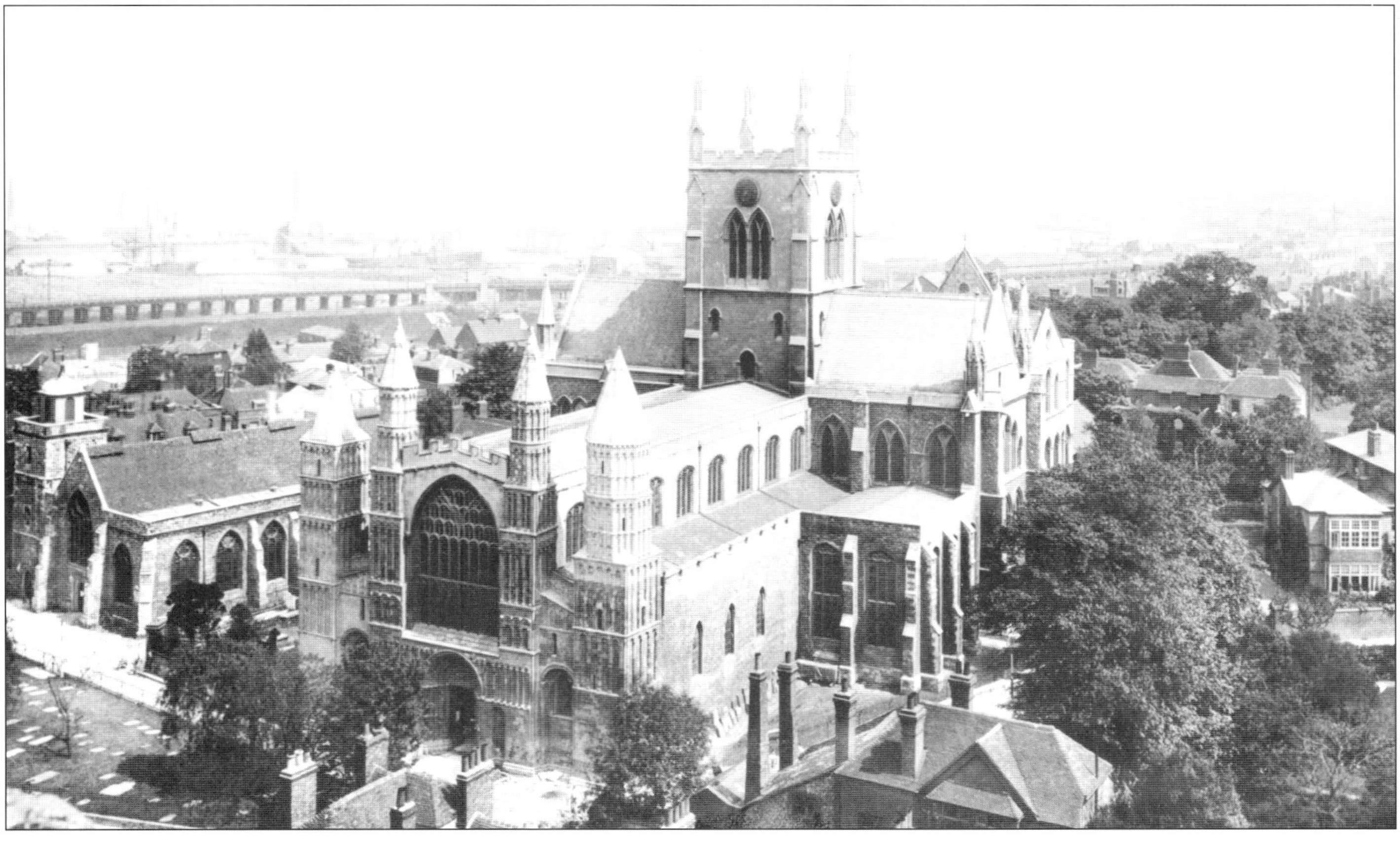

34012
A fascinating view of Rochester Cathedral taken from the castle in 1894. The central tower was rebuilt ten years later and crowned with a spire. Beyond is a glimpse of the industrial Medway.

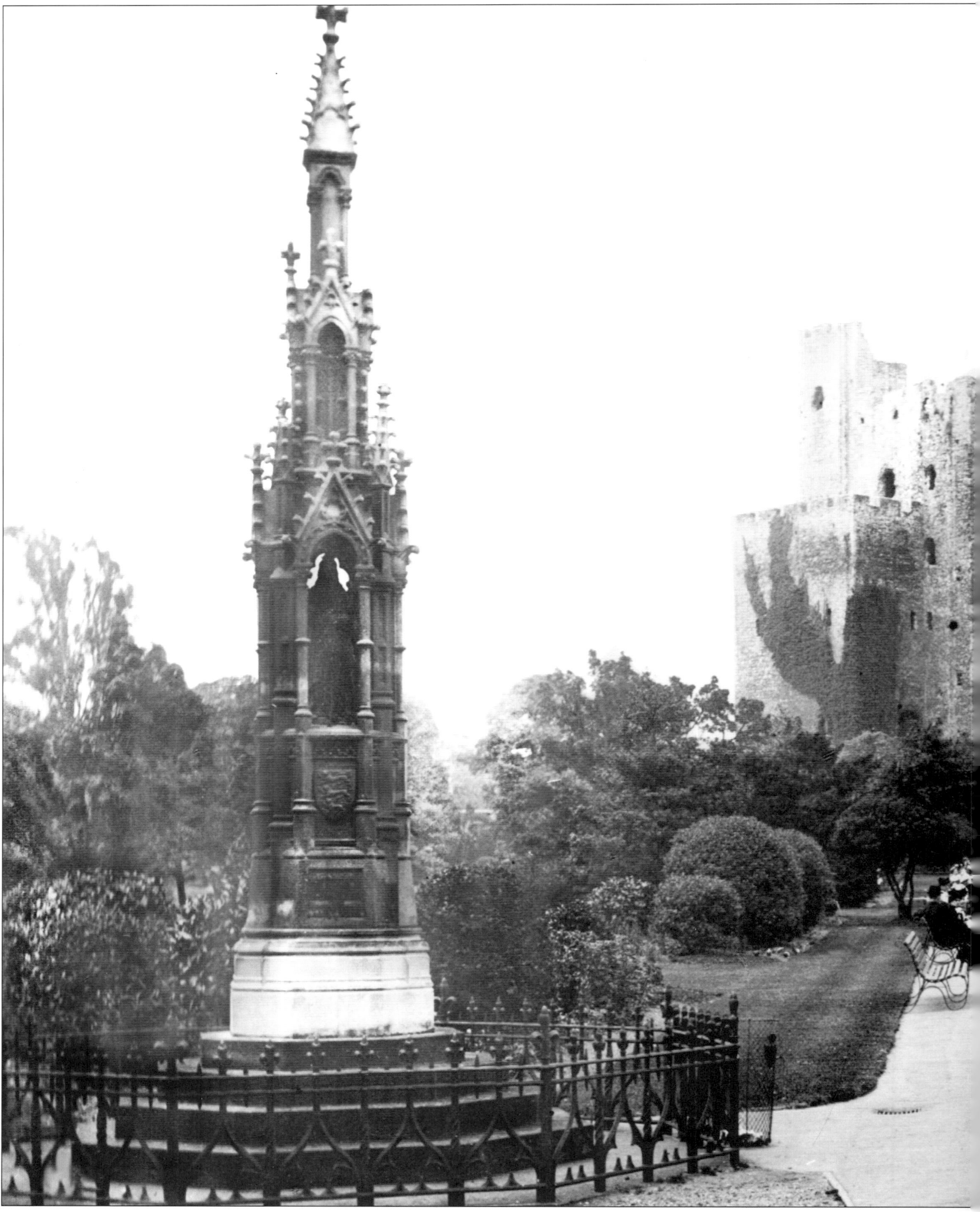

59883
The castle grounds in 1908, dominated by the Norman castle keep. the castle was besieged in 1088 when Bishop Odo fortified it against his nephew, William Rufus. The 1904 spire of the cathedral is on the left.

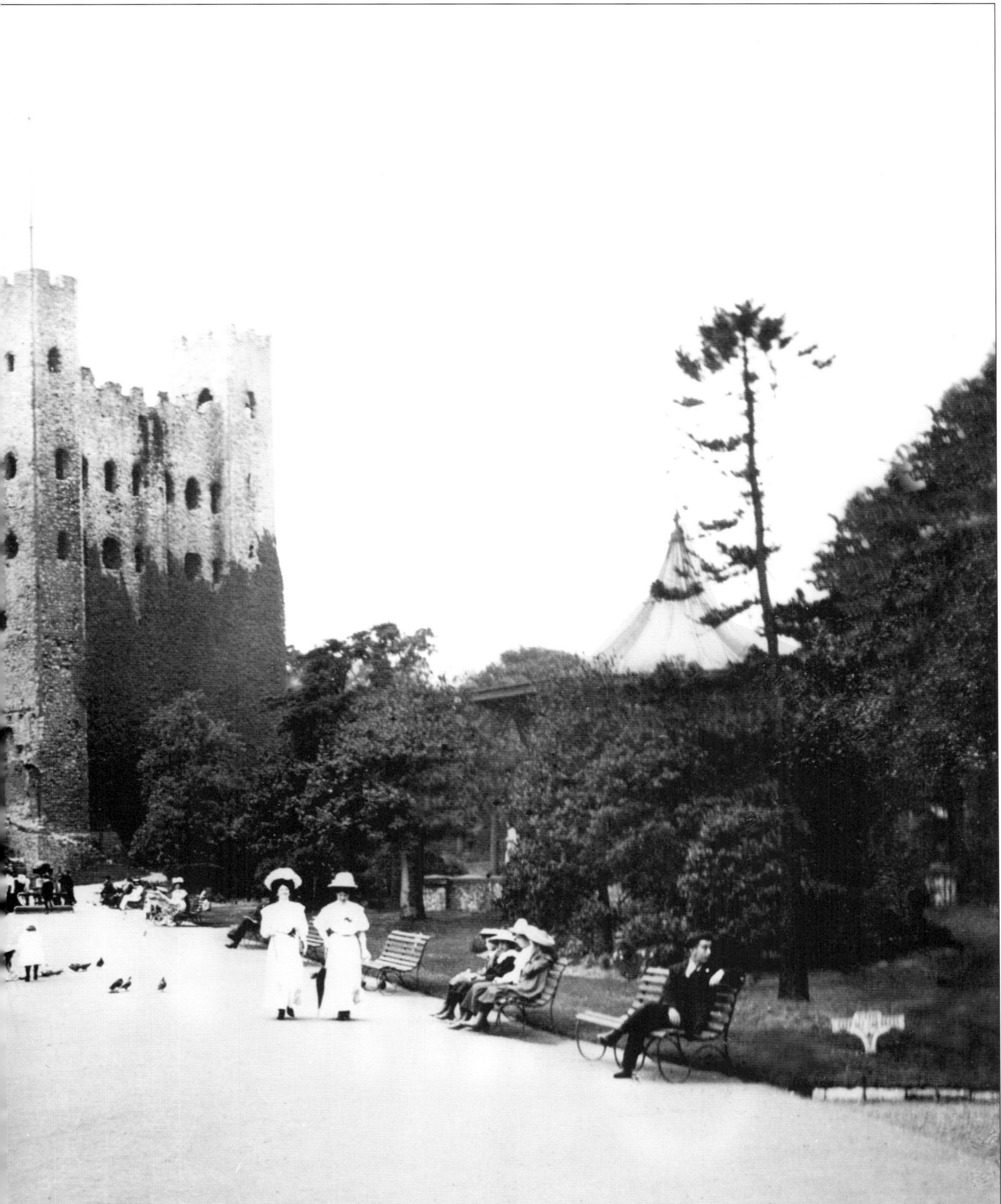

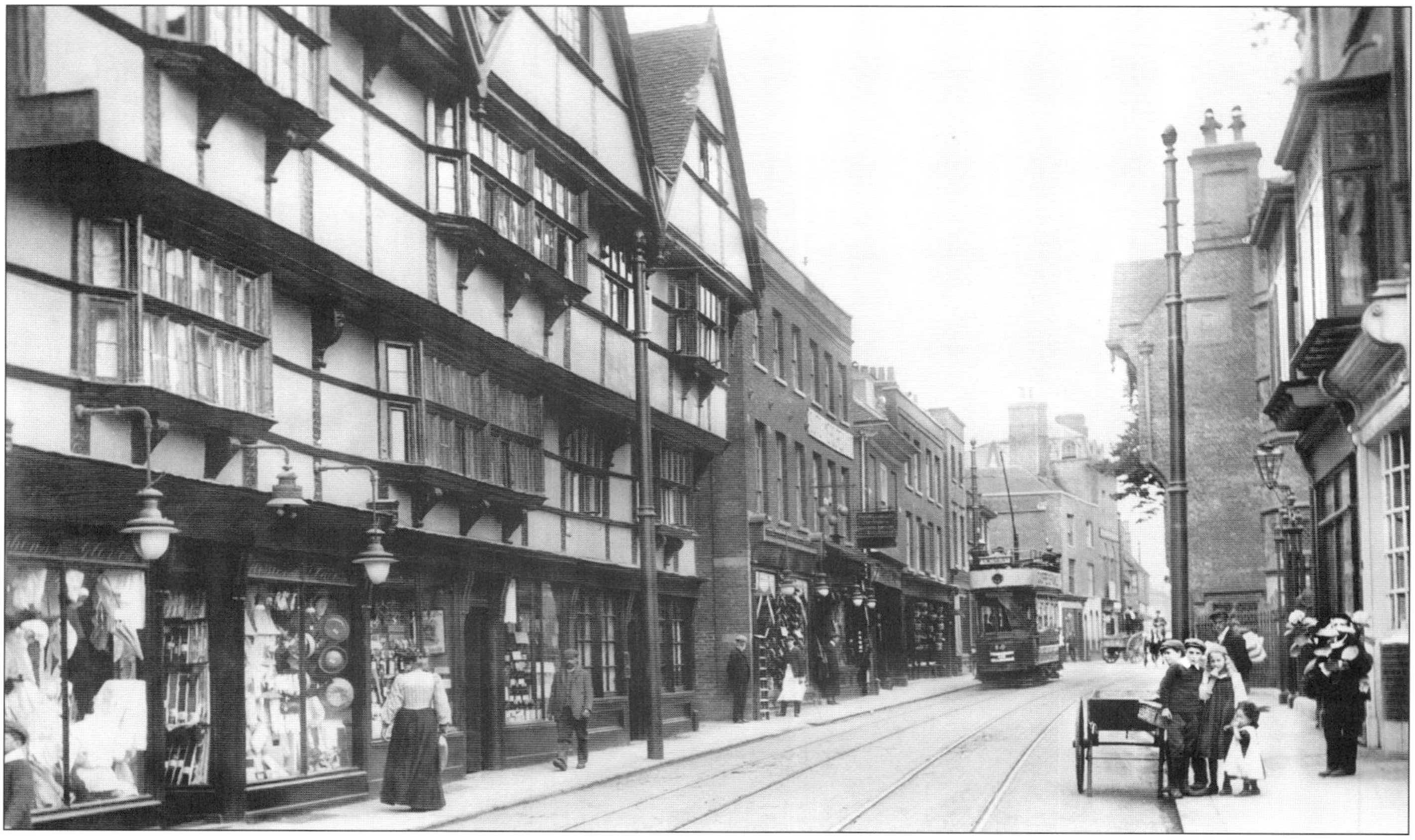

59875
Rochester's High Street runs along the famous Roman Watling Street and has not changed greatly from this 1908 view. The timber-framed house dates from the late sixteenth century. Opposite is Eastgate House of 1590, now part of the Charles Dickens Centre.

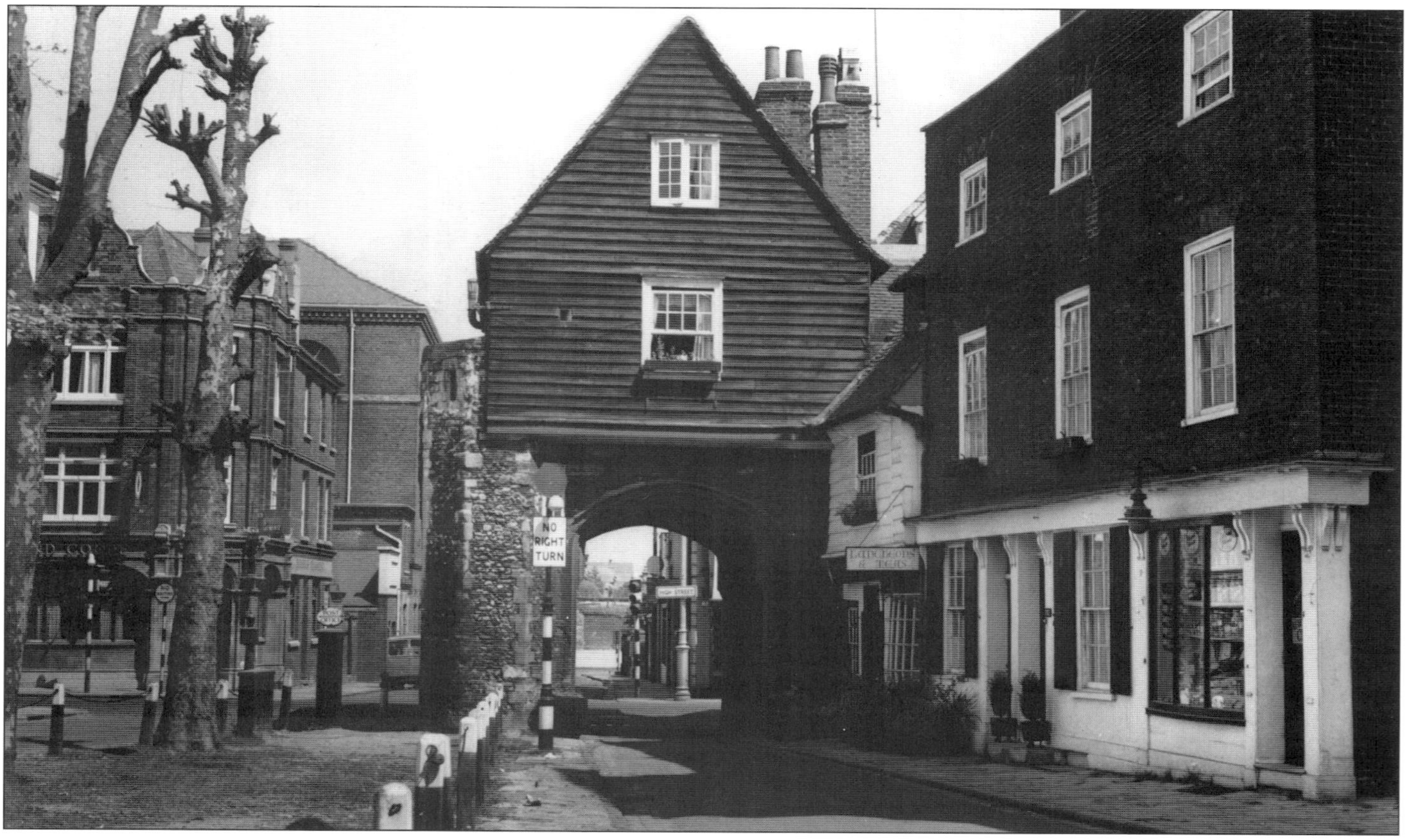


R44093
College Gate, 1955. It is one of the three remaining gates leading into the former monastic precinct. It was built in the early fifteenth century, and is also known as Chertsey's Gate or 'Jasper's Gate', by which name it appears in Dickens' novel *Edwin Drood*.

# Sandwich

Founded by the Saxons, it was once a Cinque Port at the mouth of the River Stour, but due to silting is now two miles from the sea. It reinvented itself as a cloth weaving town, and is today a quaint market town of narrow streets. The Elizabethan town hall is now the museum. The town retains two of its town gates, Barbican Gate and Fisher Gate.

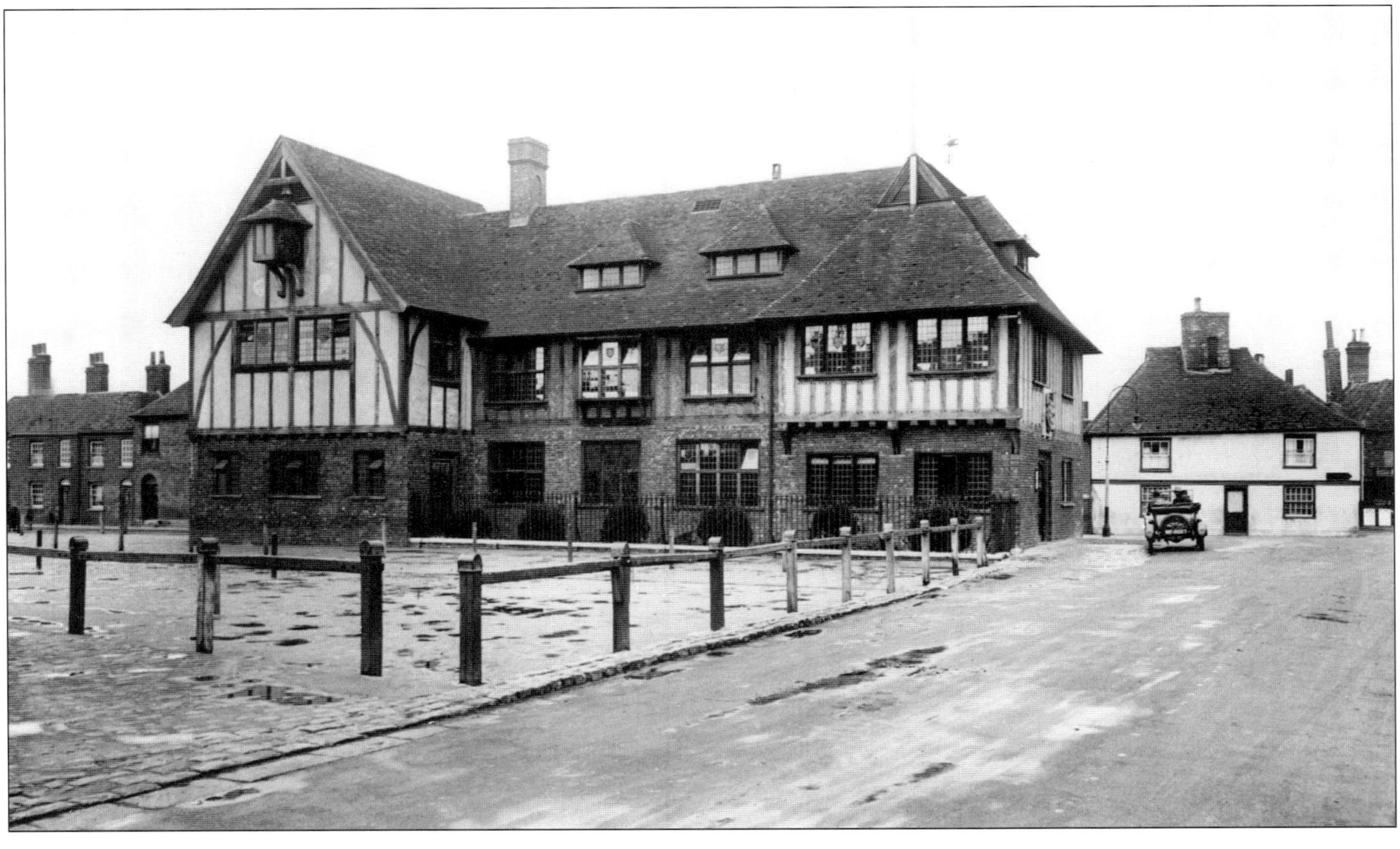

76232
The Town Hall, pictured on a wet day in 1924 - note the open-topped car on the right. This building originally went up in 1579, but its exterior was completely rebuilt in 1910-12, giving it a mock-Tudor appearance.

# Sevenoaks

A pleasing, country town situated high up on the Weald. Sevenoaks is perhaps best known for the entrance to Knole Park, built in 1456 and home of the Sackville family since the early 1600s. High Street is graced by many attractive houses dating from the seventeenth century, whilst the spacious medieval church is one of the finest in Kent.

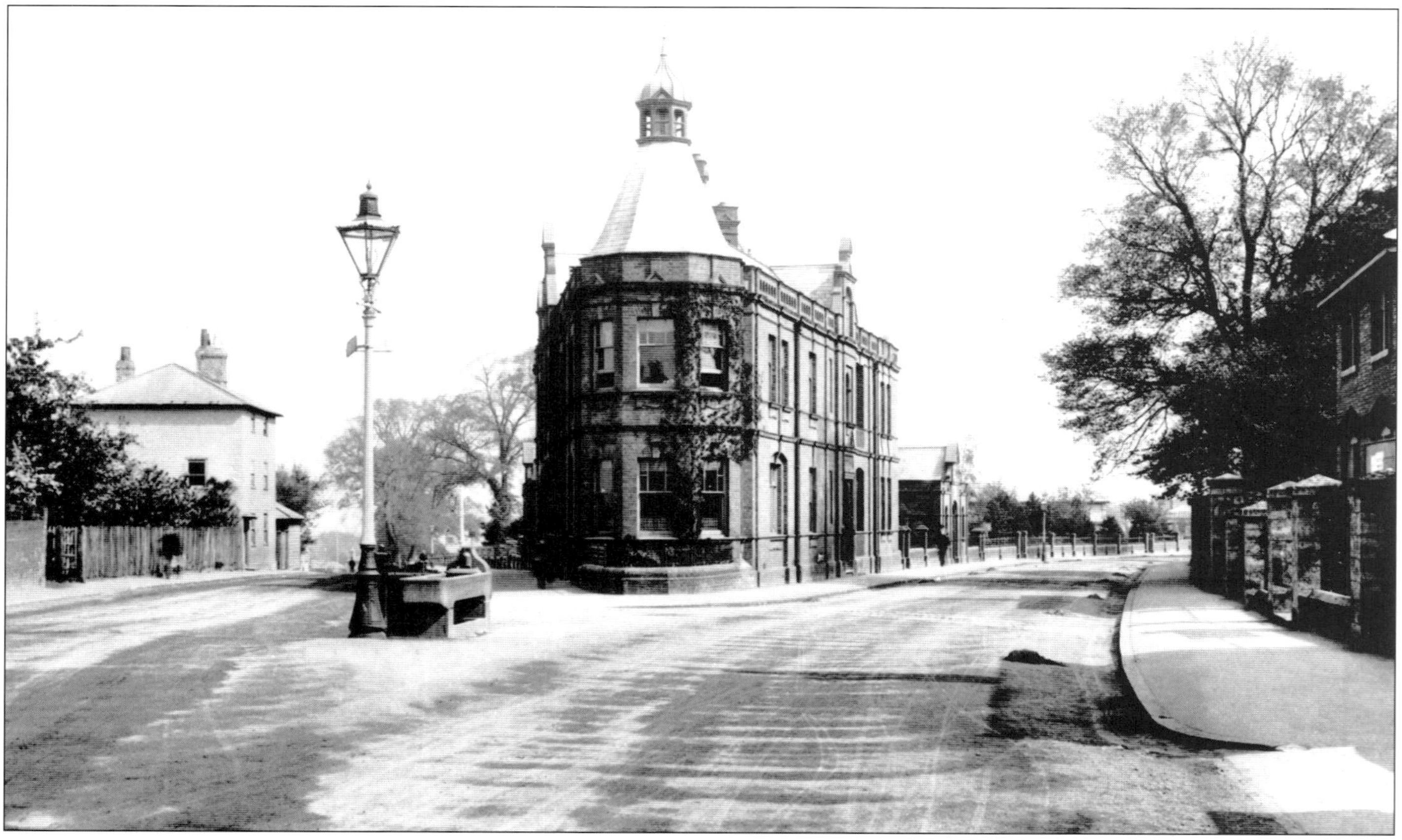

44906
This view taken in 1900, shows the Constitutional Club. Note the gas lamp and horse trough in the centre of the picture.

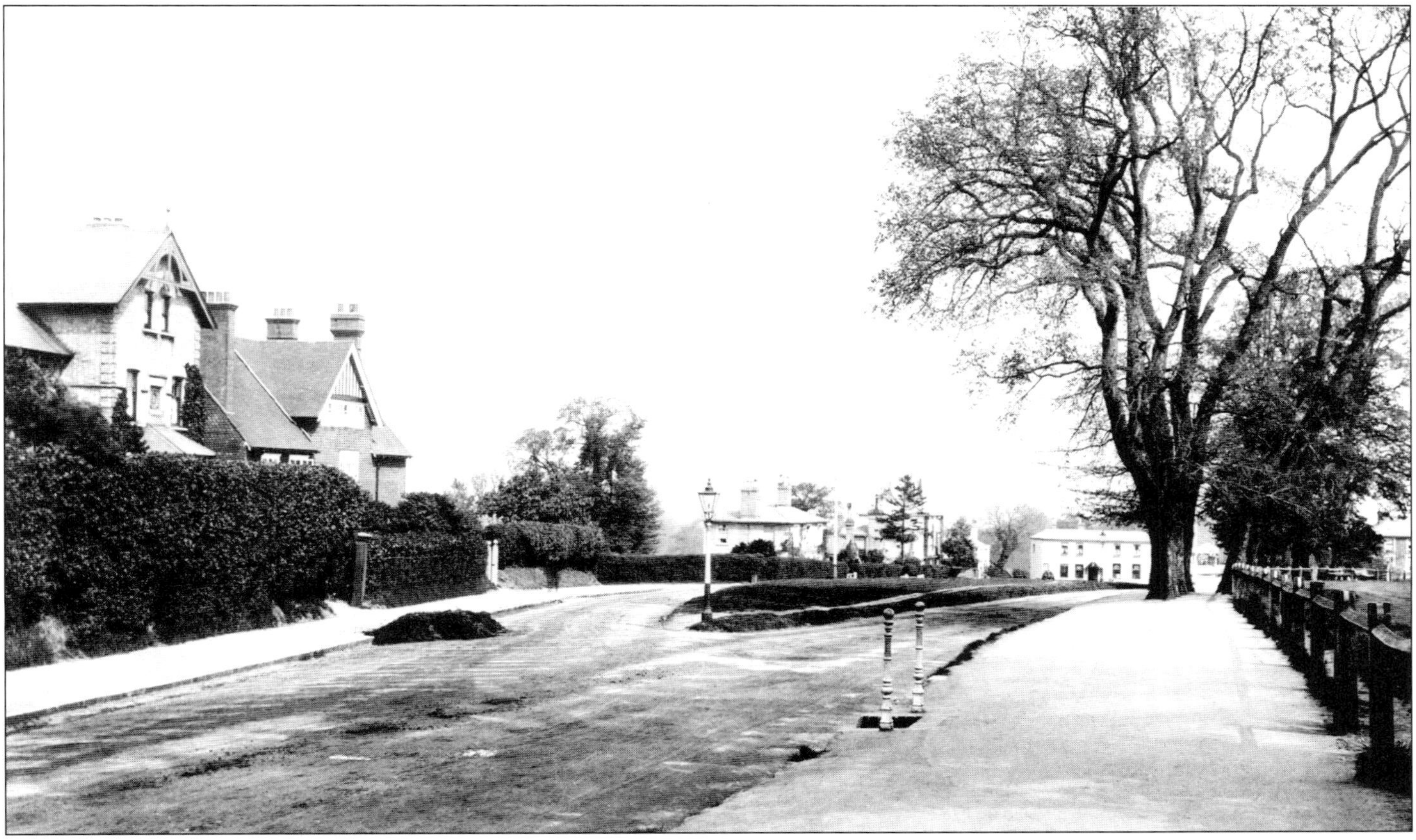

44908
Sevenoaks, in 1900. It is the burial place of William Lambarde (1536-1601), author of *Perambulation of Kent* (1570), the first topographical history of the county.

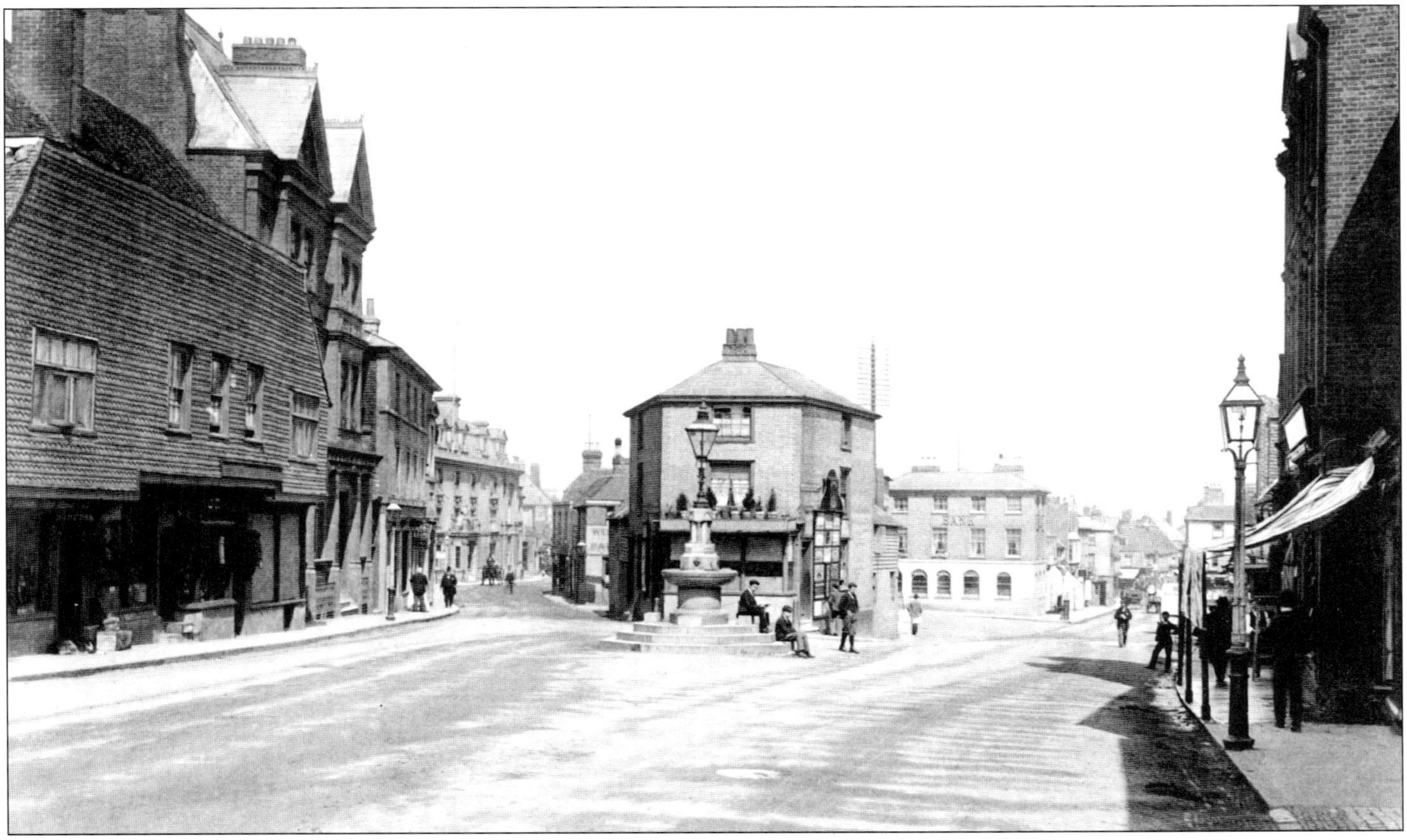

44904
Looking downhill where High Street divides, continuing on as the right hand fork. The picture was taken in 1900 and the lack of traffic is quite remarkable.

# Sheerness

A contrasting place of docks and a seaside resort situated on the Isle of Sheppey. There was a naval dockyard founded here by Pepys in the time of Charles II, but it closed in the early 1960s. The promenade, with its gardens and amusements, overlooks the beach and the Thames estuary, with views to Shoeburyness.

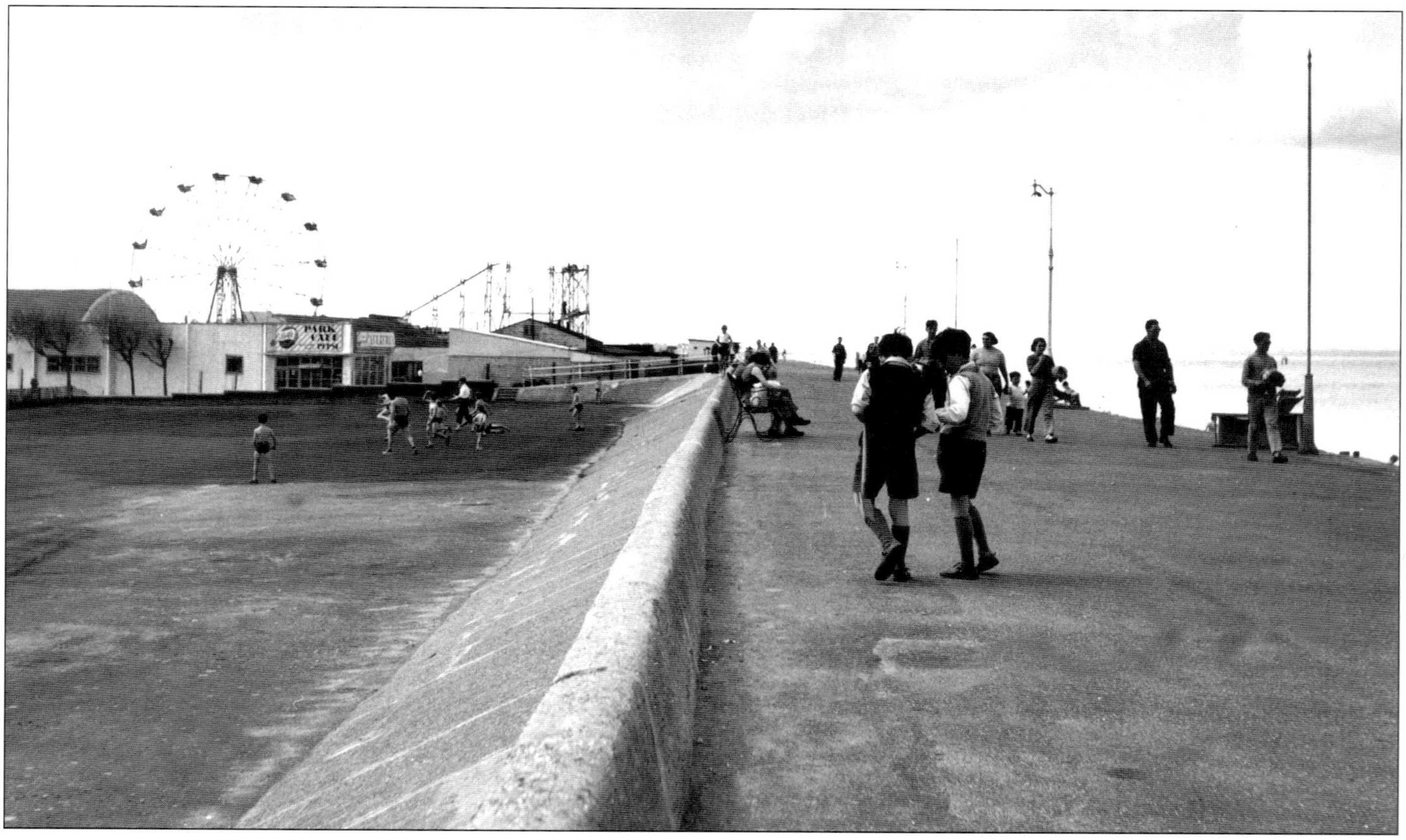

S528048
An impromptu game of football takes place in the shadow of a traditional seaside funfair, as holidaymakers stroll along the Esplanade in 1955. The beach, which has subsequently won the European 'blue flag', lies to the right.

## Sissinghurst

A charming village with a delightful main street showing a wide mixture of Kentish houses. Nearby is the ancient gateway to Sissinghurst Castle, which was founded in Tudor times. Today it is owned by the National Trust and is best known for its gardens designed by Vita Sackville-West.

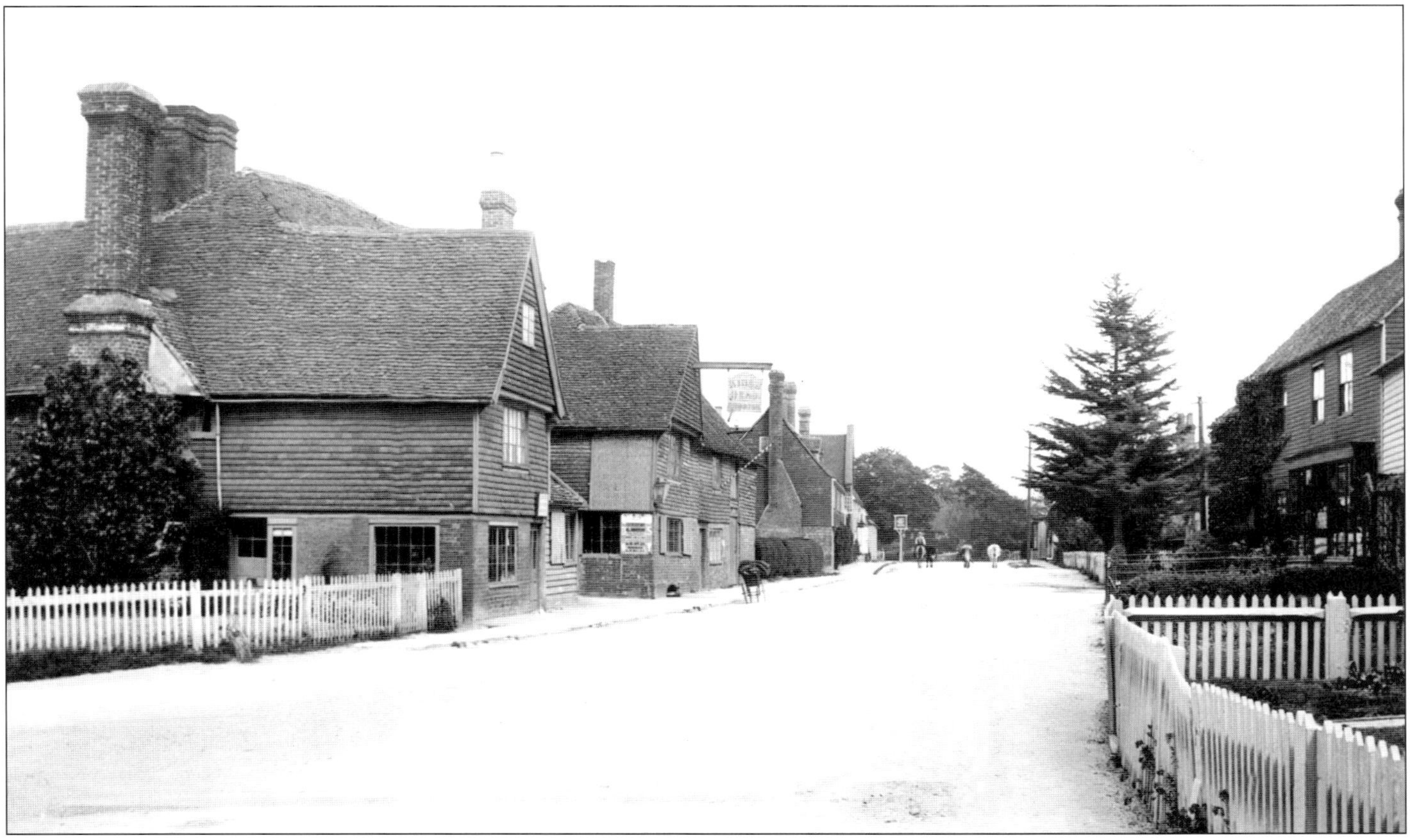

48237
Tile-hung and weatherboarded cottages pictured in Sissinghurst in 1902. The white fencing around the cottage gardens is very typical of villages in the Weald of Kent.

# Sittingbourne

An ancient place on Watling Street and the River Swale, it was an important market town and stopping place for Canterbury Pilgrims. Today, it is a thriving industrial town, and the centre of paper manufacturing and fruit packing, recalling its position at the heart of the Kentish cherry orchards.

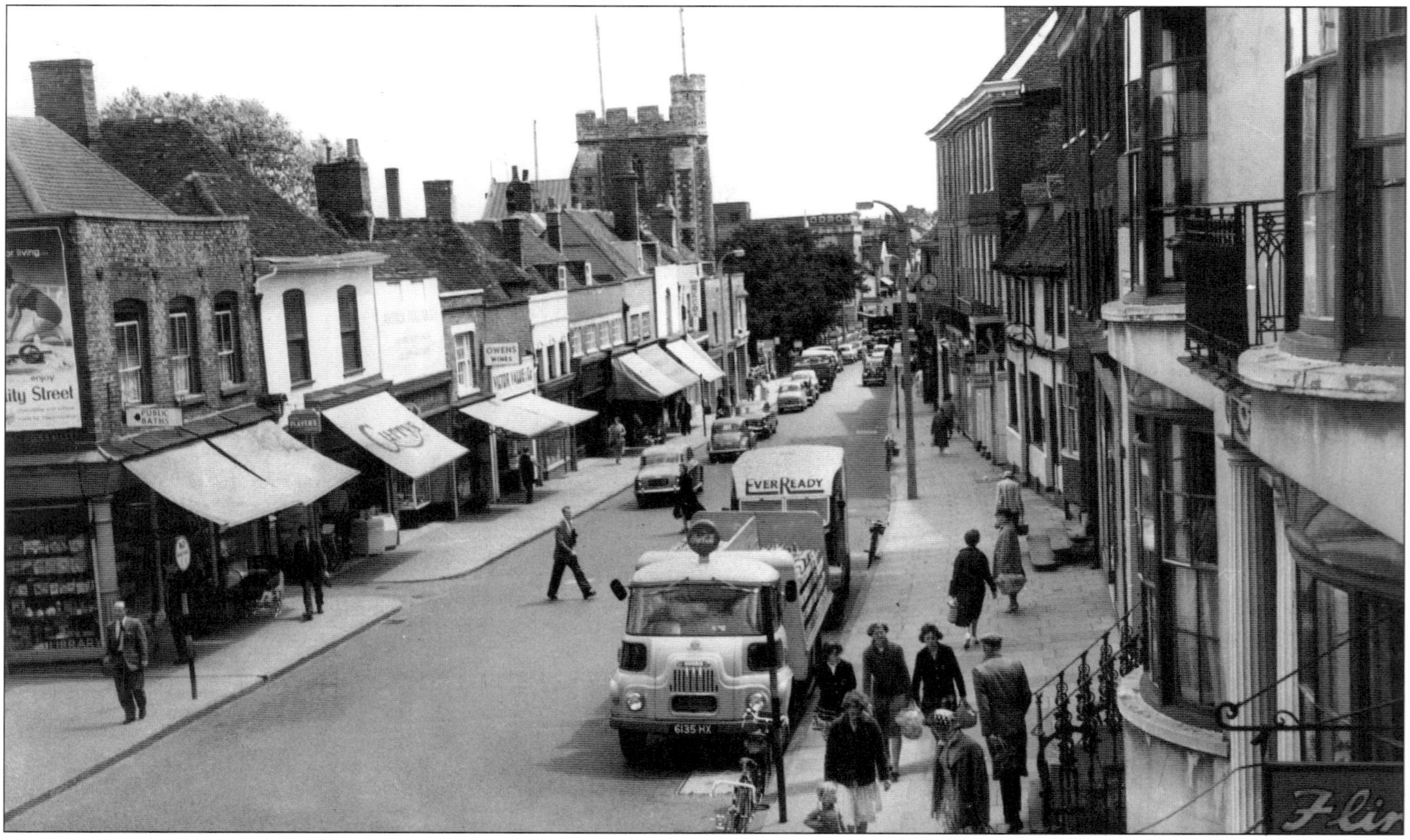


S531058
The busy, bustling High Street which runs along Watling Street, pictured in 1965. This view shows clearly, above the shopfronts with their various sun-awnings, that the street is lined with a lovely variety of Georgian and earlier architecture.

# Stansted

A scattered village found on narrow lanes in the rolling downland north of Wrotham. The church dates from the fourteenth century, but is built on a Norman site. The two bells are some of the oldest in Kent. There is an exceptional bronze war memorial.

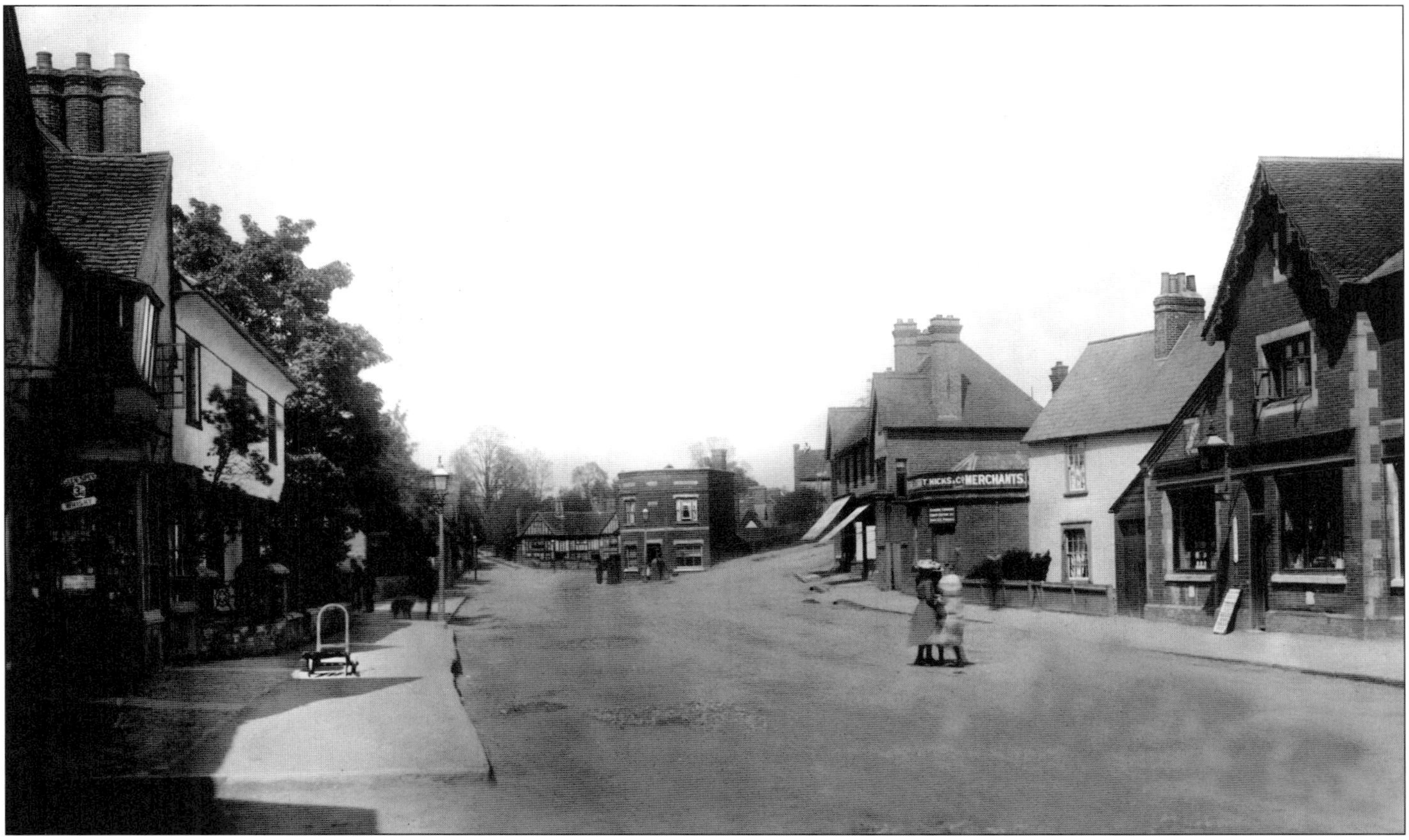


51109
An evocative view of the village centre in 1903, with children playing in the street. Today this view is dominated by the bronze war memorial erected in 1923. It was commissioned in Budapest and shows a man holding a palm branch.

## Sturry

A village situated at a crossing of the River Stour, it suffered badly from bomb damage in the Second World War. However, it retains its church, which is Norman in origin, together with its huge tithe barn, built of weatherboard and brick.

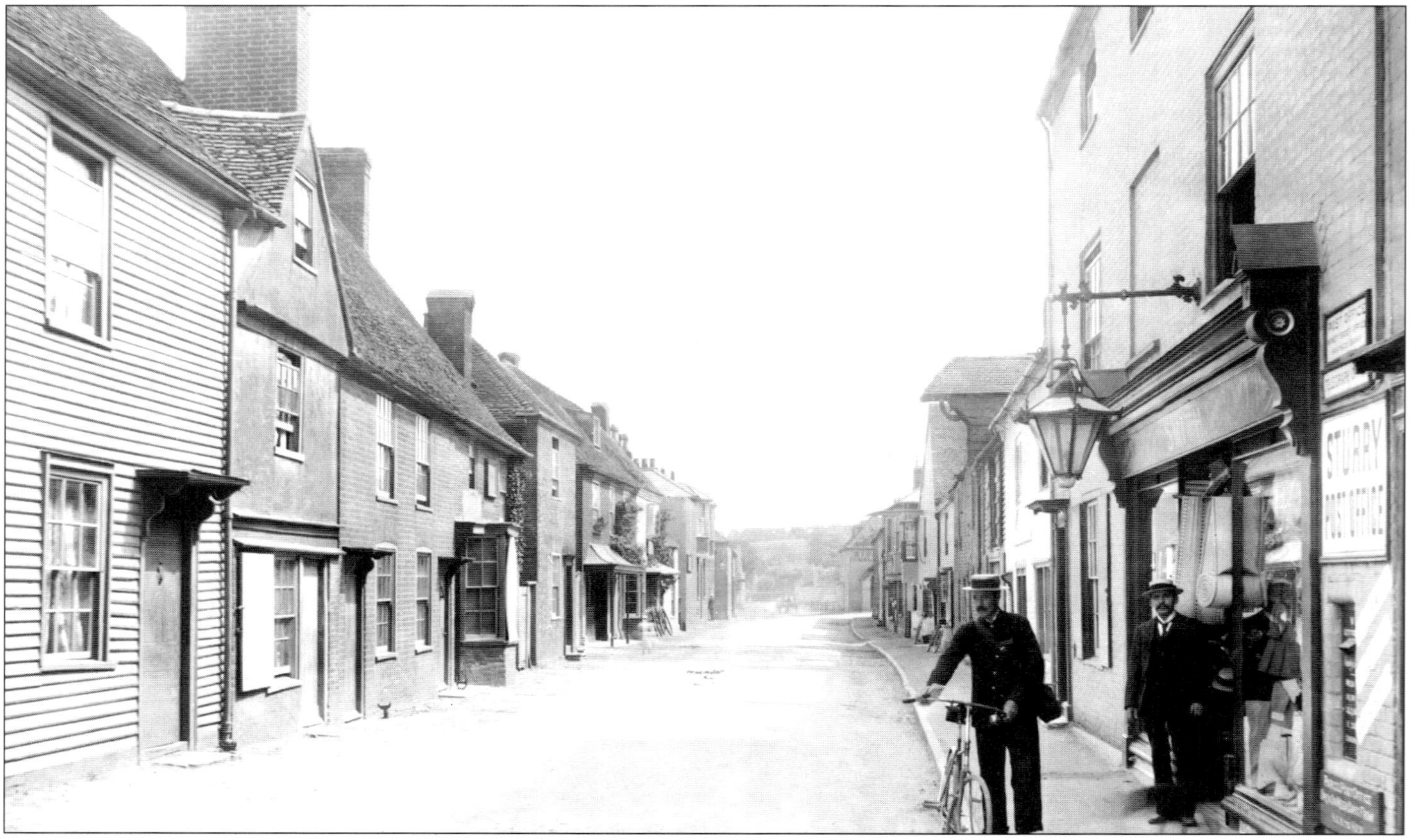


44220
An interesting picture of this Street and post office in 1899, with the village postman about to mount his bicycle. The name relates to Sturry's position on the River Stour, that is 'Stour-y'.

# Tenterden

A beautiful old Kentish town close to the Rother Levels. It grew fat in the Middle Ages on sheep, wool and weaving, and later became a market town. Its broad High Street has a pleasing mixture of half-timbered buildings and elegant Regency houses. The fine medieval church has a magnificent fifteenth century tower.

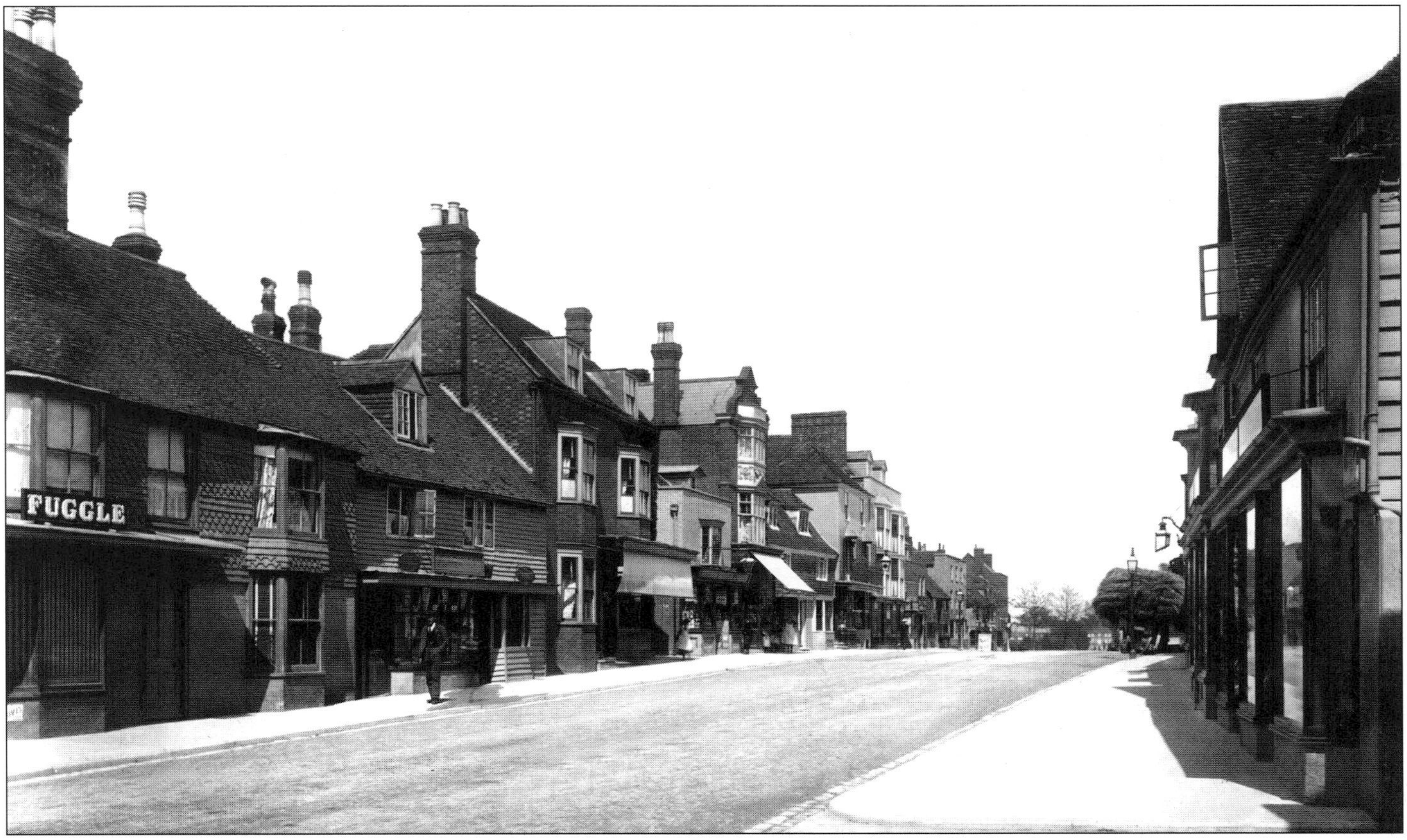


44992
The impressively wide High Street in 1900, showing a variety of architectural styles. Tenterden claims to be the birthplace of William Caxton, the first English printer.

# Tonbridge

A fine old town situated at a crossing of the River Medway, now spanned by a Victorian cast-iron bridge. It has the remains of a Norman castle, which was demolished in the Civil War - only the thirteenth century gatehouse remains, and the rest is now gardens. The High Street has many attractive eighteenth and nineteenth century buildings. Tonbridge is famous for its school, founded in Tudor times.

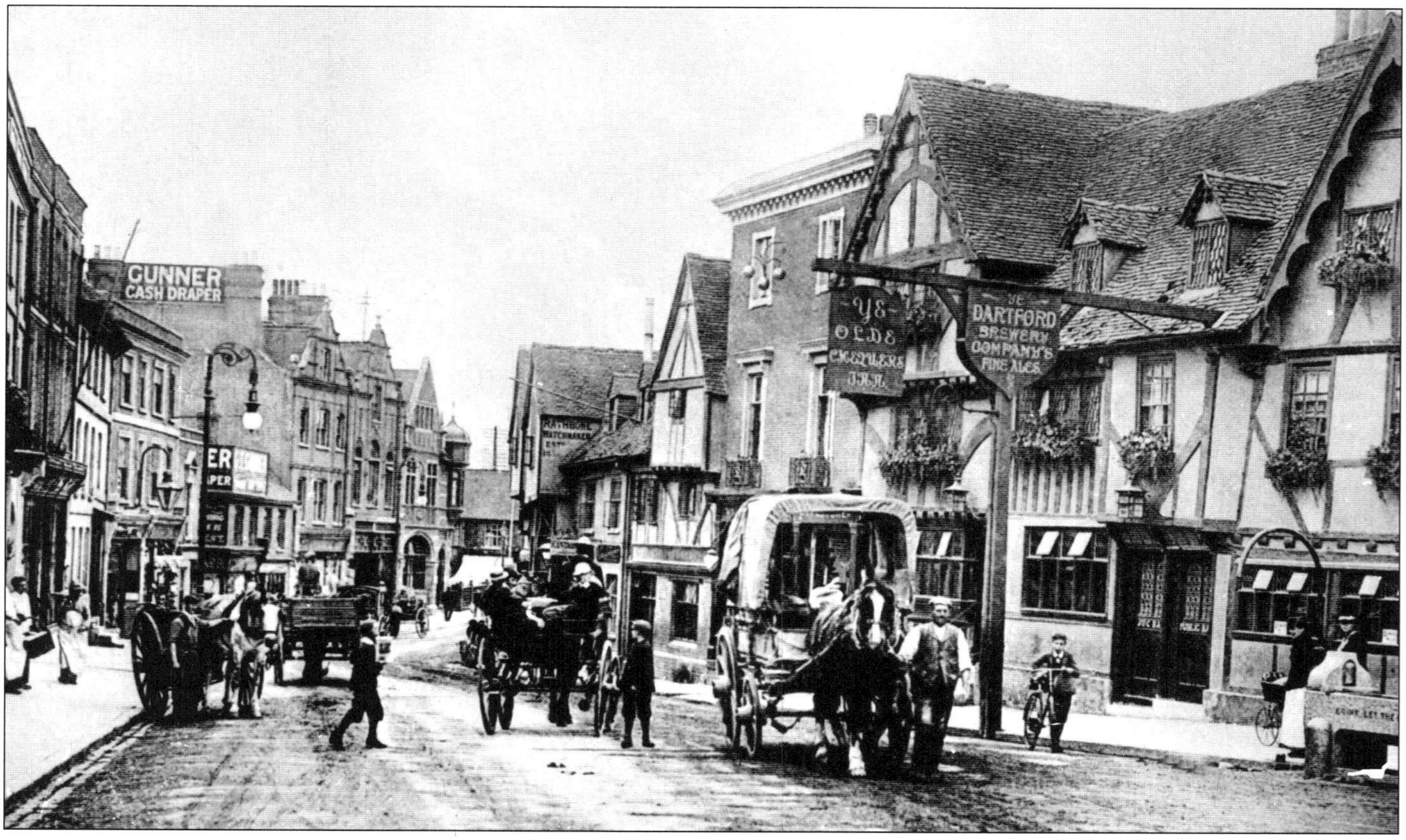


T101004

An excellent bustling view of the High Street taken in 1890. Horse-drawn wagons are plying the street. The half-timbered Chequers Inn is one of Tonbridge's oldest buildings, still there today after nearly being demolished.

# Tunbridge Wells

Tunbridge Wells was once a scattered hamlet in a forested part of the Weald, until a chalybeate spring was discovered in 1606, and it grew into a handsome spa town. Visitors camped on the common, until building began in 1638, when a promenade called the Walk was laid out. The Walk was paved and became the Pantiles.

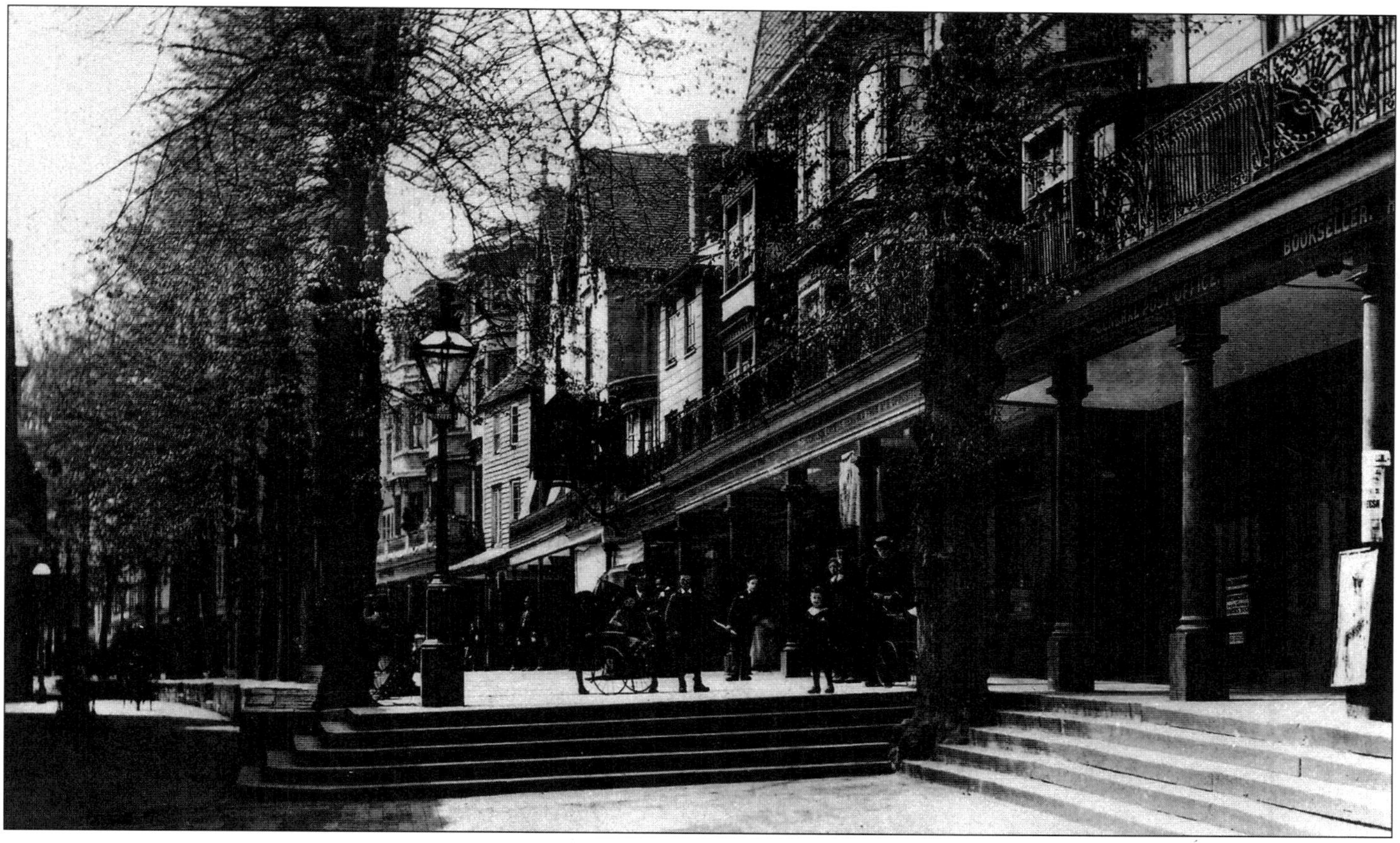


787001
An 1890s view of the most famous landmark of the Wells, the Pantiles, a terraced walk with rather superior shops behind a colonnade, flanked by limes. This was originally laid out as the Walk, and only later was it tiled.

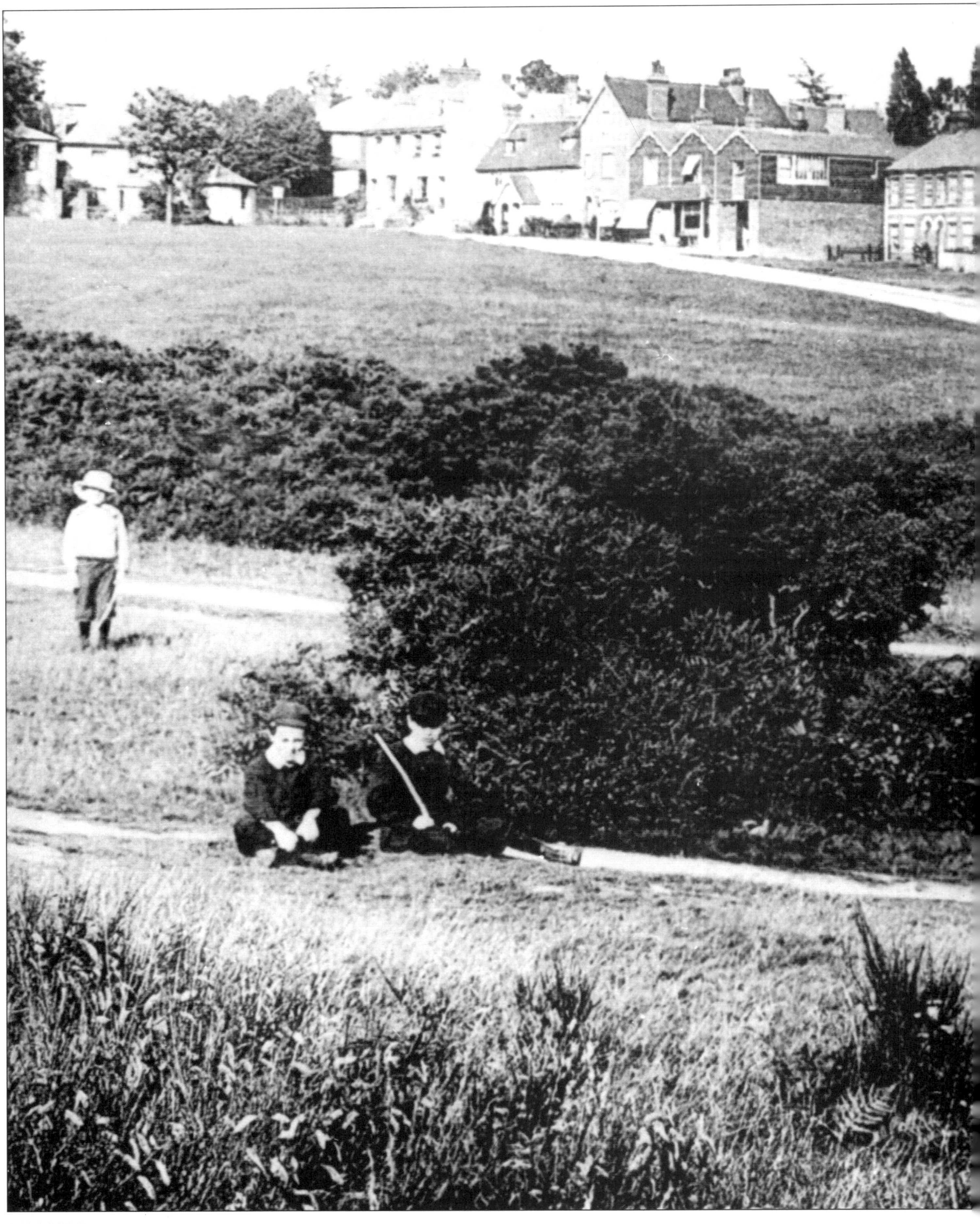

T101010
A wonderfully evocative view of Southborough Common, 1890. The common has long been a favourite place for recreation, and the children are posing attentively for the photographer.

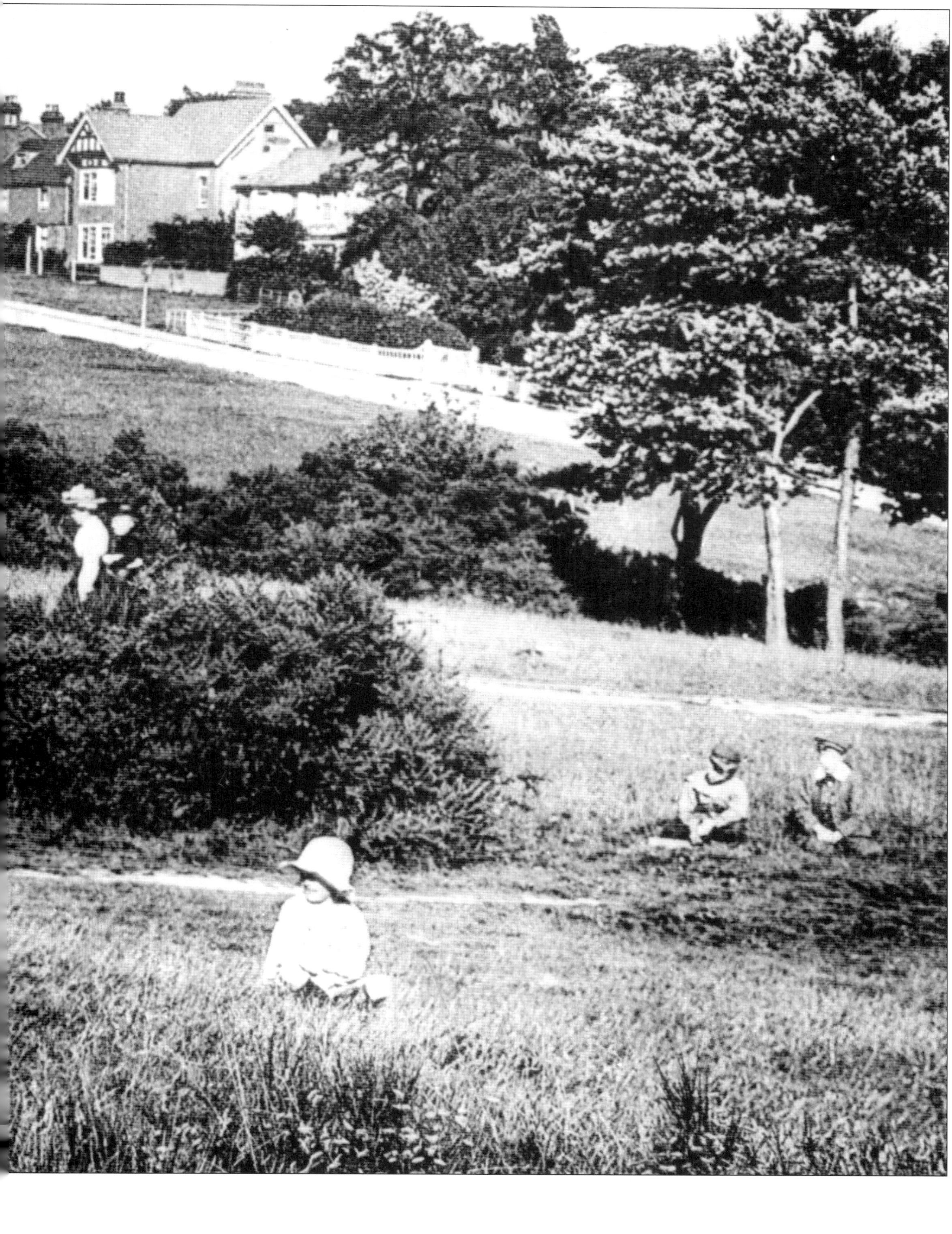

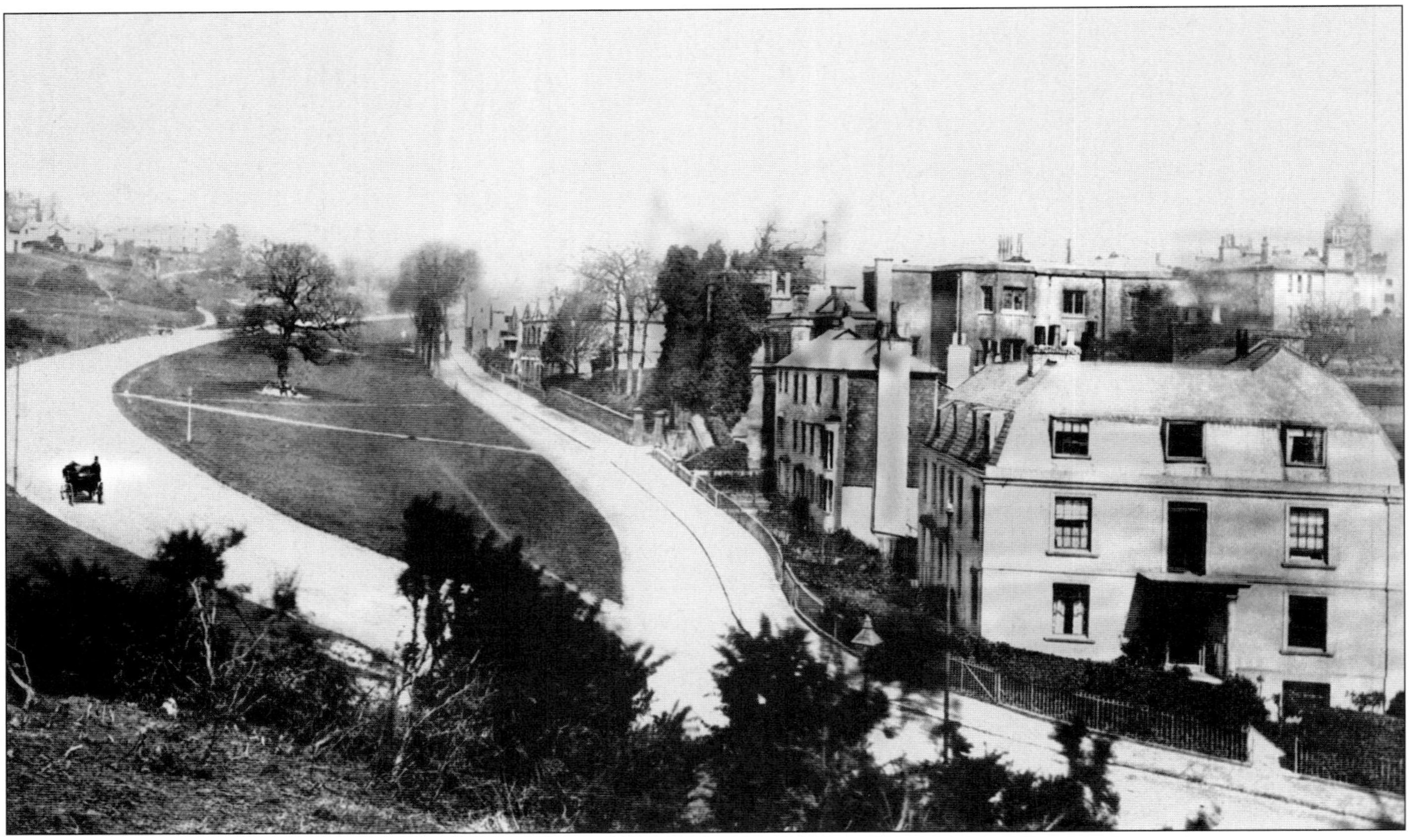

T87006
An early view of Tunbridge Wells, taken in 1875, with a lone cart ascending the hill beside the common, where early visitors like Queen Henrietta Maria had camped. The view is unmistakable, even today.

## WILLESBOROUGH

An old village, with a medieval church thought to be built on Saxon foundations. Its attractive white-boarded smock mill looks down towards the church. Today, the village is a suburb of Ashford, and is carved in two by the M20 motorway.

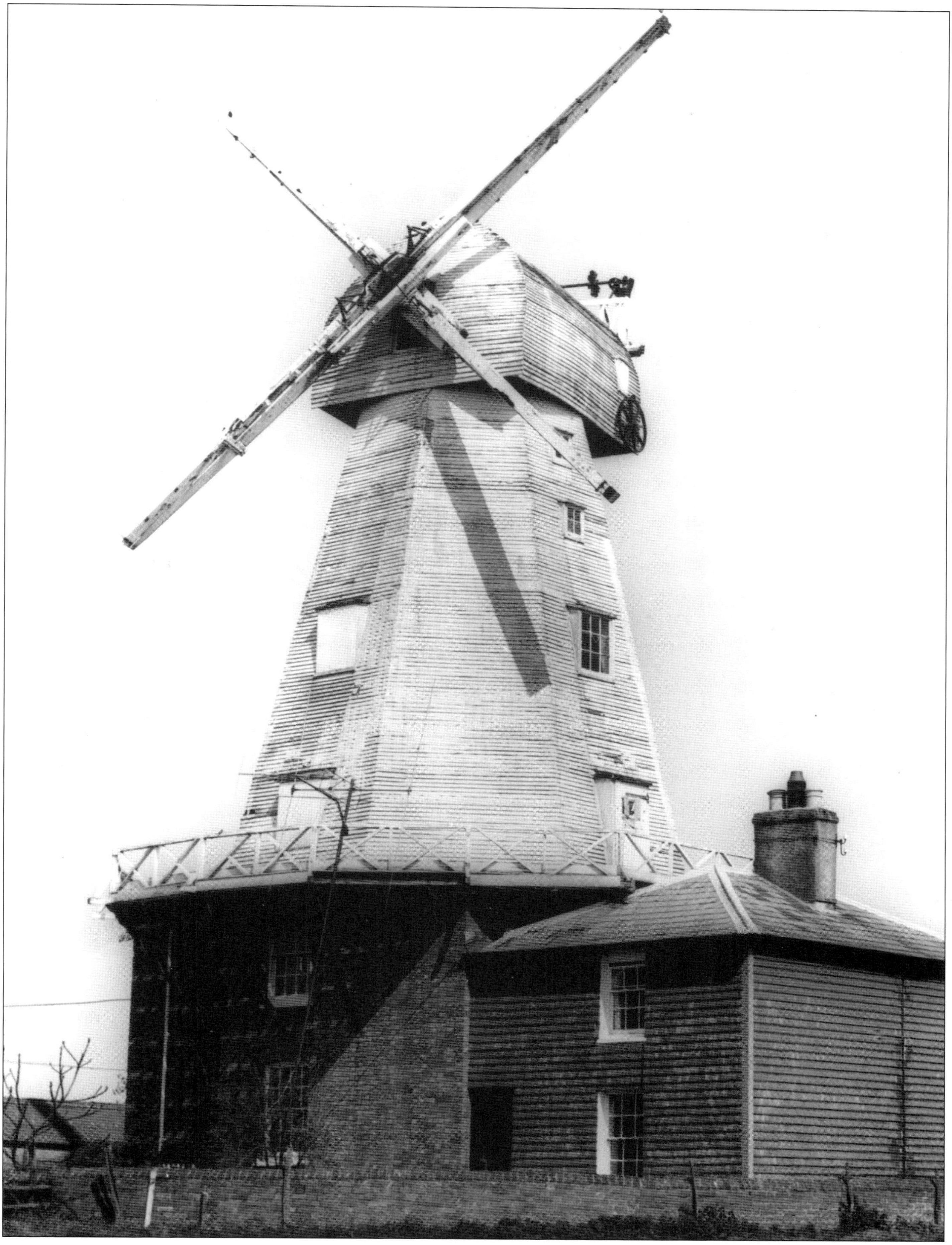

W101002
A delightful close-up view, taken in about 1955, of a typical Kentish windmill, an octagonal white-boarded smock mill. The mill was built in 1869.

# Pictorial Memories Collection

*A great new range of publications featuring the work of innovative Victorian photographer Francis Frith.*

## *1998 Titles*

*County Series* — £9.99

| ISBN | Title |
|---|---|
| 1-84125-045-7 | Berkshire |
| 053-8 | Buckinghamshire |
| 024-4 | Derbyshire |
| 077-5 | Greater London |
| 028-7 | Kent |
| 029-5 | Lake District |
| 051-1 | Lancashire |
| 031-7 | Leicestershire |
| 026-0 | London |
| 027-9 | Norfolk |
| 030-9 | Sussex |
| 063-5 | West Yorkshire |
| 025-2 | Yorkshire |

*Town & City Series* — £9.99

| ISBN | Title |
|---|---|
| 010-4 | Brighton & Hove |
| 015-5 | Canterbury |
| 079-1 | Edinburgh |
| 012-0 | Glasgow & Clydeside |
| 081-3 | Norwich |
| 040-6 | York |

*Country Series* — £9.99

| ISBN | Title |
|---|---|
| 1-84125-075-9 | Ireland |
| 071-6 | North Wales |
| 073-2 | Scotland |
| 069-4 | South Wales |

*Poster Books* — £4.99

| ISBN | Title |
|---|---|
| 000-7 | Canals and Waterways |
| 032-5 | Derbyshire |
| 001-5 | High Days and Holidays |
| 036-8 | Kent |
| 037-6 | Lake District |
| 034-1 | London |
| 005-8 | Railways |

£5.99

| ISBN | Title |
|---|---|
| 023-6 | Canterbury |
| 043-0 | Derby |

## *Titles from January to July 1999*

*County Series* — £9.99

| ISBN | Title | Month |
|---|---|---|
| 1-84125-049-x | Warwickshire | March |
| 047-3 | Staffordshire | |
| 057-0 | Devon | |
| 067-8 | Cheshire | |
| 065-1 | Nottinghamshire | |
| 059-7 | Cornwall | |
| 1-84125-101-1 | Surrey | |
| 095-3 | Hampshire | |
| 128-3 | Highlands | April |
| 149-6 | Hertfordshire | |
| 130-5 | North Yorkshire | May |
| 150-x | Wiltshire | |

*Town & City Series* — £7.99

| ISBN | Title | Month |
|---|---|---|
| 089-9 | Maidstone | March |
| 087-2 | Bradford | |
| 083-x | Colchester | |
| 093-7 | Dublin | |
| 091-0 | Leeds | |
| 105-4 | Buxton | |
| 111-9 | Bristol | |
| 113-5 | Nottingham | |
| 011-2 | Manchester | |
| 107-0 | Matlock | |
| 009-0 | Macclesfield | April |
| 132-1 | St Ives | |
| 008-2 | Derby | |
| 113-x | Sevenoaks | |
| 014-7 | Newbury | |
| 134-8 | Bognor Regis | |
| 144-5 | Leicester | |
| 145-3 | East Grinstead | |
| 146-1 | Newark | |
| 137-2 | Sheffield | May |
| 138-0 | Cambridge | |
| 139-9 | Penzance | |
| 140-2 | Eastbourne | |
| 147-x | Llandudno | |
| 142-9 | Torquay | |
| 148-8 | Whitby | |
| 159-3 | Scarborough | June |
| 160-7 | Faversham to Herne Bay | |
| 164-x | Scilly Isles | |
| 162-3 | Dorset Coast | |
| 168-2 | Falmouth | |
| 165-8 | Newquay | |
| 154-2 | Bakewell | July |
| 163-1 | Lincoln | |
| 167-4 | Barnstaple | |
| 174-7 | Great Yarmouth | |
| 141-0 | Blackpool | |
| 207-7 | Dartmoor | |

WATERTON PRESS, WATERTON ESTATE, BRIDGEND, GLAMORGAN, CF31 3XP.
TEL: 01656 668836 FAX: 01656 668710

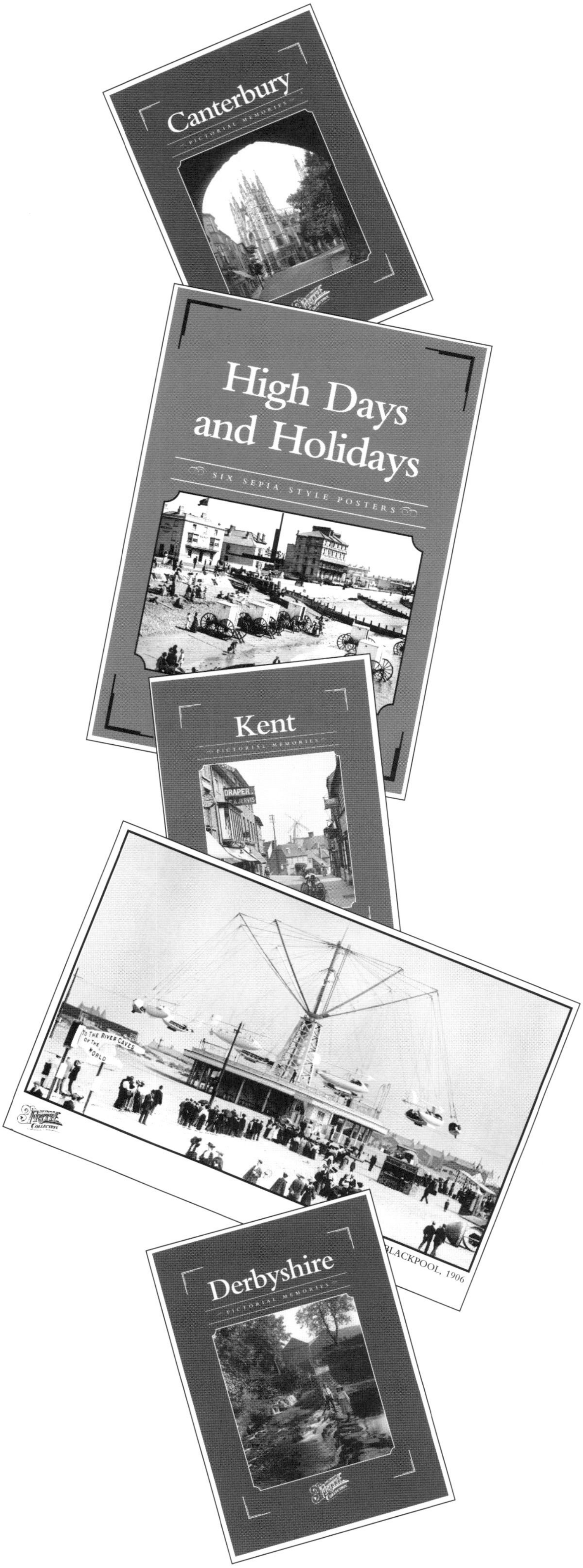


# Voucher

This voucher entitles you to a half price mounted print normally £19.95

*Mounted prints are A4 sepia, mounted in a cream mount with beval cut aperture and single burgundy ruled line, greyboard backing and cello bagged.

*Special offer price £9.97*

Simply select the view in this book that you would like to receive as a mounted print, and complete the form below.

| Page & Negative Number | Town & Description |
|---|---|
| | |

I enclose a cheque/postal order for £9.97 which includes p&p, made payable to "The Francis Frith Collection."

Name & Address:

Mr/Mrs/Miss/Ms

Initial Surname

Address

Town

County

Postcode

Daytime Telephone No.
(incase of queries)

Send your voucher and remittance to:
The Francis Frith Collection
Dept FF007, 'Friths Barn', Teffont,
Salisbury, Wilts, SP3 5QP.

# El Punto en Cuestión

Silvia C. Gómez

Chancerel

# El Punto en Cuestión

**Redacción** Ana Montero
**Diseño e ilustración** Julia Osorno
**Diseño de la cubierta** Gregor Arthur
**Fotografía** Katharine Gasparini, Picot Cassidy

**ISBN** Libro: 3-12-513344-0
**ISBN** Doble casete: 3-12-513342-4
**ISBN** Guia del profesor: 3-12-513343-2

**PN** 8 7 6 5 4 3 / 08 07 06 05 04


Impreso en Hong Kong

## Fotografías

Agencia EFE 30, 31 (2); Alcaldía Municipio Chacao 28; APA (Hong Kong) Ltd 70; Britstock-IFA Ltd 58; Picot Cassidy 66, 76; Chancerel 74, 86; Jan Chipps Photography 19, 22, 27, 36 (2), 38 (2), 50, 68, 71, 74, 90, 91; Club Med 82; Das Photo/D. Simson 6, 7, 92; Getty Images 20, 54, 88; Image Bank (The) 12, 14, 15; Katz Pictures Ltd 8; Ana Montero 36, 70 (4), 74; Panasonic UK Ltd 26 (3); "PA" News Photo Library 42; Retna Pictures Limited 40 (2); Roslin Institute 44; El Semanal 16; Michael Smith 6, 38 (3), 62 (4); South American Pictures 46, 72, 79 (2), 84, 87; Sylvia Cordaiy Photo Library Ltd 32, 34; Telegraph Colour Library 15, 18, 24, 26, 30, 38, 48, 52, 54, 64, 80, 86

# EL Punto EN Cuestión

## Textos

- El Comercio (Ecuador) *¿Un clon tiene beneficios?* 44
- El Correo Gallego (España) Cómic de Sir Cámara 93
- Cristina La Revista (México) *Te sigo amando, el debut de un talk show en las telenovelas* 20; *Acabe con el estrés antes de que acabe con usted* 52; *Las diez profesiones de más estrés* 54; *Un día en la vida de Ana* 55; *Paparazzi* 68
- Entre Estudiantes (España) *La oficina en casa* 80
- La Farola (España) Texto e ilustración, *Zapatos* 56
- Greenpeace (España) Publicidad 47
- Mariscal (España) Ilustración 51
- Mía (España) Cómic de Candela Prat, *PiliPropper* 16; *Nosotros maltratamos a la naturaleza y ella se queja* 48
- El Mundo (España) Adaptación del texto de Pedro Simón, *Vive de tus padres hasta la jubilación* 92
- La Nación (Argentina) Portada de la edición digital 7
- Gracia Nidasio (España) Cómic, *Nina* 59
- Noticias de Abya Yala (Argentina. Edición digital) *Wichí: luchando por sobrevivir en Argentina* 60
- Noticias Latin America (Londres, Gran Bretaña) *La fiesta del sol* 84
- Oficina de Turismo de México (México) Publicidad 75
- El País (Colombia) *Menores, a dormir temprano en Cali* 88
- El País (España) Cómic, *Historias de Miguelito* 35
- El País Semanal (España) Adaptación de los textos de: Fernando Franco, *El río del oro* 12; José Antonio Millán, *Internet* 24; Charo Canal, *Tocar madera. Explicaciones de sentido común para las supersticiones más famosas* 36; Luis Merino, *Turistas en masa. Los nuevos conquistadores arrasan pueblos enteros* 72
- Quino (Argentina) Cómics 23, 54, 67
- Quo (España) Fuente: Instituto Nacional Francés del Deporte y la Educación Física 15
- Revista de la Oficina de Información Diplomática (España) *Primer Congreso Internacional de la Lengua Española. Los asistentes a la cumbre de Zacatecas coinciden en que el español goza de buena salud* 8
- El Semanal (España) Adaptación de los textos de: Bernabé Tierno, *Vivir para beber* 16; Enrique Arias Vega, *La fuerza hispana* 40
- El Tiempo (Colombia. Edición digital) *'Regalo' se quedará en el Hogar Boyacá* 32
- Tiempo de VIAJAR (España) *La ciudad infinita* 64
- El Universo (Ecuador) *Irene Sáez Conde. Ex Miss Universo sueña con ser presidenta* 28
- Visión - La revista Latinoamericana (Argentina) *Machu Picchu, la ciudad escondida* 76

Hemos buscado y solicitado los derechos de los artículos y anuncios publicitarios que se encuentran en este libro, y agradecemos la amabilidad de cuantos nos han respondido y autorizado la reproducción.

# ÍNDICE

# ÍNDICE

En España y Latinoamérica hay publicaciones diarias, semanales y mensuales. Su objetivo es informar a los lectores sobre los acontecimientos políticos y sociales así como los relacionados con los deportes y el tiempo libre.

## PERIÓDICOS

Los periódicos o diarios son la principal fuente de difusión de las noticias de actualidad. La dura competencia con los medios de comunicación audiovisual (televisión y radio) ha reducido el número de estas publicaciones durante las últimas décadas.

En España los periódicos de calidad se publican en formato pequeño. Existen unos 124 diarios; hay diarios provinciales, regionales y nacionales. *El País*, fundado en 1976, es el periódico de mayor tirada (el que más vende), con un promedio de 421,000 ejemplares al día. Le siguen *ABC*, fundado en junio de 1905, y *El Mundo* cuyo primer número apareció en octubre de 1989. Tanto en España como en Latinoamérica ningún periódico alcanza el medio millón de ejemplares diarios. Únicamente *El País* de los domingos logra vender un millón de ejemplares gracias a los suplementos. Además de noticias, los periódicos contienen comentarios, pasatiempos, artículos literarios y viñetas de humor y chistes. Quino de Argentina y Romeu de España son dos humoristas muy conocidos.

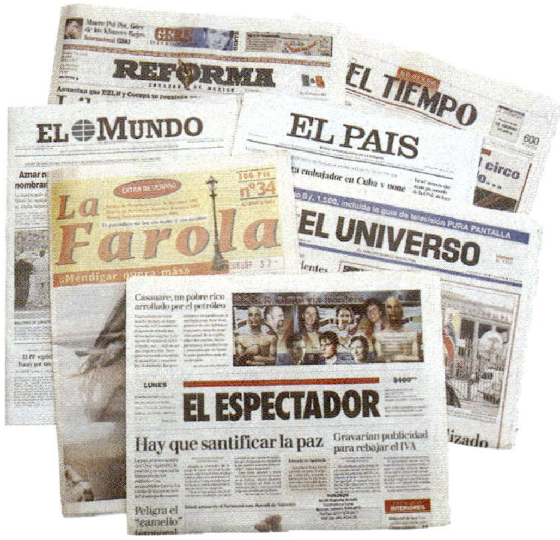


En América Latina se publican diarios de importante tirada y con gran influencia en la opinión pública de sus respectivos países. *Ejemplos: Clarín*, *La Nación* en Buenos Aires (Argentina); *Excelsior*, *El Universal* en Ciudad de México; *El Mercurio* en Santiago de Chile; *El Tiempo*, *La República* en Montevideo (Uruguay).

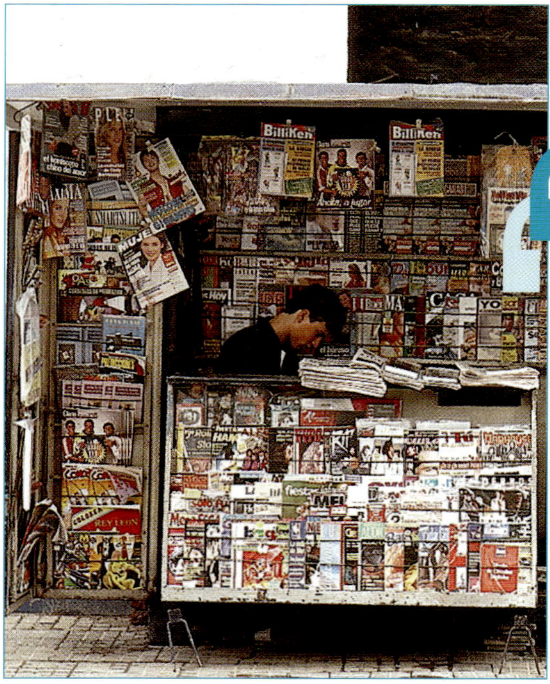

**"Los fines de semana compro El País con el suplemento porque es muy completo. La revista dominical tiene secciones muy variadas y artículos interesantes. Me gusta mucho la sección de humor de Quino. Además siempre regalan coleccionables muy útiles".**

**"No compro periódicos porque prefiero leer la versión electrónica en Internet. Es más cómodo y fácil estar al día y ahorras papel. En el futuro creo que no habrá periódicos impresos".**

## Revistas

Otro gran sector son las revistas de publicación semanal destinadas a un público general. Contienen noticias de actualidad relacionadas sobre todo con la política, pero también incluyen la cultura y el ocio. *Ejemplos: Tiempo, Cambio 16, Época, Tribuna* en España; *Semana* en Colombia; *Visión* en Argentina.

La llamada prensa del corazón se ocupa de la vida privada de personajes públicos del mundo del espectáculo y de la alta sociedad. Las revistas españolas *Hola*, *Diez Minutos*, *Semana* y *Pronto* constituyen una parte importante en el mercado de revistas. En México la revista *Alarma*, de carácter sensacionalista, vende más de un millón de ejemplares.

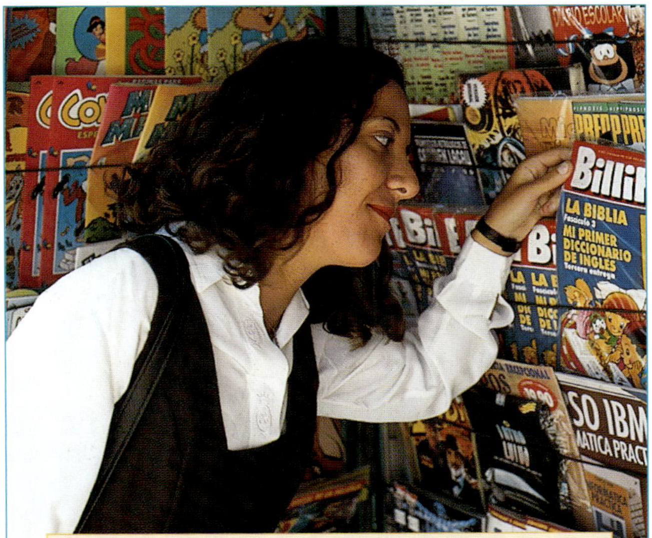


Ha aumentado el número de revistas especializadas en temas científicos, sobre la naturaleza y actividades de tiempo libre como viajes, deporte, las revistas relacionadas con la salud y, por supuesto, las revistas informáticas o de computación.

## Por vía digital

Las nuevas tecnologías están transformando el mundo de la información. Ahora es posible recibir la versión electrónica de un periódico en cualquier parte del mundo a través de Internet.

Para acceder a una publicación digital sólo tienes que escribir la dirección en el recuadro y hacer clic con el ratón en el botón de búsqueda.

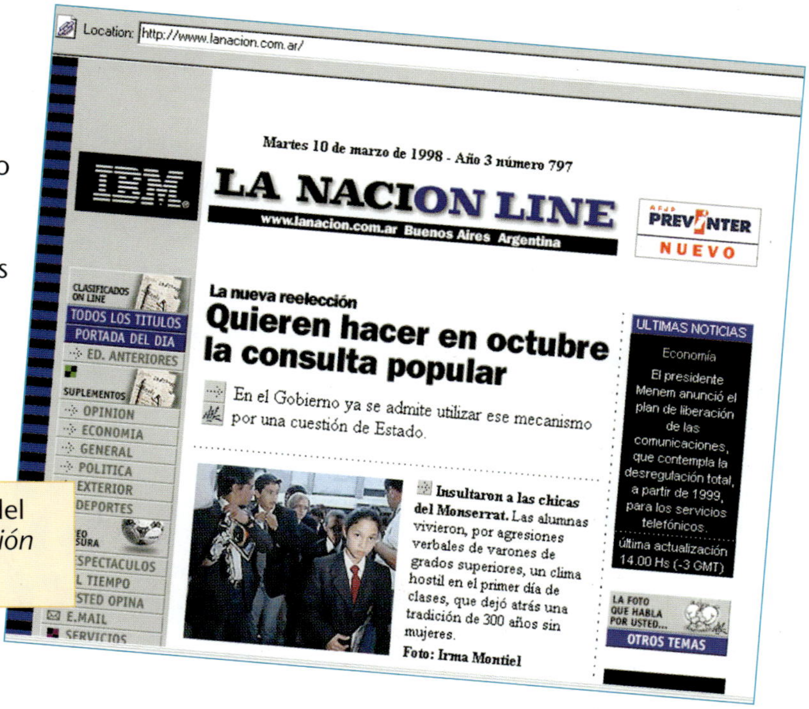

Location: http://www.lanacion.com.ar/

Martes 10 de marzo de 1998 - Año 3 número 797

IBM

LA NACION LINE

www.lanacion.com.ar Buenos Aires Argentina

PREVINTER NUEVO

CLASIFICADOS ON LINE
TODOS LOS TITULOS
PORTADA DEL DIA
ED. ANTERIORES
SUPLEMENTOS
OPINION
ECONOMIA
GENERAL
POLITICA
EXTERIOR
DEPORTES
ESPECTACULOS
EL TIEMPO
USTED OPINA
E.MAIL
SERVICIOS

La nueva reelección

**Quieren hacer en octubre la consulta popular**

En el Gobierno ya se admite utilizar ese mecanismo por una cuestión de Estado.

**Insultaron a las chicas del Monserrat.** Las alumnas vivieron, por agresiones verbales de varones de grados superiores, un clima hostil en el primer día de clases, que dejó atrás una tradición de 300 años sin mujeres.

Foto: Irma Montiel

ULTIMAS NOTICIAS

Economía

El presidente Menem anunció el plan de liberación de las comunicaciones, que contempla la desregulación total, a partir de 1999, para los servicios telefónicos.

Última actualización 14.00 Hs (-3 GMT)

LA FOTO QUE HABLA POR USTED...

OTROS TEMAS

Esta es la página principal del periódico argentino *La Nación* en su versión on-line.

## PUNTO DE MIRA

**1** ¿Por qué motivos estudias español?

**a** porque es una asignatura del colegio
**b** por tu trabajo/profesión
**c** porque te gusta
**d** porque vas de vacaciones a un país de habla española

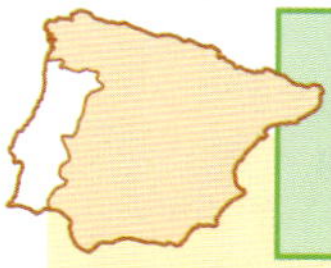

Cada vez hay más gente que estudia el español (o castellano) como lengua extranjera. Lee este artículo para conocer algunos aspectos de la lengua de Cervantes.

*Primer Congreso Internacional de la Lengua Española*

# LOS ASISTENTES A LA CUMBRE DE ZACATECAS COINCIDEN EN QUE EL ESPAÑOL GOZA DE BUENA SALUD

*Más de un centenar de lingüistas, escritores, periodistas, cineastas y empresarios y técnicos de la comunicación de una veintena de países se reunieron en la ciudad mexicana de Zacatecas para analizar el presente y el futuro de la lengua española.*

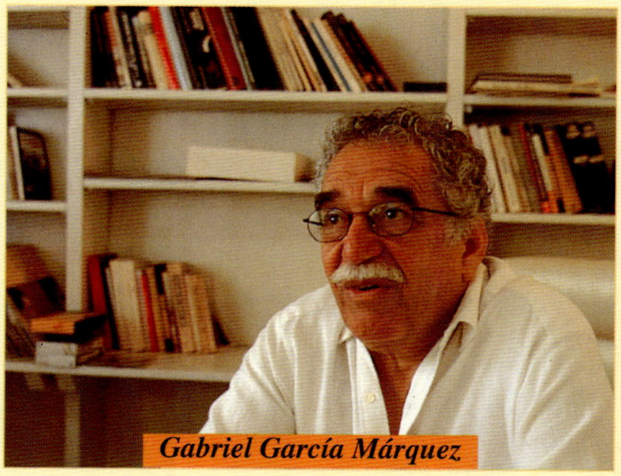

*Gabriel García Márquez*

El español es la lengua oficial en 21 países que en la actualidad suman más de 345 millones de habitantes. Además, hay que añadir los 30 millones de hispanohablantes que residen en Estados Unidos y Filipinas, que convierten a nuestro idioma en el cuarto del mundo, después del chino, el inglés y el hindi. El prestigio cultural de la lengua española, puesto de manifiesto en los diez premios Nobel de Literatura obtenidos por escritores hispanohablantes, así como su riqueza y variedad, hacen que sea una de las grandes lenguas de comunicación internacional.

El Congreso de Zacatecas estuvo dedicado a "La lengua y los medios de comunicación". En la sesión inaugural, el Rey de España afirmó que los medios de comunicación son una de las principales fuentes de renovación del idioma y que, por ello, una de sus metas debe ser el cuidado de la lengua. También señaló, refiriéndose a la comunidad iberoamericana, que la lengua española es "el gran vínculo de unión de nuestros pueblos". Advirtió que el castellano puede tener un excelente futuro si se aprovecha en su beneficio las nuevas tecnologías y se crea un nuevo territorio para nuestra lengua.

El presidente de México, apeló también a la responsabilidad de la prensa en la defensa de la unidad básica de la lengua y en el respeto por sus variantes nacionales y regionales.

En el convento de San Agustín de Zacatecas, sede del encuentro, también estuvieron presentes los premios Nobel de Literatura Camilo José Cela (España), Gabriel García Márquez (Colombia) y Octavio Paz (México), aunque este último a través de una grabación en vídeo debido a su delicada salud.

## ¿LO HAS ENTENDIDO?

**1** ¿Cuáles son los idiomas más hablados del planeta?

**2** ¿Cuál fue el tema del Congreso de Zacatecas? ¿Qué personalidades estuvieron presentes en él?

**3** ¿Por qué es el español una lengua internacional? ¿Cuántas personas lo hablan?

**4** Según el rey Juan Carlos, ¿qué deben hacer los medios de comunicación?

## TOMA NOTA

**Diferencias lingüísticas entre España y Latinoamérica**

Hay muchas variaciones de español. En España viajas en ***autobús***, en México en ***camión***, en Argentina en el ***colectivo***, en Venezuela en la ***guagua*** y en Perú en la ***góndola***.

Otra diferencia es el uso de la segunda persona plural de los verbos. En España la forma plural de ***tú*** es ***vosotros***, pero en toda Latinoamérica utilizan ***ustedes***. Así un latinoamericano se dirige a sus amigos, colegas o hermanos con ***"Hola, ¿cómo están ustedes?"***. Y un español dice ***"Hola, ¿cómo estáis?"***.

Aquí tienes una lista de palabras que se utilizan en España. Relaciónalas con sus equivalentes de América Latina.

*Ejemplo*

**beber** = *tomar*

**coche – conducir – beber – aquí – el metro – amigos – bonito – gustar – cómics – apartamento – gafas – patatas – zumo – ¡date prisa!**

*jugo* (México) – *lindo* – *acá* – *departamento* – *papas* – *carro* – *anteojos* (Argentina) – *historietas* – *manejar* – *"subte"* (Argentina) – *¡apúrate!* – *provocar* (Colombia) – *cuates* (México) – *tomar*

### AMPLÍA TU VOCABULARIO

**Cervantes** (Miguel de Cervantes, 1547-1616) escritor español. Autor de *Don Quijote de la Mancha*, considerada como la primera novela moderna de la literatura universal
**suman** totalizan, hacen un total de
**hispanohablantes** de habla hispana
**residen** viven
**puesto de manifiesto** reflejado
**hacen que sea** lo convierten en
**sesión inaugural** sesión que abre el congreso
**por ello** por esa razón
**metas** objetivos
**señaló** indicó
**vínculo de unión** punto común, unidad
**advirtió** informó
**se aprovecha** utiliza, explota
**apeló** se refirió
**variantes** variaciones

## Y TÚ, ¿CÓMO LO VES?

**1** ¿Te gusta aprender español? ¿Hablas otras lenguas? ¿Es importante saber idiomas extranjeros?

**2** ¿Qué métodos empleas para mejorar tus conocimientos de un idioma? ¿Qué resultado tienen?

- **a** leer revistas, periódicos, novelas
- **b** ver la televisión, películas, vídeos
- **c** visitar el país de vacaciones
- **d** hacer un curso en el país

**3** La *Real Academia de la Lengua Española* es una institución que establece las reglas (ortografía, gramática, puntuación, léxico...) y el uso correcto del idioma español. ¿Crees que estas instituciones son necesarias? ¿Por qué? ¿Existe una institución similar en tu país?

LENGUA Y CULTURA

## EN LA ONDA

**1** El cine, la literatura, la pintura, la música. ¿Cuál te parece más importante en la cultura de un país? ¿Cuál prefieres tú?

**2** Lee la información.

**A** ¿Podrías relacionar los datos de cada autor correctamente?

**B** ¿Cuáles de esas novelas han sido adaptadas al cine? ¿Las conoces?

**AUTORES**
**Laura Esquivel**
**Isabel Allende**
**Gabriel García Márquez**

**NOVELAS**
**1** *Crónica de una muerte anunciada*
**2** *Como agua para chocolate*
**3** *La casa de los espíritus*
**4** *Cien años de soledad*
**5** *Eva Luna*
**6** *La ley del amor*

**PAÍSES**
**a** Colombia
**b** Chile
**c** México

**3** Escucha la conversación de tres estudiantes durante un descanso. Luego escoge la frase más apropiada.

**A** Los estudiantes hablan de
**a** sus estudios.
**b** un autor literario.

**B** El realismo mágico consiste en
**a** mezclar realidad y fantasía.
**b** escribir historias reales.

**C** *Crónica de una muerte anunciada* está basada en
**a** un hecho real ocurrido en Colombia.
**b** una película.

**D** El protagonista, Santiago Nasar, era
**a** joven y delgado.
**b** de pelo rizado y rubio.

## ¡TIENES LA PALABRA!

**1** En parejas escoge uno de estos papeles. Utiliza la información del folleto de la *Academia Cervantes*.

**Director de estudios**

Entrevistas a un estudiante interesado en tu academia. Pregúntale desde cuándo estudia español y qué necesita (cuántas horas, actividades culturales, nivel…). Dale información sobre el curso.

**Estudiante**

Te interesa hacer un curso en la *Academia Cervantes* porque has oído que tiene buena fama. Habla con el director de estudios para obtener información. Explícale qué quieres.

### *Academia Cervantes*

Cursos de Español para Extranjeros
Clases durante todo el año

- Niveles: Inicial, Medio, Avanzado, Superior.
- Horas lectivas: 15/20 horas semanales. Lengua Española (teoría y práctica, composición escrita), Cultura Contemporánea Española/ Latinoamericana, Conversación (vocabulario y expresiones coloquiales, debates),
- Opciones (nivel Avanzado y Superior): Literatura Española, Historia Española/ Latinoamericana, Español Comercial, Arte español e Hispanoamericano, Costumbres y Tradiciones.

Máximo 10 alumnos en cada clase.

Amplio programa de actividades de ocio y diversión. Conferencias, películas y vídeos, fiestas, visitas y excursiones con guía. Aulas equipadas con vídeo.

**2** Mira la ilustración.

**A** ¿En qué países se habla español?

**B** ¿Crees que es un idioma con un rico pasado y un buen futuro? ¿Por qué?

**C** ¿Tu lengua se habla en otros países? ¿Está influenciada por otras lenguas?

**D** ¿Qué factores contribuyen a expandir un idioma?

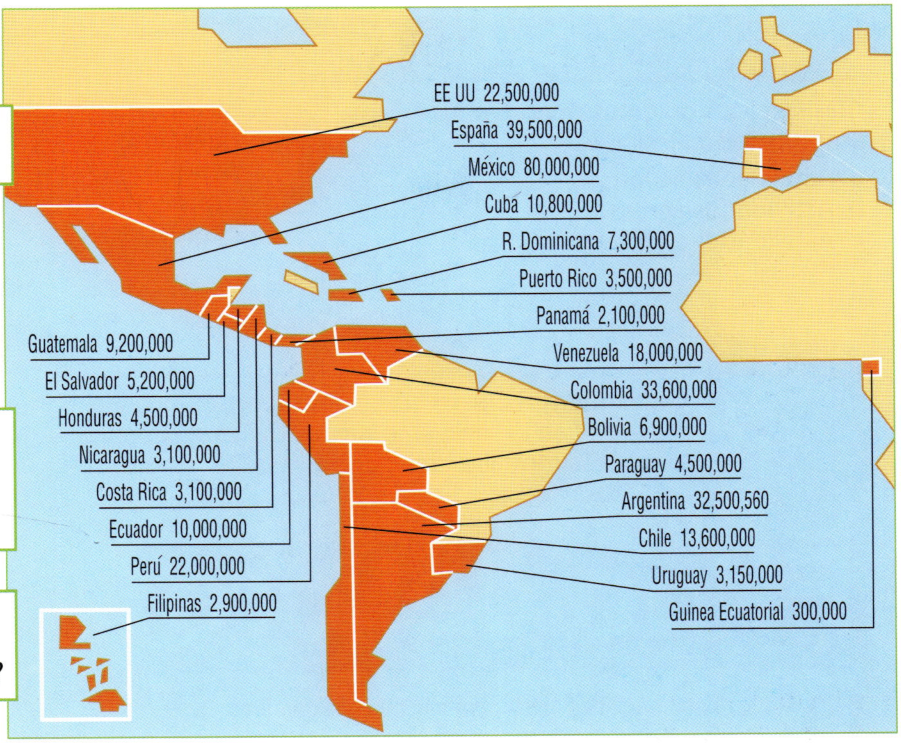


**3** Entre toda la clase comenta tus opiniones sobre estos temas.

**Los jóvenes inventan sus propias expresiones -a veces incomprensibles para los mayores. ¿Qué o quién influye en el lenguaje de los jóvenes?**

**¿Influyen los medios de comunicación en la lengua? ¿Cómo ?**

**¿Hay moda también en el lenguaje? ¿Por qué hay expresiones que de repente se ponen de moda?**

## POR ESCRITO

**1** Diseña un folleto en español para promocionar tu lengua y tu cultura en España y Latinoamérica. Menciona las ventajas de aprenderla, visitar tu país y convivir con una familia/otros estudiantes.

**2** Haz una lista de los aspectos fáciles y difíciles de aprender una lengua extranjera. ¿Qué ventajas tiene hablar idiomas?

**3** Escribe la biografía de un escritor hispano o de tu país.

*Ejemplo*

*Gabriel García Márquez nació en 1928 en el pueblito de Arataca, en la costa atlántica de Colombia. Se crió con sus abuelos maternos. Su abuelo era coronel y fue la persona más importante en su vida. Durante años trabajó como periodista y vivió en diferentes ciudades, como corresponsal. Su primera novela,* ***La Hojarasca****, fue publicada en 1955. Pero fue* ***Cien años de soledad*** *(1967) la novela que le hizo famoso. En 1982...*

## PUNTO DE MIRA

Clasifica los siguientes deportes en estas tres categorías.

**a** Actividades acuáticas
**b** Actividades aéreas
**c** Actividades terrestres

hípica
senderismo
rafting
ala delta
escalada

bicicleta
puenting
piragüismo
submarinismo
parapente

surf
tenis
vuelo sin motor
descenso de cañones
baloncesto

ciclismo extremo
caída libre
esquí
windsurf
vela

Hay gente que busca emociones fuertes en el deporte. Lee este artículo para saber más sobre las nuevas modalidades deportivas.

# El río del oro

Para los habitantes de Sort, un pueblecito en la comarca de Pallars (Pirineo leridano), su río Noguera Pallaresa sólo era idóneo para pescar. Sin embargo, en poco tiempo, nacía uno de los mejores paraísos en Europa para la práctica de los deportes-aventura, los nuevos deportes, en los cuales el individuo persigue la magia de la sensación. Entre los deportes que se pueden desarrollar en la zona, cuatro conciernen al río: rafting, hydrospeed, kayak y puenting.

El rafting es la actividad reina. Consiste en bajar la corriente sobre una lancha neumática y deslizarse sobre los rápidos. Por razones de seguridad, la lancha debe ser muy resistente, y no deben embarcarse más de ocho personas.

Para practicar el rafting es obligatorio el uso de casco y chaleco salvavidas, y para evitar ser catapultados al exterior, los tripulantes se sujetan con los pies a unas agarraderas llamadas *straps*.

En el hydrospeed, una sola persona se tumba sobre un flotador hidrodinámico con dos asas y se lanza rápidos abajo. Hay que ponerse salvavidas, casco y aletas, y agarrarse fuerte.

El kayak es el más tradicional de los deportes del río, pero también uno de los más espectaculares. Exige una enorme técnica. Fueron los esquimales los primeros en inventarlo, y los ingleses, los encargados de importarlo al Viejo Continente. Desde las antiguas piraguas de cuero hasta hoy, el kayak ha sufrido una enorme evolución. Ya no son un medio de transporte, sino una excusa para hacer deporte y experimentar el sabor de la aventura.

Si para alguno toda esta actividad no es suficiente, siempre podrá tirarse desde un puente. Atado, por supuesto. El puenting, controlado por monitores, no implica ningún peligro, pero sí una gran emoción.

Sort se ha convertido en la meca del aventurero, del buscador de emociones, y de todo aquel que quiere escapar a la rutina para descargar ese exceso de adrenalina acumulada.

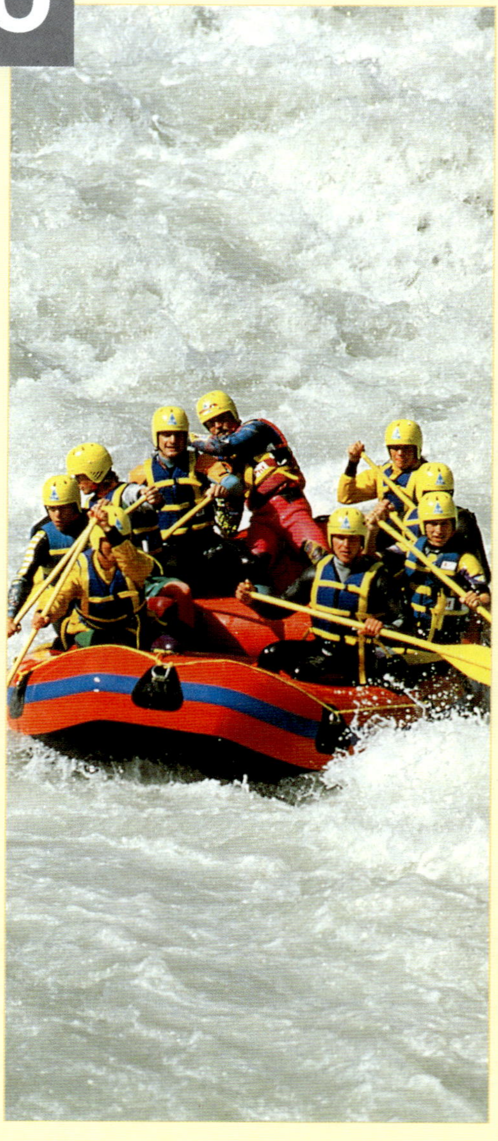

## ¿LO HAS ENTENDIDO?

**1** ¿Verdadero o falso? Lee estas frases y corrige la información incorrecta.

**A** El número de personas es importante para practicar el rafting.

**B** Los esquimales inventaron el hydrospeed.

**C** Los antiguos kayaks eran de madera.

**D** Los ingleses viajaron al Viejo Continente en kayak.

**2** ¿Cuáles de los deportes mencionados se practican en grupo y cuáles de forma individual?

**3** ¿Qué tienen en común los nuevos deportes?

**4** ¿Cuáles piensas que tienen más riesgo?

**5** ¿Qué busca la gente que practica estos deportes?

## TOMA NOTA

Fíjate en las construcciones.

| Se usan con el infinitivo | | Se usan con el sustantivo | |
|---|---|---|---|
| ***debe***<br>***hay que***<br>***es obligatorio*** | *usar* | ***es necesario***<br>***es obligatorio***<br>***exige*** | *el uso de* |

***Debe, hay que, es obligatorio, es necesario*** y ***exige*** son construcciones que indican obligación. Búscalas en *El río del oro.* ¿Conoces otras construcciones similares?

**1** ¿Verdadero o falso? Lee las frases. Corrige la información falsa, usando otras estructuras que indican obligación.

*Ejemplo*

*Para mantenerse en forma* ***hace falta*** *comer chocolate.*

*Falso.* ***No hay que*** *comer chocolate.*
***Es necesario*** *hacer ejercicio.*

**A** Es necesario tener 15 años para votar.

**B** Es obligatorio el uso del cinturón de seguridad para conducir.

**C** Para aprobar los exámenes no hace falta estudiar.

**D** El rafting no exige el uso de chaleco salvavidas.

**E** Para esquiar bien hace falta practicar mucho.

### AMPLÍA TU VOCABULARIO

**comarca** territorio, provincia
**idóneo** ideal
**persigue** intenta obtener
**lancha** embarcación
**deslizarse** descender
**se tumba** se pone boca abajo
**agarrarse** sujetarse
**exige** necesita
**encargados** responsables
**Viejo Continente** Europa
**piraguas** canoas
**tirarse de** lanzarse de
**monitores** instructores
**descargar** aliviar

## Y TÚ, ¿CÓMO LO VES?

**1** ¿Qué buscas en el deporte?

**a** emoción y aventura
**b** mejorar tu forma física
**c** relajarte de las tensiones y divertirte
**d** nada, no lo practicas

**2** ¿Te atraen los deportes de aventura y riesgo? ¿Por qué?

**3** ¿Eres una persona activa o sedentaria? Explica lo que haces normalmente en tu tiempo libre.

## EN LA ONDA

**1** Mira la tabla de información. ¿Realizas alguna actividad física? ¿Es adecuada para tu edad?

**2** ¿Qué beneficios se obtienen del deporte (a nivel físico y psíquico)? ¿Qué peligros existen?

**3** ¿Qué precauciones hay que tomar antes de hacer una actividad fuerte?

### AMPLÍA TU VOCABULARIO

**aconsejados** recomendados
**desaconsejados** no recomendados

**¿Qué actividad física conviene practicar a cada edad?**

| Edad | Deporte/Actividad | Efecto |
|---|---|---|
| **16-25 años** | | |
| *Aconsejados:* | Cualquiera | En personas sin problemas. |
| *Desaconsejados:* | Maratón<br>Squash | Problemas cardiovasculares. |
| **35-45 años** | | |
| *Aconsejados:* | Carrera / Ciclismo | Con práctica no intensiva. |
| | Natación | Favorable contra las lesiones óseas y musculares. |
| | Excursionismo | Relajación antiestrés. |
| *Desaconsejados:* | Maratón<br>Squash | Posibles problemas cardiovasculares. |
| **45-60 años** | | |
| *Aconsejados:* | Natación | Favorable contra las lesiones óseas y musculares. |
| | Golf | Relajación antiestrés. |
| *Desaconsejados:* | Maratón<br>Squash<br>Bicicleta todo terreno | Posibles problemas cardiovasculares. |

**4** Escucha a Susana y Enrique que piden información en un club deportivo y responde.

**A** ¿Qué es el cicloturismo?

**B** ¿Quién puede practicarlo? ¿Es un deporte caro? Explica.

**C** ¿Qué es necesario para practicar el hydrospeed?

**D** ¿Por qué es un deporte de emoción y riesgo?

**5** Escucha la cinta otra vez y responde.

**A** Anota todos los beneficios que se obtienen de practicar el cicloturismo.

**B** ¿En qué consisten las normas de seguridad del hydrospeed? ¿Por qué son necesarias?

**C** ¿Cuál de los dos deportes te atrae más? ¿Por qué? ¿Cuáles son para ti las ventajas y los inconvenientes de ambos deportes?

## ¡TIENES LA PALABRA!

**1** ¿En qué forma física están tus compañeros de clase? Formula las preguntas apropiadas para cada caso y busca a alguien que

- tiene una bicicleta.
- practica la natación.
- es miembro de un gimnasio.
- hace ejercicio regularmente.
- va a clase a pie.
- practica la relajación (yoga, por ejemplo).
- nunca ha fumado.
- corre/hace jogging los fines de semana.
- juega en un equipo (de fútbol, béisbol...).

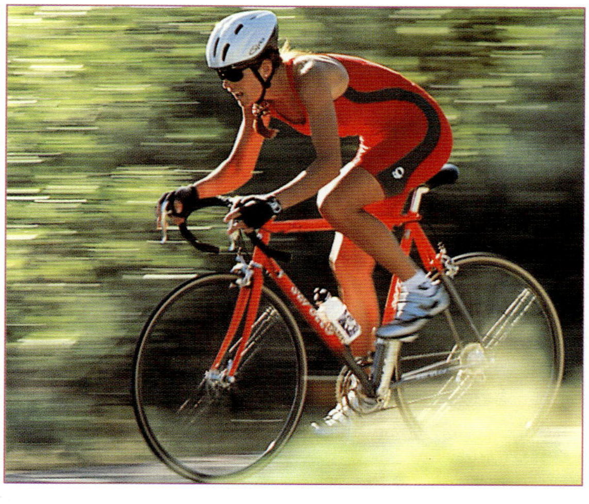

**2** Entrevista a una estrella del deporte. En parejas escoge uno de estos papeles.

**Admirador/a**

Tu club de fans te da la oportunidad de entrevistar a tu ídolo deportivo. Pregúntale sobre su vida y su carrera profesional (cómo empezó, qué fue lo más duro, sus éxitos...).

**Deportista**

Eres una famosa estrella del deporte y el ídolo de muchos jóvenes. Habla con tu admirador/a sobre tu vida y tu deporte.

## *RIESGO MUY ALTO*

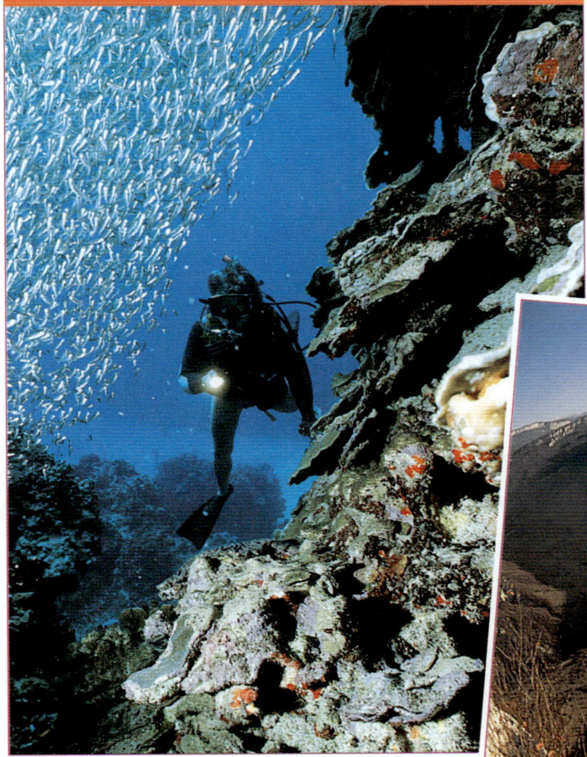

**3** Algunos deportes como el salto base (salto al vacío y apertura manual del paracaídas) están prohibidos en algunos países por su alto riesgo; pueden resultar en la muerte del deportista. ¿Crees que merece la pena jugarse la vida por un deporte? ¿Deporte y riesgo van siempre unidos? ¿Existe algún deporte sin riesgo? ¿Por qué hay tanto interés por estas actividades? Entre toda la clase comenta tus opiniones.

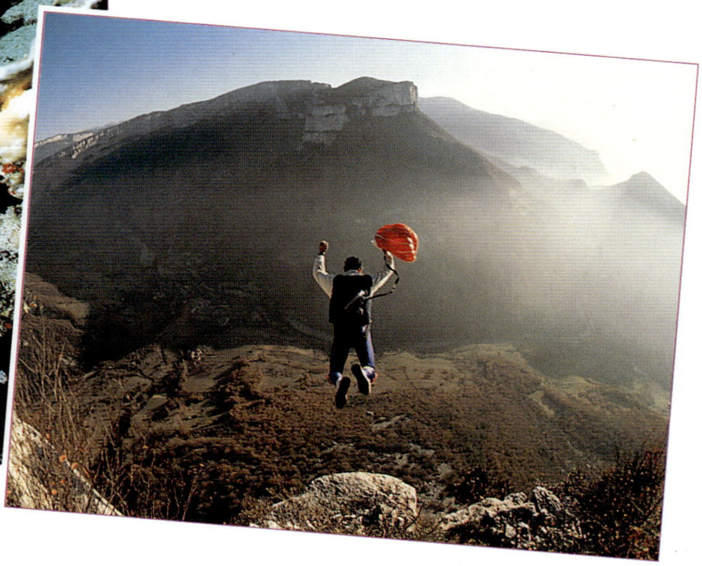

## POR ESCRITO

**1** Escribe una lista de normas utilizando las expresiones de obligación

**a** para los usuarios de una piscina.
**b** para los usuarios de una biblioteca.

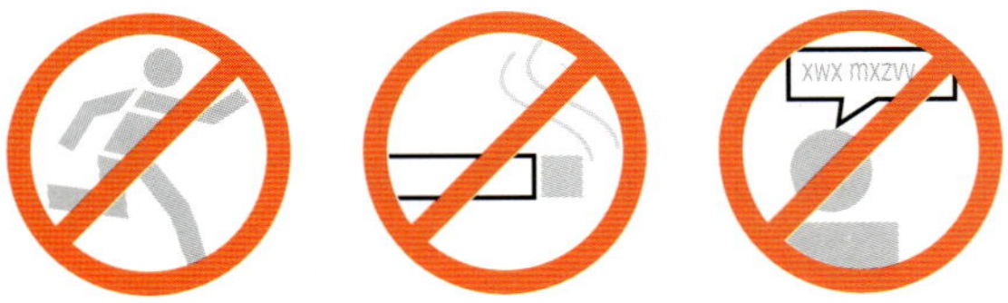

**2** Diseña un póster para promocionar el deporte. Piensa en un lema o frase para tu campaña.

**3** ¿Has practicado alguna vez un deporte de riesgo o aventura? ¿Dónde y cómo fue? ¿Qué sensaciones tuviste? ¿Lo harías otra vez? Escribe sobre la experiencia. (100-200 palabras)

## PUNTO DE MIRA

Observa el cómic. ¿Qué hace Pilar cuando está en el bar? ¿Crees que tiene una adicción? A su amiga le gusta beber café. ¿Tiene un problema de dependencia? ¿Por qué?

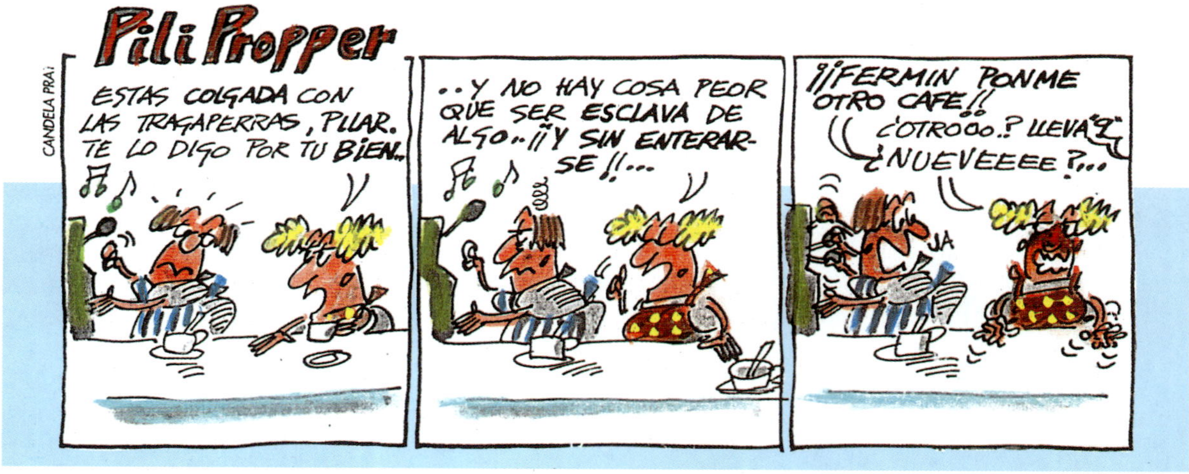


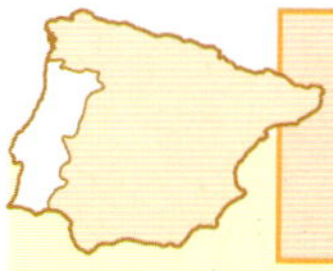

¿Por qué hay tantos jóvenes atrapados por el alcohol? Lee la carta de esta chica dirigida al consultorio del psicólogo Bernabé Tierno.

# *Vivir para beber*

BERNABÉ TIERNO

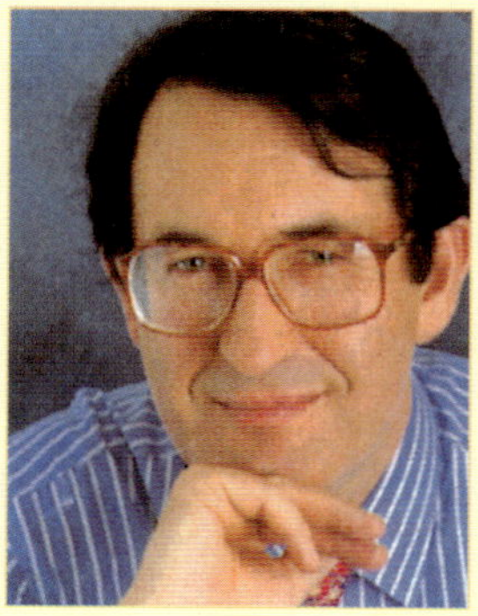

"Necesito beber. No concibo un fin de semana sin el alcohol. Me preocupa sentirme dependiente de él. Nada puedo hacer por detenerme. Sé que personas como yo hay muchas y no sabemos ayudarnos porque resulta más fácil ocultarnos tras la borrachera de cada sábado y lamentarnos el día después. Bebo desde que tenía dieciséis años y bebo cualquier cosa que sea capaz de desinhibirme y de olvidarme de mi timidez. Ahora tengo veinticinco años y conozco perfectamente los efectos letales que este odioso líquido causa en mi cerebro y, aún así, continúo. La mayoría de los jóvenes de mi edad bebe. Todo podría quedar aquí si no fuera por esas famosas drogas de diseño. Me habían hablado tanto y tan bien de ellas que pensé probarlas. Lo peor de todo es que el efecto me ha gustado. Sé que destrozan mi cuerpo y mi cerebro. Por supuesto, mis padres no saben nada, pero me gustaría decírselo y que me ayudaran. Tengo mucho miedo y necesito ayuda. He perdido el control sobre mí misma. Los días de fiesta me domina el impulso animal y puedo hacer y decir cosas que los lunes, martes, miércoles y jueves no diría ni haría. Dedique su respuesta a los chicos y chicas que, como yo, vivimos para beber".

## ¿LO HAS ENTENDIDO?

**1** ¿Qué problema tiene esta chica?

**2** ¿Por qué razones bebe?

**3** ¿Cómo se siente? ¿Es consciente de los peligros?

**4** ¿Conocen sus padres la situación?

**5** ¿En qué tono está escrita esta carta?

**a** triste **b** optimista **c** desesperado

## TOMA NOTA

Fíjate en estas palabras.

| | | |
|---|---|---|
| *drog***adicto** | *trabajo***adicto** | *tele***adicto** |
| *cocainó***mano** | *heroinó***mano** | *toxicó***mano** |
| *meló***mano** | *mitó***mano** | *cleptó***mano** |

Un ***adicto*** es una persona que tiene un problema de dependencia física y psicológica de algo. Esta palabra también se puede añadir a otras. La terminación ***-mano*** indica adicción o afición exagerada por algo. ¿Qué significan las palabras de arriba? Escribe una frase con cada una.

Completa estas frases con la palabra correcta. Utiliza las expresiones de arriba.

**A** Carlos tiene la colección completa de todas las óperas famosas del mundo. Es un auténtico ______.

**B** Los ______ pueden contagiarse enfermedades por el intercambio de jeringuillas.

**C** En mi clase había una chica que era ______ . Siempre nos faltaban cosas de las bolsas.

**D** Le ingresaron en un centro de rehabilitación para ______ . Consumía drogas desde pequeño.

### AMPLÍA TU VOCABULARIO

**estás colgada** estás obsesionada
**las tragaperras** las máquinas de juego
**sin enterarse** inconscientemente
**concibo** entiendo
**ocultarnos** refugiarnos
**tras** detrás de
**borrachera** resultado de beber alcohol en exceso
**desinhibirme** perder las inhibiciones
**timidez** falta de seguridad en uno mismo
**letales** mortales
**odioso** malo
**aún así** sin embargo, a pesar de todo
**drogas de diseño** drogas sintéticas como el *speed*
**destrozan** destruyen, causan daño
**cerebro** órgano central del sistema nervioso
**por supuesto** claro
**los días de fiesta** los fines de semana

## Y TÚ, ¿CÓMO LO VES?

**1** En tu país, ¿hay mucho consumo de bebidas alcohólicas entre los jóvenes? Cuando estás con amigos, ¿hay más presión para beber, fumar o, incluso, hacer cosas que no harías normalmente?

**2** Beber alcohol es un hábito normal y aceptado en nuestra sociedad. Mira la tabla. ¿Cuáles son los motivos para consumirlo?

**Motivos para consumir alcohol**
- para relajarse de las tensiones
- para estar más alegre y estimularse
- para vencer la timidez
- para celebrar algo
- por costumbre
- para acompañar la comida

## EN LA ONDA

**1** Entre toda la clase decide cuáles de estas cosas pueden causar obsesión o dependencia y discute los motivos y consecuencias.

### OBSESIONES

compras – alcohol – videojuegos – televisión – moda – chocolate – tabaco
teléfono – dieta – trabajo – deporte – lotería – ordenador – ídolos musicales

### POSIBLES CAUSAS

problemas laborales o familiares – falta de autoestima – por timidez
falta de estímulos en la vida – personalidad inmadura – por costumbre
para sentirse parte del grupo – miedo a estar solo – para divertirse

### CONSECUENCIAS

problemas económicos, deudas – problemas de salud – ruptura familiar
problemas en las relaciones personales – soledad – falta de vida social

**2** Escucha esta charla informativa en un colegio con motivo de la celebración del *Día Mundial Contra La Droga* y responde a las preguntas.

**A** ¿Qué es *Proyecto Hombre*?

**B** ¿Qué efectos tienen las drogas de laboratorio?

**C** ¿Cómo pueden ayudar los padres para que sus hijos no tengan graves problemas con la droga?

**D** ¿Para qué es el número 900 16 15 15?

## ¡TIENES LA PALABRA!

**1** **A** ¿A quién va dirigida la publicidad de alcohol y tabaco? ¿Debería prohibirse?

**B** ¿Qué modelos o imágenes de comportamiento ofrecen la publicidad, los medios de comunicación y el cine? ¿Qué impacto tienen estas imágenes en los jóvenes?

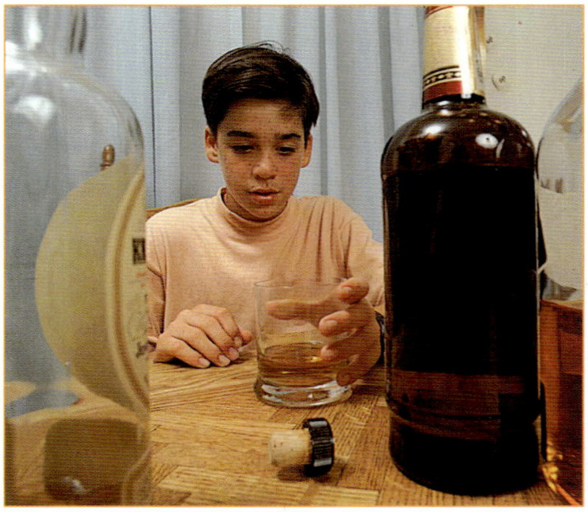

**2** Entre toda la clase defiende tu opinión a favor o en contra. Utiliza la información del recuadro para justificarte.

## *¿Beber o no beber?*

- El alcohol es la primera droga legalizada.
- El alcohol provoca la mitad de los accidentes de tráfico.
- Si un joven consume alcohol sólo los fines de semana puede llegar a convertirse en un adicto.
- El abuso del alcohol daña el hígado, el corazón, el cerebro y el riñón, y causa graves enfermedades como la hepatitis y la cirrosis.
- El vino es el alcohol más recomendable. Tomado con moderación mejora la digestión y eleva el colesterol bueno.
- Beber es un acto social que reúne a la gente.
- Los jóvenes beben para ser adultos.
- Beber puede formar parte de una vida sana si se hace de forma inteligente.
- Mucha gente bebe para evadirse de sus problemas.

**3** En grupos de tres escoge uno de estos papeles.

**PiliPropper**

Tienes la necesidad compulsiva de comprar cosas innecesarias y gastar dinero. Al principio ibas de compras para aliviar tus tensiones y frustraciones, pero ahora se ha convertido en una obsesión. Habla con tus amigos para contarles lo que te pasa.

**Víctor**

Te gusta jugar a las máquinas tragaperras. No puedes resistirlo. También juegas a la lotería y al bingo. Gastas mucho dinero en estas aficiones y eso te preocupa. Habla con tus compañeros.

**Sara**

Habla con tus amigos de sus problemas y ofréceles consejos.

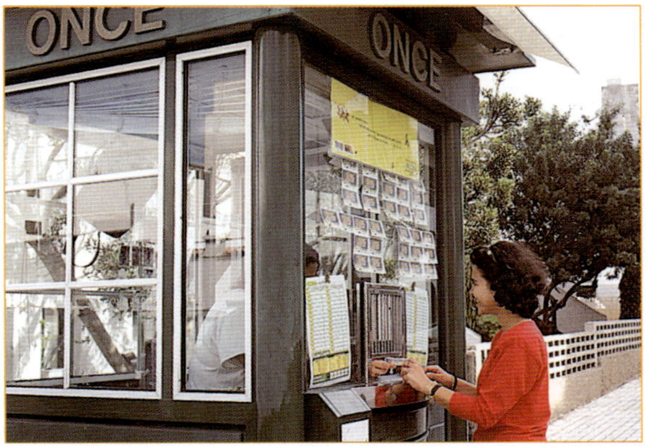


**❮Estas expresiones te ayudarán❯**

Buscar ayuda profesional
Descubrir el origen de la necesidad
Reflexionar antes de comprar algo
Evitar la tentación
No llevar dinero en el bolsillo

## POR ESCRITO

**1** Son las fiestas de Navidad y hay muchas celebraciones. Elabora un folleto para prevenir a la gente de las posibles consecuencias de beber, comprar y comer en exceso.

**2** Escribe una respuesta a la chica que tiene problemas con la bebida y las drogas de diseño. Ofrécele consejos sobre lo que puede hacer. (150 palabras)

**3** ¿Es el fin de semana una excusa para beber alcohol en exceso? Describe cómo se divierten los jóvenes en tu país. (250 palabras)

## PUNTO DE MIRA

**1** ¿Cuáles son tus programas favoritos en la televisión?

**2** ¿Cuántos canales de televisión hay en tu país? ¿Son públicos, privados/comerciales o de pago?

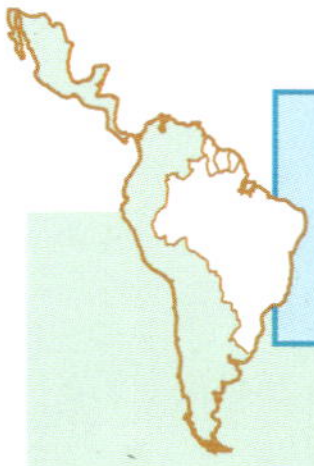

Las telenovelas gozan de una enorme popularidad en toda Latinoamérica. Lee este artículo sobre una nueva idea para hacer novelas.

# Te sigo amando

## el debut de un *talk show* en las telenovelas

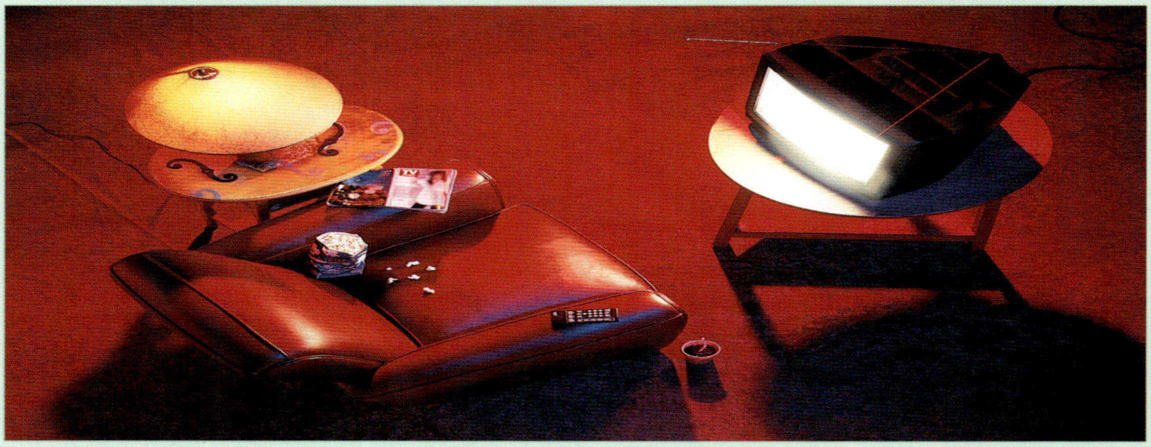

La telenovela *Te Sigo Amando* no es una historia de amor cualquiera. Su productora Carla Estrada decidió incluir en la trama al Show de Cristina. "Escogí a Cristina porque es una mujer muy talentosa, trabajadora e inteligente, con un gran dominio de su profesión y del público. Los personajes de la vida real le dan más veracidad a la historia. Resulta muy atractivo ver cómo se mezclan los personajes con ella y con su público".

*Te Sigo Amando* cuenta la historia de un apasionado triángulo amoroso cuyo vértice es *Yulissa*. A ella se la disputan *Ignacio Aguirre*, un rico hacendado, y *Luis Ángel*, un prestigioso médico.

En la historia, el Show de Cristina realiza un programa en el que interviene *Luis Ángel*. Al aparecer él en televisión, la trama da un vuelco total para la protagonista.

"Me encantó trabajar en esta telenovela", aseguró Cristina. "Ahora admiro mucho más a los artistas que entrevisto porque me di cuenta de que la perfección con que se realizan las novelas, repitiendo escenas y cuidando hasta el último detalle, requiere de personas muy profesionales. Siempre he pensado que las novelas, como mi programa, son un reflejo de la vida real y qué bueno que ambos factores ahora se junten en *Te Sigo Amando*".

¿Será un *Talk Show* la próxima trama de una novela de Carla Estrada? "No se me había ocurrido", dice Carla. "Creo que es una magnífica idea; con la cantidad de historias que nos cuentan los entrevistados se podría hacer mil historias".

## ¿LO HAS ENTENDIDO?

**1** ¿Quién es Carla Estrada?

**2** ¿Cuál es la historia de *Te Sigo Amando* y quiénes son sus principales protagonistas?

**3** ¿Qué efecto tiene la intervención de *Luis Ángel* en el Show de Cristina?

**4** ¿Qué opina Cristina de las telenovelas y de los *talk shows*?

## TOMA NOTA

Fíjate en estas palabras.

**Palabras compuestas**

| | | |
|---|---|---|
| ***tele****audiencia* | ***corta****uñas* | ***saca****corchos* |
| ***tele****vidente* | ***abre****botellas* | ***guarda****espaldas* |

Las palabras compuestas se pueden formar:

**Por fusión:** ***compra****venta* (sustantivo + sustantivo) ***peli****rrojo* (nombre + adjetivo) ***media****noche* (adjetivo + nombre) ***pasa****tiempo* (verbo + nombre).

**Por unión:** ***hombre*** *rana* (sustantivo + sustantivo). El plural en estos casos afecta sólo a la primera palabra (*los* ***hombres*** *rana*).

**1** ¿Qué significan las palabras del recuadro? Escribe una frase con cada una.

**2** Relaciona los elementos de las dos columnas para formar palabras compuestas. Después completa las frases con las palabras apropiadas.

| | |
|---|---|
| **saca** | *calle* |
| **rasca** | *puntas* |
| **sofá** | *día* |
| **medio** | *equipajes* |
| **boca** | *cielos* |
| **porta** | *cama* |

**A** Este _____ tiene cincuenta pisos.

**B** He puesto las maletas en el _____ .

**C** Mi lápiz no tiene punta. ¿Tienes un _____ ?

**D** En el salón tenemos un _____ .

**E** Se levantó más tarde del _____ .

**F** El semáforo está en la siguiente _____ .

### AMPLÍA TU VOCABULARIO

**trama** historia de una novela/película
**dominio** conocimiento profundo
**le dan más veracidad** parecen más reales
**resulta** es
**vértice** ángulo
**se la disputan** compiten entre los dos para obtenerla
**hacendado** que tiene fincas o haciendas
**interviene** participa
**da un vuelco total** cambia completamente
**protagonista** personaje principal
**me di cuenta** noté
**se junten** se unan
**no se me había ocurrido** no lo había pensado
**cantidad** número

## Y TÚ, ¿CÓMO LO VES?

**1** ¿Cuántas horas al día ves la televisión? ¿Podrías vivir sin verla? ¿Te roba tiempo para hacer otras cosas? ¿En qué actividades utilizarías el tiempo?

**2** ¿Qué tipo de programas gozan de popularidad en tu país? ¿A quién van dirigidos? ¿Cuáles son las series de máxima audiencia? ¿Por qué crees que tienen tanto éxito?

**3** En un *talk show* el público participa y cuenta sus intimidades y vivencias. ¿Por qué le gusta a la gente ver y participar en estos programas? ¿Te gustaría aparecer en televisión? ¿Por qué?

**4** ¿Crees como Cristina que la televisión refleja la vida real o al revés?

## EN LA ONDA

**1** Muchas teleseries alcanzan tanta popularidad que crean una moda y un estilo a imitar. ¿Cuáles son las series o personajes más imitados en tu país? ¿Influye la televisión en la vida de la gente? ¿Qué personas son más vulnerables a esta influencia? ¿Es el mundo como lo vemos en la televisión? ¿Qué trucos emplean las cadenas para atraer o mantener los niveles de audiencia?

**2** ¿Verdadero o falso? Escucha la conversación de dos amigas sobre una popular telenovela y decide si estas afirmaciones son verdaderas o falsas. Corrige la información incorrecta.

**A** A Lidia le encanta *Enamorada.*

**B** La telenovela tiene un índice de audiencia muy bajo.

**C** Rosaura conoce muy bien la trama.

**D** Los protagonistas son Angela, Roberto y Juan Enrique.

**E** Angela no tiene padres.

**F** Uno de los galanes trabaja de guardaespaldas.

**G** Algunas chicas se visten y peinan como Angela.

**H** Los telespectadores ven su vida reflejada en las historias de las telenovelas.

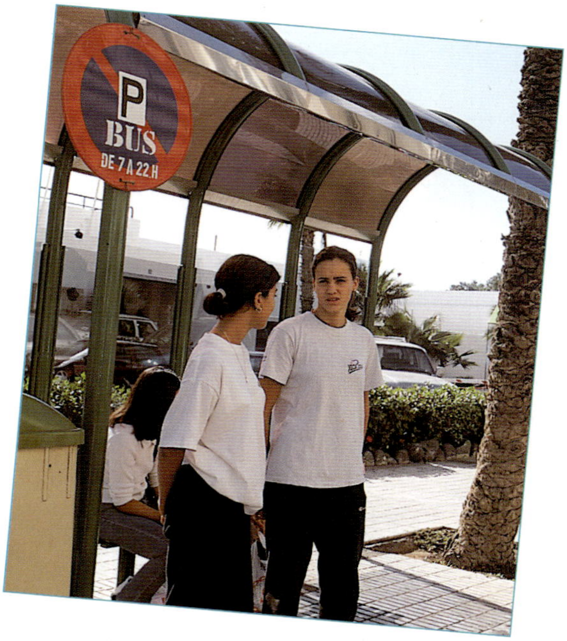


## ¡TIENES LA PALABRA!

**1 A** Mira los diferentes programas televisivos. ¿Cuáles prefieres ver y por qué?

**B** Observa la programación televisiva. En grupos de tres decide a qué tipo de programa corresponde cada uno y a qué público van dirigidos (infantil, juvenil, adulto). Explica por qué.

**C** Entre toda la clase discute qué ventajas e inconvenientes ofrece la televisión para

- **a** los niños
- **b** los jóvenes
- **c** los adultos
- **d** los ancianos

**PROGRAMACIÓN** *sábado 4 de mayo*

**CANAL 2**

**11.00 Barrio Sésamo**
**12.30 Club Infantil:** *Batman, Aventuras del joven D´Artagnan*
**13.30 El equipo A.** Serie de acción
**14.30 Lingo.** Programa concurso
**15.00 Noticias**
**15.30 National Geographic:** *Viajes por la naturaleza*
**16.30 Tarde de cine**
**18.00 El programa de Ana.** Tema a debate: la lotería
**19.00 Cosas de casa.** Comedia familiar
**20.00 Campeonato de Atletismo**

**TIPOS DE PROGRAMAS**

telecomedias y teleseries – dibujos animados
debates públicos (*talk shows*) – infantiles
documentales – películas – culturales
concursos – deportes – informativos

**2** Observa y lee la historieta y luego contesta a las preguntas.

**A** La televisión por sí sola no genera violencia pero, ¿qué efecto tiene contemplar actos violentos día tras día? ¿Crees que la gente puede volverse más violenta por ello?

**B** ¿Qué efecto provoca la violencia en la tele en ti y en las personas que te rodean?

**C** En tu país, ¿los padres ejercen un estricto control sobre los programas que ven sus hijos?

**D** Si encuentras algo ofensivo en la tele, ¿dónde y cómo puedes quejarte?

**E** ¿La televisión influye en la cultura? Se dice que las generaciones más jóvenes pertenecen a la cultura audiovisual. ¿Qué significa esto?

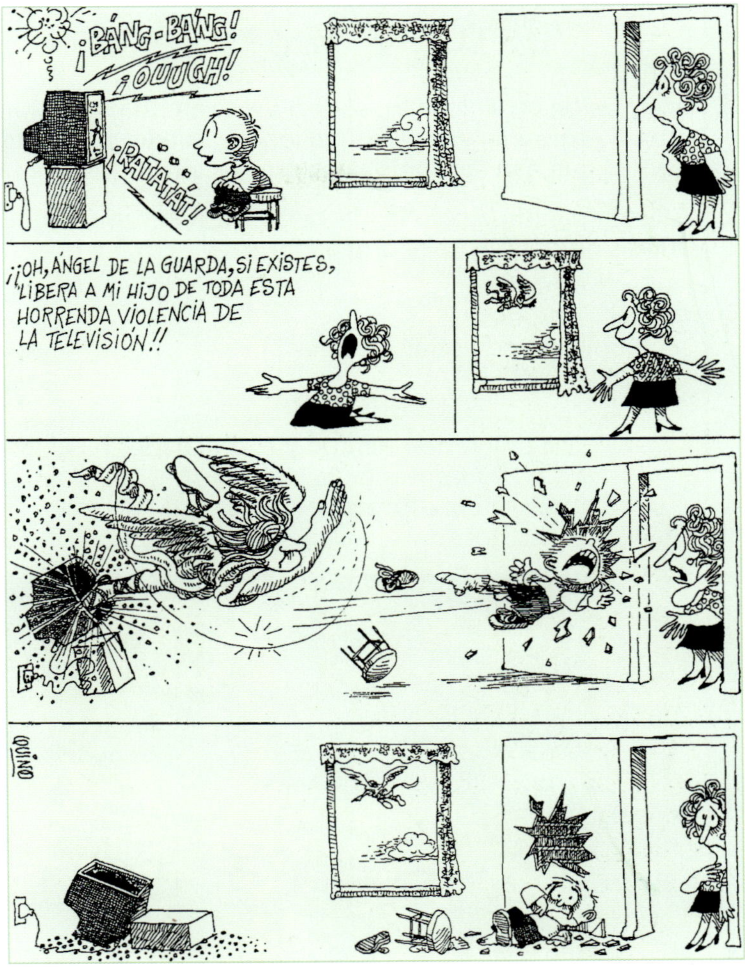


**3** Entre toda la clase comenta tus opiniones sobre estos temas.

***Con la televisión interactiva será posible elegir personalmente la programación, participar en concursos televisivos desde casa e incluso hacer compras. ¿Cuál de estas opciones te atrae más? ¿Te parece un invento positivo o negativo?***

***¿Es la televisión motivo de discusiones familiares? ¿Crees que contribuye a la armonía o, por el contrario, destruye el diálogo y separa a la familia? ¿Crees que la televisión sirve para unir socialmente a las personas?***

## POR ESCRITO

**1** En grupos de tres imagina una escena típica de telenovela. Prepara y escribe el diálogo de cada personaje y representa la escena en clase al día siguiente. (250-300 palabras)

**2** Escribe sobre tus programas y series favoritas de televisión. Explica por qué te gustan. (200 palabras)

**3** La televisión, ¿enseña o divierte? (250 palabras)

## PUNTO DE MIRA

**1** Hace más de un siglo la invención del teléfono revolucionó la forma de comunicarse de las personas. ¿Puedes nombrar otros inventos que han facilitado la comunicación en el planeta?

**2** ¿Estás preparado/a para la nueva era de la información? ¿Utilizas normalmente el ordenador para

**a** jugar solamente?
**b** trabajar/estudiar?
**c** comunicarte con otras personas?

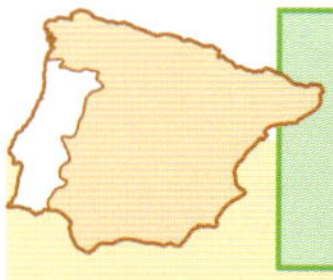

La unión del teléfono y el ordenador ha abierto el camino a las autopistas de la información. Lee el artículo para saber más sobre este apasionante tema.

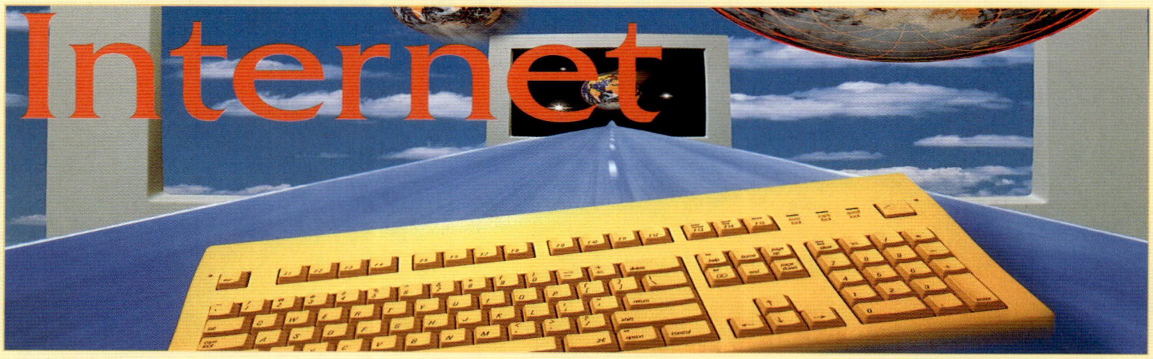


Un océano baña la puerta de todas nuestras casas. Contiene peces grandes y pequeños, algas y también tesoros. Además es un océano mágico; todos sus habitantes están a la misma distancia: al alcance de la mano. Y otra maravilla más: nadie puede agotar sus recursos.

El océano es la Internet, su localización: al otro lado de nuestros aparatos telefónicos, sus habitantes: palabras, sonidos, imágenes, datos. ¿Quién los ha puesto allí?: cualquiera. ¿Quién los puede coger?: cualquiera. ¿Qué utilidad tienen?: depende de cada uno. ¿Cuánto cuesta coger alguna cosa?: nada, lo que cuesta es el acceso. ¿Quién manda en la Internet? Nadie. ¿Y cómo es posible que exista algo así en nuestro mundo?

¿Qué contiene la Internet? Imaginemos un tablón de anuncios gigantesco y abierto a todos. Las instituciones oficiales lo utilizan para difundir sus puntos de vista; las empresas, para darse a conocer; las universidades, para proyectar su enseñanza; los jóvenes, para ponerse en contacto; los coleccionistas, para localizar a otros; los artistas, para exhibir su obra; los ociosos, para divertirse; los trabajadores, para trabajar; los vendedores, para vender; los consumidores, para comprar; los ladrones, para robar a unos y a otros. Como en la vida misma.

Una de las características de este universo electrónico es que está lleno de conversaciones y contactos. Aparte del correo electrónico, hay programas de charla, grupos de noticias para gente que comparte una afición, foros y debates.

¿Cuál es el futuro de este mundo sorprendente? Por el momento, la Internet ha aumentado la comunicación entre los habitantes del planeta, pero también el ruido; ha aumentado el conocimiento, pero también los peligros. Este mundo abierto, anárquico, ilimitado, es el mundo del futuro.

## ¿LO HAS ENTENDIDO?

¿Verdadero o falso? Lee estas frases y corrige la información incorrecta.

**A** A la red de Internet se accede a través del teléfono.
**B** En Internet hay gran cantidad de información: no existe un tema tabú.
**C** Sólo pueden utilizarlo las instituciones.
**D** La filosofía de la red es compartir el conocimiento.
**E** Con Internet hay menos comunicación entre las personas.
**F** Todo lo que circula por la red está perfectamente controlado.

## TOMA NOTA

Fíjate en estas palabras.

***¿Qué? ¿Quién? ¿Cómo? ¿Cuál? ¿Cuánto?***

Las palabras de arriba son pronombres interrogativos. Sirven para formular preguntas. Busca los ejemplos en el artículo y escríbelos.

**¡Atención!** ***¿Cuál?*** + ***ser*** es para pedir información específica cuando hay varias posibilidades. ***¿Qué?*** + ***ser*** se utiliza cuando necesitamos una definición.

**1** Formula las preguntas de estas afirmaciones.

*Ejemplo*
*Hay **dos horas** de viaje.*
*¿**Cuánto** tiempo hay de viaje?*

**A** Ha venido ***María***.
**B** El accidente fue ***a causa de la lluvia***.
**C** Me gustó más ***la primera***.
**D** Viajé a Francia ***en avión***.
**E** Tengo ***cinco mil pesetas***.

**2** Lee la información sobre Perú. Utiliza los pronombres interrogativos para formular preguntas.

*Capital:* Lima
*Población:* seis millones de habitantes
*Moneda:* nuevo sol
*Idioma:* español (oficial) y lenguas autóctonas (quechua y aymará)
*Plato típico:* cebiche (pescado crudo con limón verde y cebolla)

### AMPLÍA TU VOCABULARIO

**algas** plantas marinas
**tesoros** riquezas, cosas de gran valor
**al alcance de** cerca
**agotar** terminar
**recursos** materiales
**cualquiera** cualquier persona
**difundir** extender
**puntos de vista** opiniones
**darse a conocer** hacer publicidad
**localizar** encontrar
**ociosos** los que tienen mucho tiempo libre
**programas de charla** grupos de conversación
**afición** pasatiempo, interés
**ilimitado** sin límite

## Y TÚ, ¿CÓMO LO VES?

**1** Lee otra vez el último párrafo del artículo. ¿Estás de acuerdo con las conclusiones del autor? Razona tu respuesta.

**2** En tu opinión, ¿qué beneficios se obtienen de utilizar los ordenadores y la red Internet en los centros educativos/en el lugar de trabajo? Haz una lista.

**3** El tener acceso a cantidades increíbles de información, ¿cómo está cambiando nuestra vida, nuestra forma de aprender y de trabajar? Da ejemplos concretos.

## EN LA ONDA

**1** ¿Crees que en el siglo XXI en los colegios los ordenadores

**a** se utilizarán para enseñar informática solamente?
**b** sustituirán a los profesores?
**c** se utilizarán como complemento de los profesores para aprender ciencias, idiomas, arte...?

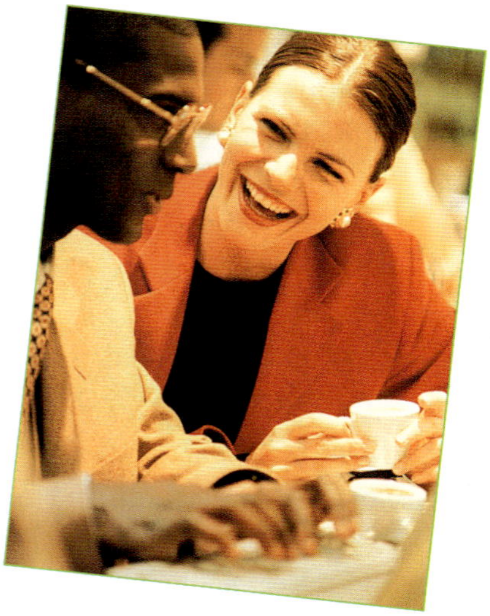

**2** Escucha a estas personas en una feria sobre nuevas tecnologías aplicadas a la educación y contesta.

**A** Nombra al menos cuatro de las tecnologías mencionadas.

**B** ¿Por qué es importante conocer bien la red Internet?

**C** ¿Qué ventajas ofrece Internet a sus usuarios?

**3** Escucha la cinta otra vez y responde.

**A** ¿Cómo son las nuevas tecnologías?

**B** ¿Qué opina el estudiante de los nuevos métodos?

**C** ¿Qué puedes hacer si estás conectado a Internet?

## ¡TIENES LA PALABRA!

**1** Aquí tienes una lista de algunos de los inventos de nuestra era. En grupos comenta tus opiniones sobre estos temas.

- *el walkman*
- *la videocámara*
- *el fax*
- *el telemando*
- *el horno microondas*
- *el compac-disc*

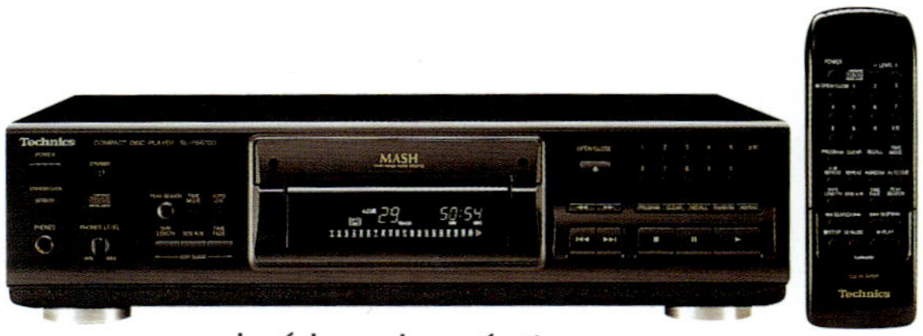


el vídeo doméstico

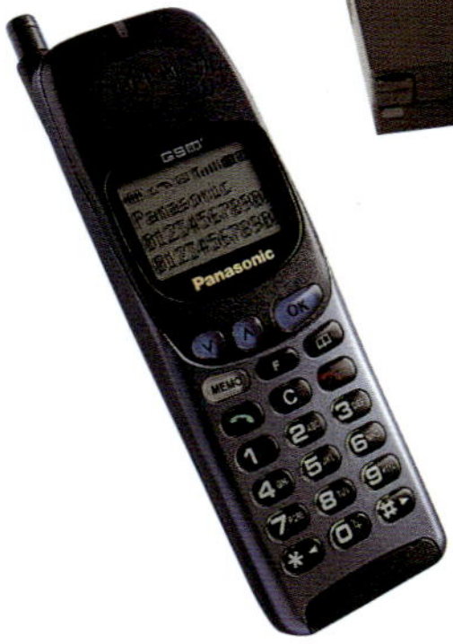


el teléfono móvil

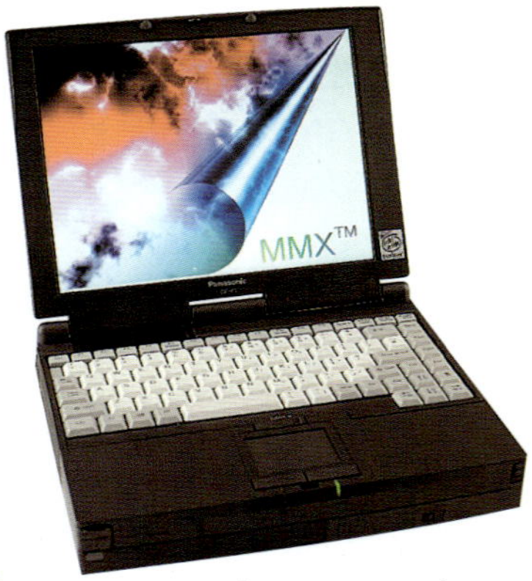


el computador portátil

**¿Eres esclavo de los aparatos? ¿Podrías vivir sin ellos? ¿Te parecen positivos o negativos?**

**¿Cuáles utilizas diariamente? ¿Dónde y para qué los utilizas?**

**2** En la tienda de informática. En parejas escoge uno de estos papeles.

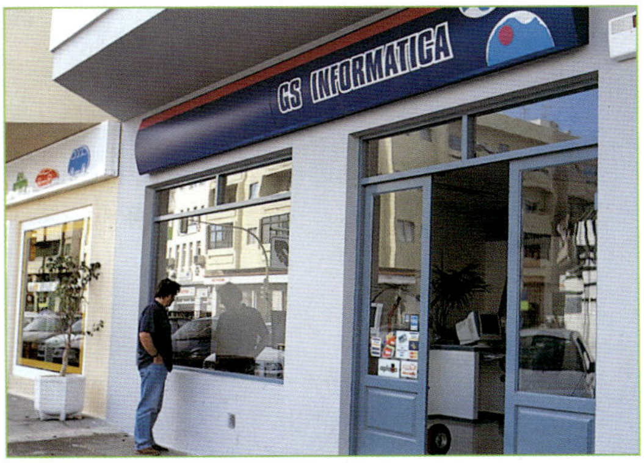


**Cliente**

Has oído hablar de las maravillas de estar conectado a la red. Te interesa recibir más información porque estás pensando en comprarte un ordenador. Infórmate sobre todo lo que necesitas y qué beneficios obtendrás.

**Vendedor/a**

Te encanta todo lo relacionado con los ordenadores. Gracias a la red Internet estás siempre al día de todo lo que pasa en el mundo. Aconseja a tu pareja sobre el tema: el tipo de ordenador que necesita, los programas, el coste, las ventajas, etc.

**Estas expresiones te ayudarán**

Conectarse a la red
Acceder a información
Navegar por el ciberespacio
El cibernauta
El correo electrónico

**3** Aquí tienes diversas opiniones de personas que participaron en el debate *"Internet, ¿un bien o una maldición?"* impulsado por *El País digital*. Trabaja en grupos. Cada uno debe analizar las implicaciones de una de las opiniones. ¿Están todos de acuerdo con lo que en ellas se dice? Explica tus ideas al resto de la clase.

> **Encontrar exactamente la información que nos interesa es a veces bastante difícil por la cantidad de datos inútiles que hay.**

*Fernando Celorrio, Valladolid (España)*

> **Internet es un consuelo para los solitarios, un juguete para los tecnológicos, un instrumento de formidable utilidad para los escritores, los artistas y los niños.**

*Vicente Verdú. Escritor y periodista español*

> **Internet contribuye a acrecentar las diferencias y desigualdades entre ciudadanos de un mismo país, y habitantes de un mismo planeta. Entre inforricos e infopobres.**

*Ignacio Ramonet. Profesor de teoría de la Comunicación. Universidad de París VII*

## POR ESCRITO

**1** Escribe una lista de las cosas que haces (o te gustaría hacer) con el ordenador y otra de las cosas para las que utilizas (o te gustaría utilizar) la red Internet.

**2** Describe cómo ha cambiado la forma de aprender en las escuelas. ¿Qué ventajas tiene utilizar el ordenador en el colegio, en casa o en el trabajo?

**3** El teléfono, el fax, el móvil, el correo electrónico, la red Internet, la televisión por cable y por satélite.... Explica de qué forma estos adelantos tecnológicos han mejorado la comunicación entre las personas y el acceso a la información. ¿Cómo han cambiado nuestros hábitos?

## PUNTO DE MIRA

¿Los hombres y las mujeres son diferentes

**a** emocionalmente?
**b** intelectualmente?

Razona tu respuesta.

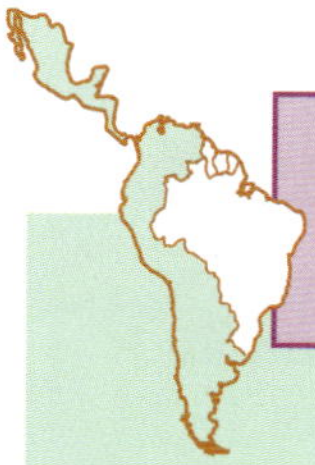

Las mujeres tienen cada vez más participación en la política. Lee este artículo sobre una persona muy admirada en Venezuela.

# Irene Sáez Conde

## EX MISS UNIVERSO SUEÑA SER PRESIDENTA

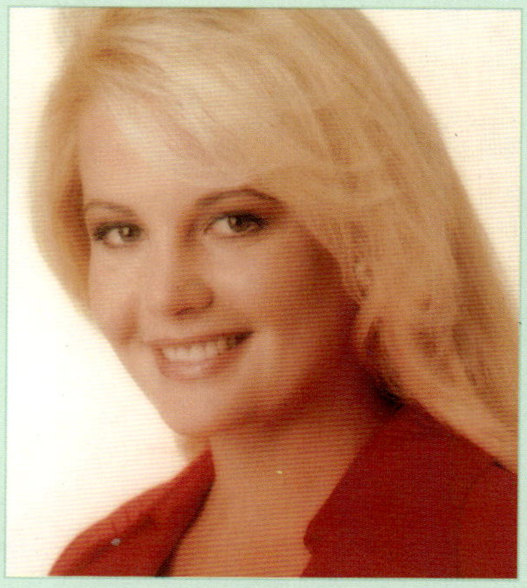

Irene Sáez es graduada en Ciencias políticas.
Habla español e inglés.
Desde que está al frente del Ayuntamiento de Chacao, ha conseguido reducir los delitos en más de un 50%.

La ex Miss Venezuela y Miss Universo 1981, Irene Sáez Conde, convertida en política, no sólo se contenta con tener el cargo de alcaldesa de Chacao, sino que ahora se está preparando para ser candidata a presidenta de su país.

Guapa y culta, Sáez de 36 años se mantiene tan esplendorosa como cuando obtuvo el mayor título de belleza mundial.

A diferencia de muchas otras ex reinas venezolanas que se valieron de su corona para saltar a la fama como modelos, actrices o empresarias de la moda, esta joven llevó su carisma hasta las masas populares para incursionar en el campo político.

La ambición de Sáez no fue entrar al cine, ni a la televisión y se negó a las ofertas que le hicieron firmas comerciales, directores y productores, aunque le prometían buenos sueldos.

Desde 1993 asumió la dirección del municipio de Chacao, uno de los más ricos de Venezuela, y ahora cuenta con el respaldo de la ciudadanía que reconoce que ha contribuido aún más al engrandecimiento de esa ciudad.

En Chacao es un personaje querido y en el resto de Venezuela es una de las figuras más distinguidas y tomadas en cuenta en el plano político.

Pero Sáez también tiene opositores que critican su línea de trabajo porque dicen que no está capacitada para estar al mando de una nación con tantos problemas, sobre todo de tipo sociales y económicos.

Otros de los reclamos que sus contrarios le hacen a la ex Miss Universo, es que todo lo que ha logrado hasta el momento en la política, ha sido posible sólo por su hermosa y dulce imagen de mujer, que encanta al público.

A Sáez no le interesa demasiado lo que piensan sus contrarios y ahora está preocupada pensando qué cosas le convienen para preparar su plataforma política hacia la primera magistratura de Venezuela.

## ¿LO HAS ENTENDIDO?

**1** ¿Quién es Irene Sáez? ¿Qué espera ser en el futuro?

**2** ¿Qué diferencia a Irene Sáez de otras reinas de belleza?

**3** ¿Qué opinión tiene el público de su trabajo como alcaldesa?

**4** ¿Con qué tipo de problemas se enfrentará si llega a la presidencia de Venezuela?

## TOMA NOTA

Fíjate en estas frases del texto.

> *"...se **valieron de** su corona para saltar a la fama...".*
> *"...se **negó a** las ofertas que le hicieron las firmas comerciales...".*
> *"...ahora **cuenta con** el respaldo de la ciudadanía...".*

Estos verbos necesitan ciertas preposiciones para formar una frase.

Completa estas frases utilizando la preposición apropiada.

**por** **de** **con** **en**

**A** No dejaré de hacer deporte cada día.
**B** Ha vendido su casa por bastantes millones.
**C** Se ha convertido en el candidato ideal para el puesto.
**D** Enrique soñó de el puesto de director de su empresa.
**E** No gasto mucho dinero por comprar ropa.
**F** ¿En qué piensas?
**G** Me encontré Con Alicia en la fiesta.
**H** No sale de casa desde que tuvo el accidente.
**I** El ladrón entró por la parte de atrás.
**J** Vamos de vacaciones a la playa.

### AMPLÍA TU VOCABULARIO

**está al frente del** está al mando del
**el cargo** la posición, el puesto
**alcaldesa** primera autoridad política de un municipio
**culta** con estudios y cultura
**se valieron de** utilizaron
**saltar a la fama** hacerse famosas
**incursionar** introducirse
**campo** área
**se negó a** declinó
**sueldos** dinero, salarios
**cuenta con** tiene
**respaldo** apoyo
**ciudadanía** el conjunto de ciudadanos
**capacitada** preparada

## Y TÚ, ¿CÓMO LO VES?

**1** ¿Crees que Irene Sáez sería un buen líder para Venezuela? ¿Por qué?

**2** ¿Son necesarios los líderes? ¿Quiénes son los principales líderes en tu país? ¿Qué opinas de ellos?

**3** ¿Quiénes son las mujeres más importantes/famosas en tu país? ¿Qué ocupación tienen? ¿Qué tipo de trabajos desempeñan las mujeres en tu país?

**4** ¿Te interesa el mundo de la política? ¿Sigues las campañas electorales en tu país?

## EN LA ONDA

**1** ¿Cuáles son las profesiones tradicionales para los hombres y las mujeres? Haz una lista para ambos y compáralas. ¿Crees que hay trabajos sólo para hombres o sólo para mujeres? Razona tu respuesta.

*Ejemplo*

**Profesiones para el hombre**
- bombero
- soldado

**Profesiones para la mujer**
- ama de casa
- enfermera

**2** Escucha una clase de historia sobre Eva Perón y completa estas frases.

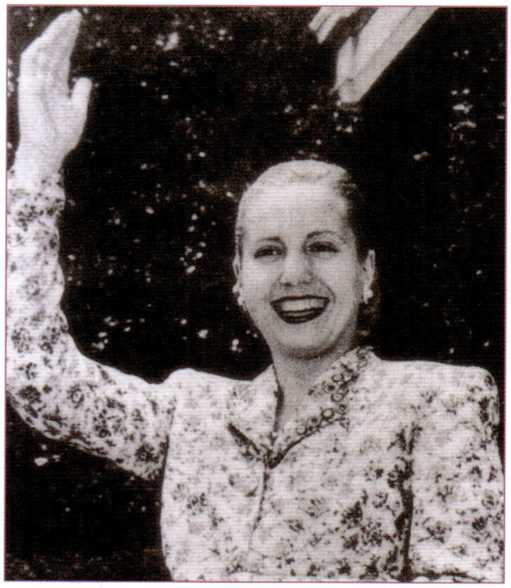

**A** La familia de Eva era _____ .
**B** De joven su ambición era ser _____ .
**C** Con 16 años se fue a _____ .
**D** Argentina estaba gobernada por _____ .
**E** Juan Perón era _____ y tenía _____ .
**F** Eva se identificó con los intereses de la clase _____ .
**G** Eva llegó a la _____ de la República con tan sólo _____ años.
**H** Eva fue el ídolo de _____ pero las clases poderosas _____ .
**I** Como líder de su país impulsó la participación en la política de los _____ y las _____ .
**J** Murió joven, enferma de _____ y sus funerales fueron _____ .

**3** Escucha la información otra vez y anota lo que ocurrió en estas fechas.

| | | | | | |
|---|---|---|---|---|---|
| **1919** | **1935** | **1944** | **1945** | **1946** | **1952** |

## ¡TIENES LA PALABRA!

**1** En grupos de tres discute cuáles son las cualidades más importantes de un líder. Ordena esta lista de cualidades por orden de importancia. ¿Son las mujeres mejores líderes que los hombres? ¿Por qué? ¿Quiénes son más organizados?

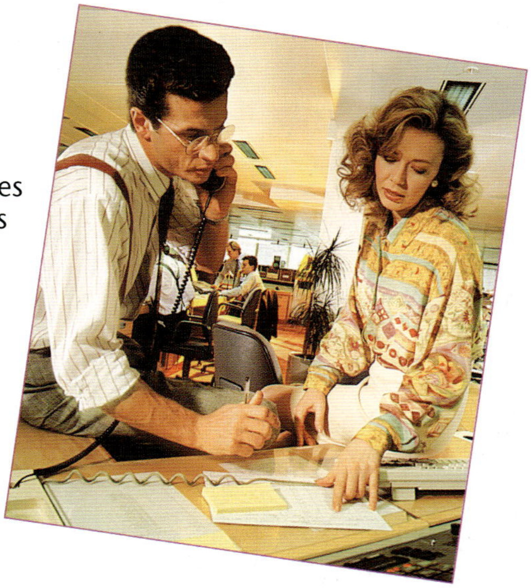

**a** carisma y personalidad atrayente
**b** poder de persuasión y comunicación
**c** capacidad para resolver conflictos
**d** capacidad para tomar decisiones
**e** inspirar respeto/admiración
**f** poseer conocimientos y sabiduría
**g** saber hablar en público (elocuencia)
**h** estar abierto al diálogo

**2** Entre toda la clase observa las fotos y lee la información sobre estas mujeres. ¿Crees que reflejan una imagen típica? ¿Por qué?

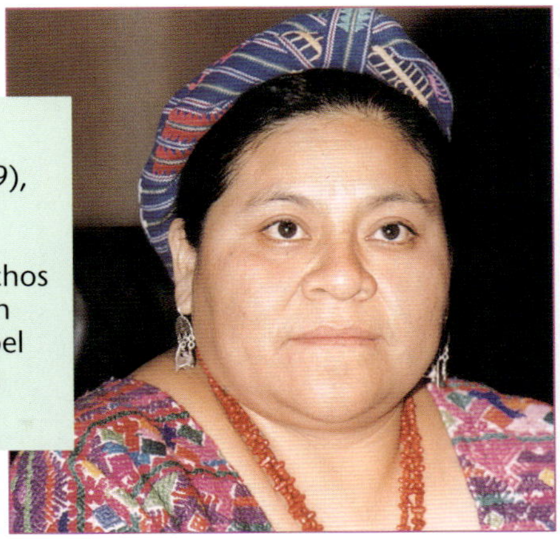

**Rigoberta Menchú**

Nacida en Guatemala (1959), es líder del movimiento en defensa de los derechos humanos, la paz y los derechos de los pueblos indígenas. En 1992 recibió el Premio Nobel de la Paz, siendo la persona más joven en recibirlo.

**Cristina Sánchez**

Hija de torero, numerosos profesionales de prestigio le ayudaron en su ascensión en un mundo taurino hostil a la presencia femenina.
Ha conquistado numerosas plazas de prestigio.

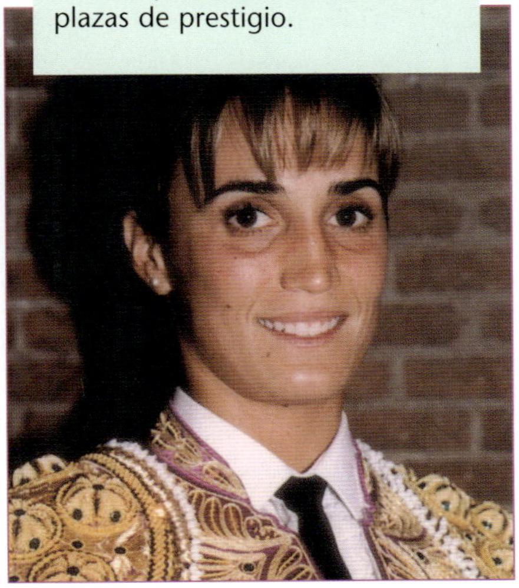

**AMPLÍA TU VOCABULARIO**

**taurino** relativo al mundo de los toros
**hostil** contrario, poco favorable
**prestigio** gran fama, reputación

**3** Entre toda la clase comenta tus opiniones sobre estos temas.

***¿Los hombres y las mujeres son considerados iguales en nuestra sociedad? ¿Existe algún tipo de discriminación contra el hombre o la mujer?***

***¿Quién tiene más capacidad de trabajo, el hombre o la mujer? ¿O eso depende de cada persona y no del sexo? ¿Se valora por igual a la mujer en el trabajo?***

***¿Qué entiendes por machismo? ¿Hay actitudes machistas hacia las mujeres en tu lugar de estudio/de trabajo...?***

## POR ESCRITO

**1** Haz una lista comparativa de las características que más admiras en un hombre y en una mujer. Haz otra lista de las que detestas. ¿Hay diferencias entre ambos? (150 palabras)

**2** Describe a algún líder de tu país. Incluye información sobre su personalidad, sus triunfos profesionales y la opinión pública. (200 palabras)

**3** ¿De qué forma han cambiado los papeles tradicionales del hombre y la mujer? ¿Qué logros han obtenido las mujeres de tu país en los últimos 50 años? Explica. (250 palabras)

## PUNTO DE MIRA

¿Te gustan los animales? ¿Cuál es tu animal favorito? ¿Por qué? ¿Tienes alguna mascota en casa?

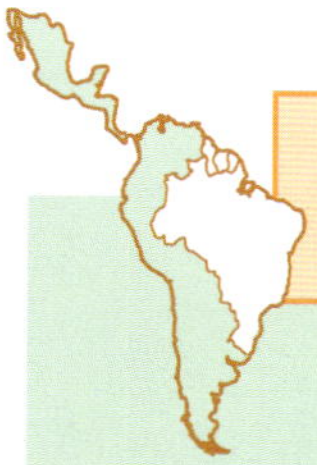

¿Qué derechos tienen los animales? Lee esta curiosa historia que sucedió en Colombia.

# 'Regalo' se quedará en el Hogar Boyacá

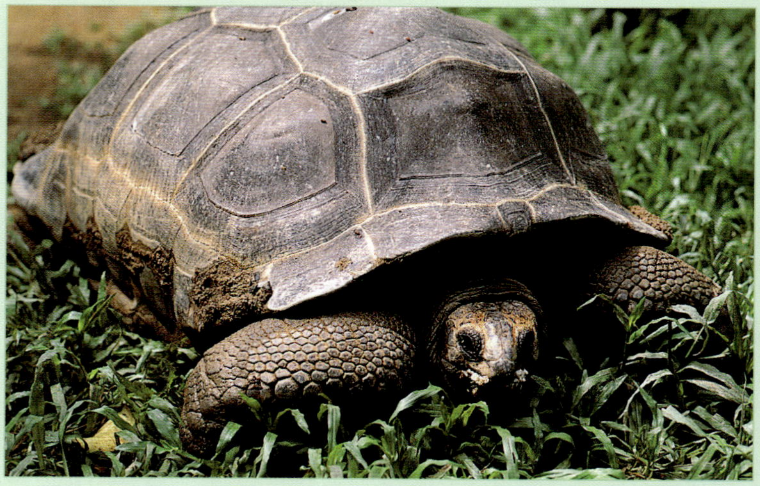

'Regalo' se quedará en casa por solicitud del presidente de la República.

Este macho de tortuga Galápago vive desde hace más de 50 años en el Hogar Boyacá, un albergue de enfermos en el municipio de Agua de Dios (Cundinamarca).

El primer mandatario viajó hasta allí el sábado para visitar al animal. Antes, solicitó al director de la Corporación Autónoma Regional de Cundinamarca (CAR) que cesara las acciones encaminadas a sacarlo del lugar.

Con esto dio por terminada una historia que comenzó hace más de seis meses, cuando la Asociación de Protectores de la Fauna Colombiana (Aprofac) se enteró de que la tortuga vivía en condiciones inadecuadas para su especie, y dio aviso a la CAR.

El día en que ambas entidades visitaron el lugar para llevar a la tortuga al Zoológico de Medellín, los enfermos se resistieron a dejarla ir. Con piedras, y otros artefactos, hicieron una barricada frente a la puerta. "Ella no sale viva de aquí", decían algunos.

Distrajeron a los policías que acompañaban a la autoridad ambiental y bajaron a 'Regalo' del vehículo.

El administrador del Hogar explicó que estaban dispuestos a todo. Le cambiarían la papa y el arroz por verduras frescas y hasta lo sacarían a pasear por el prado.

Según Víctor Vélez, biólogo de la CAR, presenta síntomas de desnutrición y deshidratación. Un biólogo francés experto en reptiles explicó que ni está desnutrida, ni es Galápago, sino una tortuga común. De todos modos, tal parece que permanecerá allí por el resto de su vida, que podría durar entre 300 y 400 años.

## ¿LO HAS ENTENDIDO?

**1** ¿Quién es el protagonista de la disputa entre la CAR y el Hogar Boyacá?

**2** ¿Por qué razón quería la CAR sacarlo del albergue?

**3** ¿Qué hicieron los enfermos para impedir que se llevaran a 'Regalo'?

**4** ¿Qué harán para mejorar las condiciones de vida de la tortuga?

## TOMA NOTA

Fíjate en estas frases del texto.

> *"Este macho de tortuga Galápago vive **desde hace** más de 50 años...".*
> *"Con esto dio por terminada una historia que comenzó **hace** más de seis meses".*

***Desde hace*** indica duración de tiempo. Se utiliza con sustantivos en plural o numerados.
***Hace*** + **periodo de tiempo** utilizado con el verbo en pasado indica cuándo tuvo lugar la acción.

**1** Completa estas frases con ***desde hace*** o ***hace***.

**A** Vive en la ciudad ____ tres años.
**B** Vendimos la casa ____ tres semanas.
**C** Lidia te llamó por teléfono ____ un momento.
**D** No veo a mi familia ____ un mes.

Fíjate en esta frase del texto.

> *"...**ni** está desnutrida, **ni** es Galápago, sino una tortuga común".*

***Ni*** indica negación. Se debe repetir antes de cada elemento de una lista. Cuando va después del verbo éste debe ir en forma negativa.

**2** Escribe estas frases en forma negativa.

*Ejemplo*
*Tenemos leche, pan y chocolate.*
***No** tenemos **ni** leche, **ni** pan, **ni** chocolate.*

**A** Teresa es alta y gorda.
**B** Rosa y Adriana vinieron a la fiesta.
**C** Raúl puede comer leche, huevos y mantequilla.

### AMPLÍA TU VOCABULARIO

**por solicitud** por petición personal
**macho** masculino
**albergue** refugio
**municipio** provincia
**el primer mandatario** el presidente
**cesara** parara
**encaminadas a** dirigidas a
**dio por terminada** terminó
**se enteró de que** tuvo noticias de que
**inadecuadas** no apropiadas
**dio aviso a** informó a
**ambas** las dos
**entidades** organizaciones
**estar dispuesto a** estar preparado para
**la papa** (*Am Lat*) la patata (*Esp*)

## Y TÚ, ¿CÓMO LO VES?

**1** ¿Qué beneficios tiene la compañía de animales para las personas? ¿Crees que los animales tienen un efecto terapéutico en la gente?

**2** A algunas personas tener un animalito en casa les cambia la vida. ¿Para quiénes puede ser beneficioso tener un animal de compañía?

**3** ¿Te preocupan los derechos de los animales? ¿Utilizas cosméticos y productos de limpieza no probados con animales? ¿Qué opinas de las personas que tienen animales exóticos como mascotas?

## EN LA ONDA

**1** Haz una lista de los animales que se pueden tener como mascota. Explica las ventajas e inconvenientes que presenta cada uno.

*Ejemplo*

CABALLO

| Ventajas | Inconvenientes |
| --- | --- |
| Puedes practicar la equitación.<br>Puedes acariciarlo y comunicarte con él. | Es muy caro comprarlo y mantenerlo.<br>Necesita atención y cuidados especiales. |

**2** Escucha estas encuestas a unos jóvenes que hablan de sus mascotas y responde.

**A** ¿Crees que al chico le gustan los animales? ¿Por qué?

**B** ¿Cómo cuida el chico de sus perros? ¿Qué adjetivos y frases utiliza para describir su carácter?

**C** ¿Comparte la chica la misma opinión sobre tener animales en casa? ¿Por qué?

**3** En el lenguaje popular hay muchas expresiones que hacen referencia a animales.

*Ejemplo*
***Ser un gallina*** significa ser un cobarde, no tener suficiente valor.

En parejas mira la lista de animales y completa las expresiones con uno de ellos. ¿Sabrías explicar el significado de estas frases? ¿Conoces otras expresiones de este tipo?

**avispa** **gato** **tortuga** **lince** **lobo** **elefante** **lirón** **cabra** **ostra** **gallina**

**A** Ser lento como una ____.
**B** Tener vista de ____.
**C** Tener memoria de ____.
**D** Dormir como un ____.
**E** Tener más vidas que un ____.
**F** Poner la piel de ____.
**G** Aburrirse como una ____.
**H** Tener hambre de ____.
**I** Tener cintura de ____.
**J** Estar más loco que una ____.

## ¡TIENES LA PALABRA!

**1** Regalar un cachorro de perro como mascota está de moda. Muchos terminan abandonados en las calles a los pocos meses. ¿Por qué crees que ocurre esto? ¿Se abandonan muchos perros en tu país? ¿Qué hacen con ellos? ¿Cómo se podría evitar esto? ¿Hay en tu país alguna organización que defiende los derechos de los animales? ¿Te parecen necesarias este tipo de organizaciones?

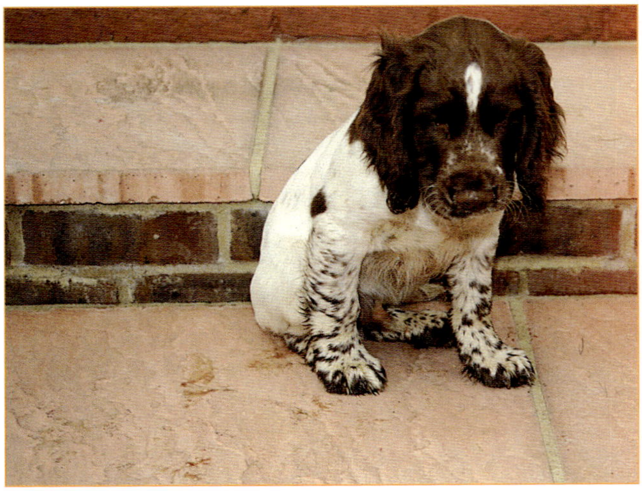

## HISTORIAS DE MIGUELITO

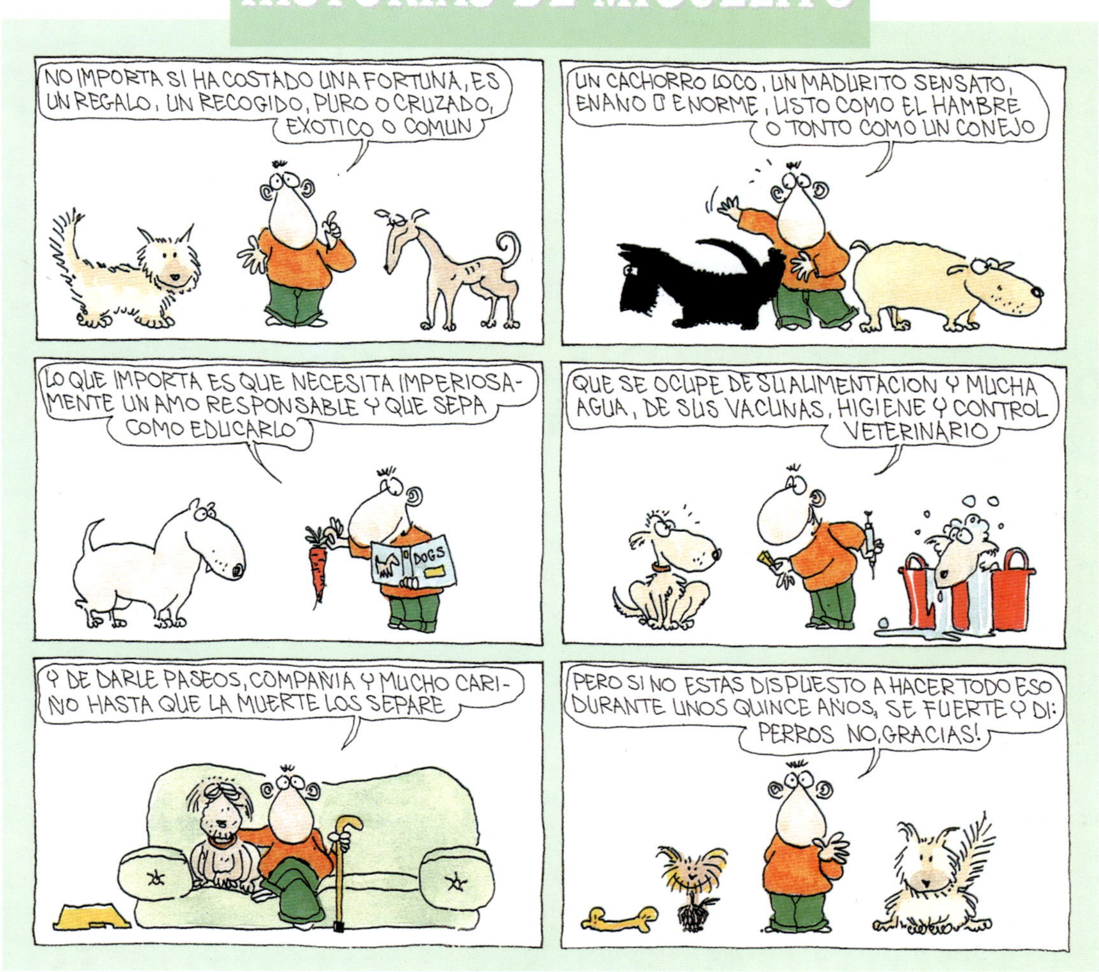


**2** Lee *Historias de Miguelito*. Luego escoge la frase que mejor resume su contenido.

**a** No importa el perro que tengas: todos necesitan los mismos cuidados y atenciones.
**b** Tener un perro supone una gran responsabilidad; hay que aceptarla con todas sus consecuencias.

**3** ¿Estás de acuerdo con la conclusión de Miguelito? ¿Por qué?

### AMPLÍA TU VOCABULARIO

**cachorro** perro recién nacido
**madurito** adulto
**sensato** responsable
**enano** muy pequeño
**imperiosamente** urgentemente
**amo** propietario
**vacunas** inyecciones

## POR ESCRITO

**1** Escribe sobre los animales que tienes, cómo son, qué haces para cuidarlos y por qué te gusta tenerlos. (150 palabras)

**2** Inventa una historia o un diálogo donde puedas utilizar algunas de las expresiones con animales que has aprendido.

**3** Inventa un diálogo entre el dependiente de una tienda de animales y un cliente que quiere comprar una mascota para regalar a una persona mayor. Incluye consejos sobre el tipo de animal apropiado y sus cuidados. (200 palabras)

## PUNTO DE MIRA

¿Eres supersticioso/a? ¿Tienes algún amuleto o talismán para atraer la buena suerte?

Cada país tiene sus propias creencias populares. Lee este texto para conocer algunas de la cultura española.

# Tocar madera

## Explicaciones de sentido común para las supersticiones más famosas

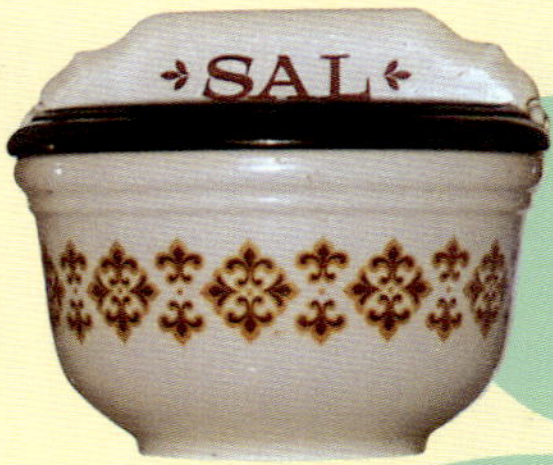


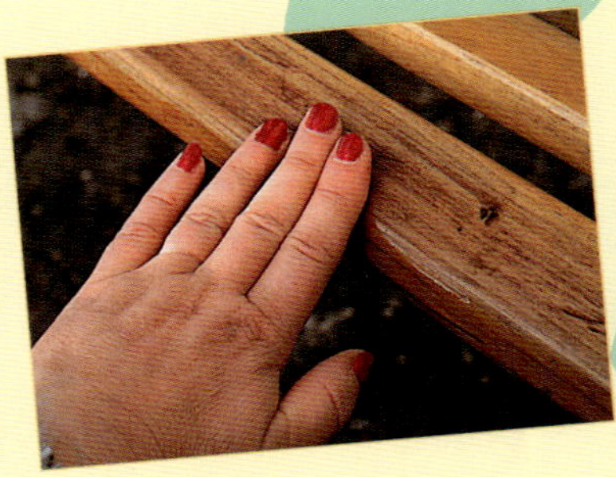

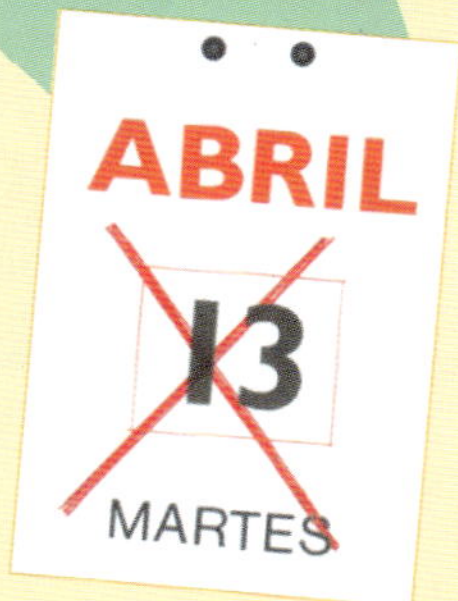


**Derramar la sal.** La sal es un producto extraído del mar, un mundo desconocido que escapa a nuestro dominio. En algunas zonas existe la creencia de que la sal puede propiciar la fecundidad, pero también puede atraer desastres.

La sal es el símbolo de la amistad. Si se derrama, la amistad se rompe. Para neutralizar este mal augurio basta con echar un poco de sal derramada sobre el hombro izquierdo tres veces.

La palabra salario proviene de la paga que se les daba a los soldados para que compraran la sal, un producto caro y muy escaso.

**El viernes y el martes.** El viernes es un día con mala reputación en todo el mundo anglosajón por ser el día en que, dicen, murió Cristo. En España, sin embargo, la fecha fatídica se traslada al martes, sobre todo si es 13. El martes, además, está asociado al dios de la guerra, Marte. "El martes, ni te cases ni te embarques", dice el refrán. Ese día tampoco es aconsejable cambiarse de casa o cortarse el pelo y las uñas.

**Tocar madera.** Es una forma de conjurar maleficios. Siempre que nos jactemos de nuestra buena suerte es recomendable tocar madera, y también cuando queramos que un deseo se realice.

Los árboles eran dioses para los paganos; por tanto, con el gesto de tocar madera nos ponemos bajo su protección.

**El trébol de cuatro hojas.** Se considera un poderoso amuleto para la persona que lo encuentra. Pero no se debe regalar, ni siquiera se debe enseñar. Puede colocarse entre las hojas de un libro para que se seque, pero también es recomendable llevarlo siempre consigo. Dicen que quien encuentra un trébol de cuatro hojas encontrará pronto el amor. Cuenta la leyenda que Eva, al ser expulsada del paraíso, se llevó consigo esta planta.

## ¿LO HAS ENTENDIDO?

**1** ¿Qué poderes se le atribuyen a la sal?

**2** ¿Qué cosas no debes hacer si es martes y 13 en España según el proverbio?

**3** ¿Qué significado tiene tocar madera?

**4** ¿Qué poderes tiene el trébol de cuatro hojas?

**5** ¿Qué es lo que se debe y no se debe hacer con él?

## TOMA NOTA

Fíjate en estas expresiones.

| | |
|---|---|
| ***es recomendable***<br>***es aconsejable***<br>***no se debe*** | **infinitivo** |

***Es recomendable, es aconsejable*** y ***no se debe*** son expresiones que utilizamos para ofrecer consejos o recomendaciones. Hay varios ejemplos en el texto. Búscalos. ¿Conoces otras expresiones similares?

Escribe en una lista los consejos que se dan en el artículo para cada creencia.

*Ejemplo*

**Trébol de cuatro hojas**
***No es aconsejable regalarlo.***

**El viernes y el martes**

**Tocar madera**

**Derramar la sal**

### AMPLÍA TU VOCABULARIO

**derramar** dejar caer
**dominio** control
**propiciar** favorecer
**fecundidad** fertilidad
**augurio** señal de un suceso futuro
**basta con** es suficiente con
**salario** sueldo, paga
**anglosajón** de habla inglesa
**fatídica** que conmemora un hecho fatal
**refrán** proverbio
**conjurar** expulsar, repeler
**maleficios** mala suerte, daños causados por magia
**jactemos de** estemos demasiado orgullosos/presuntuosos
**por tanto** por consiguiente
**poderoso** que tiene mucho poder
**ni siquiera** tampoco
**enseñar** mostrar
**colocarse** ponerse
**consigo** con uno mismo

## Y TÚ, ¿CÓMO LO VES?

**1** ¿Algunas de las creencias mencionadas en el artículo son comunes a tu cultura? ¿Qué otras supersticiones hay en tu país? ¿Qué importancia y significado tienen para ti? ¿Qué explicación tienen este tipo de creencias?

**2** ¿Haces algo especial para atraer o repeler la mala suerte?

**3** ¿Crees en el horóscopo? ¿Cuál es tu signo? ¿Tienes la costumbre de leer o consultar las predicciones del horóscopo? ¿Por qué?

**4** ¿Qué formas de interpretar el pasado y predecir el futuro conoces? ¿Crees en alguna de ellas?

**5** ¿Crees que se puede saber cómo es una persona simplemente leyendo su mano (quiromancia), estudiando su escritura (grafología) o su carta astral (astrología)? ¿O piensas que todo esto sólo son tonterías sin ninguna validez científica?

# SUPERSTICIONES

## EN LA ONDA

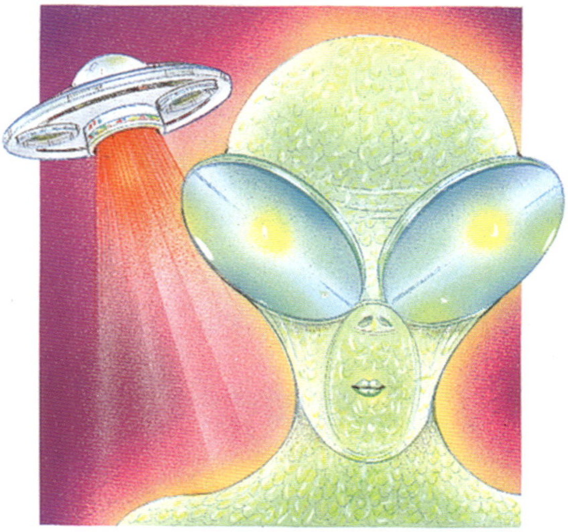

**1** ¿Crees en los fenómenos sobrenaturales o piensas que todo tiene una explicación científica? ¿Crees que existe/n

**a** los OVNIs?
**b** los extraterrestres?
**c** el yeti?
**d** los espíritus/los fantasmas?
**e** los vampiros?

**2** ¿Hay actualmente una fiebre o moda de lo paranormal? ¿Por qué este tipo de fenómenos ejercen tanta atracción sobre las personas?

**3** Escucha las noticias sobre los ataques de un extraño animal llamado *chupacabras* y responde.

**A** ¿A quién ataca el llamado *chupacabras*?
**B** ¿Qué hace con sus víctimas?
**C** ¿Cómo ha reaccionado la población? ¿Qué explicación tienen para lo que está pasando?
**D** Da tres detalles de la descripción de la criatura (ojos/cuerpo/extremidades).
**E** ¿Qué dicen los expertos en genética?

## ¡TIENES LA PALABRA!

**1** Entre toda la clase mira la ilustración.

**A** ¿Qué objetos o situaciones traen mala suerte y cuáles traen buena suerte?
**B** ¿Qué números y colores son afortunados en tu país? ¿Cuáles son importantes para ti?

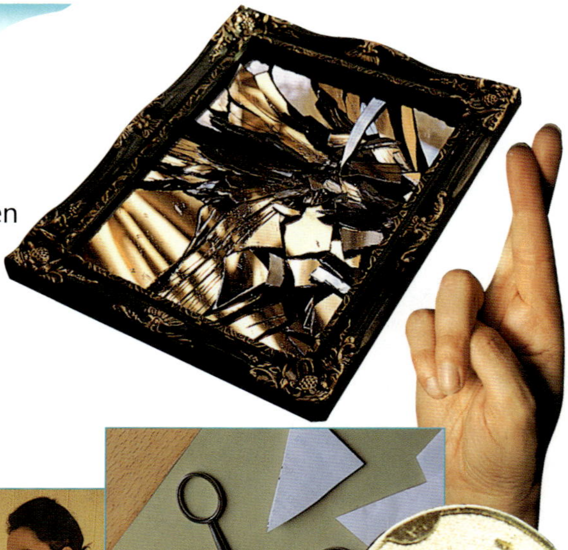

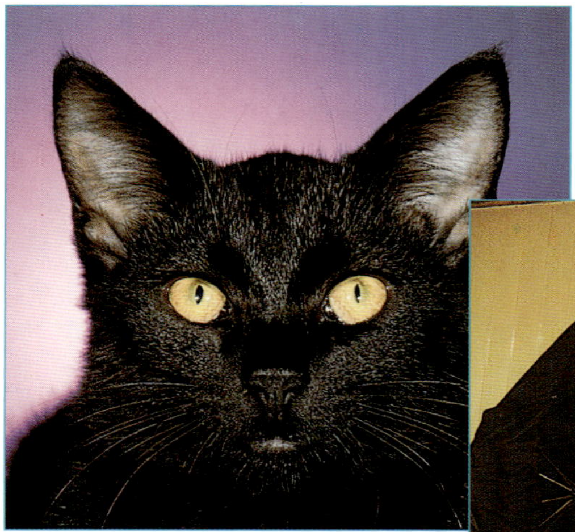

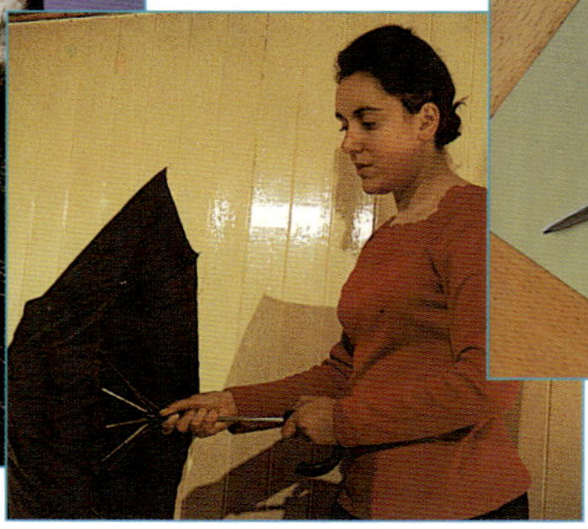

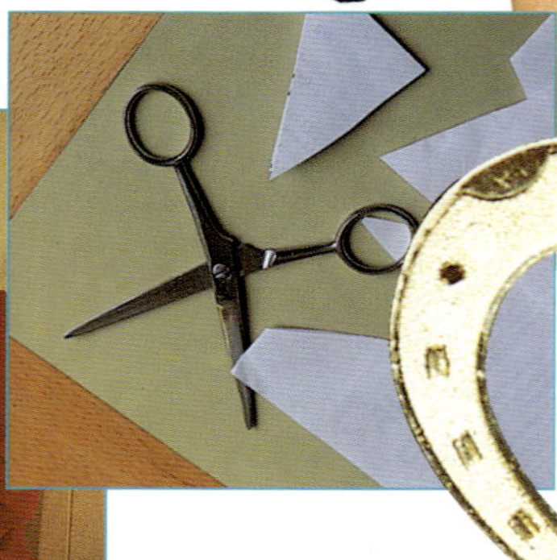

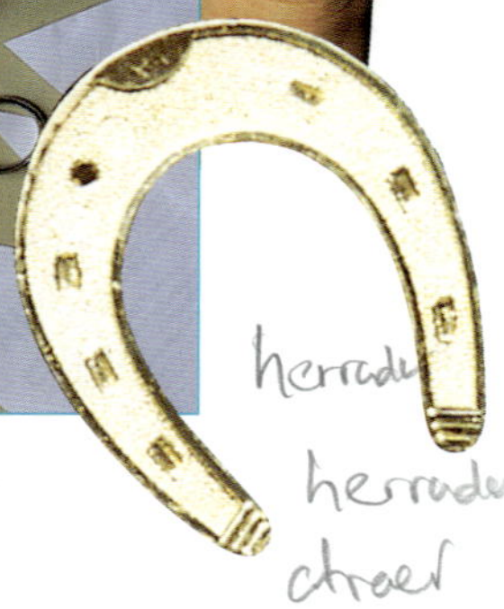

herradu
herradura
atraer
buena

**2** Los refranes o dichos tienen un origen muy antiguo y reflejan la filosofía popular y la sabiduría de los mayores.

**A** En grupos de tres relaciona estos proverbios con la explicación apropiada y discute su significado.

**B** Escoge tres proverbios. Imagina situaciones de la vida real en las que podrían aplicarse.

**C** ¿Hay expresiones similares en tu lengua?

### Refranes

1. *Más vale pájaro en mano que ciento volando.*
2. *En boca cerrada no entran moscas.*
3. *No es oro todo lo que reluce.*
4. *Dime con quién andas y te diré quién eres.*
5. *A la tercera la vencida.*
6. *Más vale tarde que nunca.*
7. *Pan para hoy y hambre para mañana.*
8. *A palabras necias oídos sordos.*
9. *Más vale prevenir que lamentar.*
10. *A suerte mala, paciencia y buena cara.*

### Explicaciones

**a** Es preferible hacer algo tarde a no hacerlo nunca.
**b** Las apariencias pueden ser falsas. No debemos fiarnos.
**c** Es mejor tomar precauciones.
**d** Las personas o compañías que frecuentamos nos influencian.
**e** Es mejor una cosa segura que muchas posibilidades en el aire.
**f** Es una solución temporal a un problema grave.
**g** A pesar de las adversidades hay que mantener el buen espíritu y el buen humor.
**h** Hay que callarse para no ser imprudente.
**i** La tercera vez que intentamos algo lo conseguimos.
**j** No debemos escuchar ni dar importancia a palabras estúpidas.

**3** Entre toda la clase comenta tus opiniones sobre estos temas.

**¿Hay vida en otros planetas? ¿Existe una civilización tecnológicamente superior a la nuestra en otras galaxias?**

**La astrología, ¿es para gente ingenua? ¿Crees que tiene una base científica?**

## POR ESCRITO

**1** Inventa un diálogo entre una adivinadora y una persona que quiere consultar su futuro. (150-200 palabras)

**2** Describe tu signo y los aspectos positivos/negativos de tu personalidad según tu horóscopo. ¿Estás de acuerdo con todo lo que se dice de tu signo? (200 palabras)

**3** Imagínate un día en la vida de una persona supersticiosa y escribe una historia. Puedes utilizar algunos de los refranes que has aprendido. (250 palabras)

## PUNTO DE MIRA

¿Cuánto sabes de los ídolos de España y Latinoamérica? Pon a prueba tus conocimientos. Responde a este sencillo cuestionario.

**1** La cantante Gloria Estefan es de origen
- **a** mexicano.
- **b** chileno.
- **c** cubano.

**2** ¿En qué película no actúa Antonio Banderas?
- **a** *Entrevista con el vampiro*
- **b** *Los reyes del mambo*
- **c** *Como agua para chocolate*

**3** La cantante Selena era la reina
- **a** del pop español.
- **b** de la balada romántica.
- **c** de la música tejana o tex-mex.

**4** Joaquín Cortés es
- **a** cantaor de flamenco.
- **b** bailaor de flamenco.
- **c** modelo.

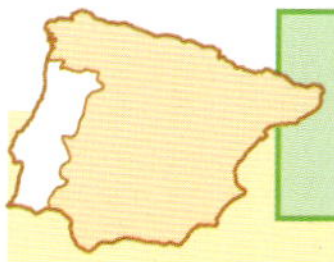

Música, cantantes, actores, directores de cine.... ¿Está de moda lo latino? Lee este artículo para descubrirlo.

# La fuerza hispana

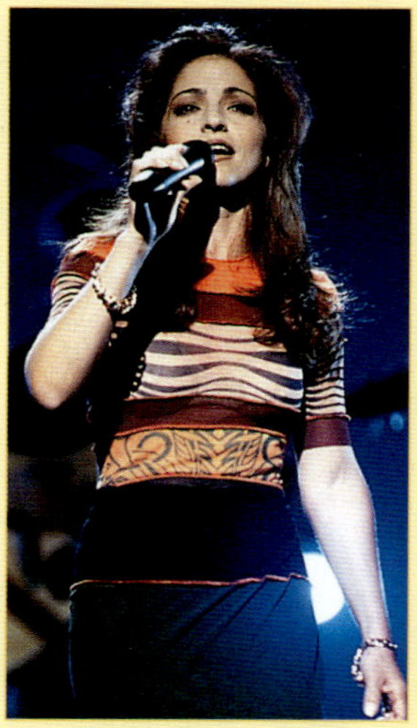

La revista *People*, una de las más populares en Estados Unidos, acaba de sacar una edición en castellano. Para celebrar su incursión en el creciente mercado hispano, ha elaborado su relación de las diez estrellas latinas del momento.

Además de Banderas, otro español figura en la lista: Enrique, el hijo de Julio Iglesias. Les acompañan cinco mujeres y tres hombres: Gloria Estefan, Cristina Saralegui, Thalía, Jennifer López, Salma Hayek, Francisco Gattorno, Jimmy Smits y Luis Miguel.

La cultura y los intereses de los puertorriqueños de Nueva York, los cubanos de Miami o los chicanos de California no son los mismos. Pero su empuje conjunto convierte a este grupo social (los hispanos) en una fuerza determinante. Y sus mitos, sus valores y sus ídolos se traspasan al resto de la sociedad norteamericana.

Lejos quedan los tiempos en que los artistas de origen hispano eran algo exótico. Hoy la cantante Gloria Estefan es quizás el valor en activo más incontestable, tanto en castellano como en inglés. Su fama es tal que, según cuentan, la correspondencia que le dirigen poniendo sólo su nombre, sin dirección, le llega sin ningún problema.

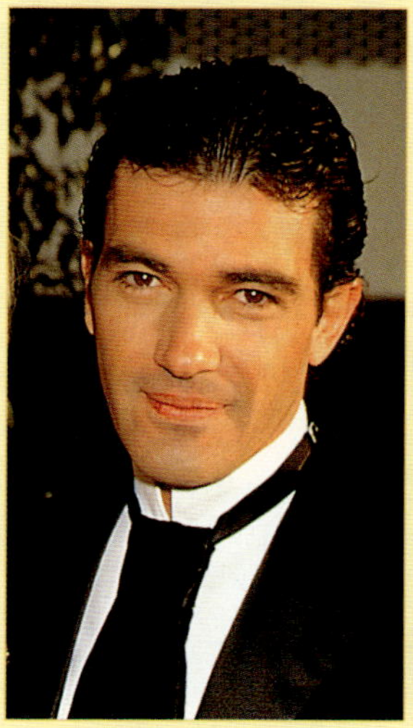

El número uno indiscutible entre los actores es Antonio Banderas. Es verdad que su físico le abrió las primeras puertas. Pero no es menos cierto que tiene ya una importante filmografía en Estados Unidos.

Una de las razones del éxito de este colectivo es el crecimiento demográfico y económico de la minoría de origen hispano. Según cifras oficiales, este grupo social, con 27 millones de ciudadanos, es el que aumenta más rápidamente en el país. Hoy es la minoría más mayoritaria entre los jóvenes y antes de 2010 se calcula que será la más importante de Estados Unidos.

El nivel de renta de la minoría hispana aún está por debajo de la media del país, pero crece año a año. Por eso, la publicidad se orienta cada vez más a ese mercado.

## ¿LO HAS ENTENDIDO?

1 ¿En qué idiomas se puede leer la revista *People*? ¿La lee mucha gente?

2 ¿Cómo ha celebrado el lanzamiento de su nueva edición?

3 ¿Qué prueba hay de que la cantante Gloria Estefan es famosa y tiene un enorme éxito?

4 ¿Qué revelan las estadísticas sobre la población hispana en Estados Unidos?

## TOMA NOTA

Fíjate en estas palabras del texto.

| | | | |
|---|---|---|---|
| ***castellano*** | ***aumentar*** | ***figurar*** | ***crecer*** |
| ***minoría*** | ***éxito*** | ***razones*** | ***por debajo de*** |

Relaciónalas con sus sinónimos (***aumentar*** – ***aparecer*** – ***motivo*** – ***español***)
Relaciónalas con sus opuestos (***mayoría*** – ***fracaso*** – ***por encima de*** – ***disminuir***)

**1** Sustituye las palabras subrayadas por un sinónimo.

**A** ***El motivo*** de su éxito es su gran talento como actriz.

**B** Ricky Martin canta tanto en ***castellano*** como en inglés.

**C** Su nuevo disco ***aparece*** en todas las listas de éxitos de varios países.

**D** Su número de fans ***crece*** cada día.

**2** Expresa lo contrario de estas frases.

**A** Su nueva película fue un gran fracaso comercial.

**B** El interés por la cultura hispana disminuye cada día.

**C** Las personas que tienen el español como primera lengua son minoría.

**D** Sus intereses personales están por debajo de sus intereses comerciales.

### AMPLÍA TU VOCABULARIO

**acaba de sacar** ha publicado recientemente
**incursión** penetración, introducción
**creciente** cada vez más grande
**chicanos** personas de origen mexicano que viven en Estados Unidos
**empuje** fuerza, impulso
**conjunto** común, unido
**determinante** decisiva, importante
**se traspasan** se transmiten
**incontestable** incuestionable
**cierto** verdad
**éxito** triunfo
**colectivo** grupo
**cifras** estadísticas
**aumenta** crece
**mayoritaria** más grande
**nivel de renta** nivel económico, nivel de vida
**se orienta** está dirigida

## Y TÚ, ¿CÓMO LO VES?

1 ¿Conoces a alguno de los artistas mencionados en el artículo? ¿De qué los conoces?

2 ¿Tienes algún ídolo? ¿A qué personaje famoso te gustaría conocer? ¿Por qué?

3 ¿Perteneces a algún club de fans? ¿Alguna vez has escrito a alguien famoso?

4 ¿Qué influencias latinas o hispanas hay en tu país? ¿Hay una fiebre por la música, el cine o la cultura española o hispana? ¿Hay influencias culturales de algún otro país, por ejemplo en la comida, la ropa, la música...? Explica.

5 En tu opinión, ¿por qué es importante para los hispanos mantener sus mitos, valores, ídolos y tradiciones culturales?

ÍDOLOS

## EN LA ONDA

**1** ¿Tienes algún ídolo o persona que admiras mucho en la música, el cine o el deporte? ¿Admiras a esa persona por

**a** su físico?
**b** su trabajo?
**c** su talento?
**d** su personalidad?

**2** ¿Qué cualidades se necesitan para ser famoso? Haz una lista de los rasgos que hacen a una estrella. ¿Cuáles de estas cualidades te parecen positivas/negativas? ¿Por qué?

**Para llegar a la fama tienes que**

- ser ambicioso
- ser creativo y original
- ser extrovertido
- ser muy trabajador
- ser egocéntrico
- tener suerte
- tener confianza en sí mismo
- tener buenos contactos

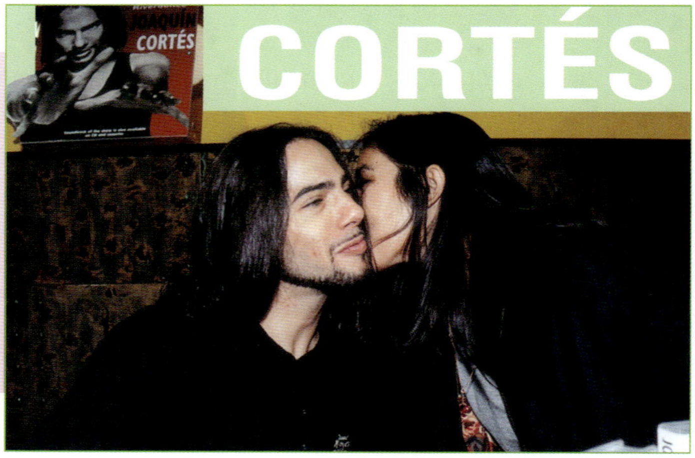


**3** Escucha a unos jóvenes que hablan de sus gustos e ídolos musicales y responde.

**A** ¿Qué evidencia hay del éxito de Selena?
**B** ¿De qué tragedia hablan?
**C** ¿Qué tipo de canciones canta Luis Miguel?
**D** ¿Cuándo comenzó su carrera artística?
**E** ¿De dónde es el grupo Ketama?
**F** ¿Cómo es la música de Ketama?

**4** Escucha la cinta por segunda vez y anota las características de los tres estilos musicales: tejano, bolero y nuevo flamenco.

## ¡TIENES LA PALABRA!

**1** En parejas describe tu cantante, actor, ídolo o película favoritos sin decir el nombre. Tu pareja tiene que adivinar quién o qué película es. Si lo descubre cambia de papeles.

**Estas palabras te ayudarán**

**Tipos de música**
rock – pop – balada – ranchera
bolero – salsa – indi – flamenco
tex mex (música tejana)
pop – clásica

**Tipos de películas**
de acción – romántica – policíaca
de aventuras – de ciencia-ficción
de suspense – comedia – histórica
de terror

**2** En grupos mira la cartelera de espectáculos y decide dónde quieres ir y por qué. Habla con tus compañeros para llegar a un acuerdo sobre cuál es la mejor propuesta.

**Guaycán y Merenglass**
*Teatro Metropólitan*
Lo mejor del ritmo salsero, la cumbia, el pasodoble y el bolero.
- Miércoles 20:30 horas.

**La Unión**
*Teatro Metropólitan*
Una de las agrupaciones más importantes del rock en español se presenta con lo más reciente de su producción discográfica.
- Sábado, 20:00 horas.

**Las Tapas**
*Hotel Camino Real*
Show de música flamenca con grupos en vivo y bailarinas. Cocina española.
- De las 19:00 a las 1:00 horas.

**La Guitarra de Chamín**
*Londres 25*
Sitio bohemio con las actuaciones de Chamín Correa, Los Cinco Reales y Martha Eugenia. Interpretan boleros de siempre.
- Viernes y sábado a partir de las 22:00 horas.

**3** Entre toda la clase comenta tus opiniones sobre estos temas.

**¿Qué importancia tienen los mitos e ídolos? ¿Para qué sirve tener un ídolo? ¿Crees que puede causar obsesión?**

**Si pudieras ser una estrella, ¿quién te gustaría ser? ¿Por qué?**

**¿Crees que la fama cambia a las personas?**

**¿Qué ventajas e inconvenientes tiene ser famoso?**

## POR ESCRITO

**1** Haz una lista de tus diez artistas/películas favoritas. Explica los motivos de tu elección. (200 palabras)

**2** ¡Enhorabuena! Has ganado el concurso *Pasa un día con tu ídolo*. Cuenta tus planes para tan importante cita y prepara una lista de preguntas que te gustaría hacerle. (250-300 palabras)

**3** Eres crítico de cine para una revista española. Escribe la reseña de dos películas que conoces. Incluye esta información: título, actores principales, tipo de película, argumento y calificación (regular, buena, excelente...). (200 palabras)

## PUNTO DE MIRA

En el siglo XXI la ciencia y la tecnología marcarán una nueva era. Pero, ¿qué impacto tuvieron estos inventos para la humanidad?

**a** la rueda
**b** la imprenta
**c** los rayos X
**d** las vacunas
**e** el automóvil
**f** el avión

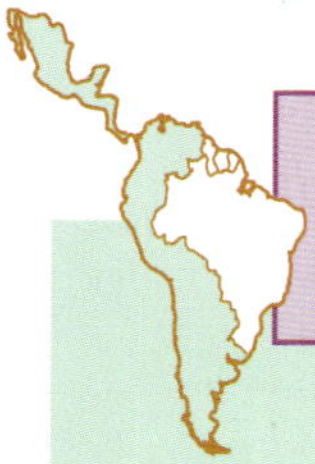

La biotecnología tendrá un papel esencial en las próximas décadas. Lee este artículo sobre algunas aplicaciones de esta ciencia.

# ¿Un clon tiene beneficios?

La histórica llegada a la escena internacional de la oveja Dolly desencadenó una serie de preguntas sobre para qué puede servir un clon.

Más allá de los temores sobre los peligros para la humanidad, los resultados obtenidos por el equipo escocés en el Instituto Roslin de Edimburgo, abren perspectivas reales en el campo de la medicina.

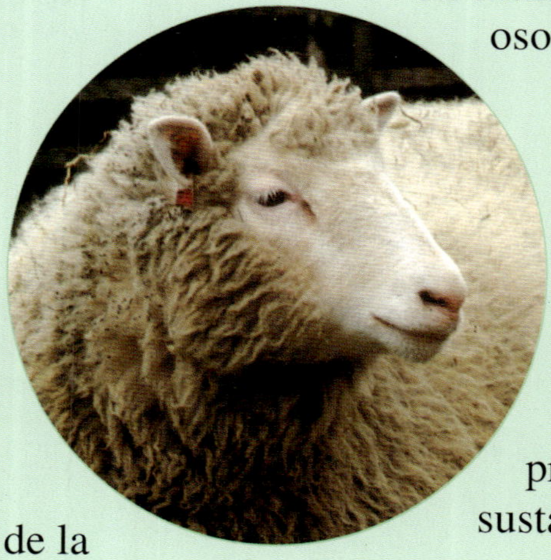

Entre otras: fabricación de medicamentos, hormonas y órganos humanizados a partir de animales, modelos más eficaces para estudiar las enfermedades humanas y un mejor conocimiento de los cánceres.

Estos también pueden ser aprovechados en la agricultura (rendimiento, gusto, calidad) y para la salvaguarda de especies en extinción, como los osos panda.

La empresa PPL Therapeutics, propietaria de la técnica 'Dolly', está especializada en corderos transgénicos, productores de sustancias terapéuticas.

Los animales transgénicos permiten fabricar productos para el tratamiento de enfermedades pulmonares. La clonación de estos animales mejoraría la producción y la obtención de órganos para transplantar al humano. **AFP**

## ¿LO HAS ENTENDIDO?

**1** ¿Quién ha creado a Dolly?

**2** ¿Qué ha provocado el descubrimiento de Dolly?

**3** ¿Es importante la clonación en la medicina?

**4** ¿En qué otros campos se aplica la clonación?

**5** ¿Para qué sirven los animales transgénicos?

## TOMA NOTA

Fíjate en estas palabras.

| | | | |
|---|---|---|---|
| *fabricar* | *la fabrica**ción*** | *tratar* | *el trata**miento*** |
| *investigar* | *la investiga**ción*** | *nacer* | *el naci**miento*** |

A partir de un verbo y con la ayuda de los sufijos ***-ción*** y ***-miento*** puedes obtener nuevas palabras y ampliar de este modo tu vocabulario. Las palabras terminadas en ***-ción*** son siempre femeninas y las terminadas en ***-miento*** masculinas.

Algunas de estas palabras aparecen en el artículo. ¿Sabrías formar los verbos o sustantivos que faltan?

| **VERBO** | **SUSTANTIVO** |
|---|---|
| ____ | reproducción |
| rendir | ____ |
| conocer | ____ |
| ____ | obtención |
| sustituir | ____ |
| ____ | pensamiento |
| producir | ____ |

| **VERBO** | **SUSTANTIVO** |
|---|---|
| clonar | ____ |
| ____ | aplicación |
| aprovechar | ____ |
| ____ | entendimiento |
| seguir | ____ |
| extinguir | ____ |
| descubrir | ____ |

### AMPLÍA TU VOCABULARIO

**biotecnología** conjunto de técnicas para alterar las características de los organismos vivos
**desencadenó** provocó
**temores** preocupaciones
**eficaces** eficientes, que consiguen el efecto deseado
**ser aprovechados** ser utilizados beneficiosamente
**rendimiento** producción
**gusto** sabor
**salvaguarda** protección
**fabricar** elaborar, producir
**pulmonares** relativas al pulmón
**mejoraría** haría mejor, potenciaría

## Y TÚ, ¿CÓMO LO VES?

**1** Pronto los científicos sabrán qué genes son responsables de 4.000 enfermedades hereditarias. ¿Crees que este descubrimiento es bueno o malo? ¿Por qué? ¿Será más fácil en el siglo XXI controlar nuestro destino?

**2** Gracias a los avances en la higiene y la medicina vivimos mucho más tiempo que nuestros antepasados. En el futuro la tecnología podría alargar la vida humana hasta límites increíbles. ¿Te gustaría vivir más tiempo? ¿Crees que nuestros descendientes morirán a los 200 ó 300 años? ¿Qué repercusiones tendría esto?

## EN LA ONDA

**1** Cuando vas al supermercado, ¿te fijas en las etiquetas de los productos que compras? ¿Qué tipo de información esperas encontrar?

**2** El pan, el vino, la cerveza y el queso son tradicionales productos biotecnológicos. Escucha esta conferencia de prensa sobre la nutrición. Anota la información para los siguientes puntos.

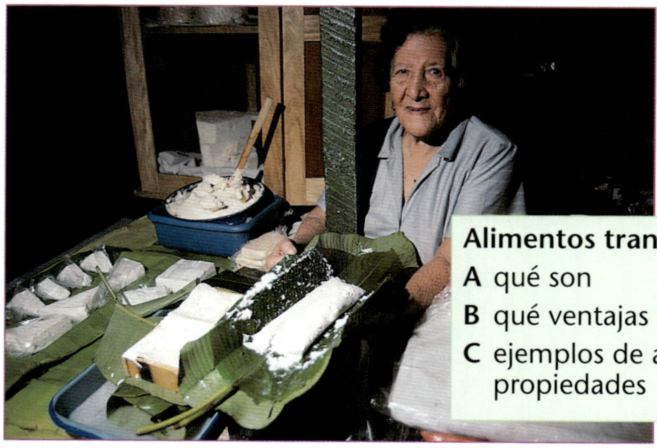

**Dieta del futuro**
**A** tipo de dieta
**B** productos que se comerán

**Alimentos transgénicos**
**A** qué son
**B** qué ventajas tienen
**C** ejemplos de alimentos y propiedades

**Biotecnología**
consecuencias de su aplicación

## ¡TIENES LA PALABRA!

**1** En grupos lee las ventajas y riesgos de la clonación y de las aplicaciones de la biotecnología. ¿Ayudará a disminuir el hambre en el mundo? ¿Qué beneficios tendrán para el consumidor los alimentos transgénicos? Defiende tu opinión a favor o en contra.

### Ventajas

- animales resistentes a los virus y enfermedades
- alimentos con proteínas para tratar enfermedades
- animales donantes de órganos
- ganadería y agricultura más rentables y productivas
- plantas transgénicas que necesitan poca agua y nutrientes
- aumento de la producción mundial de alimentos
- prevención de miles de enfermedades hereditarias

### Riesgos

- pérdida de la diversidad genética: cultivo de una o dos variedades por especie vegetal
- propagación de enfermedades en animales del mismo clon. Posible transmisión a las personas
- mal uso: posible clonación de seres humanos
- fabricación de armas biológicas
- reacciones alérgicas a las sustancias de los alimentos transgénicos
- impacto negativo en el medioambiente

**2** Observa el anuncio de *Greenpeace*. Entre toda la clase discute la biotecnología. ¿Es una esperanza para la humanidad o una potencial amenaza? La clonación de animales y plantas es ya una realidad. Pero, ¿podrían algún día fabricarse seres humanos? ¿Te parece ético? ¿Se debe prohibir la clonación humana?

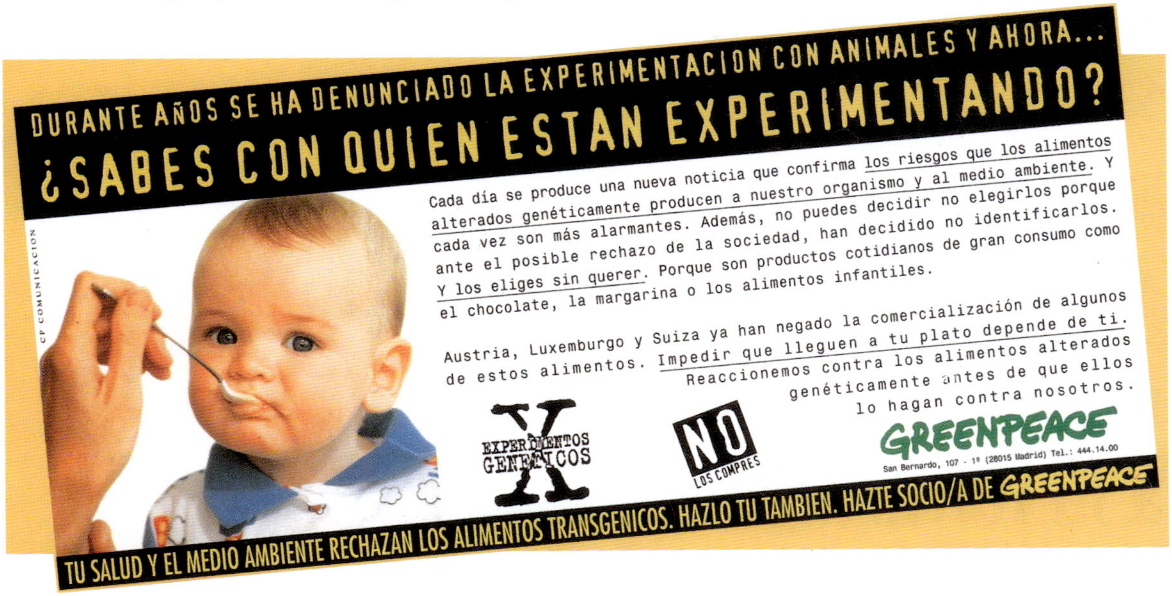


**3** Mira la tabla de predicciones para el año 2100. ¿Cuáles de ellas te parecen más probables? ¿Por qué? ¿Viviremos algún día en el espacio? ¿Qué predicciones harías tú para el siglo XXI?

**Para el año 2100 habrá**

- edificios inteligentes (controlados por ordenador)
- ciudades artificiales sobre los océanos
- elección genética de la reproducción
- implantación de órganos biónicos en enfermos
- aumento de la esperanza de vida y de la población
- planetas artificiales para vivir (estaciones orbitales)
- realidad virtual creíble
- turismo en el espacio y vehículos aéreos

## POR ESCRITO

**1** ¿Cómo te imaginas la vida dentro de dos siglos? Describe un día en la vida de un estudiante/trabajador de ese tiempo.

**2** Pregunta a personas mayores de tu entorno (padres, tíos, abuelos) sobre los cambios que han visto en la alimentación y en la comida de los supermercados. Escribe las conclusiones de tu investigación en español. (250 palabras)

**Ejemplos de preguntas**

¿Qué alimentos se comían más? (carne, pescado...)

¿Había comida precocinada?

¿Es la dieta más variada ahora?

¿Cómo han cambiado los envases y etiquetas?

¿Consideran los cambios positivos o negativos?

PUNTO DE MIRA

¿Cuánto sabes sobre el reciclaje? Haz una lista de los materiales que pueden reciclarse. ¿Cuáles son los más utilizados?

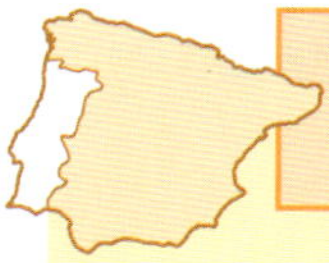

¿Respetamos la naturaleza como se merece? Lee el siguiente texto para descubrirlo.

# Nosotros maltratamos a la naturaleza y ella se queja

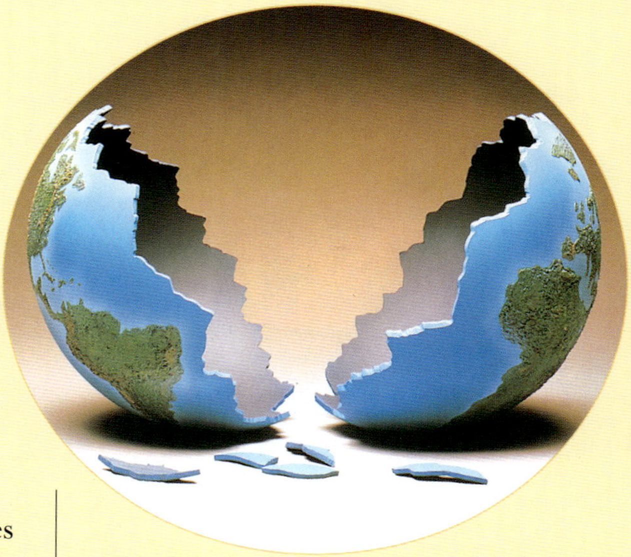

La mayoría de los avances técnicos no ha respetado la naturaleza; al contrario, han contribuido a la desaparición de las especies naturales o a la destrucción de la atmósfera. Frecuentemente olvidamos que el hombre es parte integrante de la naturaleza y que lo que le afecte a ella también nos acabará haciendo daño a nosotros. Estas son algunas de las *quejas* de la naturaleza.

**Cambio climático.** El clima está sufriendo serias modificaciones. Lo hemos podido notar en los largos períodos de sequía o de lluvias torrenciales que destrozan nuestros campos, temperaturas cada vez más extremas... Los expertos evitan sacar conclusiones sobre si se trata de una causa natural o provocada por el hombre, pero reconocen que los coches, fábricas, etc, emiten diariamente gases nocivos con capacidad para alterar el clima del planeta.

**Agujero en la capa de ozono.** Cada año, los datos sobre la destrucción de la capa de ozono son más alarmantes. El ozono en la atmósfera es vital para que la vida en el planeta continúe: nos protege de las nocivas radiaciones ultravioletas que acompañan a los rayos de sol. La causa de este deterioro es el uso masivo de gases que contienen los *sprays* de las lacas y los ambientadores, los congeladores y también los aparatos de aire acondicionado.

**Contaminación de los mares.** Los océanos se han convertido en los basureros de la actividad industrial. A los vertidos de las industrias hay que añadir la contaminación procedente de la atmósfera, que acaba depositándose en el mar arrastrada con la lluvia.

**Desertización.** El suelo cada vez es más pobre a causa de las talas indiscriminadas de árboles, los incendios forestales y el uso de abonos químicos.

**Contaminación atmosférica.** El uso del automóvil es la principal fuente de contaminación urbana. Los niveles de monóxido de carbono en la atmósfera son cada vez mayores y el efecto *smog* –la nube grisácea que cubre las ciudades– ha aumentado.

## ¿LO HAS ENTENDIDO?

**1** ¿Qué impacto ha tenido el progreso en la naturaleza?

**2** ¿Qué efectos tienen los gases emitidos por los automóviles y las fábricas?

**3** ¿De qué forma ha cambiado nuestro clima?

**4** ¿Por qué es importante el ozono?

**5** ¿Cuáles son los peligros para nuestros bosques?

**6** ¿Por qué hay tanta contaminación en las ciudades?

## TOMA NOTA

Fíjate en estas frases del texto.

*"...temperaturas **cada vez más** extremas...".*
*"El suelo **cada vez** es **más** pobre...".*

***Cada vez más/cada vez menos*** es una forma de comparación utilizada con verbos y adjetivos. Se utiliza para enfatizar su significado (porque indica progresión ascendente/descendente).

Completa estas frases con ***cada vez más*** o ***cada vez menos***.

*Ejemplo*
*Luis ha perdido mucho peso últimamente. **Cada vez** está **más** delgado.*

**A** Circulan demasiados coches por la ciudad. _____ hay _____ contaminación.
**B** Está llegando la primavera. _____ hace _____ calor.
**C** Debido a los incendios forestales _____ hay _____ árboles en nuestros bosques.
**D** Muchos utilizan el mar como basurero. Las playas están _____ sucias.
**E** Últimamente tengo mucho trabajo. Salgo _____ por la noche.
**F** ¡Cómo suben los precios en el supermercado! _____ está todo _____ caro.
**G** La gente es más consciente ahora y _____ recicla _____ .
**H** Los aerosoles con gases nocivos se utilizan _____ .

### AMPLÍA TU VOCABULARIO

**quejas** problemas, lamentos
**sequía** falta de agua
**reconocen que** admiten que
**nocivos** perjudiciales, malos, que causan daño
**datos** información
**lacas** productos para fijar el pelo
**ambientadores** para perfumar el ambiente
**basureros** lugares donde se depositan los residuos
**vertidos** basura, residuos
**arrastrada** llevada, transportada
**talas de árboles** cortar los árboles
**abonos químicos** fertilizantes
**grisácea** de color gris

## Y TÚ, ¿CÓMO LO VES?

**1** ¿Te preocupas por los problemas ambientales de la Tierra? ¿Qué haces tú personalmente para mejorar la situación?

**2** ¿Reflexionas antes de comprar algo si tienes verdadera necesidad de ello?

**3** ¿Eres miembro de alguna asociación ecologista o de defensa de la naturaleza?

**4** ¿Crees que el progreso implica necesariamente ir contra los intereses de la naturaleza? ¿Es posible encontrar un equilibrio entre ambos? Explica.

**5** ¿Cómo ves el futuro de nuestro planeta?

## EN LA ONDA

**1** ¿Cuánto te preocupas por el medio ambiente? En parejas responde ***sí, no*** o ***a veces*** a estas preguntas.

**A** ¿Haces las compras con tu propia bolsa?

**B** ¿Usas productos reciclados?

**C** ¿Compras alimentos biológicos?

**D** ¿Usas cosméticos no probados en animales?

**E** ¿Depositas las botellas y las latas en un contenedor?

**F** ¿Depositas los periódicos y revistas en un contenedor de papel?

**G** ¿Compras productos de limpieza ecológicos?

**H** ¿Reutilizas cosas que tienes o compras otras nuevas?

**I** ¿Apagas la luz cuando no la necesitas?

**J** ¿Te bañas más que te duchas?

**2** Manifestación ecologista: campaña *"Salvemos el Planeta Azul"*. Escucha a los líderes de este movimiento ecologista y responde.

**A** ¿De qué dos formas podemos ahorrar agua en nuestros hábitos de higiene personal?

**B** ¿Qué ventajas tiene la bicicleta como medio de transporte?

**C** ¿Qué tenemos que hacer con la basura doméstica?

**3** Escucha otra vez los consejos y completa estas frases con las ideas mencionadas.

| ACCIÓN | CONSECUENCIA |
|---|---|
| *Ejemplo* | |
| *Si te bañas* | *_____ mucha agua.* |
| *Si te bañas* | ***gastarás*** *mucha agua.* |
| **A** Si te _____ | ahorrarás mucha agua. |
| **B** Si pones la _____ | _____ 200 litros de agua. |
| **C** Si viajas en _____ | es más _____ y _____ . |
| **D** Si _____ | harás deporte también. |
| **E** Si _____ | salvarás muchos árboles. |

## ¡TIENES LA PALABRA!

**1** En parejas piensa en ideas para

**a** proteger los bosques.
**b** disminuir la contaminación en las ciudades.
**c** evitar la contaminación de los mares.
**d** reducir el volumen de basura.

Explica tus ideas al resto de la clase.

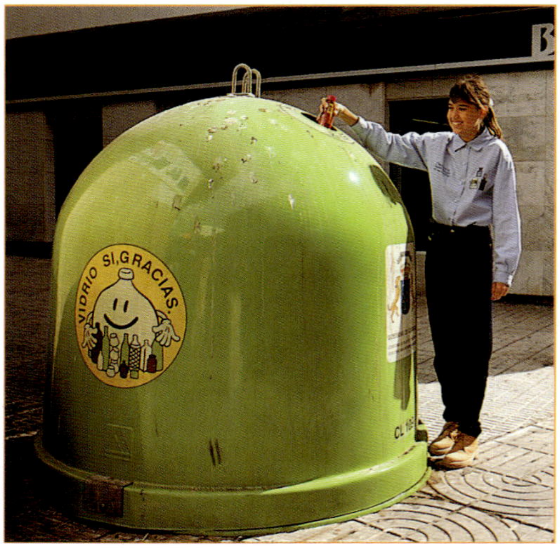

**EL SEÑOR MUNDO MARISCAL**

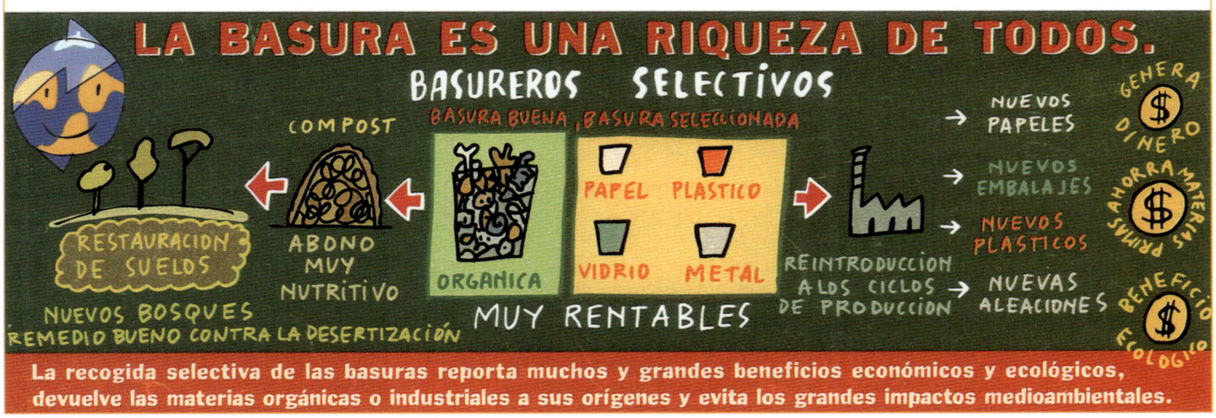


**2** En grupos observa la ilustración de Mariscal para *El Señor Mundo*. ¿Qué opinas de ella? ¿Te parece divertida, seria, informativa, clara, precisa.... ¿Cuál es su mensaje principal? ¿Qué quiere comunicarnos Mariscal con su ilustración? ¿Crees que lo hace de forma efectiva? ¿Por qué? ¿Estás de acuerdo con sus ideas?

### AMPLÍA TU VOCABULARIO

**riqueza** bien, tesoro
**nutritivo** con mucho alimento
**rentables** beneficiosos
**embalajes** paquetes
**materias primas** recursos naturales
**aleaciones** mezcla de metales

**3** Entre toda la clase comenta tus opiniones sobre estos temas.

**¿Por qué es necesario reciclar?**

**¿Piensas que estamos destruyendo nuestro planeta? ¿Cómo?**

**¿Qué posibilidades de reciclaje ofrece tu ciudad? ¿Las utilizas al máximo?**

**¿Es importante la participación de toda la sociedad para salvar el futuro del planeta Tierra? ¿Por qué?**

## POR ESCRITO

**1** Diseña un póster con fotos o ilustraciones para animar a la gente a usar el transporte público/reciclar más. Piensa en un lema o frase para tu campaña.

**2** Escribe una guía de cómo ser un buen ecologista. (200 palabras)

**3** ¿Te preocupas realmente por el medio ambiente? Escribe lo que haces para aliviar los problemas, lo que no haces y los hábitos que deberías cambiar. Explica las razones. (250-300 palabras)

**4** *"El hombre es el peor enemigo de la naturaleza"*. ¿Estás de acuerdo con esta afirmación? Discute. (300 palabras)

## PUNTO DE MIRA

Ante estas situaciones:

**a** un examen importante
**b** una discusión familiar / con los amigos
**c** un viaje en metro / tren lleno de gente
**d** una entrevista de trabajo

**¿Cómo reaccionas?**
con ansiedad
con frustración
con mal/buen humor
con tensión

**¿Cómo te sientes?**
nervioso/a
irritable
tranquilo/a
angustiado/a

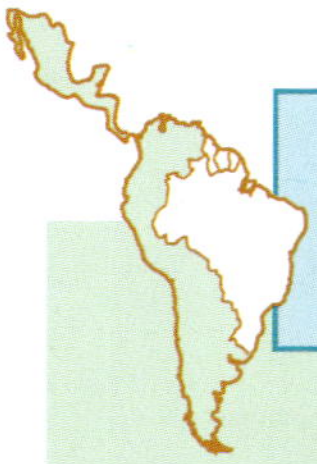

¿Es nuestra vida diaria una carrera contra el reloj? Vas a leer un artículo sobre las presiones de la vida moderna.

# Acabe con el ESTRÉS antes de que acabe con USTED

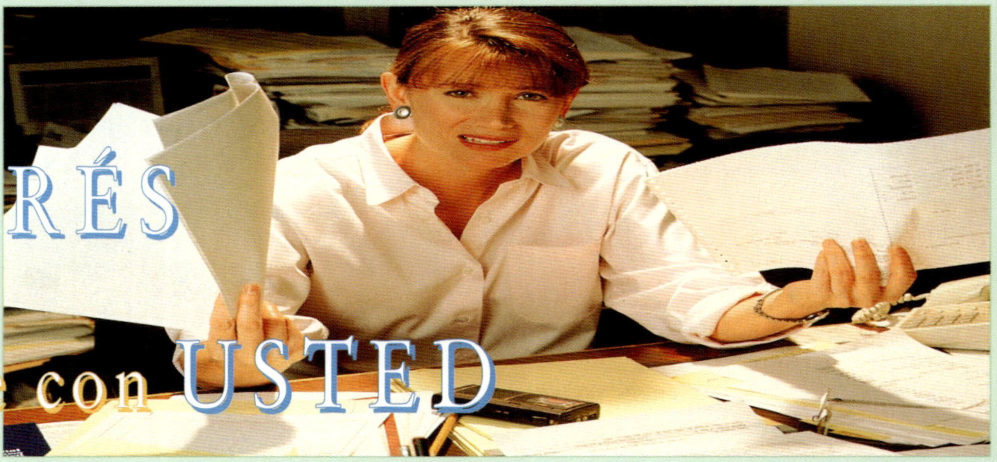

La tecnología moderna ha transformado el mundo. Hoy en día, las computadoras, el teléfono celular y los *beepers* están sobre la mesa del comedor, al lado de la cama, en el carro... y también en los restaurantes, en los cines y en la playa. La carrera contra el tiempo y las múltiples responsabilidades están acabando con la vida de los ejecutivos, las secretarias, los obreros y las amas de casa. El mundo parece estar al borde de un ataque de nervios. Según informes estadísticos, en los países industrializados una de cada cuatro personas padece de cansancio crónico.

El estrés se ha convertido en el principal motivo por el cual las personas acuden a ver al médico. Los síntomas del estrés varían en cada persona. Pueden ser pasajeros o transformarse en una enfermedad crónica. Las manifestaciones pueden empezar con un dolor de cabeza, una parálisis muscular, presión alta, problemas digestivos, depresión, e inclusive culminar en un ataque al corazón.

Y aunque el hombre igual que la mujer sufre de este mal, es ella la que está llevando la peor parte. La tensión nerviosa que le causa trabajar fuera, atender la casa y ocuparse de los hijos se está convirtiendo en una bomba a punto de estallar. Pero, ¿es posible resistir por mucho tiempo esa tensión nerviosa? Los expertos consideran que no.

Si bien la vida moderna nos exige mucho, existen algunos métodos para combatir el estrés. ¿Qué hacer? Dedíquese cinco minutos de su tiempo. Las técnicas para combatir el estrés se aplican de acuerdo al grado de tensión nerviosa: pequeñas sesiones de ejercicios, masajes, meditación, yoga.

## ¿LO HAS ENTENDIDO?

**1** ¿Cuál es el gran problema que afecta a los países industrializados?

**2** ¿Por qué motivos puede la vida moderna producir altos niveles de ansiedad?

**3** Explica de qué forma es la mujer más vulnerable a los efectos del estrés.

**4** ¿Con qué métodos se puede combatir el estrés?

## TOMA NOTA

Fíjate en la estructura.

***Estar*** **+ participio de presente (gerundio)**

**-AR: *-ando***
*hablar - habl**ando***
*estudiar - estudi**ando***

**-ER/-IR: *-iendo***
*tener - ten**iendo***
*vivir - viv**iendo***

**Irregulares**

*leer - le**yendo*** *oir - o**yendo*** *ir - **yendo***

El presente progresivo describe acciones que están en proceso de realizarse en el momento presente. Esta forma es mucho más frecuente en el lenguaje hablado en Latinoamérica que en España. Hay tres ejemplos de esta forma verbal en el artículo. Búscalos.

En grupos de tres utiliza la mímica y gestos para representar acciones. Practica el presente progresivo de esta forma.

*Ejemplo*
Estudiante 1°: *¿Qué **estoy haciendo**?*
Estudiante 2°: ***Estás comiendo** una manzana.*
Estudiante 3°: *¿Qué **estoy haciendo**?*
Estudiante 1°: ***Estás...***

### AMPLÍA TU VOCABULARIO

**hoy en día** actualmente
**las computadoras** (*Am Lat*) los ordenadores (*Esp*)
**los *beepers*** (*Am Lat*) los "busca" personas (*Esp*); pequeños aparatos electrónicos de comunicación
**carro** (*Am Lat*) coche, auto
**obreros** trabajadores
**padece de** sufre de
**cansancio** fatiga
**acuden** van
**pasajeros** temporales
**llevando la peor parte** estar en peor situación
**si bien** aunque
**exige** demanda, requiere
**de acuerdo al** dependiendo de, según

## Y TÚ, ¿CÓMO LO VES?

**1** ¿Tienes tiempo libre para hacer lo que te gusta o, por el contrario, siempre estás muy ocupado/a? ¿Para qué te gustaría tener más tiempo libre?

**2** Con el ritmo de vida actual es raro no tener un día sin encontrar algún tipo de estrés. ¿Qué situaciones te producen estrés? ¿Cómo reaccionas ante esas situaciones? Haz una lista y después presenta tus ideas al resto de la clase.

**3** ¿Qué haces para relajarte de las tensiones?

**a** escuchar música
**b** tomar un baño
**c** hablar con amigos
**d** leer
**e** ir al gimnasio

## EN LA ONDA

**1** Mira la lista de las diez profesiones. Escoge tres de ellas y explica qué tensiones se sufren a consecuencia de esas ocupaciones. ¿Qué otras profesiones podrías añadir a esa lista? Justifica tu opinión.

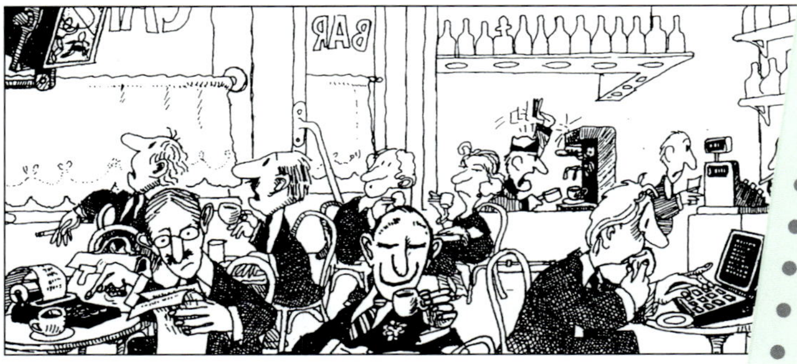

**Las 10 Profesiones de Más Estrés**

- Operadores de tráfico aéreo
- Médicos y enfermeras
- Abogados
- Policías
- Periodistas
- Secretarias
- Profesores
- Amas de casa
- Meseros
- Entrenadores de deportes

**2** Escucha a estas dos personas que acuden a la consulta del médico. Anota los problemas y consejos que se mencionan para cada uno.

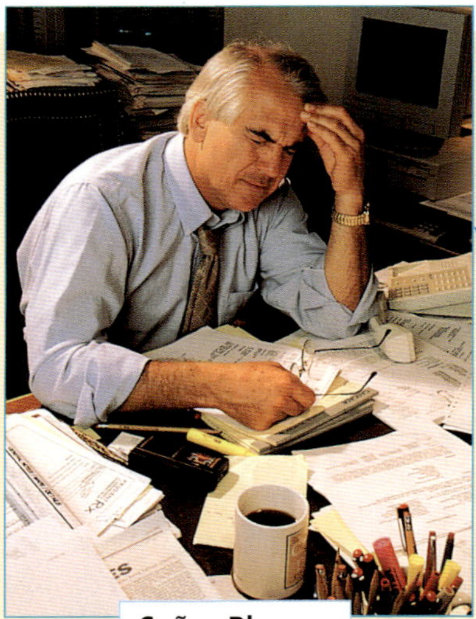

Señor Blanco

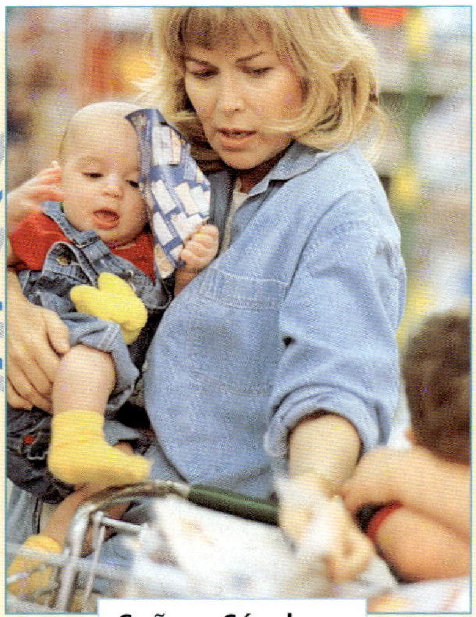

Señora Sánchez

***Problemas***

***a*** *falta de apetito*
***b*** *dolores de cabeza*
***c*** *cansancio, fatiga*
***d*** *falta de concentración*
***e*** *irritabilidad, mal humor*
***f*** *dificultad para dormir bien*
***g*** *dolor de espalda*
***h*** *dolor de estómago*

***Consejos***

***a*** *tomar unos días de descanso*
***b*** *hacer ejercicio físico*
***c*** *recibir sesiones de masaje*
***d*** *nadar*
***e*** *practicar la relajación*
***f*** *cultivar una actividad/pasatiempo*
***g*** *tomar vitaminas*
***h*** *caminar en compañía*

## ¡TIENES LA PALABRA!

**1** Lee *Un día en la vida de Ana.* ¿Crees que Ana padece de estrés? ¿Por qué?

**2** En la consulta del médico. En parejas utiliza la información de *Un día en la vida de Ana* para hacer los papeles de paciente y médico. Ana cuenta sus problemas y el médico debe proponer soluciones.

**3** ¿Es posible vivir sin estrés? Entre toda la clase piensa en técnicas que se pueden aplicar para controlar los niveles de estrés de forma efectiva.

### AMPLÍA TU VOCABULARIO

**la madrugada** las primeras horas de la mañana
**niñera** persona que cuida a niños
**almuerza** come
**disfruta de** goza de
**acuesta** pone a dormir
**se acuesta** va a la cama

### Un día en la vida de Ana

Ana Traveras fue abandonada por su marido. Sola y con una hija de meses, Ana se vio obligada a tener dos trabajos en diferentes panaderías. Su día empieza a las 4 de la mañana y termina a la una de la madrugada. Un día en la vida de Ana es así:

**4:00 a.m.** Toma una ducha.
**4:30** Prepara a la niña para salir.
**5:00** Espera el bus para ir a la casa de la niñera.
**6:00** Deja a la niña.
**6:10** Toma el autobús para ir al trabajo.
**1:00 p.m.** Almuerza.
**4:00** Sale del trabajo.
**5:00** Llega a casa de la niñera. Y disfruta de unos cortos minutos junto a su hija.
**5:15** Espera el bus para ir a su segundo empleo.
**9:30** Sale del trabajo.
**9:40** Toma el bus.
**10:25** Recoge a la niña.
**11:30** Llega a su casa y acuesta a la niña.
**12:00** Hace algo de comer y cena.
**1:00 a.m.** Se acuesta a dormir.

**4** Defiende tu opinión. ¿Estás de acuerdo con las siguientes afirmaciones?

> ***Es bueno tener cierto grado de tensión, puesto que hace nuestro trabajo más interesante y agradable. Por el contrario, la falta de tensión total sólo conduce al aburrimiento.***

> ***El estrés es la enfermedad de la vida moderna.***

> ***El estrés y la tensión nos empujan a crear, a mejorarnos y tener éxito.***

## POR ESCRITO

**1** Escribe un resumen de un día típico en tu vida y anota tus emociones.

| **Hora** | **Actividad** | **Cómo me siento** |
|---|---|---|
| *7a.m.* | *Me levanto* | *¡Fenomenal! Hoy va a ser un gran día.* |

**2** Imagina que eres Ana. Utiliza la información del texto para escribir una redacción sobre los problemas que tienes para trabajar y mantener a tu hija. Describe cómo te sientes y qué te gustaría cambiar en tu vida. (250 palabras)

## PUNTO DE MIRA

¡Ponte a prueba! ¿Cuántas palabras sabes sobre la ropa y los complementos? Clasifica las palabras en las categorías siguientes:

**Mujer**: *falda, bolso...* / **Hombre**: *corbata, americana...* / **Unisex**: *vaqueros, mochila...*

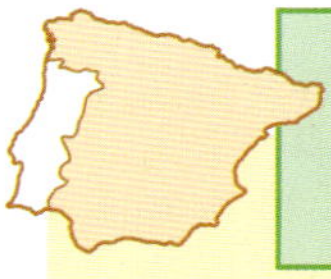

¿Una imagen vale más que mil palabras? Vas a leer una anécdota sobre la experiencia de un hombre que sale a la calle.

# *Zapatos*

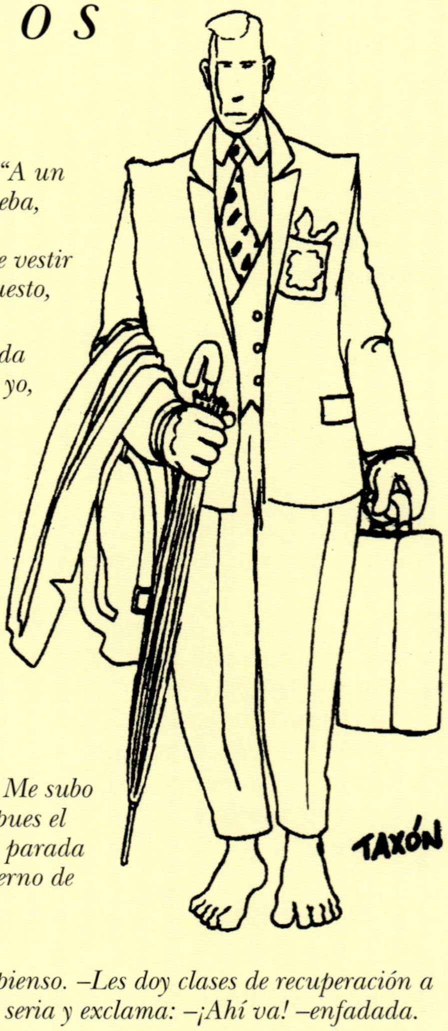


*Decidí, un día, salir sin zapatos a la calle.*

*Y decidí esto porque en una ocasión alguien me dijo: "A un tío sin zapatos no lo quiere nadie". Para hacer la prueba, pues, me afeité, puse gomina en mis cabellos, elegí un elegante pantalón de color café con leche y me acabé de vestir con una camisa blanca planchada para la ocasión y, por supuesto, una fina corbata. Pero sin zapatos.*

*Nada más salir de casa ya noto como todo el mundo se queda mirando. Incluso los que van por la otra acera hasta señalan; yo, ni vuelvo la cabeza: de nunca me ha interesado la gente maleducada.*

*Voy a entrar en una panadería.*

*–Buenos días. ¿Me da un donuts, por favor?*

*Y, dando la vuelta al mostrador, sale el gorila –se trata de un tipo de unos noventa o cien kilos– me coge del hombro y me dice:*

*–¡Mire, váyase, no quiero problemas!*

*–¡Pero si sólo quiero un donuts! ¡Mire, tengo dinero! –le enseño al gorila un billete de mil.*

*Y qué va, el bestia me conmina a salir del establecimiento.*

*Llego hasta una marquesina. Espero al autobús. Ya viene. Me subo no muy convencido; sin embargo, esta vez no tengo problema, pues el conductor ni me ha mirado. Ocupo un asiento. En la próxima parada sube una chica y se sienta a mi lado. Lleva un libro y su cuaderno de apuntes.*

*–Hola, ¿vas a estudiar? –me presento.*

*–Sí –se vuelve y sonríe. "¡Qué bien! Por fin un altruista", pienso. –Les doy clases de recuperación a unos chicos y... –es entonces cuando mira hacia abajo, se pone seria y exclama: –¡Ahí va! –enfadada. Se levanta y se va.*

*Ya no lo puedo soportar más. ¡Cómo es la gente! Tienes la desgracia de no tener zapatos y huyen de ti como de un apestado. No pretendía hacer de esto una cuestión personal, sólo era un experimento. En fin, si no me creéis haced la prueba, pero el que me lo dijo llevaba más razón que un santo: sin zapatos no te quiere nadie.*

## ¿LO HAS ENTENDIDO?

**1** ¿Por qué razón salió a la calle sin zapatos esta persona? ¿Qué quería comprobar?

**2** ¿Cómo describes la forma en que se prepara para salir a la calle?

**a** sin interés especial en su aspecto
**b** cuidadosa, con atención al detalle

**3** ¿Cuál es la primera reacción de la gente en la calle ante su aspecto?

**4** ¿Cuántas veces intenta establecer contacto con otras personas? ¿Cuál es el resultado? ¿Tiene éxito?

**5** ¿Cómo se siente el autor después de esta experiencia?

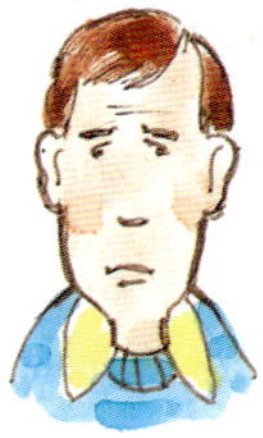

**a** desilusionado y triste

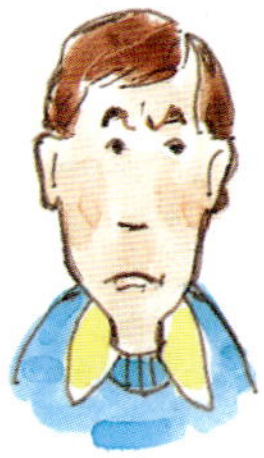

**b** ofendido y enfadado

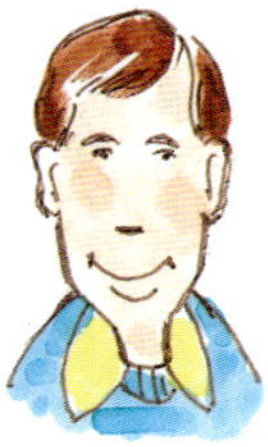

**c** feliz y satisfecho

## TOMA NOTA

Fíjate en estos verbos del texto.

**Verbos pronominales (y reflexivos)**

| | | |
|---|---|---|
| ***me*** *afeité* | ***se*** *sienta* | ***se*** *pone* |
| ***me*** *subo* | ***se*** *vuelve* | ***se*** *levanta* |

Los **verbos pronominales** llevan un pronombre de la misma persona que el sujeto del verbo.

Los **verbos reflexivos** indican que la acción del verbo incide sobre el mismo sujeto. Son fáciles de reconocer porque llevan -***se*** en el infinitivo.

En grupos de cuatro haz una lista de los verbos reflexivos que conoces. Luego, practica los pronombres reflexivos ***me, te, se***. Se debe añadir un nuevo verbo después de la tercera persona (***se***).

*Ejemplo*

Estudiante 1°: *Por las mañanas* ***me despierto*** *y* ***salgo*** *de casa.*

Estudiante 2°: *Por las mañanas* ***te despiertas*** *y* ***sales*** *de casa.*

Estudiante 3°: *Por las mañanas* ***se despierta*** *y* ***sale*** *de casa.*

Estudiante 4°: *Por las mañanas* ***me despierto, me levanto*** *y* ***salgo*** *de casa...*

### AMPLÍA TU VOCABULARIO

**tío/a** (*coloq*) individuo, persona
**gomina** crema para fijar el pelo
**planchada** lisa
**nada más salir** justo al salir
**acera** parte de la calle destinada a los peatones
**me conmina** me obliga
**marquesina** cubierta para la parada del bus
**altruista** humanitario, filántropo
**soportar** tolerar, aguantar
**huyen** escapan
**apestado** infectado de una enfermedad
**llevar más razón que un santo** tener toda la razón, ser correcto en lo que dice

## Y TÚ, ¿CÓMO LO VES?

**1** ¿Qué te parece más importante en una persona? Razona tu respuesta.

**a** su aspecto físico (belleza, atractivo...)
**b** cómo viste (la ropa que lleva)
**c** su personalidad (cómo es de carácter)

**2** ¿Cómo reaccionarías si te encontraras por la calle con una persona sin zapatos o mal vestida?

**3** ¿Qué estilo de ropa prefieres y qué colores te gustan?

## EN LA ONDA

**1** ¿Compras habitualmente ropa
- **a** porque te queda bien y refleja tu personalidad?
- **b** por el prestigio de la marca?
- **c** porque te gusta cambiar de imagen a menudo?

**2** Escucha esta entrevista a una joven actriz española en un estudio de televisión y decide si
- **a** sigue su propio estilo. / es una víctima más de la moda.
- **b** es muy presumida, pasa horas y horas preparándose. / prefiere lo natural, no pierde el tiempo delante del espejo.

**3** En parejas escoge uno de estos papeles.

**Periodista**

Trabajas para una revista de moda. Tienes que entrevistar a una persona famosa sobre su forma de vestir. (Puedes utilizar como modelo las preguntas de la entrevista que acabas de escuchar).

**Personaje famoso**

Un periodista quiere entrevistarte sobre tu forma de vestir. Responde a sus preguntas. (Puedes utilizar como modelo las respuestas de la entrevista que acabas de escuchar).

## ¡TIENES LA PALABRA!

**1** En parejas decide el tipo de ropa que llevarías en cada una de las siguientes situaciones. ¿Qué diferencias de opinión hay entre tu compañero/a y tú?
- **a** primera cita con un chico o una chica
- **b** entrevista de trabajo
- **c** boda familiar
- **d** fiesta de amigos

**Estas palabras te ayudarán a expresarte**

**Estilos**
deportivo
cómodo
informal
sencillo
juvenil

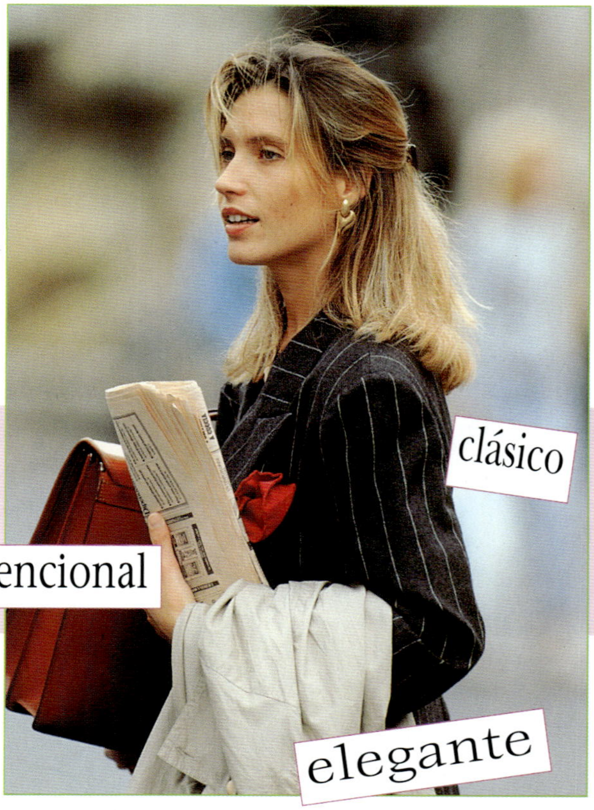


**Escala de colores**

cálidos | vivos | oscuros | claros | llamativos

**2** Lee esta historieta y luego contesta a las preguntas.

**A** Mira el cómic.
¿Te preocupas por tu imagen?
¿Qué haces para cuidarla?
¿Eres presumido/a?

**B** ¿Estás de acuerdo con la conclusión de la historieta?

**C** ¿Es importante la imagen que proyectamos a otras personas? ¿En tu país se da mucha importancia a la imagen externa? ¿De qué forma?

2 *Nina* Grazia Nidasio

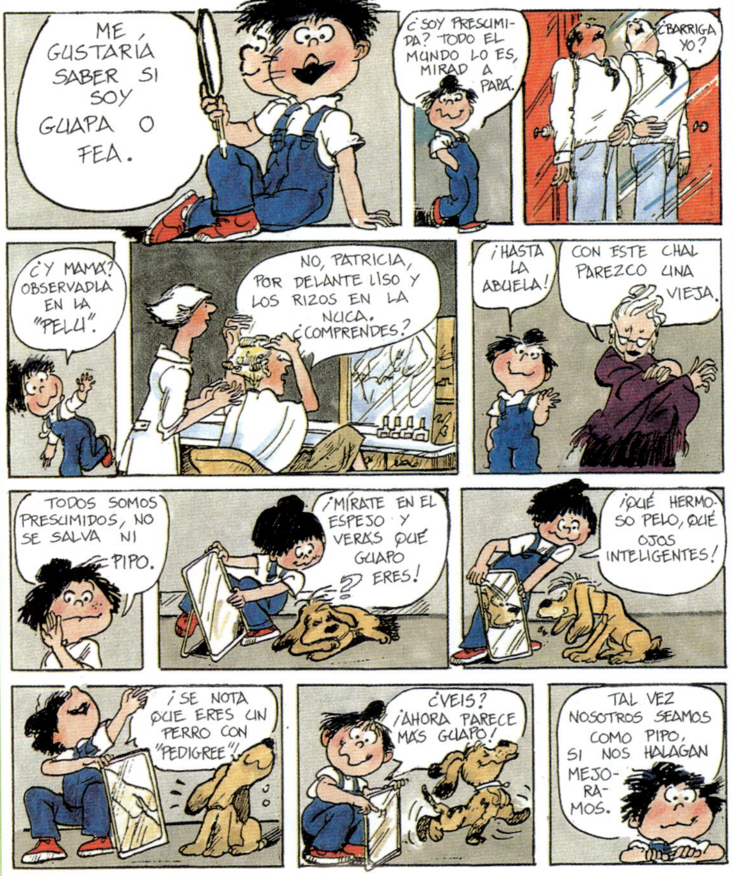


## AMPLÍA TU VOCABULARIO

**presumida** vanidosa
**barriga** estómago
**"pelu"** abreviatura de peluquería
**se nota que** se ve que
**tal vez** probablemente
**halagan** destacan las buenas cualidades de una persona
**mejoramos** nos hacemos mejor

**3** Trabaja en grupos. Cada uno debe defender una de las siguientes opiniones.

> **Hoy vestir con lujo significa exhibir las marcas con la misma pretensión que cuando se conduce un Mercedes.**

*M. Gatel, profesor de Historia de la Moda Contemporánea, Universidad Politécnica, Madrid*

> ***Lo último entre los jóvenes es tener un gran vestuario por poco dinero; poder decir a tus amigos: 'Mira, por 1.000 pesetas he comprado estos pantalones'.***

*Carlos Serrat, diseñador de la firma Crazy de Barcelona dedicada al reciclaje de ropa usada*

## POR ESCRITO

**1** Haz una encuesta entre la gente de tu edad sobre sus gustos de moda y cuidados de la imagen. Prepara un cuestionario de diez preguntas. Escribe las conclusiones en unas líneas.

**2** Escribe un final diferente para *Zapatos* o inventa otra historia similar. (250 palabras)

**3** Escribe un reportaje de moda sobre las tendencias de este año, con fotos de revistas como ilustración. Escoge una temporada. (100/150 palabras)

**a** otoño
**b** invierno
**c** primavera
**d** verano

## PUNTO DE MIRA

¿Cuánto sabes sobre la cultura indígena de América Latina?
Responde a este sencillo cuestionario.

**1** El quechua y el aymará son

- **a** platos típicos de Latinoamérica.
- **b** lenguas habladas por la población indígena.
- **c** instrumentos musicales de los Andes.

**2** Los antiguos habitantes del Perú eran los

- **a** aztecas.
- **b** mayas.
- **c** incas.

**3** Los otavalo son

- **a** una minoría étnica de Ecuador.
- **b** unas montañas famosas.
- **c** un animal en peligro de extinción.

**4** El quetzal es

- **a** un pájaro exótico y símbolo de Guatemala.
- **b** una lengua de los pueblos andinos.
- **c** una bebida alcohólica.

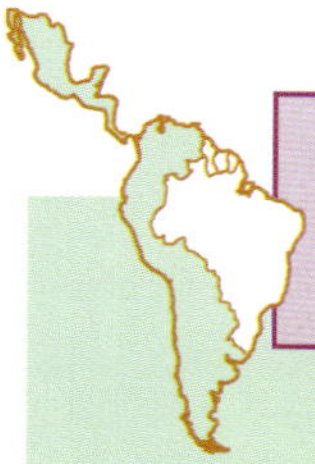

La vida de muchos pueblos indígenas de Latinoamérica es una constante lucha por la supervivencia. Lee el siguiente artículo.

# Wichí: Luchando Por Sobrevivir En Argentina

Durante 90 años, los Wichí han sufrido la invasión gradual de extranjeros en su territorio. Lo que fue una vez una tierra fértil llena de árboles y arbustos se ha convertido en un desierto seco. Junto con otras plantas, varios tipos de animales que los Wichí cazaban han desaparecido. Hoy en día, los Wichí no están en peligro de extinción, pero su forma de vivir tradicional está desapareciendo. Como respuesta los Wichí están organizándose y luchando desesperadamente por asegurar su territorio.

Desde el comienzo del siglo XX, los Wichí han sufrido malos tratos así como serios ataques violentos en que muchos indígenas murieron. Los colonizadores siempre armados, no sólo han introducido enfermedades, sino también ganado que perjudica la tierra frágil y árida de los Wichí.

Son todavía una población numerosa entre 20,000 a 50,000 personas que viven en el sudeste de Bolivia y noreste de Argentina, en una región semiárida conocida como el Chaco. Las comunidades Wichí tienen su propio territorio, pero frecuentemente seis o siete comunidades comparten las regiones. En la sociedad Wichí cada comunidad incluye uno o más clanes, los hombres se van a vivir en la comunidad de su esposa cuando se casan.

Tienen una relación muy estrecha con sus alrededores. Sus casas pequeñas hechas de lodo y ramas se adaptan fácilmente a las altas temperaturas de 50 grados centígrados bajo sombra en el verano. Durante los meses del invierno seco, dependen del pescado. En los veranos húmedos, cultivan maíz, frijol y calabazas que crecen en sus jardines que están protegidos de las invasiones del ganado de los colonizadores con espinas.

Para los Wichí, la desertificación se traduce en hambre debido a que sus recursos tradicionales alimenticios están desapareciendo. Muchas veces los jardines protegidos con espinas son pisoteados por el ganado de los colonizadores.

Como resultado del deterioro del medio ambiente, los criollos están evitando que los indígenas tengan control sobre las pocas tierras productivas que quedan. Les prohiben cazar animales y, en algunos casos, les han negado el acceso a los pozos de agua que son básicos para sobrevivir.

## ¿LO HAS ENTENDIDO?

**1** ¿Qué problemas sufren los Wichí?

**2** ¿Cómo ha cambiado su hábitat? (Tierra, plantas, animales).

**3** ¿Qué consecuencias ha tenido la presencia de colonizadores para los Wichí? Menciona tres.

**4** ¿Dónde viven los Wichí? ¿Cuál es su estructura social?

**5** ¿Cómo construyen sus casas?

**6** ¿Qué problemas crea la desertificación para los Wichí? ¿De qué forma hacen los criollos la vida imposible para los indígenas?

## TOMA NOTA

Fíjate en la estructura.

**Pretérito perfecto = presente de *haber* + participio de pasado**

| | | |
|---|---|---|
| ***he*** **hablado** | ***has*** **comprado** | ***ha*** **estado** |
| ***hemos*** **tenido** | ***habéis*** **leído** | ***han*** **salido** |

El pretérito perfecto es una forma verbal compuesta. Describe una acción completa y terminada que se inicia en el pasado pero que continúa en el momento actual. Busca los ejemplos en el artículo.

En parejas practica el pretérito perfecto. Responde negativamente a las preguntas.

*Ejemplo*

*¿Te* ***has levantado*** *pronto esta mañana?*
*No, me* ***he levantado*** *tarde.*

**A** ¿Has ido al colegio/a la oficina en autobús?

**B** ¿Habéis llegado pronto a la conferencia?

**C** ¿Han comido ustedes carne?

**D** ¿Ha leído Luis el periódico?

**E** ¿Han trabajado mucho Roberto y Cristina hoy?

## AMPLÍA TU VOCABULARIO

**lo que fue una vez** lo que antes era
**arbustos** plantas de poca altura
**asegurar** establecer
**ganado** animales
**perjudica** hace daño, destruye
**árida** muy seca
**clanes** grupos sociales formados por familias
**lodo** barro, mezcla de tierra y agua
**frijol** (*Am Lat*) judía, planta legumbre
**calabazas** frutos secos y redondos
**espinas** pinchos que sirven de protección
**pisoteados** destruidos
**deterioro** pérdida de calidad
**criollos** colonizadores, descendientes de europeos
**cazar** capturar animales salvajes
**les han negado** les han prohibido
**pozos** perforación en la tierra que contiene agua

## Y TÚ, ¿CÓMO LO VES?

**1** Ser solidario implica concienciarse de los problemas que sufren los más necesitados y ayudar. ¿Eres solidario/a? ¿Te preocupas por los problemas y derechos de las personas más necesitadas y vulnerables? ¿Realizas algún tipo de trabajo social voluntario? (Cuidar ancianos, colaborar en campañas de concienciación...).

**2** ¿Hay minorías étnicas en tu país? ¿Cuáles son? ¿Dónde viven? ¿Cómo son sus condiciones de vida? ¿Sufren problemas de discriminación y racismo?

**3** Cada año desaparece un pueblo indígena. ¿Crees que es importante preservar las culturas tradicionales de estos pueblos? ¿Por qué? ¿Qué relación tienen ellos con la tierra y la naturaleza? ¿Es diferente de nuestra relación?

## EN LA ONDA

**1** ¿Te gustan los objetos hechos a mano? ¿Qué objetos tienes en casa? (De decoración, ropa, joyas, muebles...). ¿Conoces la artesanía de Latinoamérica?

**2** ¿Compras artesanía porque
- **a** la coleccionas?
- **b** quieres ayudar a los pueblos indígenas?
- **c** te parece un regalo original y atractivo?

**3** Escucha a esta chica en una tienda de artesanía indígena de Latinoamérica. Mira las fotos y relaciona los nombres con los objetos. Después escucha otra vez la conversación y anota para cada objeto la información que oigas.

**Quitapenas – retablo – tumi – joyas/adornos**

**A**

*Nombre:*
*País:*
*Materiales:*
*Se usa para:*

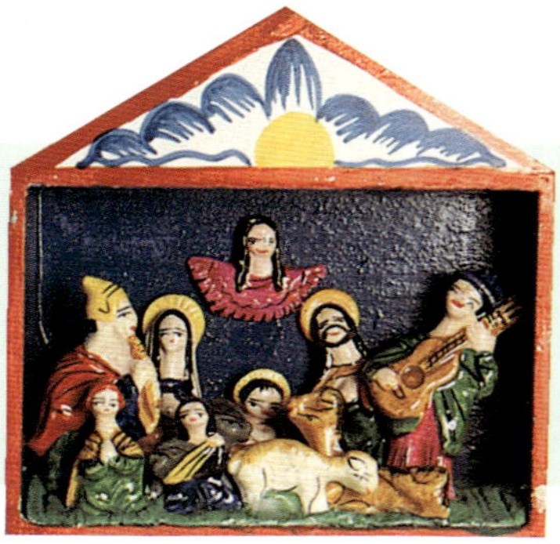

**C**

*Nombre:*
*País:*
*Materiales:*
*Se usa para:*

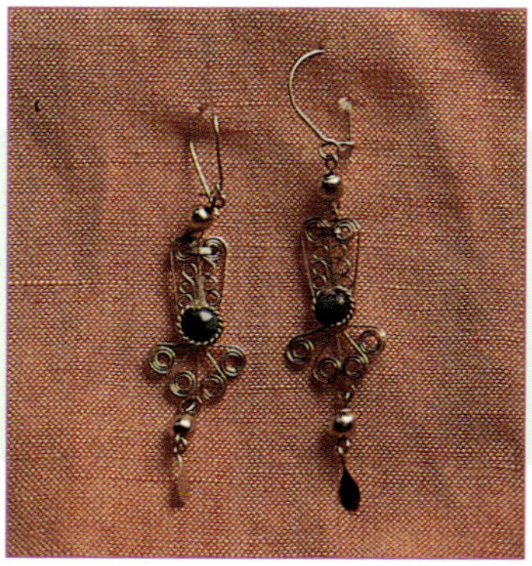

**B**

*Nombre:*
*País:*
*Materiales:*
*Se usa para:*

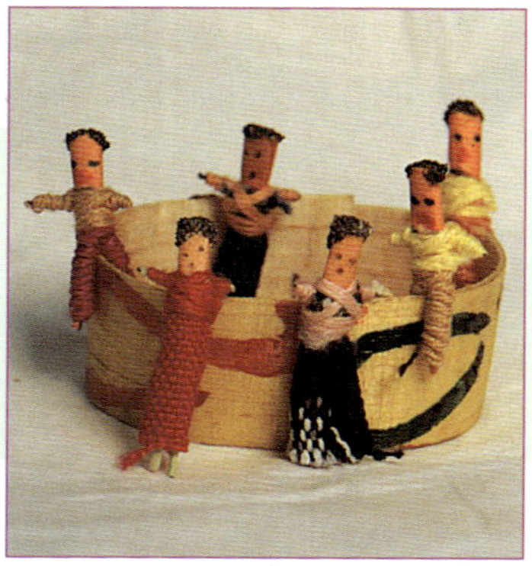

**D**

*Nombre:*
*País:*
*Materiales:*
*Se usa para:*

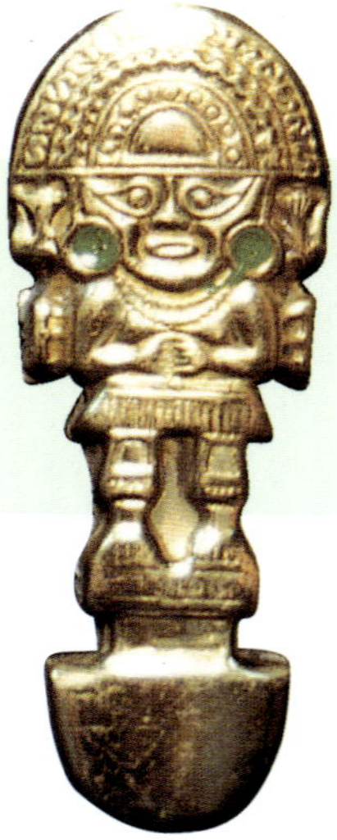

## ¡TIENES LA PALABRA!

**1** Entre toda la clase comenta tus opiniones sobre estos temas.

**Hay tiendas de comercio justo y equitativo con diferentes grupos del tercer mundo. ¿Qué ventajas tiene comprar en esas tiendas? ¿Existen en tu país? ¿Qué cosas se pueden comprar? ¿Crees que debería haber más establecimientos como éstos? ¿Por qué?**

**¿Puedes nombrar alguna organización humanitaria? ¿En qué consiste su trabajo? ¿Qué organizaciones existen en tu país? ¿Colaboras con alguna de ellas?**

**2** En grupos cada uno representa a un pueblo amenazado. Explica los problemas que sufren y defiende sus derechos. Intenta proponer soluciones.

**Quechuas**

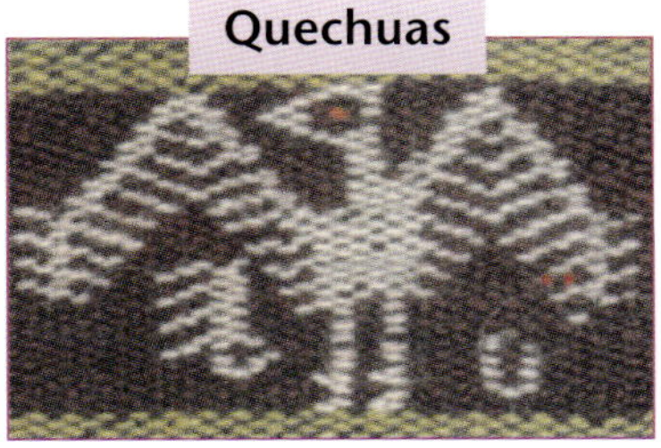

***País***: Perú y Bolivia

***Idioma***: quechua. Son descendientes de los antiguos incas

***Formas de vida***: agricultores y pastores

***Problemas***: sufren la invasión de sus tierras, racismo y destrucción de su cultura

**Yanomamis**

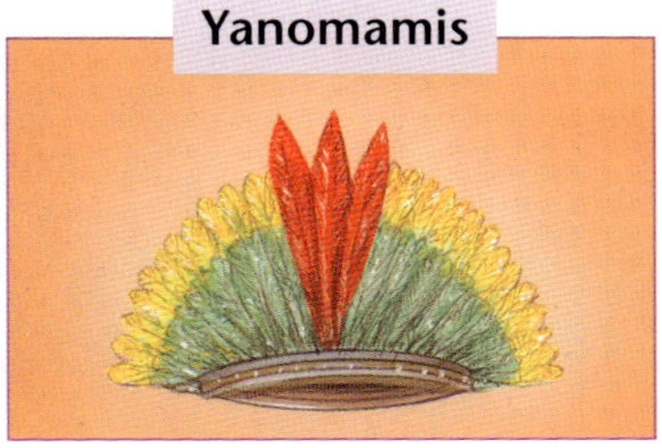

***País***: Venezuela y Brasil. Viven en la selva amazónica

***Formas de vida***: recolectan frutos, cultivan la tierra, cazan y pescan

***Problemas***: están amenazados por la deforestación de la selva amazónica y los buscadores de oro que contaminan sus ríos

**Mayas**

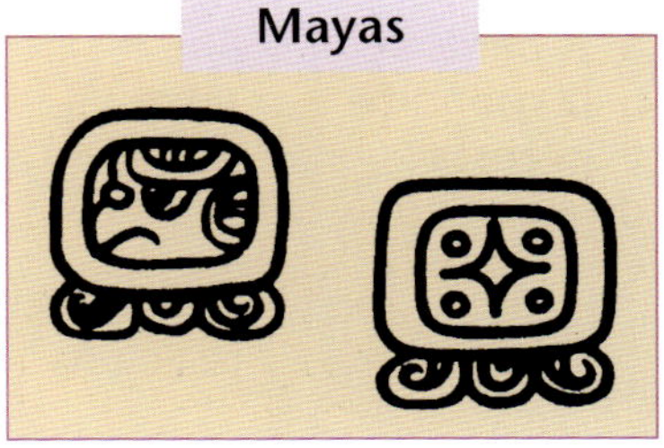

***País***: México y Guatemala. Son descendientes directos de los antiguos mayas, hoy forman más de la mitad de la población de Guatemala

***Formas de vida***: campesinos

***Problemas***: están amenazados por la pérdida de sus tierras y la destrucción de su cultura

**3** Pobreza, hambre, injusticia, guerra, racismo, xenofobia.... ¿Qué podemos hacer para cambiar y mejorar la sociedad en que vivimos? En grupos piensa en soluciones para estos problemas.

- escribir cartas a gente importante (presidentes...) o a los periódicos.
- hacerse socio de una *ONG* -una *Organización No Gubernamental* (independiente)- que da ayuda efectiva a quien lo necesita.
- colaborar en campañas de concienciación de la sociedad en tu ciudad/comunidad/colegio.
- formar/unirse a un grupo de presión a favor de los derechos humanos.
- recaudar dinero para las personas/los países necesitados.
- no comprar cosas que explotan comercialmente a las personas/los recursos naturales de esos países.
- comprar café, artesanía, etc. en tiendas de comercio justo.

## POR ESCRITO

**1** Escribe una carta al gobierno de Argentina/Bolivia para protestar sobre la situación de los Wichí. Pide que se defiendan sus derechos. Utiliza la información del artículo para ayudarte. Aquí tienes un modelo de carta.

**2** Eres periodista. Prepara un informe sobre las condiciones de vida de un pueblo indígena de Latinoamérica (historia, formas de vida, comida, cultura, costumbres e idioma). Utiliza fotos y gráficos como ilustración. Si lo prefieres, escribe sobre una minoría étnica de tu país.

*Señor Presidente:*

*Le escribo para llamar su atención sobre* _____ *.*
*Los* _____ *llevan mucho tiempo soportando* _____ *por parte de* _____ *.*

*Le recuerdo que es un grave atentado contra los derechos humanos y una clara amenaza para la supervivencia de* _____ *.*

*Atentamente le saluda,*

## PUNTO DE MIRA

¿Cuál es tu lugar ideal para vivir? ¿Por qué?

**a** el campo
**b** la montaña
**c** la costa
**d** la ciudad
**e** el pueblo

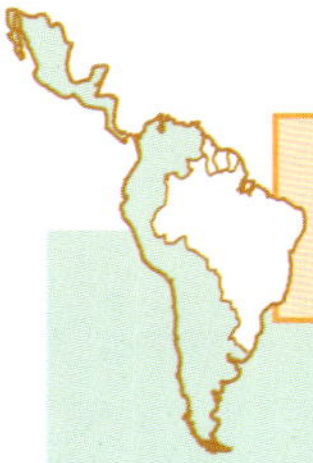

Algunas ciudades tienen un encanto y atractivo especial. Lee este artículo sobre una de ellas.

# La ciudad infinita

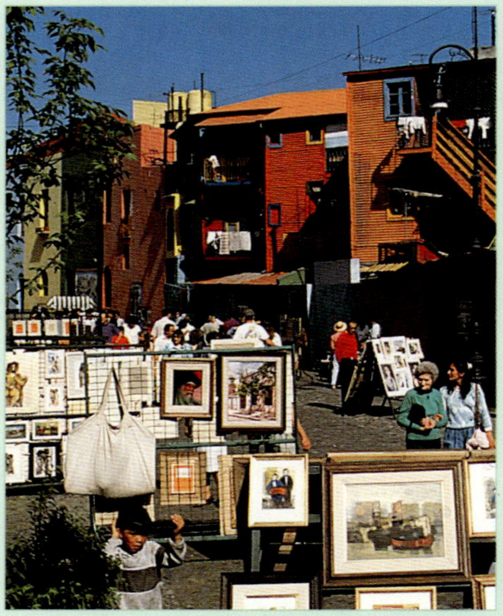

Nunca duerme esta urbe nacida del tango y la alegría, amante del arte y la modernidad. Se enorgullece de ser la más europea de las ciudades hispanoamericanas, pero bañada con un acento peculiar y genuinamente hispano.

Polifacética, privilegiada, ambiciosa, rica y extrovertida. Esta gran urbe cosmopolita es, para residentes y visitantes, una ciudad entrañable. Sobre la Pampa, a orillas del Río de la Plata, todo en ella trasluce la herencia europea.

El pequeño rincón francés de las calles *Arroyo*, *Alvear* o de *Plaza San Martín*, el aire italiano que se respira caminando por aceras adoquinadas de La Boca o el entusiasmo español que rezuman los restaurantes o cafés de la *Avenida de Mayo*. Elegante, colonial o posmoderna, misteriosa e infinita, nos atrae.

Los porteños, hombres y mujeres, son como la urbe que habitan. Apasionados, buenos conversadores, vanidosos y seductores, les encanta mirar y ser mirados. Pasear por Buenos Aires es encontrarse a cada paso con una nueva representación de la ciudad y de su gente.

Hablar de Buenos Aires es hablar del aire de vitalidad que se respira en todos sus rincones, del ritmo cosmopolita en las calles, del bullicio con que se acoge a la noche y sus promesas. Los jardines y palmeras de la *Plaza de Mayo*, el centro vivo de la ciudad, testigo de los hechos históricos más importantes del país, compiten con la exótica arboleda de la *Plaza San Martín*, una de las zonas más atractivas y elegantes, por las que pasan todas las personalidades internacionales. Aquí siempre se tiene la sensación de que no alcanza el tiempo y de que dos ojos son pocos para ver todo lo que se desea.

## ¿LO HAS ENTENDIDO?

1 ¿Dónde está situada Buenos Aires?

2 ¿Cómo se llaman los habitantes de Buenos Aires? ¿Cómo son?

3 ¿Qué ofrece la ciudad a las personas que viven en ella?

4 ¿Cómo es la Plaza de San Martín?

5 ¿Qué impresión general tienes de Buenos Aires?

- **a** un lugar poco interesante y aburrido
- **b** una ciudad alegre, atractiva y llena de vida
- **c** una ciudad moderna y europea

## TOMA NOTA

Fíjate en esta frase.

*__Nadar__ es un buen ejercicio para la espalda.*

El infinitivo se utiliza en español como sujeto de una oración. Hay dos ejemplos en el artículo. Búscalos.

**1** Relaciona las frases de estas dos columnas.

- **A** Ser tolerante
- **B** Beber mucha agua
- **C** Proteger las especies en peligro
- **D** Independizarse de los padres
- **E** Vivir en el campo
- **F** Ir a la universidad

- **1** es el objetivo de esta organización ecologista.
- **2** es difícil para los jóvenes sin trabajo.
- **3** te ayuda a mejorar tu educación.
- **4** resulta más tranquilo que vivir en la ciudad.
- **5** significa respetar las opiniones de los demás.
- **6** es bueno para la salud.

**2** Completa estas frases con tus propias ideas.

- **A** Viajar...
- **B** Estudiar idiomas...
- **C** Vivir en una gran ciudad...
- **D** Hacer ejercicio...
- **E** Ver la televisión...
- **F** Comprar en las rebajas...

### AMPLÍA TU VOCABULARIO

**urbe** ciudad
**se enorgullece** se siente orgullosa de
**polifacética** que ofrece muchas cosas
**entrañable** afectuosa, cariñosa
**a orillas de** situada al lado de
**trasluce** refleja
**herencia** legado cultural, influencia
**rincón** lugar pequeño
**aceras adoquinadas** parte de la calle destinada a los peatones cubierta de piedras rectangulares
**rezuman** poseen, transpiran
**porteños** habitantes de Buenos Aires
**bullicio** animación, ruido de mucha gente
**se acoge** se recibe
**no alcanza** no es suficiente

## Y TÚ, ¿CÓMO LO VES?

1 En tu país, ¿en qué tipo de vivienda prefiere vivir la gente?

- **a** en un piso
- **b** en bloques de apartamentos
- **c** en casas con jardín
- **d** en un bungaló

2 ¿Cómo es tu vivienda? ¿Qué es lo que más te gusta del lugar donde vives? ¿Y lo que menos? ¿Qué cambiarías? ¿Cómo es para ti la casa perfecta?

3 ¿En qué ciudad del mundo te gustaría vivir? ¿Por qué?

4 Para ti, ¿dónde hay más calidad de vida, en la ciudad o en el campo? ¿Por qué?

## EN LA ONDA

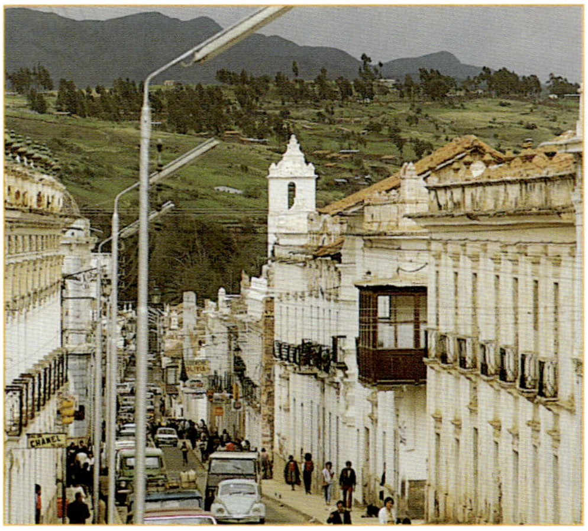

**1** ¿Qué aspectos te parecen más importantes en una ciudad/un pueblo? Pon estos factores en orden de preferencia.

**a** el clima/estar cerca del mar o la montaña
**b** la oferta cultural y actividades de ocio
**c** la seguridad ciudadana
**d** los espacios verdes/zonas peatonales
**e** la arquitectura y buen desarrollo urbanístico
**f** la red de transporte y comunicaciones
**g** el precio de la vivienda (compra y alquiler)
**h** la tranquilidad y la paz

**2** ¿Verdadero o falso? Escucha la conversación entre Miguel, un chico de Barcelona, y su amigo mexicano, Alejandro. Decide si estas afirmaciones son verdaderas o falsas.

**A** Es la segunda vez que Alejandro visita Barcelona.
**B** A Alejandro le interesa el arte.
**C** A Miguel le gusta vivir junto al mar.
**D** Los mexicanos llaman a Ciudad de México el DC.
**E** En la capital mexicana los turistas no son bienvenidos.
**F** Para Miguel vivir en la ciudad no es positivo.
**G** Según Alejandro hay más problemas sociales en la ciudad.
**H** A Miguel le gusta escaparse de la vida urbana a veces.

**3** En parejas habla con tu compañero/a de estos temas.

**A** ¿Qué te gusta de tu pueblo/ciudad?
**B** ¿Qué aspectos positivos/negativos tiene?
**C** ¿Qué hace la gente en el tiempo libre?
**D** ¿Qué atracciones tiene para el visitante?

## ¡TIENES LA PALABRA!

**1** En parejas mira los anuncios de *Inmobiliaria Hicasa* y escoge uno de estos papeles.

### Cliente

Por tus estudios/trabajo vas a vivir a una ciudad de habla española. Necesitas alquilar un piso. Prepara una lista de todo lo que necesitas y de las condiciones (depósito, alquiler mínimo...). Pide más información al encargado de la inmobiliaria.

### Agente inmobiliario

Tienes varios apartamentos que pueden interesar a tu cliente. Inventa el resto de la información (precio...) para responder a las preguntas del cliente. Explícale las condiciones y pregunta cuándo quiere verlos.

**INMOBILIARIA HICASA**

Se alquila apartamento céntrico. 2 habitaciones, baño, sala-comedor, cocina equipada, balcón y ascensor. Totalmente amueblado. $50m^2$. Precio negociable.

Apto. para alquilar en el barrio de Granada. Aparcamiento, antena parabólica, teléfono, 2 dormitorios, baño, cocina, sala. Espacioso. Amueblado completamente. Buen precio.

Apartamento soleado, zona tranquila residencial con piscina, $110\ m^2$. Excelente estado, quinto piso. 3 habitaciones, sala-comedor, cocina, baño, terraza. Sin amueblar. Alquiler mínimo 6 meses.

**2** En grupos observa y lee el cómic. Luego contesta a las preguntas.

**A** Describe brevemente la escena.

**B** ¿Qué efecto pretende conseguir el director de la oficina? ¿Crees que el resto de los empleados tiene la misma opinión? ¿Por qué?

**C** Neurosis, estrés, ansia.... ¿Qué efectos negativos tiene vivir en una gran ciudad?

**D** ¿Cómo podemos hacer la vida en las grandes ciudades más soportable y agradable?

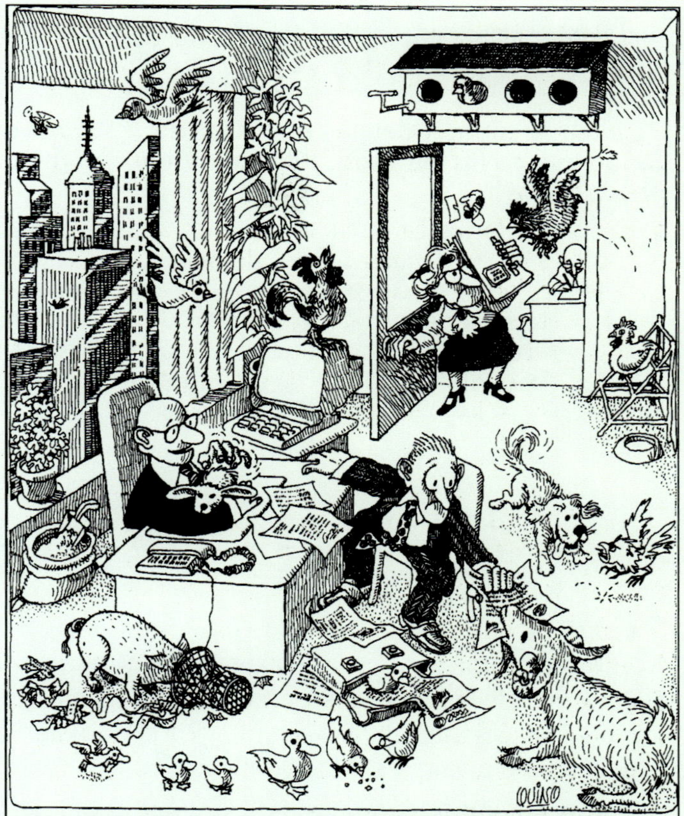


–SI, CLARO, NO ES COMO VIVIR EN EL CAMPO, PERO NO ME DIRÁ QUE EN MEDIO DE TODA LA LOCURA, EL ANSIA, LA NEUROSIS Y EL STRESS QUE PRODUCE LA CIUDAD, TRAER UN POCO DE ESTA SERENA PAZ RURAL NO LE CALMA EL ESPÍRITU A CUALQUIERA.

### AMPLÍA TU VOCABULARIO

**locura** estado de loco, alienación
**ansia** preocupación, agitación
**paz** tranquilidad
**rural** del campo
**calma** tranquiliza
**cualquiera** cualquier persona

**3** Entre toda la clase comenta tus opiniones sobre estos temas.

**¿Crees que algún día será posible vivir en el espacio, en la Luna o en algún otro planeta?**

**¿Cómo te imaginas la ciudad del futuro?**

**¿Cómo será la casa del futuro? ¿Estará todo controlado por computador? ¿Qué ventajas tendría vivir en una casa cibernética?**

## POR ESCRITO

**1** ¿Cómo sería tu vivienda ideal? Describe la casa de tus sueños. Incluye información sobre su localización, las habitaciones, la decoración y todo lo que sea importante. (200 palabras)

**2** Describe detalladamente el lugar donde vives: el tipo de vivienda, el ambiente, la gente, la calidad de vida y las actividades culturales que hay. (250-300 palabras)

**3** ¿Campo o ciudad? Escribe sobre las ventajas e inconvenientes de vivir en una gran ciudad y vivir en un pueblo. (250 palabras)

| **Ciudad** | **Pueblo** |
| --- | --- |
| *pros/contras* | *pros/contras* |

## PUNTO DE MIRA

1 ¿Te interesa conocer detalles de la vida de tus ídolos y de los famosos? ¿Qué te gusta saber de ellos?

2 ¿Te gusta hojear o leer las revistas del corazón? ¿Por qué?

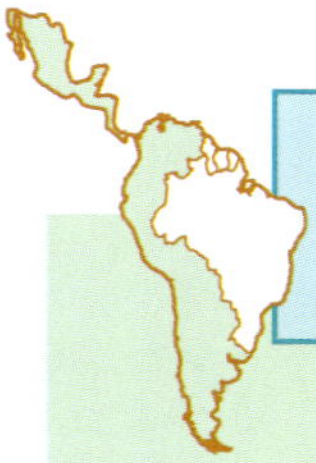

La vida de los ricos y famosos despierta el interés y la atención de mucha gente. Pero, ¿es también un negocio millonario? Lee el siguiente artículo.

# PAPARAZZI

Como los vampiros, viven al acecho de su presa. Se ocultan, se disfrazan de meseros, policías o enfermeros, pasan 24 horas sin dormir, vigilando la entrada o salida de algún famoso, y hasta se cuelgan de un helicóptero, cámara en mano, pues no les importa arriesgar la vida si obtienen *la* foto. Unos se especializan en la realeza. Otros persiguen a los políticos. Son los *paparazzi*.

Con sus cámaras fotográficas o de vídeo, y sus lentes de largo alcance, persiguen y asaltan a las celebridades. "Nuestra meta es conseguir la imagen más caliente o comprometedora", dice un fotógrafo de un semanario sensacionalista. "La foto te puede reportar ganancias de hasta seis figuras". Es por eso que los "vampiros del lente" ya no se limitan a perseguir la noticia; ahora la *fabrican*.

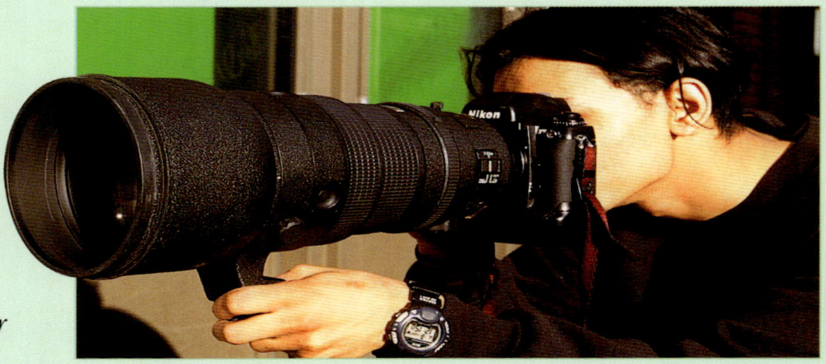


Hasta el momento los tribunales han fallado *a favor* de las víctimas del acoso. En Francia y otros países de Europa, así como en muchos de América Latina, el derecho a la protección de la vida privada figura en la legislación nacional. Sin embargo, en Inglaterra y Estados Unidos no es así.

Un caso que demuestra exactamente hasta qué punto son capaces de llegar los "vampiros del lente" es el del Príncipe Felipe de España y Gigi Howard. Cuando una revista española descubrió que el príncipe se veía con Howard, montó una prodigiosa cacería que, partiendo de España, llegó a la isla de San Martín, continuó a Miami y culminó en Nueva York, donde un grupo de detectives privados se dedicó a vigilar la residencia de Howard. Fotos de los jóvenes en la playa despertaron el interés de otras revistas... Y el asunto estalló cuando se descubrió que habían estado interceptando llamadas del teléfono de la joven. El periodista español Carlos Hugo Arriazu fue condenado en un tribunal de Nueva York a seis meses de prisión. Al justificar su decisión, el juez afirmó que "la privacidad de la joven y el código ético de la profesión periodística fueron violados por el acusado".

## ¿LO HAS ENTENDIDO?

**1** ¿Qué son los *paparazzi* y cuál es su objetivo?

**2** ¿Con quién se compara a los *paparazzi*?

**3** ¿Qué hacen para obtener las fotos de los famosos?

**4** ¿En qué países es ley el derecho a la protección de la vida privada? ¿En qué países no lo es?

**5** ¿A quién perseguía Carlos Hugo Arriazu? ¿Cómo terminó todo?

## TOMA NOTA

Fíjate en la estructura.

| ***Ser*** **(pretérito indefinido)** + | **participio de pasado** | | |
|---|---|---|---|
| ***fui*** | *entrevistado/a* | ***fuimos*** | *acosados/as* |
| ***fuiste*** | *examinado/a* | ***fuisteis*** | *arrestados/as* |
| ***fue*** | *preguntado/a* | ***fueron*** | *perseguidos/as* |

Se utiliza esta estructura verbal para formar el pretérito de la voz pasiva. La voz pasiva indica un cambio de énfasis en la frase. Hay dos ejemplos de esta estructura en *Paparazzi*. Búscalos.

**1** Completa estas frases con el pretérito indefinido de ***ser*** y el participio de pasado.

**A** El *paparazzo* _____ (***ser*** + ***arrestar***) por acosar a su víctima.

**B** La guapa modelo _____ (***ser*** + ***descubrir***) cuando tenía sólo 13 años.

**C** Los atracadores del banco _____ (***ser*** + ***perseguir***) por la policía.

**2** Transforma estas frases de activa a pasiva. Haz todos los cambios necesarios.

**A** El jurado galardonó la película con el premio a la mejor dirección y fotografía.

**B** El actor demandó al periodista por intrusión en la vida privada.

**C** El profesor castigó a sus alumnos sin recreo por llegar tarde.

### AMPLÍA TU VOCABULARIO

**al acecho de** vigilando
**presa** víctima
**se disfrazan de** se visten de
**meseros** (*Am Lat*) personas que sirven las mesas en bares y restaurantes; camareros (*Esp*)
**se cuelgan de** se suspenden de
**arriesgar** poner en peligro
**la realeza** la familia real
**meta** objetivo
**semanario** publicación semanal, revista
**reportar ganancias** dar beneficios económicos
**acoso** persecución
**cacería** persecución
**estalló** explotó
**fueron violados** fueron infringidos

## Y TÚ, ¿CÓMO LO VES?

**1** Los *paparazzi* son capaces de cualquier cosa con tal de obtener una foto indiscreta. ¿Qué opinas de su trabajo? ¿Qué consecuencias tienen sus acciones? Si fueras un famoso, ¿cómo reaccionarías ante ellos?

**2** ¿Qué atracción tiene leer las revistas del corazón y ver los programas de televisión donde se cuentan las intimidades y escándalos de los famosos? ¿Por qué hay tanto interés por la vida de estas personas? ¿Crees que es un gran negocio? ¿A quién beneficia?

**3** Hablar de los demás, lo que se conoce también como el "cotilleo" o "chisme", es una costumbre normal en nuestra sociedad. ¿Por qué le gusta a la gente cotillear? En tu opinión, ¿quiénes son más cotillas, los hombres o las mujeres?

## EN LA ONDA

**1** Hay distintos tipos de publicaciones: revistas, periódicos, semanarios.... ¿Cuál prefieres leer y por qué? Da ejemplos concretos sobre publicaciones en tu país que te gustan.

- de interés político
- de actualidad
- de economía
- de deportes
- de informática/computación
- de música
- de cine
- de fotografía
- de belleza y moda
- del corazón

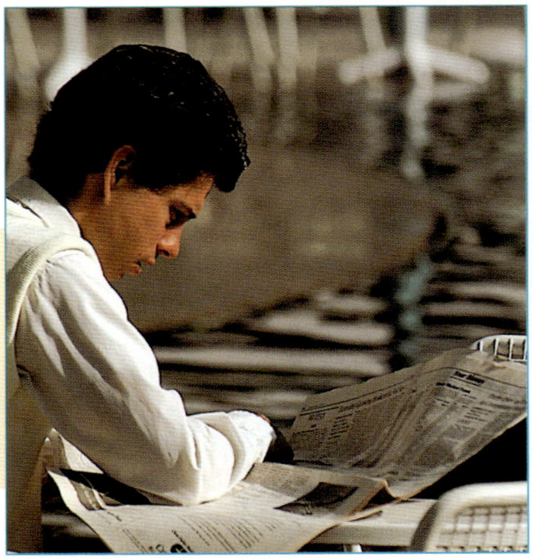

**2** Escucha a dos amigos, Guadalupe y Miguel, que se encuentran casualmente en el vestíbulo del *Hotel Continental*. Completa con toda la información apropiada.

**A** Miguel está en el hotel porque tiene que _____ .

**B** Miguel estudió _____ en la universidad y fue _____ del _____ . Ahora trabaja para _____ .

**C** Para ser un buen periodista hay que tener _____ y saber _____ .

**D** A Miguel le gusta su trabajo porque es _____ y le ofrece la oportunidad de _____ .

**E** Un aspecto negativo de su profesión es que es _____ .

**F** Los fotógrafos hacen su trabajo para satisfacer _____ .

**G** Los famosos son _____ . La explotación de sus vidas se ha convertido en un _____ .

**H** A la gente le gusta hablar de los famosos porque es un modo de _____ .

## ¡TIENES LA PALABRA!

**1** En grupos de tres observa las portadas de estas publicaciones y decide de qué tipo son (de cultura, políticas, económicas, del corazón, deportivas, para jóvenes...).

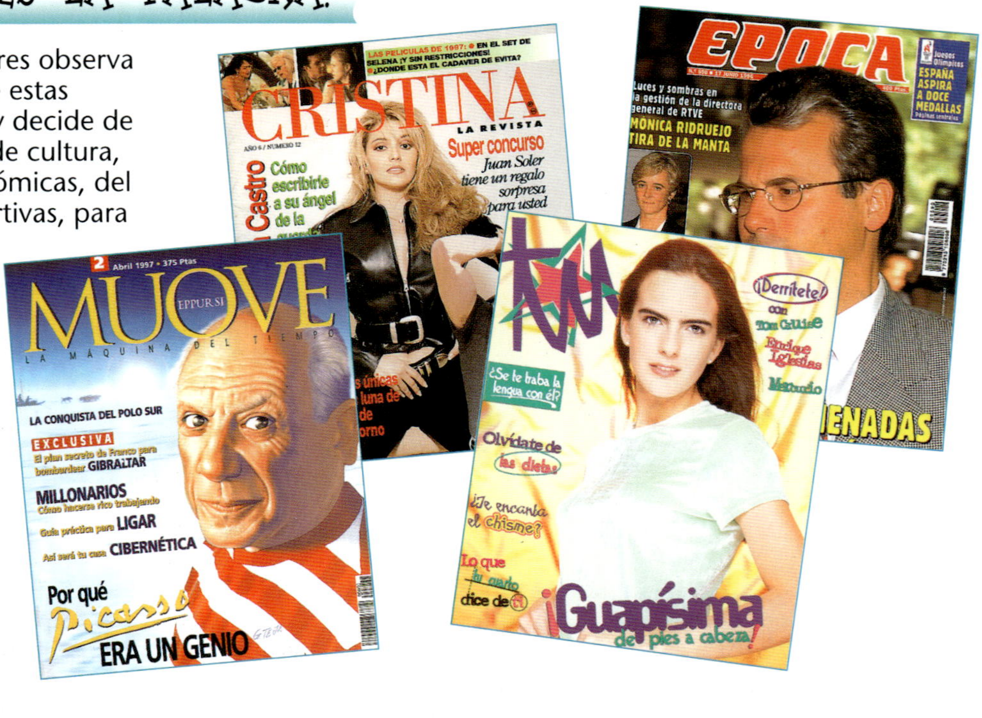

**2** Entre toda la clase comenta tus opiniones sobre estos temas.

¿Tiene la prensa demasiado poder?

¿Qué responsabilidad y función tienen los medios de comunicación ante la sociedad?

¿Dónde debe estar el límite entre información y privacidad? ¿Qué leyes hay en tu país sobre este tema?

¿Por qué la prensa sensacionalista es un gran negocio? ¿Es la ley de la oferta y la demanda?

**3** Se divide la clase en dos grupos, **los famosos** y **los *paparazzi***, para defender el tema *Derecho a la vida privada, ¿sí o no?*

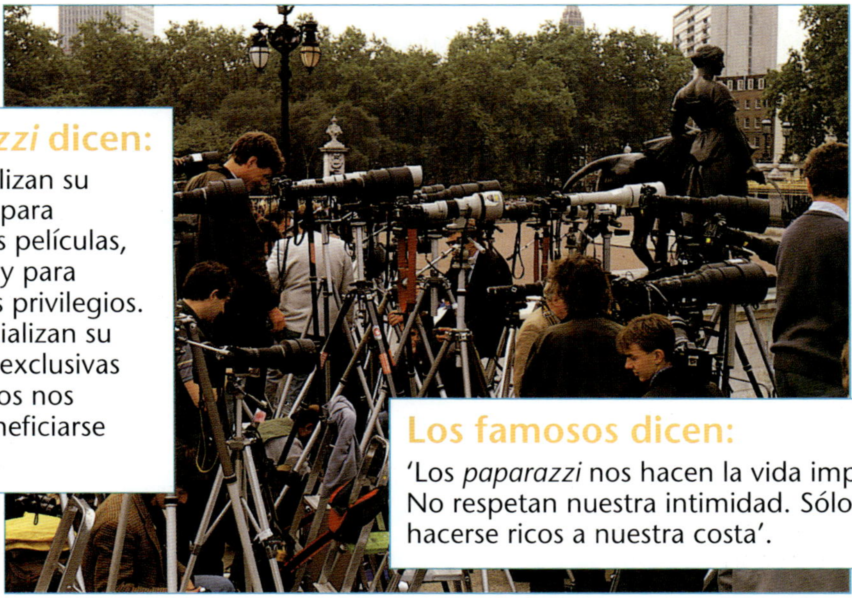

### Los *paparazzi* dicen:

'Los famosos utilizan su imagen pública para promocionar sus películas, sus canciones... y para obtener muchos privilegios. Algunos comercializan su vida vendiendo exclusivas a las revistas. Ellos nos utilizan para beneficiarse personalmente'.

### Los famosos dicen:

'Los *paparazzi* nos hacen la vida imposible. No respetan nuestra intimidad. Sólo buscan hacerse ricos a nuestra costa'.

## POR ESCRITO

**1** Escribe una lista de las diferencias entre la prensa seria y la sensacionalista. Da ejemplos de publicaciones de tu país.

| Título | Formato | Contenido | Tipo de lector |
|---|---|---|---|
| | | | |

**2** *"Periodista condenado a seis meses de cárcel"*. Elabora la noticia de este titular. (150-200 palabras)

**3** Muchos jóvenes sueñan con ser periodistas. ¿Qué atractivos e inconvenientes tiene esta profesión para ti y qué medio informativo prefieres? (prensa escrita, radio, televisión...).

## PUNTO DE MIRA

**1** ¡Ponte a prueba! Anota todos los medios de transporte que conozcas en estos tres grupos:
**Por tierra:** bicicleta... / **Por agua:** canoa... / **Por aire:** globo...
¿Cuál es tu medio de transporte favorito?

**2** ¿Qué entiendes por
**a** turismo cultural?
**b** turismo verde/rural o ecoturismo?
**c** turismo de masas?

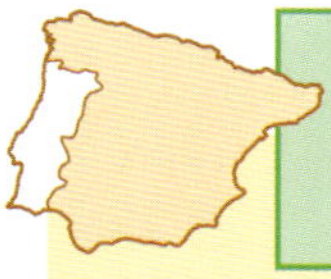

Viajar amplía nuestros horizontes y enriquece nuestras mentes. Vas a leer un texto sobre la otra cara del turismo.

# Turistas en masa

## Los nuevos conquistadores arrasan pueblos enteros

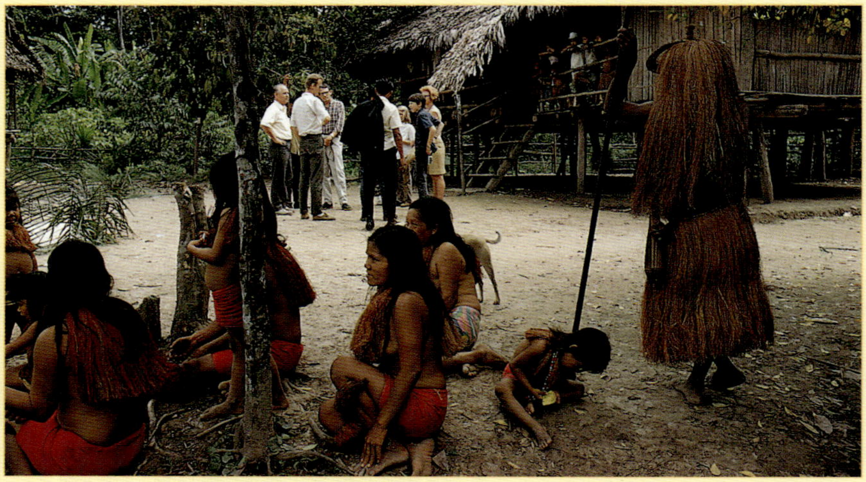

El turismo será la mayor industria mundial antes de fin de siglo. Cada año se realizan alrededor de 500 millones de viajes que producen enormes beneficios. Según la Organización Mundial del Turismo, unos 118 millones de personas viven de esta industria.

Semejante monstruo no se detiene ante nada ni ante nadie. Tras haber exprimido las buenas condiciones turísticas de los países ricos buscan ahora los lugares más remotos, donde pueden encontrar algo distinto a lo cotidiano: otros países, otra naturaleza, otros pueblos.

Los maka de Paraguay, por ejemplo, eran un grupo indígena nómada del Chaco, con una rica cultura.

Ahora viven atrapados en una reserva-islote de 335 hectáreas. Con la pérdida de sus tierras y su progresiva dependencia del turismo, han olvidado muchos de sus antiguos conocimientos.

Para complacer a los turistas, las jóvenes se pintan la cara con pinturas de guerra hechas con lápiz de labios. Como ésta hay mil historias patéticas que demuestran hasta qué punto el turismo puede ser la nueva versión de las conquistas de siglos pasados, que arrasaron pueblos enteros.

La organización Survival International, de ayuda a los pueblos indígenas, está desarrollando una campaña para dar a conocer el enorme impacto del turismo masivo. Para Survival, "la palabra clave es control; los pueblos indígenas no sólo tienen derecho a sus tierras, sino también a decidir lo que pase en ellas".

Pero hay otras maneras de que el turismo se acerque a los pueblos indígenas. En Australia, los aborígenes de Queensland del Norte son los guías turísticos dentro de sus reservas.

Algunos pueblos indígenas deciden voluntariamente mostrar su cultura para compartir con personas de otros países sus problemas o su identidad amenazada. Así lo han hecho pueblos del Tíbet, Indonesia o Tailandia.

## ¿LO HAS ENTENDIDO?

**1** La industria turística, ¿va a crecer o disminuir en el futuro? ¿Cuál es su objetivo en estos momentos?

**2** ¿Ha afectado el turismo a los maka de Paraguay? ¿De forma positiva o negativa?

**3** ¿Con qué se compara el turismo? ¿Por qué? Razona tu respuesta.

**4** ¿Existen otras formas de viajar más positivas? ¿Cuáles son? ¿Qué diferencias tienen con el turismo masivo?

## TOMA NOTA

Fíjate en estas frases del texto.

*"Los maka de Paraguay, por ejemplo,* ***eran*** *un grupo indígena nómada.... Ahora viven atrapados en una reserva-islote...".*

Utilizamos el imperfecto para contrastar entre el presente y el pasado. También se utiliza para hacer descripciones generales en el pasado y para hablar de los recuerdos de la infancia.

**1** ¿Qué más cosas han cambiado en la vida de los maka? Lee otra vez el texto y exprésalas utilizando el imperfecto.

**2** *"Cuando era pequeño...".* ¿Qué recuerdas de tu infancia? (escuela, vacaciones, pasatiempos...). ¿Cómo ha cambiado tu vida? Escribe una lista de las cosas que hacías antes y coméntalas con tu compañero/a.

**3** Entre toda la clase hay que inventar una historia descriptiva en el pasado. Cada estudiante añade una frase nueva hasta completar la historia. Se puede empezar así:

*Ejemplo*

Estudiante 1°: *Ayer en el tren* ***había*** *un hombre.*

Estudiante 2°: *El hombre* ***llevaba*** *un abrigo gris.*

Estudiante 3°: ...

### AMPLÍA TU VOCABULARIO

**semejante** (con sentido enfático) tan grande
**exprimido** explotado
**remotos** distantes, apartados
**cotidiano** de todos los días
**indígena** habitante nativo de un país
**nómada** que viaja de un sitio para otro
**islote** isla pequeña
**hectáreas** medida agraria; comprende 100 áreas
**complacer** agradar, gustar
**arrasaron** destruyeron
**clave** esencial
**se acerque** se aproxime, contacte
**amenazada** en peligro

## Y TÚ, ¿CÓMO LO VES?

**1** ¿Te gusta viajar porque

- **a** te interesa conocer otros pueblos y culturas?
- **b** quieres relajarte en la playa y divertirte por la noche?
- **c** te atrae la aventura de lo exótico y desconocido?

**2** ¿Cómo y dónde pasas tus vacaciones normalmente? ¿Qué es lo que más te interesa de los sitios que visitas? (los monumentos, la gastronomía, las tradiciones, el ambiente nocturno...). Explica.

**3** ¿Prefieres viajar en un grupo organizado por una agencia o por tu cuenta, con mochila y a la aventura? ¿Qué ventajas e inconvenientes tienen ambas modalidades de hacer turismo?

## EN LA ONDA

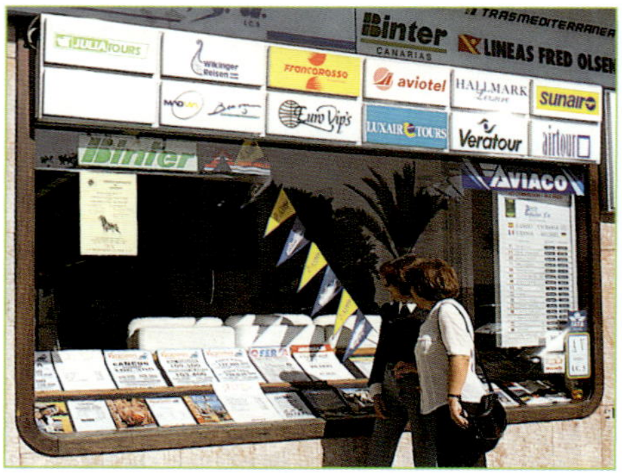


**1** Antes de salir de viaje,

**a** ¿vas a la oficina de turismo para pedir información?
**b** ¿te compras una guía del país o lugares que vas a visitar?
**c** ¿planeas con todo detalle el itinerario de cada día?
**d** si viajas a otro país, ¿intentas aprender unas frases útiles del idioma para comunicarte mejor?

**2** ¿Verdadero o falso? Escucha a estas personas en una agencia de viajes y decide si las siguientes afirmaciones son verdaderas o falsas. Corrige la información incorrecta.

**A** El cliente está interesado en el turismo alternativo.
**B** *Arco Iris* es una agencia de viajes convencional.
**C** Ahora la gente prefiere el turismo verde.
**D** El ecoturismo destruye el paisaje y las culturas tradicionales.
**E** El ecoturista se aloja en grandes hoteles lujosos.
**F** En los viajes de convivencia los grupos son pequeños.
**G** El turista ecológico quiere disfrutar de la naturaleza sin perjudicarla.

**3** Escucha otra vez la conversación y responde.

**A** ¿Cuál es la filosofía del ecoturismo?
**B** ¿Qué diferencias ves entre un viaje comercial y los viajes de convivencia?
**C** En tu opinión, ¿qué ventajas e inconvenientes tiene el ecoturismo?

## ¡TIENES LA PALABRA!

**1** En grupos escoge una ciudad/una zona del mundo que te gustaría visitar. Planea tu viaje ideal (de aventura, exótico, ecológico, de convivencia, deportivo...). Piensa en el itinerario para cada día y lo que necesitas llevar. Luego cada grupo lo cuenta al resto de la clase.

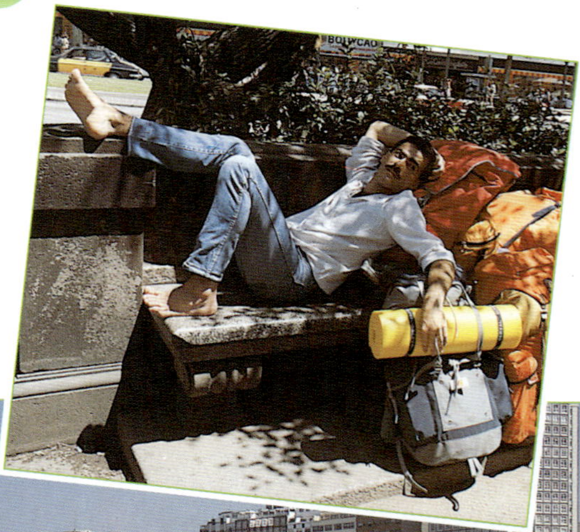

**ITINERARIO**

- Destino
- Transporte
- Fecha/duración
- Equipaje
- Alojamiento
- Sitios de interés
- Actividades
- Compras

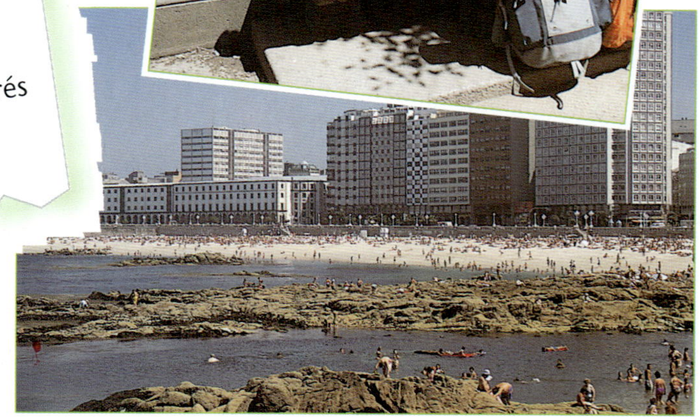

**2** En la agencia de turismo. En grupos de tres escoge uno de estos papeles.

**Agente de viaje**

Trabajas en una agencia de turismo. Pregunta a los clientes qué les interesa hacer en sus vacaciones. Utiliza la información de México para aconsejarles sobre sus destinos ideales.

**Turista 1°**

Te interesan los viajes activos para practicar deportes acuáticos y actividades al aire libre. Pregunta en la agencia qué destinos son buenos para tus preferencias.

**Turista 2°**

Te gusta observar a los animales. Prefieres unas vacaciones en contacto con la naturaleza. ¿Qué ofertas hay para ti?

**RUTAS ECOTURÍSTICAS. MUCHO MÁS QUE NATURALEZA EN VIVO: UN MUNDO POR DESCUBRIR.**

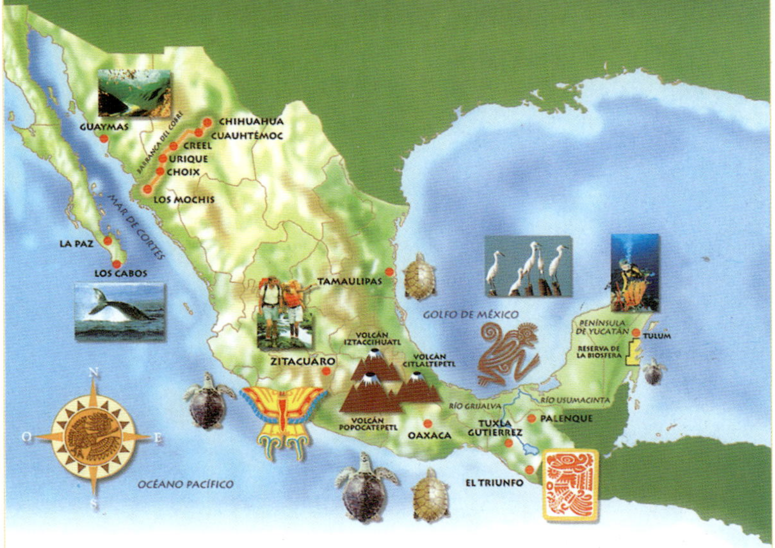


Déjate sorprender por todas las posibilidades de unas vacaciones en México. Combina la tranquilidad de las más bellas playas con la cultura, la historia, el arte, la arquitectura y el alegre carácter mexicano. Porque en México todo es nuevo y sorprendente, ¡ven a conocerlo!... tienes todo un mundo por descubrir. Para más información, consulta en tu agencia de viajes.

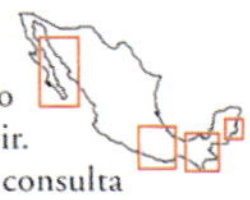

**3** Entre toda la clase comenta tus opiniones sobre estos temas.

***¿Cuáles son los destinos preferidos por los turistas en tu país? ¿Por qué? ¿Qué busca el típico turista de tu país en sus vacaciones?***

***¿Qué aspectos positivos y negativos tiene el turismo para los países y las personas que lo reciben?***

***¿Cómo podemos desarrollar un turismo responsable, de sensitividad cultural hacia los lugares visitados?***

## POR ESCRITO

**1** Diseña un anuncio como el de México para promocionar tu país y atraer a turistas españoles y de Latinoamérica.

**2** Imagina que eres uno de los maka de Paraguay. Describe cómo el turismo ha cambiado la vida y las costumbres de tu tribu y cómo ves el futuro de tu pueblo.

**3** Trabajas como guía turístico durante el verano mostrando a los turistas españoles y latinoamericanos tu ciudad/región. Prepara una presentación con los lugares de interés. Incluye información sobre las actividades que pueden realizar en cada uno. (250 palabras)

## PUNTO DE MIRA

¿Qué significa la historia para ti? Razona tu respuesta.

**a** una de las asignaturas del colegio
**b** algo realmente apasionante e interesante
**c** un instrumento para conocer nuestro pasado y el comportamiento de las personas
**d** algo que afecta a nuestro futuro

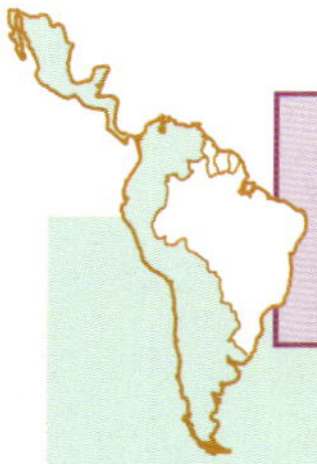

Latinoamérica conserva un rico pasado histórico de sus antiguas culturas. Lee este texto para descubrir un lugar misterioso y espectacular.

# Machu Picchu

## La ciudad escondida

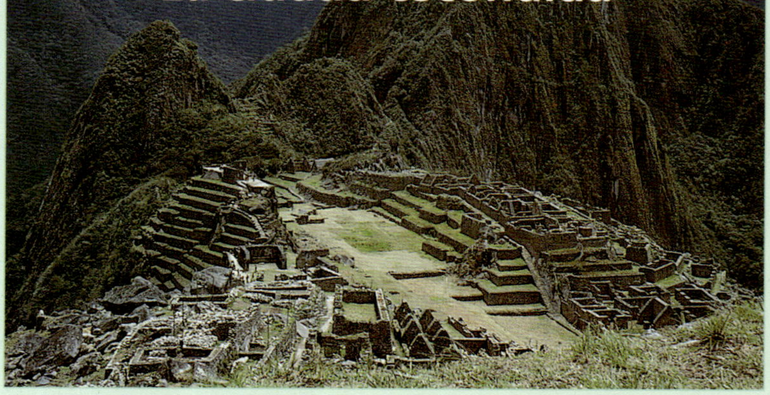

Durante siglos permaneció en silencio. Erigido piedra sobre piedra, Machu Picchu es el monumento arquitectónico más importante del Perú, y uno de los más extraordinarios de la humanidad.

La ciudad perdida de los incas, situada a 2.400 metros sobre el nivel del mar (en el sur del Perú, a 112 kilómetros de Cusco), fue pensada para encajar armónicamente en un paisaje montañoso estrecho y de difícil acceso.

Machu Picchu significa "cerro viejo". "¿Me creerá alguien lo que aquí descubrí?", escribió Hiram Bingham en su diario de viaje luego de hallar, el 24 de julio de 1911, las ruinas incaicas. Bingham llegó al Perú en una expedición organizada por la Universidad de Yale, buscando la ciudad de los descendientes de los soberanos incas.

Cuando llegó al valle del Urubamba, en la desolada localidad de Mandorbamba, el campesino Melchor Arteaga le contó que en lo más alto del cerro Machu Picchu se encontraban unas ruinas. El investigador había escuchado sobre diversas ciudades perdidas en el Perú, e insistió ser conducido a las mismas. Bingham también descubrió otros complejos arquitectónicos de la región.

A pesar de que hay varias versiones sobre el enigma de Machu Picchu, no hay duda, por la forma de su construcción, los objetos de alfarería y de metalurgia, que las ruinas datan del período de apogeo de la cultura inca (1438-1532), la última de las culturas andinas, con una tradición de 3.000 años.

La silenciosa ciudad, centro de culto y ceremonias, está compuesta por dos zonas bien diferenciadas: el sector agrario y el urbano. Durante la época de la conquista española, los incas jamás revelaron el secreto de Machu Picchu. Su estratégica ubicación hace suponer que habría sido un puesto de avanzada en los esfuerzos de hegemonía inca por dominar la región del Amazonas, que se inicia precisamente en Cusco.

También se encontraron 135 esqueletos: 109 de mujeres, 22 de hombres y el resto de niños. A raíz de esto, Bingham supuso que los últimos habitantes de Machu Picchu habrían sido las "vírgenes del sol" o Acllas.

## ¿LO HAS ENTENDIDO?

**1** ¿Qué es Machu Picchu y dónde se encuentra?

**2** ¿Quién era Hiram Bingham? ¿Por qué fue al Perú?

**3** ¿Qué le dijo Melchor Arteaga a Bingham?

**4** ¿Qué se encontró en las ruinas de la ciudad inca?

## TOMA NOTA

Fíjate en estas frases del texto.

> *"Durante siglos **permaneció** en silencio".*
> *"El investigador **había escuchado** sobre diversas ciudades perdidas en el Perú...".*

El pretérito indica acciones realizadas y completadas en el pasado. También se utiliza para una acción continuada durante un periodo de tiempo de duración finita.

El pluscuamperfecto se forma con el imperfecto del verbo ***haber*** y el participio de pasado. Se utiliza para acciones o sucesos que preceden a otra acción en el pasado.

**1** Vuelve a leer el texto y anota los verbos en el pasado.

**2** Completa esta información sobre los aztecas utilizando el pretérito.

**A** Los aztecas _____ (***ser***) feroces guerreros. _____ (***llegar***) al Valle de México en el siglo XII y su imperio _____ (***ocupar***) México central entre 1300 y 1521.

**B** En 1325 los aztecas _____ (***fundar***) su capital en Tenochtitlán.

**C** La civilización azteca _____ (***desarrollar***) una cultura muy compleja en las artes, la arquitectura y el comercio.

**D** El conquistador español Hernán Cortés _____ (***desembarcar***) en las costas mexicanas en 1519.

### AMPLÍA TU VOCABULARIO

**erigido** construido
**arquitectónico** relativo a la arquitectura de los edificios
**encajar** integrarse
**cerro** monte
**hallar** descubrir
**soberanos** reyes
**campesino** persona que trabaja el campo
**a pesar de que** aunque
**enigma** misterio
**alfarería** cerámica
**apogeo** esplendor, época dorada
**andinas** de los Andes
**agrario** agrícola
**época** periodo
**ubicación** situación
**a raíz de esto** por esta razón
**Acllas** vírgenes consagradas al dios sol

## Y TÚ, ¿CÓMO LO VES?

**1** Al hombre siempre le interesó investigar el origen de las cosas. ¿Te interesa el pasado? ¿Por qué? ¿Qué sabes de tus antepasados familiares? ¿Te interesaría conocer la historia de tu familia? ¿Qué sentido tiene explorar el pasado?

**2** ¿Son necesarios los museos? ¿Qué función cumplen? ¿Qué museos hay en tu ciudad? ¿Qué se exhibe en ellos? ¿Qué tipo de museos prefieres? (De ciencia, de historia natural, de arte ...).

**3** ¿Te parece importante preservar las ruinas y los restos de las civilizaciones pasadas? ¿Por qué?

**4** ¿Qué atractivo tiene para el turista visitar lugares míticos e históricos? ¿Te atrae esta modalidad de viajes? Explica.

## EN LA ONDA

**1** En grupos de tres descubre qué letras faltan para completar estas palabras.

| La expedición | Los participantes | Los objetivos |
|---|---|---|
| r_t_ | _ _plor_dor | in_ _ _tigar |
| _tiner_rio | _ _queólog_ | expl_ _ _ción |
| _ _ario de viaj_ | historia_ _ _ | descubrim _ _ _to |
| tr_ _spor_ _ | _ven_ _rero | estu_ _ _ |
| equi_ _ | in_ _ _tigador | r_ _nas |
| m_p_ | _ _tudioso | civili _ _ _ión |

**2** Escucha a Mónica, guía de un museo, mostrando a los visitantes los tesoros culturales de México. Completa estas frases con la información que oigas.

**A** Tulum y Chichén Itzá fueron centros _____ y de _____ .

**B** Tulum es una _____ amurallada situada sobre el _____ . La vista allí es _____ .

**C** Chichén Itzá está en la _____ del Yucatán, en el _____ de México. Allí hay una _____ dedicada a Quetzalcóatl, el _____ de los _____ . Tiene _____ escaleras. Quetzalcóatl es representado en forma de _____ .

**D** Los sacerdotes mayas _____ los misterios del _____ . Vivían en gigantescos _____ de _____ .

**E** Los _____ construyeron _____ astronómicos e inventaron un _____ muy _____ .

**F** Los colores _____ de los mayas eran _____ , _____ , _____ y _____ .

## ¡TIENES LA PALABRA!

**1** En la embajada cultural del Perú. En parejas escoge uno de estos papeles.

**Visitante**

Tienes intención de hacer una expedición a pie para ver Machu Picchu. Pide información sobre el lugar, cómo se puede ir, cuál es la mejor opción y qué precauciones tienes que tomar.

**Asistente**

Trabajas de relaciones públicas en la embajada. Lee esta información sobre el Camino del Inca y responde a las preguntas del visitante. Infórmale sobre los tipos de expediciones que hay, el precio y las precauciones para el viaje.

### MACHU PICCHU
### CAMINO DEL INCA

#### Historia

Perú es uno de los países más misteriosos de Latinoamérica. Para llegar a Machu Picchu hay que recorrer el tradicional Camino del Inca. Éste puede realizarse de varias formas:

#### Consejos

***Independientemente:*** se necesita equipo de montaña y alimentos.

***Con agencias poco fiables:*** una caminata o *trekking* de tres días. Entre $100 y $150 todo incluido.

***Con una agencia acreditada y de prestigio:*** $300. Incluye: cuatro días de caminata, buen equipo de montaña, comida y guía para enseñar Machu Picchu.

#### Precauciones

Respete la altitud. No tome comidas pesadas ni beba alcohol. Si le afecta el soroche (mal de las alturas) descanse y tome té de coca.

**2** Las misteriosas líneas de Nasca (Perú), los gigantescos *moais* de la Isla de Pascua.... Entre toda la clase comenta tus opiniones sobre estos temas.

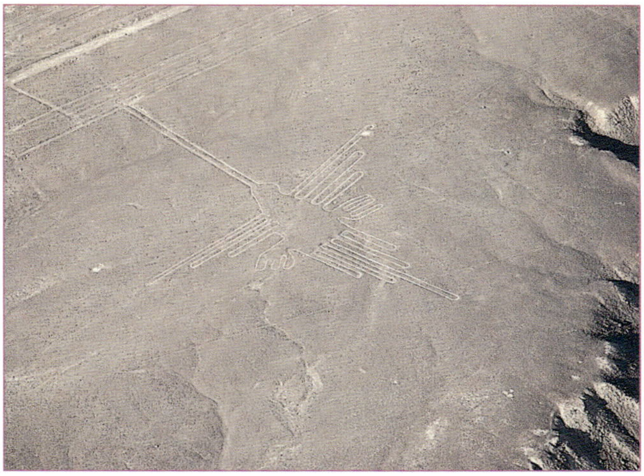

**¿Podemos aprender algo de las civilizaciones antiguas?**

**Imagina que tienes que hacer una cápsula del tiempo. ¿Qué objetos incluirías para simbolizar y representar la vida en el siglo XX? Explica las razones.**

**¿Crees que los edificios y monumentos del siglo XX durarán más de 1000 años? ¿Qué visitará la gente en el siglo XXII?**

## POR ESCRITO

**1** En grupos investiga sobre una de las civilizaciones: inca, azteca o maya. Después realiza una exposición oral en clase con ayuda de fotografías, pósters o ilustraciones. Puedes exponer el trabajo en tu aula de español.

*Ejemplo*

La arquitectura maya es impresionante. Construyeron pirámides, palacios y templos. Los sacerdotes vivían en los templos para estudiar los misterios del cosmos y adorar a los dioses del sol, la lluvia y la luna.

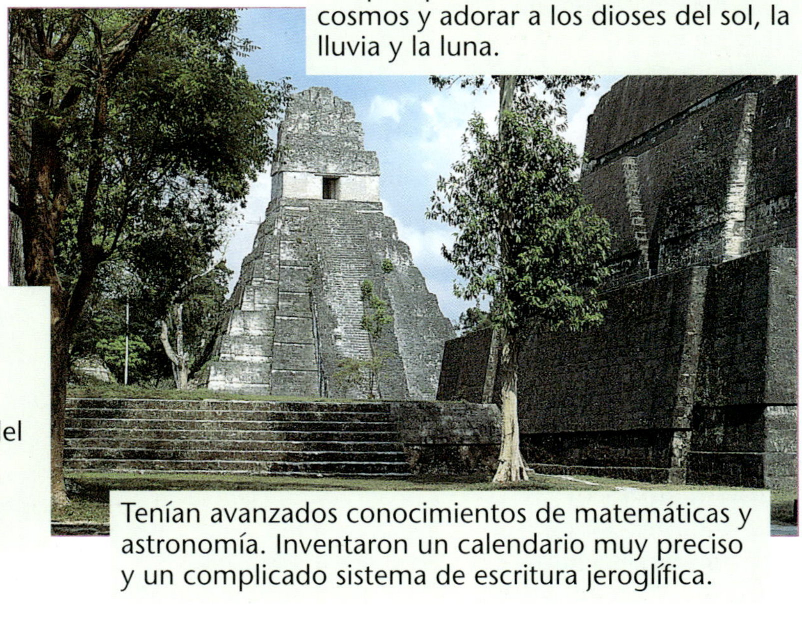

Los mayas fueron una antigua civilización. Su poder e influencia se extendía por el sur de México y la península del Yucatán, Guatemala, Belice y parte de Honduras y El Salvador.

Tenían avanzados conocimientos de matemáticas y astronomía. Inventaron un calendario muy preciso y un complicado sistema de escritura jeroglífica.

**2** ¿Cuánto sabes de tu pasado? Dibuja el árbol genealógico de tu familia y escribe unas frases con información sobre cada miembro.

**3** Imagina que eres Hiram Bingham. Escribe un día de su diario de viaje. (200 palabras)

**4** Concurso *Expedición cultural a Latinoamérica*. Para ser seleccionado escribe por qué te gustaría participar, cuál sería tu contribución personal al proyecto y por qué eres el candidato ideal. (250 palabras)

## PUNTO DE MIRA

¿Qué experiencias de trabajo has tenido? ¿Fueron positivas? ¿En qué te gustaría trabajar? ¿Por qué? ¿Qué ventajas e inconvenientes tiene ese trabajo?

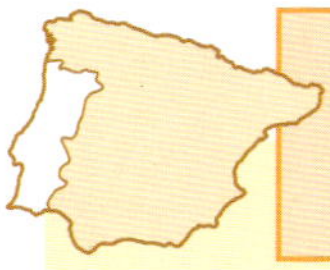

¿Será posible en un futuro trabajar sin salir de casa, libres de horarios estrictos? Lee este artículo para averiguarlo.

# La oficina en casa

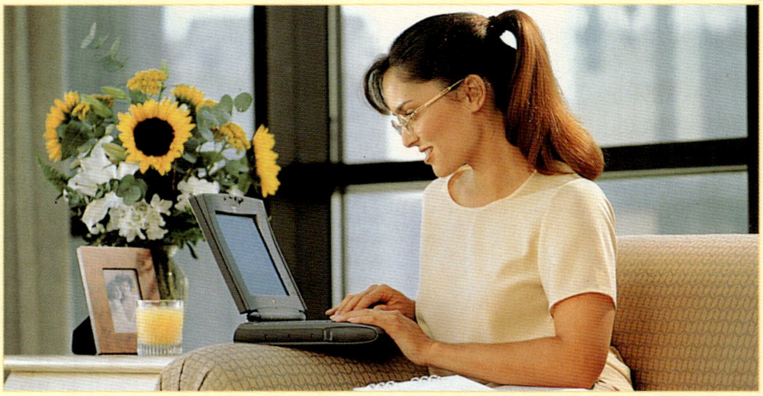

El teletrabajo se puede describir como un sistema de trabajo a distancia, donde el trabajador recibe por vía telemática las instrucciones y devuelve el resultado de su labor de la misma manera. Existen muchas formas de teletrabajar, desde la persona que realiza trabajos determinados para empresas como autónomo, pasando por las empresas que han puesto parte de su plantilla a trabajar en casa porque lo consideran más rentable, hasta llegar a aquellas personas que se buscan la vida a través de Internet.

Gracias al desarrollo de la informática y de las telecomunicaciones, millones de personas teletrabajan. En el futuro abarcará aquellos trabajos que no requieran la presencia física de una persona.

*Isabel Hoyos* trabajó durante siete años como secretaria bilingüe en una oficina. Al tener una hija decidió trabajar desde casa, ofreciéndose a varias empresas como traductora especializada en informática. Ya lleva seis años como teletrabajadora.

Entre las ventajas que le reporta trabajar en casa, *Isabel* destaca la flexibilidad de horarios, y la posibilidad de vivir donde quiera. *"Vivo en mitad del campo y es maravilloso. No tengo que perder el tiempo en transportes, ni gastar en ropas de oficina o en salir a comer a restaurantes"*. Cree que si el teletrabajo sigue prosperando podrá ayudar a sectores con problemas para encontrar empleos adecuados a sus necesidades, como las mujeres con niños o los discapacitados físicos.

Pero no todo es de color de rosa en el mundo del teletrabajo. La mayoría de profesionales trabajan por proyecto; el concepto de trabajo seguro no existe. Los teletrabajadores corren el peligro de aislarse excesivamente de la sociedad.

A decir de los expertos, se está atravesando una fase de transición de la sociedad industrial a la de la información. Labores que antes necesitaban varias personas, pueden ser realizadas ahora por una sola gracias al teletrabajo, por lo que, a corto plazo este sistema está destruyendo empleo. A medida que entremos en la sociedad de la información habrá más trabajos que se puedan hacer a distancia. Las posibilidades son grandes, pero hay que adecuarse a la tecnología.

## ¿LO HAS ENTENDIDO?

**1** ¿Qué es el teletrabajo?

**2** ¿De qué forma ha mejorado la vida de Isabel Hoyos?

**3** ¿A qué sectores de las población puede beneficiar el teletrabajo?

**4** ¿Cuáles son los peligros?

## TOMA NOTA

Fíjate en la estructura.

**El futuro simple**

| -AR / -ER / -IR | | Irregulares | |
|---|---|---|---|
| *trabajaré* | *trabajar**emos*** | *tener - ten**dré*** | *poder - po**dré*** |
| *trabajar**ás*** | *trabajar**éis*** | *salir - sal**dré*** | *decir - **diré*** |
| *trabajar**á*** | *trabajar**án*** | *hacer - **haré*** | *querer - quer**ré*** |

El futuro simple se utiliza para hacer predicciones. Las terminaciones se añaden al infinitivo. Las tres conjugaciones tienen las mismas terminaciones. Busca los ejemplos de esta forma verbal en el artículo.

Completa estas frases con el futuro simple.

**A** El 20% de la población trabajadora _____ (***producir***) el 80% de lo necesario.

**B** Un 40% _____ (***trabajar***) en empresas muy especializadas.

**C** Un 40% _____ (***ser***) teletrabajadores que _____ (***hacer***) su trabajo desde casa.

**D** _____ (***aumentar***) el trabajo a tiempo parcial. El trabajo _____ (***estar***) más repartido.

**E** El trabajador _____ (***dedicar***) tanto tiempo al trabajo como al estudio.

**F** _____ (***haber***) más tiempo libre para el ocio.

### AMPLÍA TU VOCABULARIO

**telemática** comunicación informática a distancia
**devuelve** retorna
**labor** trabajo
**empresas** compañías, negocios
**autónomo** que trabaja para sí mismo
**plantilla** personal de una empresa
**rentable** beneficioso económicamente
**desarrollo** progreso
**abarcará** comprenderá
**requieran** necesiten
**reporta** da
**destaca** distingue
**gastar** utilizar el dinero en comprar algo
**prosperando** progresando
**discapacitados** con problemas físicos
**aislarse** estar solo
**a decir de** en opinión de
**a corto plazo** a corto tiempo
**a medida que** cuando, al tiempo que
**adecuarse** adaptarse

## Y TÚ, ¿CÓMO LO VES?

**1** ¿Qué profesiones te parecen más aptas para el teletrabajo? ¿Por qué?

**2** En tu país, ¿es fácil para los jóvenes conseguir un puesto de trabajo? ¿Crees que el teletrabajo generará más empleo a largo plazo? ¿Lo ves como una posibilidad para tu futuro?

**3** El mercado laboral será cada vez más duro y competitivo. ¿Cómo te estás formando para el futuro? ¿Estás preparado/a para sobrevivir a los cambios? Explica.

**4** ¿Te parece positiva la utilización de nuevas tecnologías en el trabajo? ¿Cambiarán nuestra forma de trabajar?

## EN LA ONDA

**1** Mira esta lista de profesiones. ¿Qué conocimientos, experiencia y cualidades personales son necesarios para realizarlas? ¿Crees que estas ocupaciones serán importantes en unos años? ¿Habrá nuevos empleos en el futuro? Explica.

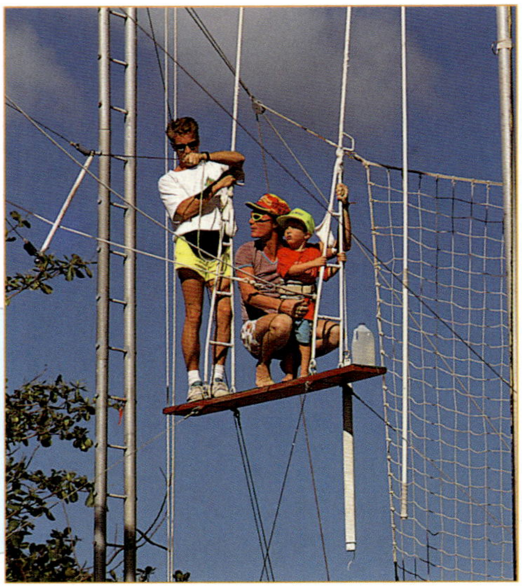

- Diseñador de programas informáticos
- Técnico en robótica e informática
- Técnico en medioambiente
- Experto en dietética y nutrición
- Monitor de deportes de aventura
- Animador sociocultural

**2** Un programa de radio está interesado en conocer qué tipo de trabajos realizan los jóvenes durante el verano. Escucha a estos chicos dejar sus mensajes en el contestador de la emisora. Anota la siguiente información para cada uno.

| | **Fernando** | **Guadalupe** | **Mireya** |
|---|---|---|---|
| ***Edad*** | | | |
| ***Estudios*** | | | |
| ***Empleo*** | | | |
| ***Responsabilidades*** | | | |
| ***Ventajas*** | | | |
| ***Inconvenientes*** | | | |

## ¡TIENES LA PALABRA!

**1** En parejas mira las ofertas de empleo y escoge uno de estos papeles.

### Candidato

Escoge una de las ofertas y demuestra tu interés en conseguir ese puesto. Habla de tus calificaciones y experiencia laboral. Pregunta sobre las condiciones (horas, salario, contrato...).

### Entrevistador

Pregunta al candidato todo lo relacionado con su formación educativa y experiencia. Ofrécele información sobre el puesto vacante.

### OFERTAS DE EMPLEO

**Importante Cadena Hotelera** necesita
**JÓVENES**
julio, agosto, septiembre
**Se requiere:** dominio de inglés, español, alemán. Conocimientos de informática. Buena presencia.
**Se ofrece:** puesto de relaciones públicas. Trato directo con los clientes. Remuneración competitiva. Alojamiento.

***Empresa Líder del sector*** precisa
**TELENCUESTADORES**

*Requisitos:*
- Conocimientos de informática
- Facilidad de comunicación
- Experiencia en servicios de atención al cliente

*Ofrecemos:*
- Formación y equipamiento a cargo de la empresa
- Trabajo desde casa
- Flexibilidad de horarios

**2** En grupos de tres lee esta información. Defiende tu posición a favor o en contra del teletrabajo.

### El teletrabajador

*Ventajas*
- jornadas y horarios más flexibles
- trabajo desde casa o centros compartidos de trabajo
- vida más relajada: más tiempo para el ocio, la familia y la autoformación

*Inconvenientes*
- inestabilidad laboral
- dominio de las nuevas tecnologías
- formación continua
- problemas psicológicos, soledad y estrés

### La sociedad

*Ventajas*
- menos tráfico y menor impacto ambiental
- incorporación de discapacitados y jubilados
- aumento de la calidad de vida
- ampliación de servicios para el ocio y el tiempo libre

*Inconvenientes*
- menos trabajo: mercado laboral duro y competitivo
- desigualdad entre los que se adaptan a las nuevas tecnologías y los que no
- frustración y aumento de la violencia en las grandes ciudades

**3** Entre toda la clase comenta tus opiniones sobre estos temas.

**Muchos estudiantes aprovechan las vacaciones del verano para trabajar y conseguir algún dinero extra. En tu país, ¿cuáles son los trabajos preferidos de los jóvenes durante el verano? ¿Por qué?**

**¿Hay problemas de desempleo en tu país? ¿A quién afecta? ¿Qué tipo de ayuda recibes si estás en el paro (desempleo)?**

**¿Es difícil encontrar un empleo si eres joven? ¿Cómo son las condiciones de trabajo? (Horas, salario, contrato...).**

**¿Crees que las nuevas tecnologías crearán una sociedad diferente?**

## POR ESCRITO

**1** Estás buscando trabajo en un país de habla hispana.

**A** Escribe tu currículo en español para las empresas.

**B** Responde a una de las ofertas de empleo anteriores.

**2** Describe cómo cambiará nuestra forma de trabajar en el futuro y cómo será la vida de los teletrabajadores. (300 palabras)

| CURRICULUM | | |
|---|---|---|
| **Datos personales** | | |
| *Nombre* | *Edad* | *Dirección* |
| *Fecha de nacimiento* | *Nacionalidad* | *Teléfono* |
| **Estudios y Calificaciones** | | |
| **Experiencia Laboral** | | |
| **Intereses** | | |
| **Otros** | | |

## PUNTO DE MIRA

¿Cuánto sabes sobre las fiestas hispanas? Pon a prueba tus conocimientos. Responde a este sencillo cuestionario.

**1** El 12 de octubre, Día de la Hispanidad, es fiesta en España y Latinoamérica porque
- **a** en ese día Cristóbal Colón llegó al Nuevo Mundo.
- **b** se conmemora una importante batalla.

**2** El Carnaval es una fiesta de tradición
- **a** indígena.
- **b** cristiana.

**3** La Noche de Muertos es una fiesta importante en
- **a** México.
- **b** Venezuela.

**4** En España se recibe el nuevo año
- **a** con fuegos artificiales.
- **b** comiendo las 12 uvas de la suerte.

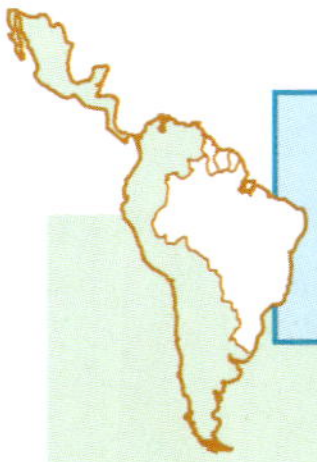

En el mundo hispano se celebran numerosas fiestas, muchas de origen muy antiguo. El siguiente texto trata de una milenaria tradición de Perú.

# LA FIESTA DEL SOL

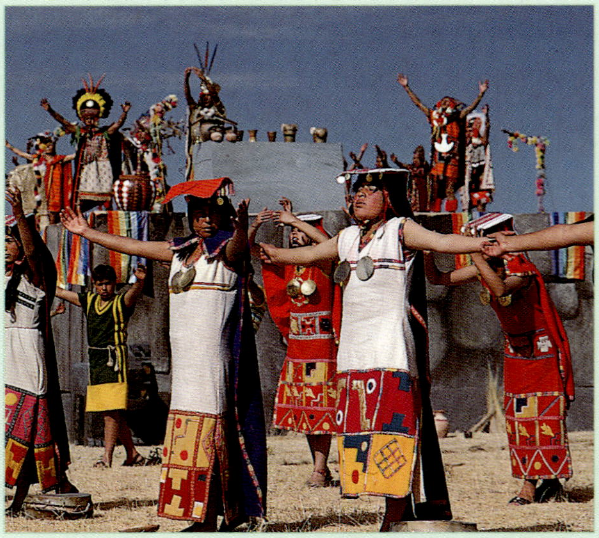

La fiesta del Inti Raymi tiene lugar todos los años en el templo de Koricancha, en Huaccaypata (plaza de armas de Cusco) y en Sacsahuamán, el antiguo fuerte militar de los incas.

La altiplanicie de Sacsahuamán situada sobre Cusco es un escenario majestuoso, ubicado a 3.600 metros, donde el Dios Sol vierte cada año su preciosa simiente para que el mundo no se sumerja en las tinieblas.

La fastuosa ceremonia se desarrolló este año en español e inglés, además de en la lengua inca (el quechua), en una bella escenificación por parte de más de 200 actores.

Se llama la Fiesta del Sol porque el 24 de junio marca el solsticio de invierno (cuando la noche es la más larga del año) y el inicio del año agrícola en buena parte de los pueblos andinos, por lo que el Inca pide que la cosecha sea buena en todo el imperio para que su pueblo no pase hambre y sea feliz y próspero.

Antiguamente, decenas de miles de pobladores llegaban cada año por estas fechas a Cusco, donde estaba el centro del arte, la sabiduría y el poder. El Inca, era el centro de la fiesta que tenía lugar en Huaccaypata, la plaza sagrada, donde el Inca rendía los honores al primer rayo de sol.

Esas ceremonias sagradas ya no se celebran en el centro de la ciudad imperial. La noche del 22 de junio se inicia la fiesta con fuegos artificiales frente a la estatua del Inca Pachacútec y finalizan con una concentración masiva en la explanada de las ruinas de Sacsahuamán.

## ¿LO HAS ENTENDIDO?

**1** ¿A qué cultura pertenece esta celebración? ¿Cuándo se celebra y por qué es importante esta fecha?

**2** ¿Qué importancia y significado tiene el sol en la fiesta del Inti Raymi?

**3** ¿Cuál era la figura principal de esta fiesta y qué misión tenía?

**4** En la actualidad, ¿quiénes representan la ceremonia?

## TOMA NOTA

Fíjate en esta frase del texto.

*"...el Inca **pide que** la cosecha **sea** buena... para que su pueblo no **pase** hambre y **sea** feliz y próspero".*

El subjuntivo se utiliza con verbos que expresan deseo como ***pedir que***, ***preferir que***, ***querer/desear que***. También se emplea con verbos que expresan órdenes, consejo, necesidad, prohibición, permiso o petición de algo. ¿Cuántos verbos conoces que siguen esta regla? Escribe una lista.

**1** Completa las siguientes frases utilizando el presente de subjuntivo.

**A** El profesor prohíbe que los alumnos _____ (***hablar***) en clase.

**B** Mi madre me pide que _____ (***ordenar***) mi dormitorio.

**C** Mi prima desea que yo le _____ (***escribir***) regularmente.

**D** El director ordena al empleado que _____ (***recibir***) a los clientes.

**2** Utiliza el presente de subjuntivo de los verbos entre paréntesis para terminar las frases.

**A** Mi profesor de español quiere que nosotros (***aprender*** *los verbos,* ***estudiar*** *el vocabulario,* ***hablar*** *más en clase,* ***participar*** *en los debates,* ***hacer*** *los ejercicios,* ***venir*** *a clase,* ***escribir*** *redacciones y* ***leer*** *revistas*).

**B** Mis padres desean que yo (***estudiar*** *más,* ***sacar*** *buenas notas,* ***ir*** *a la universidad,* ***tener*** *un buen trabajo y* ***ser*** *feliz*).

**C** Algunos padres exigen que sus hijos (***volver*** *a casa pronto,* ***ayudar*** *con las tareas domésticas y* ***estudiar*** *mucho*).

### AMPLÍA TU VOCABULARIO

**fuerte** fortificación
**altiplanicie** superficie alta y plana
**simiente** semilla
**se sumerja** se introduzca
**tinieblas** oscuridad
**fastuosa** llena de lujo y espectacularidad
**escenificación** representación teatral
**cosecha** recolección de los frutos de la tierra
**pobladores** habitantes
**sabiduría** conocimientos
**rendía los honores** ofrecía homenaje
**explanada** superficie plana, llanura

## Y TÚ, ¿CÓMO LO VES?

**1** ¿Te gustan las fiestas que conmemoran algún hecho importante o tradición antigua? ¿Por qué?

**2** ¿Qué tradiciones y fiestas hay en tu país? ¿Cuáles son las más importantes? ¿Conoces el origen de estas celebraciones? ¿Hay algunas que se celebran sólo en tu ciudad/región? Explica en qué consisten.

**3** El Inti Raymi era una fiesta sagrada. Su celebración hoy día recuerda a los descendientes de los incas la gloria de sus antepasados. ¿Te parece importante preservar este tipo de tradiciones? ¿Por qué?

## EN LA ONDA

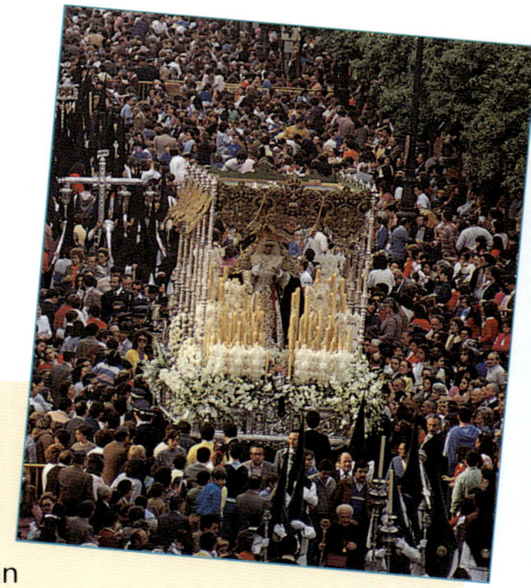

**1** ¿Cuántas fiestas españolas o latinoamericanas conoces? En parejas relaciona los elementos y tradiciones con las fiestas mencionadas.

**A** Carnaval
**B** Navidad
**C** Nochevieja
**D** Semana Santa

**ELEMENTOS**
**a** los disfraces
**b** los fuegos artificiales
**c** las procesiones religiosas
**d** los desfiles y comparsas
**e** las bandas de música
**f** el baile
**g** el belén y el árbol de Navidad

**TRADICIONES**
**1** comer uvas
**2** ir a misa
**3** hacer regalos
**4** beber champán
**5** comer turrón y mazapán
**6** representar la pasión de Jesucristo
**7** recorrer las calles bailando al ritmo de la música

**2** ¿Verdadero o falso? Escucha a un turista español hablando con un chico mexicano y decide si las siguientes frases son verdaderas o falsas.

**A** La Noche de Muertos es una fiesta triste.
**B** Se celebra el día uno de diciembre.
**C** Las casas y cementerios se adornan con flores y velas.
**D** Es tradicional comer la comida favorita del difunto.
**E** En la Noche de Muertos todos se reúnen en los cementerios para estar con sus familiares desaparecidos.
**F** Todo el mundo guarda silencio.
**G** Se comen huesos, esqueletos y calaveras hechos de azúcar.

## ¡TIENES LA PALABRA!

**1** Lee la información sobre los "sanfermines". Son la fiesta más popular de España y también atraen a muchos extranjeros. Luego contesta a las preguntas.

**A** Mira la fotografía. ¿Cuáles son los elementos principales de los "sanfermines" y qué características tienen?

**B** ¿Qué diferencias encuentras entre la fiesta del Inti Raymi y los "sanfermines"? ¿Hay alguna similitud? ¿Cuál de las dos prefieres? Razona tu respuesta.

El rojo y el blanco son los colores de la fiesta. La gente viste pantalón y camisa blancos, lleva un pañuelo y una boina rojos.

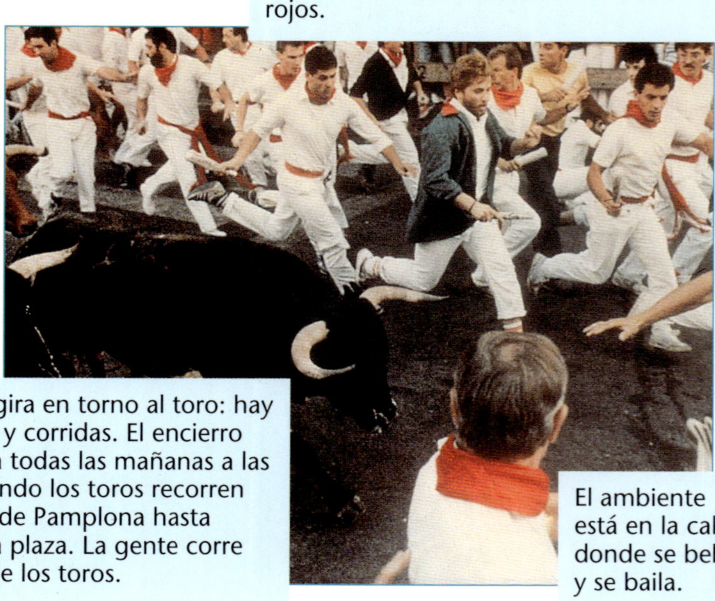

La fiesta gira en torno al toro: hay encierros y corridas. El encierro comienza todas las mañanas a las ocho cuando los toros recorren las calles de Pamplona hasta llegar a la plaza. La gente corre delante de los toros.

El ambiente está en la calle, donde se bebe y se baila.

**2** En la oficina de turismo. En parejas escoge uno de estos papeles.

**Empleado/a**

Los turistas te piden información sobre fiestas. Lee con atención este folleto turístico y después contesta a las preguntas del visitante.

**Turista**

Quieres información sobre el Carnaval de Oruro (Bolivia). Pregunta en la oficina de turismo (cuándo y dónde se celebra, qué se puede hacer, cuáles son los elementos principales de la fiesta...).

## Carnaval de Oruro

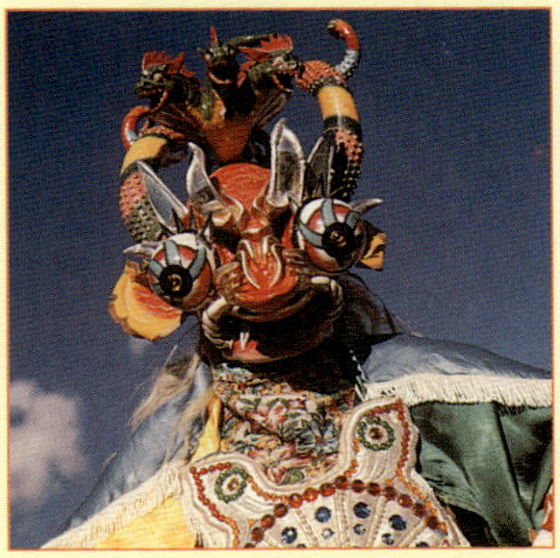

**Febrero**

*Duración*: una semana.

No se pierda este fantástico espectáculo lleno de color y alegría. Una de las fiestas más hermosas de Latinoamérica. Mezcla de tradiciones cristianas y nativas.

*Actividades*: Representación de la Diablada. Los bailarines son todos hombres. Llevan vistosos y pesados trajes y elaboradas máscaras de diablo que simbolizan los siete pecados capitales. El baile es el elemento esencial de la fiesta. Simboliza la batalla de San Miguel contra los pecados: lucha contra los diablos uno por uno y los vence.

Concurso de comparsas de bailarines: ¿quiénes llevan los mejores adornos y las mejores máscaras?

Fuegos artificiales.

**3** Entre toda la clase comenta tus opiniones sobre estos temas.

***¿Sueles dar fiestas en casa para tus amigos? ¿Qué elementos son importantes para dar una gran fiesta?***

***¿Te gusta celebrar la Navidad o el Año Nuevo? ¿Cómo se celebran en tu casa? ¿Es diferente a cómo se hace en los países de habla española?***

***Imagina que en tu país sólo permitieran celebrar una fiesta al año. ¿Cuál escogerías tú y por qué razones?***

## POR ESCRITO

**1** Quieres promocionar una fiesta de tu ciudad/país para atraer a turistas de habla española. Diseña un folleto incluyendo toda la información necesaria.

**2** En grupos escoge una o dos fiestas del mundo hispano. Infórmate bien y elabora un póster con fotos, mapas, dibujos.... Explica en qué consiste la fiesta, su origen, cuándo se celebra, qué se puede ver y qué recomiendas hacer. Puedes exponer el proyecto en clase una vez terminado.

**3** Imagina que estás visitando Cusco o Pamplona durante las fiestas. Escribe una postal a tu profesor/a de español contándole lo que estás haciendo y cómo lo estás pasando.

*Ejemplo*

*Querido profesor:*
*Estoy pasando ___ en ___ porque ___ . Ayer ___ .*
*Mañana pienso ___ . Lo que más me gusta es ___ . Lo estoy pasando ___ . La comida es ___ .*
*Recuerdos,*

## PUNTO DE MIRA

En tu país, ¿a qué edad comienzan los chicos y chicas a salir por la noche? ¿Qué hacen cuando salen? ¿Hay alguna restricción de horarios?

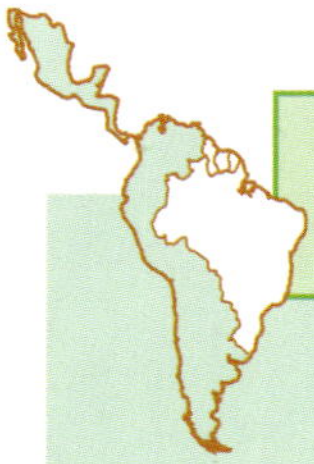

¿Cómo prevenir la delincuencia juvenil? Vás a leer sobre una medida adoptada en Cali, Colombia.

# Menores, a dormir temprano en Cali

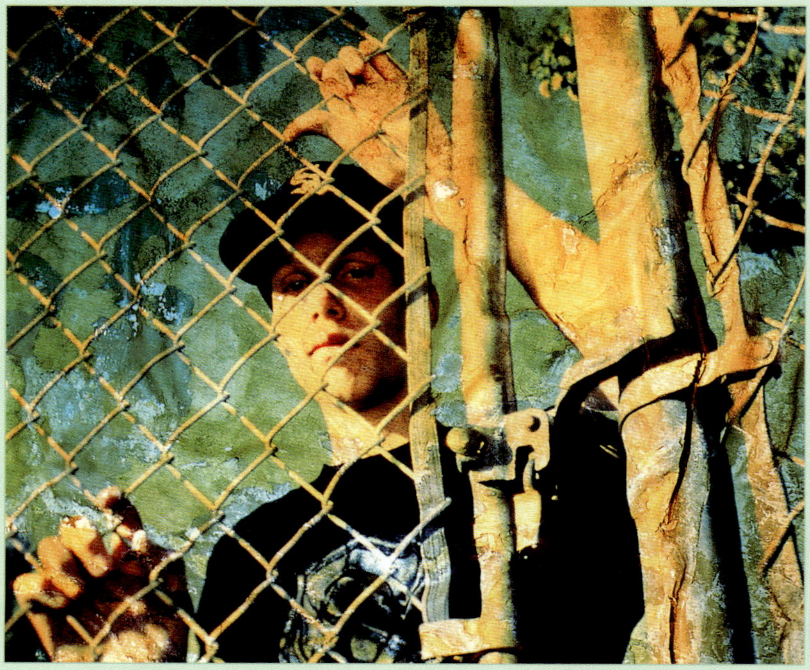

Los menores de edad tendrán que acostarse temprano y dejar de deambular las calles de Cali, a partir de la próxima semana.

En efecto, el toque de queda será implantado para menores de 16 años entre las 11 p.m. y las 6:00 a.m. por parte de la Administración Municipal.

"La medida servirá no sólo para disminuir el consumo de drogas y alcohol entre la juventud, sino para controlar a los muchachos que por el descuido de sus padres se mantienen ociosos en las calles", dijo el secretario de Gobierno, Convivencia y Seguridad.

Además, se evitará que los adolescentes caigan en la delincuencia y aprendan cosas indebidas por falta de actividades extraescolares. "Los menores de edad deben estar estudiando, trabajando o en sus casas, pero nada tienen que hacer en las calles".

La razón de la medida que se pretende implantar en la ciudad se desprende de las miles de quejas de la comunidad y de las estadísticas del Programa de Epidemiología de la Violencia realizado por la Administración Municipal, que revelan que más del 40% de los actos delincuenciales son cometidos por menores de edad.

Pese a las acciones de la Policía y de los demás organismos de seguridad del Estado, se han incrementado los delitos contra la propiedad, especialmente el hurto de vehículos.

## ¿LO HAS ENTENDIDO?

**1** ¿Qué medida quiere introducir el gobierno en Cali?

**2** ¿A quién afectará esta medida?

**3** ¿A qué hora empieza y termina el toque de queda?

**4** ¿Qué quieren las autoridades conseguir con esta medida?

**5** ¿Qué revelan las estadísticas?

**6** ¿Cuáles son los actos delictivos más comunes en Cali?

## TOMA NOTA

Fíjate en esta frase del texto.

> *"Además, **se evitará que** los adolescentes **caigan** en la delincuencia y **aprendan** cosas indebidas...".*

Las expresiones ***evitar que, impedir que, prohibir que*** y ***pedir que*** van seguidas del subjuntivo porque introducen una oración subordinada con un sujeto diferente.

Completa estas frases con el presente de subjuntivo.

**A** Se prohibirá que los adolescentes _____ (***salir***) por la noche.
**B** Se evitará que el robo de vehículos _____ (***aumentar***).
**C** Se pedirá que los padres _____ (***tener***) más responsabilidad.
**D** La policía quiere impedir que los menores _____ (***deambular***) por las calles.
**E** Los padres deben impedir que sus hijos _____ (***caer***) en el mundo de la droga.
**F** El gobierno quiere evitar que el problema de la delincuencia _____ (***agravarse***).
**G** Las autoridades prohibirán que los bares _____ (***abrir***) después de la medianoche.
**H** La sociedad pide que _____ (***existir***) más seguridad y vigilancia policial en las calles.

### AMPLÍA TU VOCABULARIO

**deambular** caminar sin dirección determinada
**toque de queda** tiempo después del cual las personas deben permanecer en sus casas hasta el día siguiente
**será implantado** será impuesto/obligado
**descuido** negligencia, falta de atención
**ociosos** que no hacen nada
**evitará** impedirá que pase
**indebidas** que no se deben hacer, inapropiadas
**se desprende de** se deduce de
**quejas** protestas
**delincuenciales** criminales
**pese a** en contra de
**delitos** ofensas criminales
**hurto** robo

## Y TÚ, ¿CÓMO LO VES?

**1** ¿Crees que es necesario que los padres impongan un horario estricto para volver a casa? ¿Por qué? ¿Alguna vez has vuelto más tarde de la hora? ¿Qué pasó? ¿Te castigaron tus padres?

**2** ¿Crees que los castigos son efectivos? ¿Cuál es el castigo que más te molesta? ¿Qué otras alternativas hay?

**3** ¿Te parece eficaz y suficiente para prevenir la delincuencia el toque de queda impuesto en Cali? ¿Qué medidas impondrías tú?

**4** En tu ciudad, ¿hay delincuencia juvenil? ¿Existen las peleas entre diferentes pandillas de jóvenes? ¿Qué problemas causa y qué medidas existen para solucionarlos?

## EN LA ONDA

**1** Mira la lista. En tu opinión, ¿cuáles son las causas de la delincuencia juvenil y la drogadicción? ¿Es posible prevenirlas?

- familias rotas o desestructuradas
- problemas en el colegio
- relaciones familiares problemáticas
- abandono de los padres
- falta de
  - un modelo familiar estable
  - seguridad
  - afecto
  - autoestima personal

**2** ¿Verdadero o falso? Escucha a Adriana Mendoza hablar sobre el proyecto de la *Casa de la Juventud* en Bogotá (Colombia) con un periodista en la radio. Decide si estas frases son verdaderas o falsas.

**A** En la *Casa de la Juventud* los menores pueden jugar y aprender cosas.

**B** No hay facilidades para practicar deportes.

**C** La *Casa de la Juventud* está abierta sólo para los adolescentes.

**D** Muchos menores se quedan solos porque sus padres trabajan.

**E** Tienen suficiente dinero para su proyecto.

**F** Quieren ampliar las facilidades del centro.

**G** Quieren abrir un hogar para los niños de la calle.

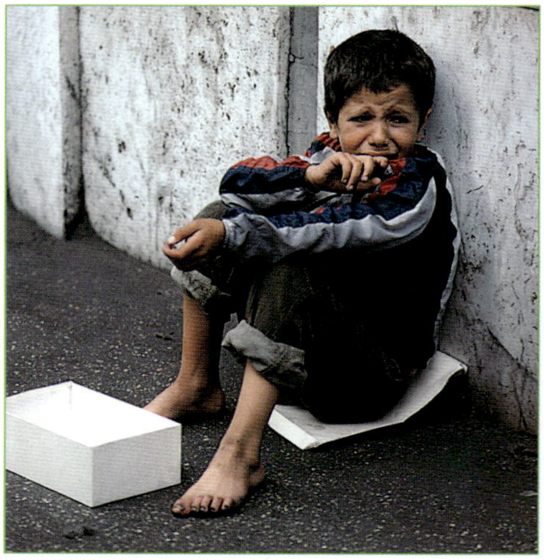

## ¡TIENES LA PALABRA!

**1** Entre toda la clase decide cuáles son los castigos más apropiados para estas faltas. Explica los motivos de tu decisión.

**Delitos**

- vandalismo y graffiti
- robar en las tiendas o grandes almacenes
- robar en las viviendas
- robar vehículos
- vender droga
- viajar en transporte público sin pagar
- conducir bajo los efectos del alcohol
- falsificar dinero
- homicidio
- terrorismo

**Castigos**

- pagar una multa
- hacer servicio comunitario
- ingresar en un centro de rehabilitación
- prisión de régimen abierto
- cadena perpetua
- pena de muerte

**2** En grupos de tres escoge uno de estos papeles.

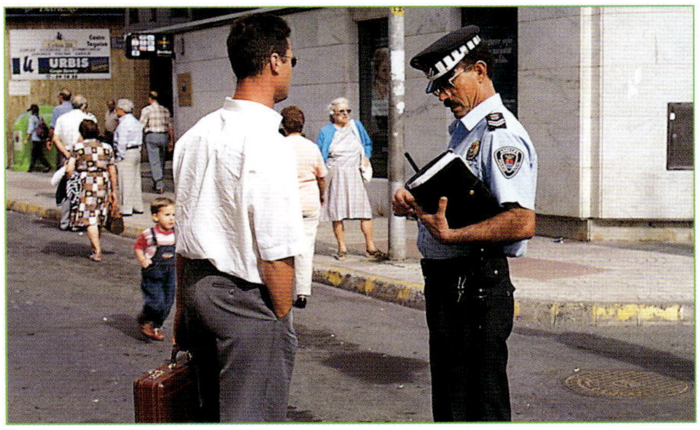

**Turista**

Tienes que denunciar el robo de tu vehículo. Responde a las preguntas de la policía. Describe tu vehículo (marca, color, matrícula), sus contenidos y dónde te pueden localizar.

**Policía**

Habla con el turista y el testigo para completar tu informe sobre el robo. Haz las preguntas necesarias para obtener la información.

**Testigo**

Viste todo lo que ocurrió desde la ventana de una cafetería. Responde a las preguntas del policía.

**3** Entre toda la clase comenta tus opiniones sobre estos temas.

***¿La justicia es igual para todos o sólo para los que pueden pagarse un buen abogado?***

***¿Está justificada la pena de muerte?***

## POR ESCRITO

**1** Observa el gráfico con la opinión de los padres sobre los mayores peligros para sus hijos. Haz una encuesta entre cinco estudiantes de tu clase sobre cuáles consideran los mayores peligros para los adolescentes. Prepara un cuestionario de cinco preguntas y escribe las conclusiones.

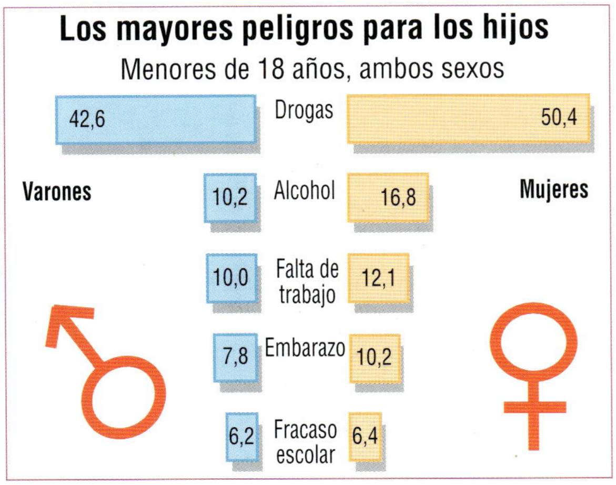


**2** ¿Qué medidas pueden contribuir a prevenir o reducir la delincuencia juvenil? Haz una lista.

**MEDIDAS**

- *aumentar la vigilancia policial*
- *abrir más hogares para los niños de la calle*
- *implantar un toque de queda*

**3** Trabajas como voluntario/a en un centro de atención para menores como la *Casa de la Juventud*. Explica qué haces, qué opinas del proyecto y qué problemas existen. (250 palabras)

## PUNTO DE MIRA

¿Qué es lo que más te preocupa o interesa en la vida? Escoge los cinco temas que más te interesan. Razona tu respuesta.

el consumo
el deporte

la salud
la familia
los estudios
la amistad

la diversión
la sinceridad
la independencia
el éxito profesional

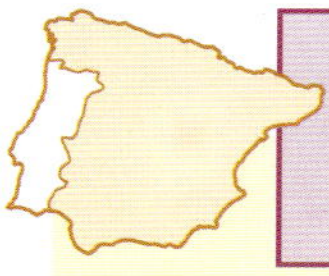

¿Todos los jóvenes quieren vivir independientemente? Vas a leer los casos de tres chicos españoles.

# Vive de tus padres hasta la jubilación

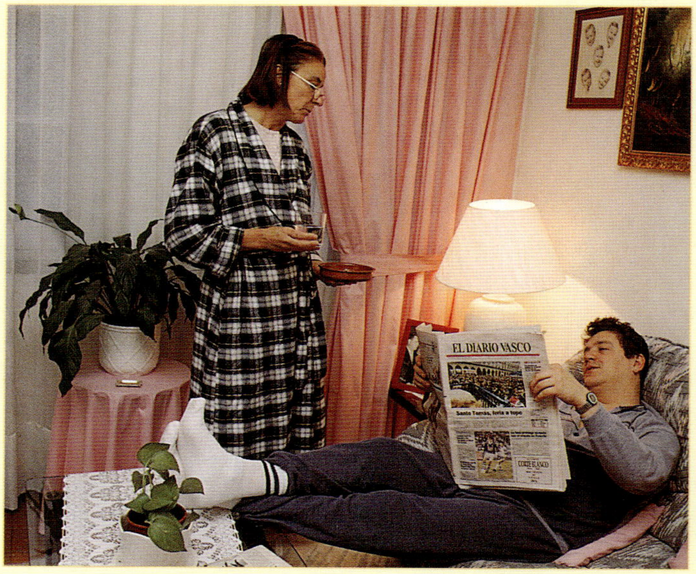


No hay quien les eche del hogar familiar. Trabajan, ganan dinero y tienen coche. Viven felices. Son los hijos. Los hijos gorrones, claro está.

La comodidad es la principal causa de que muchos jóvenes españoles que tienen suficientes recursos como para emanciparse no quieran hacerlo.

Según el informe *Juventud en España*, del Instituto de la Juventud, el 77% de los jóvenes (entre 15 y 30 años) vive con sus padres. El informe refleja que la mayoría se emancipa cuando se casa. Federico, Francisco, o Miguel no tienen excusas.

Federico tiene 28 años y su despacho está en casa. Y la cocinera, y la lavandera. Y todo lo que le haga falta. Acabó Biológicas en 1992, hizo un máster de Dirección de Empresas y trabaja desde hace más de un año en una multinacional alemana, coche de la empresa incluido. «Entro, salgo, hago lo que me apetece, no tengo gastos en casa... La gente es muy comodona». Y se muestra sincero: «Si tuviera un hijo querría que se fuese lo antes posible».

Francisco cumplió los 29. Aunque goza de independencia económica, nunca se ha planteado irse a vivir fuera de casa. «Estoy muy a gusto con mis padres y hermanas. Si viviera solo, me aburriría». Nunca ha ahorrado. Ni para un alquiler ni para comprar una vivienda. «Sólo lo haría si encontrase a una chica».

A sus 30 años Miguel es el vividor consciente: «En casa se vive como en un hotel. Te planchan, te ponen de comer...». Únicamente se queda solo los meses de julio y reconoce el calvario que supone. «Al principio muy bien, pero al final estoy deseando que venga mi madre para ver si me organiza todo».

## ¿LO HAS ENTENDIDO?

**1** ¿Qué tienen en común Federico, Francisco y Miguel?

**2** ¿Qué ventajas tiene para ellos vivir con los padres?

**3** ¿Cuál es el principal motivo por el que mayoría de los jóvenes españoles decide vivir fuera de casa? ¿Cuál es una de las razones por las que no se emancipan antes?

**4** ¿Con qué compara Miguel el hogar familiar? ¿Por qué?

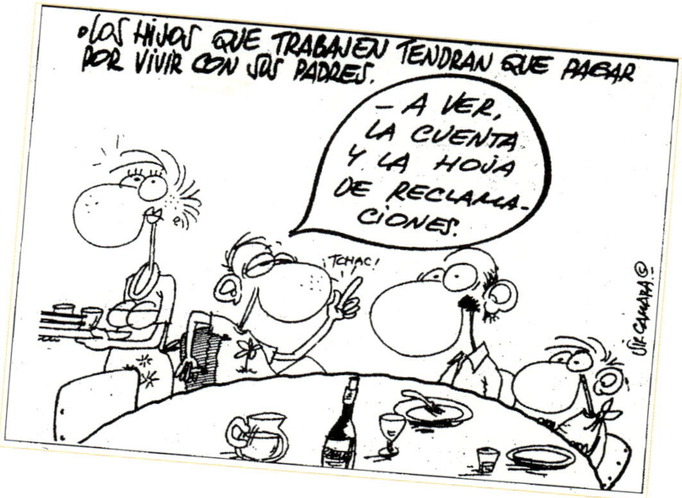


## TOMA NOTA

Fíjate en la estructura. **_Si_ + imperfecto de subjuntivo + condicional**

Las frases condicionales de este tipo expresan una condición remota o lejos de poder realizarse. Hay tres ejemplos en *Vive de tus padres hasta la jubilación*. Búscalos.

**1** Completa las siguientes frases con el condicional.

**A** Si tuviera seis meses de vacaciones...
**B** Si tuviera mucho dinero...
**C** Si hiciera más deporte...
**D** Si estudiara más...

**2** Completa las siguientes frases con el imperfecto de subjuntivo.

**A** Viviría por mi cuenta si...
**B** Aprendería español más rápido si...
**C** Invitaría a mis amigos a una fiesta si...
**D** Tendría más dinero si...

### AMPLÍA TU VOCABULARIO

**jubilación** retirarse del trabajo a los 60/65 años
**gorrones** que viven a costa de los demás
**recursos** medios económicos, dinero
**emanciparse** independizarse
**lo que le haga falta** todo lo que necesite
**gastos** expensas
**comodona** que le gusta vivir confortablemente
**goza de** disfruta de
**se ha planteado** ha pensado en
**estoy muy a gusto** estoy muy bien
**ahorrado** guardado dinero, economizado
**vividor** persona que vive a costa de los demás
**calvario** sufrimiento, tormento

## Y TÚ, ¿CÓMO LO VES?

**1** ¿Qué opinas de la actitud de los jóvenes en el artículo? ¿Si tuvieras trabajo y ganaras dinero harías lo mismo que estos chicos españoles?

**2** Si tuvieras hijos, ¿cómo reaccionarías ante una situación así?

**3** ¿Crees que los padres se sacrifican por los hijos? ¿Cómo?

**4** ¿Qué relación tienes con tus padres? ¿Te parece que son estrictos o tolerantes? Explica.

**5** ¿Para qué cosas te gustaría tener más libertad en casa?

## EN LA ONDA

**1** Haz una lista de las cosas que te permiten hacer tus padres y otra de las que no te dejan.

*Ejemplo*

**Mis padres me dan permiso para**
*traer amigos a casa.*

**Mis padres no me dejan**
*salir durante la semana.*

**2** ¿Cómo describirías a los jóvenes de tu generación? Utiliza estos adjetivos para expresarte. Razona tus respuestas.

*Ejemplo*

*Pienso que los jóvenes de mi generación son* ***tolerantes*** *porque aceptan la eutanasia.*

| | |
|---|---|
| sexistas | tolerantes |
| abiertos | igualitarios |
| competitivos | conservadores |
| idealistas | individualistas |
| estudiosos | materialistas |

**3** ¿Verdadero o falso? Escucha a estos jóvenes en la clase de ética y decide si estas afirmaciones son verdaderas o falsas.

**A** En España los jóvenes se independizan pronto.

**B** Vivir solo es barato.

**C** A Paloma le gustaría vivir por su cuenta.

**D** Es fácil independizarse si tienes un empleo.

**E** Los jóvenes mexicanos están muy unidos a sus padres.

**F** Es fácil para los jóvenes encontrar empleo.

**G** Los jóvenes valoran mucho las buenas relaciones familiares.

## ¡TIENES LA PALABRA!

**Valores que los adultos inculcan**

Menores de 18 años, ambos sexos

| | | | |
|---|---|---|---|
| Consumir | 84,1 | 15,9 | Ahorrar |
| Competir | 82,6 | 17,4 | Compartir |
| Ser comunicativo | 76,7 | 23,3 | Ser reservado |
| Ser interesado | 75,2 | 24,8 | Ser entregado |
| Ser realista | 70,4 | 29,6 | Ser idealista |
| Ser igualitario | 67,7 | 32,3 | Ser sexista |
| Ser resuelto | 66,5 | 33,5 | Ser dependiente |

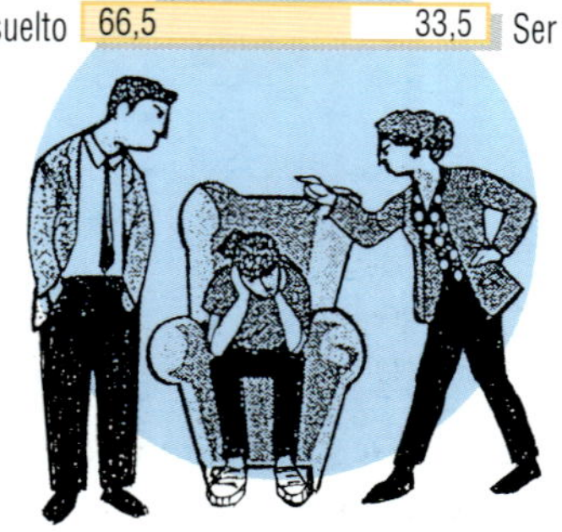

**1** En grupos observa esta información. ¿Qué valores son importantes para ti en la vida y en la familia? ¿Coinciden con los de la ilustración? ¿Cuáles son positivos y cuáles negativos?

**2** ¿Crees qué hay diferencia de valores entre los chicos y las chicas? ¿Por qué crees que existe esa diferencia?

### AMPLÍA TU VOCABULARIO

**ser interesado** que hace las cosas para beneficio propio

**ser resuelto** que no tiene miedo a las dificultades; valiente

**ser entregado** que hace las cosas para el beneficio de otras personas

**3** En grupos de tres escoge uno de estos papeles.

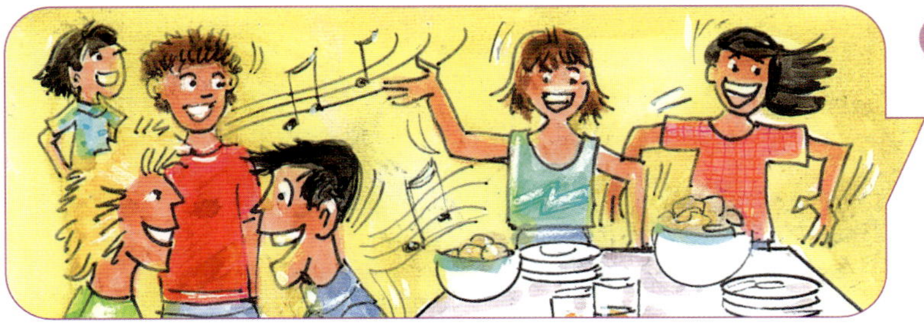

**Hijo/a**

El próximo fin de semana te gustaría dar una fiesta en casa e invitar a todos tus amigos. Tus padres estarán de viaje. Habla con ellos para convencerles.

**Madre**

La idea de tu hijo/a te parece un poco arriesgada. No quieres mucha gente extraña en casa. No quieres que pase nada malo.

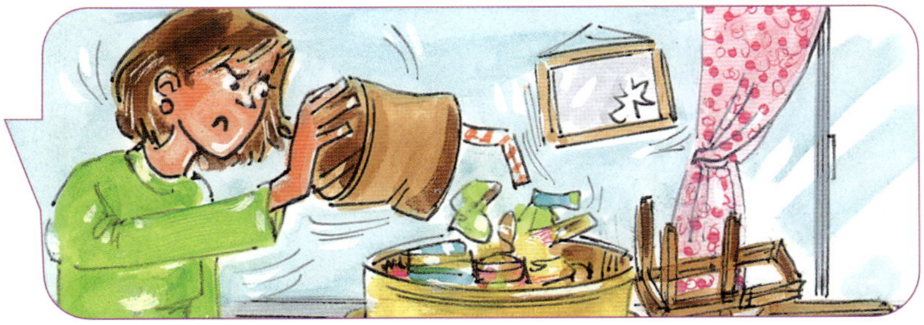

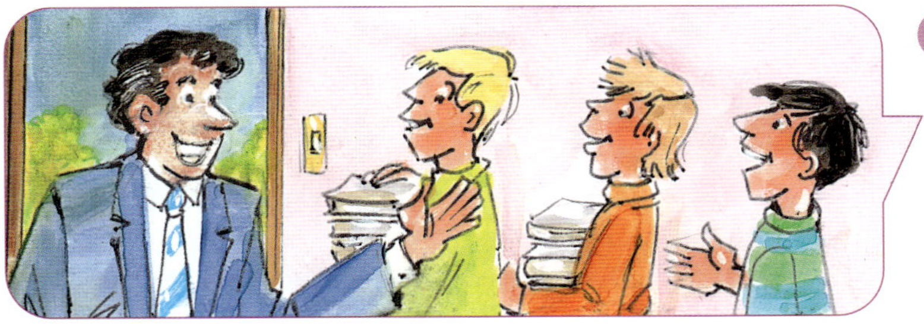

**Padre**

Conoces bien a tu hijo/a y sabes que es sensato/a. Dale consejos sobre lo que debe y no debe hacer. Intenta llegar a un acuerdo entre los tres.

**4** Entre toda la clase discute tus opiniones sobre estos temas.

***¿Es frecuente que los jóvenes vivan solos cuando terminan sus estudios?***

***¿Para quién es más fácil vivir con los padres, para los chicos o para las chicas?***

***¿Con qué dificultades se encuentran los jóvenes de tu país para independizarse de sus padres?***

## POR ESCRITO

**1** ¿Vives con tus padres? ¿Qué ventajas e inconvenientes tiene esto para ambas partes? Escríbelas en una lista.

**2** ¿Cuáles son tus planes para el futuro con respecto al trabajo y la vivienda? ¿Te gustaría vivir por tu cuenta? (250 palabras)

**3** Escribe sobre los jóvenes de tu país, cómo son, qué piensan, qué temas les preocupan y cómo se relacionan con sus padres. (200 palabras)

**4** ¿Qué importancia tienen la familia y los valores tradicionales en la sociedad actual?

KEY

| | |
|---|---|
| (*adj*) = adjective | (*prep*) = preposition |
| (*adv*) = adverb | (*pron*) = pronoun |
| (*Lat Am*) = Latin American word | (*nf*) = feminine noun |
| (*col*) = colloquialism | (*nm*) = masculine noun |
| (*Sp*) = word used chiefly in Spain | (*nm/f*) = masculine/feminine noun |
| (*ph*) = phrase | (*v*) = verb |

## A

**a corto plazo** (*ph*) *80* short-term
**a decir de** (*ph*) *80* according to
**a medida que** (*ph*) *80* as
**a orillas de** (*ph*) *64* on the banks of
**a partir de** (*ph*) *88* starting on
**a pesar de** (*ph*) *39* in spite of, despite
**a raíz de** (*ph*) *76* as a result of
**abarcar** (*v*) *80* to include
**abogado/a** (*nm/f*) *54* lawyer
**abono químico** (*nm*) *48* fertilizer
**abrebotellas** (*nm*) *21* bottle opener
**aburrimiento** (*nm*) *55* boredom
**acabar** (*v*) *48* to finish
**acabar de** (*ph*) *40* to have just done something
**acariciar** (*v*) *34* to stroke, to pat
**acceder** (*v*) *25* to access
**acera** (*nf*) *56* sidewalk, pavement
**acercarse** (*v*) *72* to approach, to come into contact with
**Aclla** (*nf*) *76* Inca virgin consecrated to the sun god
**acoger** (*v*) *64* to welcome
**aconsejar** (*v*) *14* to recommend, to advise
**acoso** (*nm*) *68* hounding, persecution
**acostar** (*v*) *55* to put to bed
**acostarse** (*v*) *55* to go to bed
**acrecentar** (*v*) *27* to increase
**acuático/a** (*adj*) *12* aquatic
**acudir** (*v*) *52* to go
**adecuarse** (*v*) *80* to adapt oneself
**adelanto** (*nm*) *27* progress, improvement
**adicto** (*adj*) *17* addicted
**adivinador/a** (*nm/f*) *39* fortune-teller
**adivinar** (*v*) *42* to guess
**adoquinar** (*v*) *64* to pave
**adorno** (*nm*) *62* decoration, adornment
**advertir** (*v*) *8* to point out, to draw attention to
**aéreo/a** (*adj*) *12* aerial
**afeitarse** (*v*) *56* to shave
**afición** (*nf*) *24* hobby, pastime
**afortunado/a** (*adj*) *38* lucky, fortunate
**agarradera** (*nf*) *12* handle
**agarrarse** (*v*) *12* to hold on
**agencia de viajes** (*nf*) *74* travel agency
**agotar** (*v*) *24* to use up, to deplete
**agrario/a** (*adj*) *76* land
**ahorrar** (*v*) *6* to save
**aislarse** (*v*) *80* to isolate oneself
**ajedrez** (*nm*) *31* chess
**al alcance de** (*ph*) *24* near, within reach
**al principio** (*ph*) *19* at first, in the beginning
**ala delta** (*nf*) *12* hang-gliding
**alargar** (*v*) *45* to lengthen, to prolong
**alarmante** (*adj*) *48* alarming, worrying
**albergue** (*nm*) *32* shelter, refuge
**alcalde/esa** (*nm/f*) *28* mayor
**alcance** (*nm*) *68* reach
**alcanzar** (*v*) *6* to attain, to reach
**aleación** (*nf*) *51* alloy
**aleta** (*nf*) *12* flipper
**alfarería** (*nf*) *76* pottery
**alga** (*nf*) *24* seaweed
**aliviar** (*v*) *19* to ease
**almorzar** (*v*) *55* to have lunch
**alojamiento** (*nm*) *74* accommodation
**alquiler** (*nm*) *66* rent
**alrededor de** (*ph*) *72* approximately, about
**alterar** (*v*) *48* to change
**altiplanicie** (*nf*) *84* high plateau
**altruista** (*nm/f*) *56* unselfish person, altruist
**ama de casa** (*nf*) *30* homemaker, housewife
**ambientador** (*nm*) *48* air freshener
**ambiental** (*adj*) *32* environmental
**ambiente** (*nm*) *51 73* environment; atmosphere
**ambos/as** (*adj*) *20* both
**amenazar** (*v*) *72* to threaten
**amistad** (*nf*) *36* friendship
**amo/a** (*nm/f*) *35* owner
**amuleto** (*nm*) *36* amulet, lucky charm
**amurallado/a** (*adj*) *78* walled
**anárquico/a** (*adj*) *24* anarchic
**andino/a** (*adj*) *76* Andean, from the Andes
**ángel de la guarda** (*nm*) *23* guardian angel
**anglosajón/a** (*adj*) *36* Anglo-Saxon
**ansia** (*nf*) *67* anxiety
**ante** (*prep*) *72* before
**antepasado/a** (*nm/f*) *45* ancestor
**anuncio** (*nm*) *24* advertisement
**añadir** (*v*) *8* to add
**aparte de** (*prep*) *24* aside from

**apasionado/a** (*adj*) *20* passionate
**apelar a** (*v*) *8* to call on
**apertura** (*nf*) *15* opening
**apestado/a** (*adj*) *56* infected
**apetecer** (*v*) *92* to strike one's fancy
**apogeo** (*nm*) *76* height, apogee
**aprobar** (*v*) *13* to pass an exam
**aprovechar** (*v*) *8* to make good use of
**apunte** (*nm*) *56* note
**arboleda** (*nf*) *64* grove
**árbol genealógico** (*nm*) *79* family tree
**arbusto** (*nm*) *60* bush, shrub
**árido/a** (*adj*) *60* arid
**arquitectónico/a** (*adj*) *76* architectural
**arrasar** (*v*) *72* to destroy, to demolish
**arrastrado/a** (*adj*) *48* carried away
**arriesgar** (*v*) *68* to endanger
**arroz** (*nm*) *32* rice
**artesanía** (*nf*) *62* craftsmanship
**asa** (*nf*) *12* handle
**asegurar** (*v*) *20 60* to affirm; to secure, to safeguard
**asignatura** (*nf*) *8* subject
**asistentes** (*nm/f*) *8* participants
**asumir** (*v*) *28* to assume, to take on
**atado/a** (*adj*) *12* tied
**atraer** (*v*) *13* to attract
**atrapar** (*v*) *16 72* to trap; to confine
**atrayente** (*adj*) *30* attractive
**augurio** (*nm*) *36* omen
**aumentar** (*v*) *7* to increase
**aún así** (*adv*) *16* even so
**autónomo/a** (*nm/f*) *80* self-employed person
**autopista de información** (*nf*) *24* information super-highway
**aventura** (*nf*) *12* adventure
**averiguar** (*v*) *80* to find out
**avispa** (*nf*) *34* wasp
**ayuda** (*nf*) *19* help

## B

**bailaor/a** (*nm/f*) *40* flamenco dancer
**bajar** (*v*) *12 32* to descend; to take down
**bajo/a** (*adj*) *22* low
**baloncesto** (*nm*) *12* basketball
**bañar** (*v*) *24 50* to bathe
**barato/a** (*adj*) *94* cheap
**barriga** (*nf col*) *59* belly, paunch
**bastar** (*v*) *36* to be enough
**basurero** (*nm*) *48* garbage dump
**batalla** (*nf*) *84* battle
**bebida** (*nf*) *19* drink
**beeper** (*nm Lat Am*) *52* pager
**béisbol** (*nm*) *14* baseball
**beneficio** (*nm*) *8* benefit
**bienvenido/a** (*adj*) *66* welcome
**biotecnología** (*nf*) *44* biotechnology
**bolsillo** (*nm*) *19* pocket
**borrachera** (*nf*) *16* drunkenness
**bullicio** (*nm*) *64* uproar, hubbub
**bungaló** (*nm*) *65* bungalow
**buscador/a** (*nm/f*) *12* searcher, seeker

## C

**cabra** (*nf*) *34* goat
**cacería** (*nf*) *68* hunt
**cachorro/a** (*nm/f*) *35* puppy
**cadena** (*nf*) *22* network
**cadena perpetua** (*nf*) *90* life imprisonment
**caída libre** (*nf*) *12* free fall
**calabaza** (*nf*) *60* pumpkin
**cálido/a** (*adj*) *58* warm
**callarse** (*v*) *39* to keep quiet
**calmar** (*v*) *67* to calm
**calvario** (*nm*) *92* torment, heavy burden
**cambiar** (*v*) *32* to change
**caminata** (*nf*) *78* hike, excursion
**campaña** (*nf*) *15* campaign
**campeonato** (*nm*) *22* championship
**campesino/a** (*nm/f*) *76* peasant
**campo** (*nm*) *28* field, sphere
**canal** (*nm*) *20* channel
**cansancio** (*nm*) *52* fatigue, exhaustion
**cantaor/a** (*nm/f*) *40* flamenco singer
**cantidad** (*nf*) *20* quantity
**capa de ozono** (*nf*) *48* ozone layer
**capacitado/a** (*adj*) *28* qualified
**capaz** (*adj*) *16* able, competent
**cargo** (*nm*) *28* duty, office
**carrera** (*nf*) *15 52* career; race
**carro** (*nm Lat Am*) *9* car
**carta** (*nf*) *16* letter
**casar** (*v*) *36* to marry
**casco** (*nm*) *12* helmet
**castellano** (*nm*) *8* Castilian, Spanish
**castigar** (*v*) *69* to punish
**cazar** (*v*) *60* to hunt
**cebolla** (*nf*) *25* onion
**centenar** (*nm*) *8* hundred
**centro de rehabilitación** (*nm*) *17* rehabilitation center
**cerebro** (*nm*) *16* brain
**cerro** (*nm*) *76* hill
**Cervantes** *8* (Miguel de Cervantes, 1547-1616), Spanish writer. Author of ***Don Quijote de la Mancha***
**cerveza** (*nf*) *46* beer
**cesar** (*v*) *32* to stop
**chal** (*nm*) *59* shawl
**chaleco salvavidas** (*nm*) *12* life jacket
**charla** (*nf*) *18* talk
**chicano/a** (*nm/f*) *40* Mexican-American
**chisme** (*nm*) *69* piece of gossip
**ciencia** (*nf*) *26* science
**cierto/a** (*adj*) *40* true, certain
**cifras** (*nf*) *40* statistics
**cinturón de seguridad** (*nm*) *13* seat belt
**cita** (*nf*) *43* date, meeting
**ciudadanía** (*nf*) *28* citizens
**clan** (*nm*) *60* clan

**clave** (*adj*) *72* key
**clon** (*nm*) *44* clone
**cobarde** (*nm/f*) *34* coward
**coleccionista** (*nm/f*) *24* collector
**colectivo** (*nm*) *40* collective, group
**colgar** (*v*) *68* to hang, to be suspended
**colocar** (*v*) *36* to place
**comarca** (*nf*) *12* region, area
**cometer** (*v*) *88* to commit
**comodón/a** (*adj*) *92* comfort-loving
**compartir** (*v*) *24* to share
**complacer** (*v*) *72* to please
**complementos** (*nm*) *56* accessories
**comportamiento** (*nm*) *18* conduct
**comprar** (*v*) *6* to buy
**compras** (*nf*) *18* shopping
**computadora** (*nf Lat Am*) *52* computer
**concebir** (*v*) *16* to conceive, to imagine
**concernir** (*v*) *12* to concern
**concurso** (*nm*) *22* competition
**conducir** (*v*) *9 76* to drive a car; to guide
**conducir a** (*ph*) *55* to lead to
**conferencia de prensa** (*nf*) *46* press conference
**confianza** (*nf*) *42* confidence
**conjunto/a** (*adj*) *40* joint
**conjurar** (*v*) *36* to exorcise
**conminar** (*v*) *56* to threaten
**conocimiento** (*nm*) *9* knowledge
**conquistador** (*nm*) *72* conqueror
**consejo** (*nm*) *19* piece of advice
**consigo** (*pron*) *36* with oneself
**consistir en** (*v*) *12* to consist of
**consuelo** (*nm*) *27* comfort
**contar** (*v*) *20* to tell
**contar con** (*v*) *28* to count on
**contenedor** (*nm*) 50 container
**contentarse con** (*v*) *28* to be satisfied with
**contrario/a** (*nm/f*) *28* opponent
**conversador/a** (*nm/f Lat Am*) *64* coversationalist
**convertirse** (*v*) *48* to be changed
**corazón** (*nm*) *7* heart
**cordero/a** (*nm/f*) *44* lamb
**corona** (*nf*) *28* crown
**corregir** (*v*) *13* to correct
**correo electrónico** (*nm*) *24* e-mail
**correspondencia** (*nf*) *40* letters
**corriente** (*nf*) *12* current, flow
**cortauñas** (*nm*) *21* nail clippers
**cosecha** (*nf*) *84* harvest
**costumbre** (*nf*) *10* custom
**cotidiano/a** (*adj*) *72* commonplace
**cotilleo** (*nm*) *69* gossip
**creciente** (*adj*) *40* growing, increasing
**creencia** (*nf*) *36* belief
**criollo** (*nm/f*) *60* person of Spanish ancestry
**crudo/a** (*adj*) *25* raw
**cruzado/a** (*adj*) *35* crossbred
**cualquier/a** (*adj*) *7* any
**cualquiera** (*pron*) *24* anybody
**cuenta** (*nf*) *93* bill
**cuero** (*nm*) *12* leather
**cuerpo** (*nm*) *16* body
**culto/a** (*adj*) *28* educated, cultured
**cumbre** (*nf*) *8* summit, meeting
**cuyo** (*adj*) *6* whose

## D

**dañar** (*v*) *19* to harm, to damage
**dar aviso a** (*ph*) *32* to tell, to inform
**dar por terminado/a** (*ph*) *32* to end
**dar un vuelco total** (*ph*) *20* to change drastically
**darse a conocer** (*ph*) *24* to make a name for oneself
**darse cuenta de** (*ph*) *20* to realize
**dato** (*nm*) *48* fact, piece of information
**de acuerdo al** (*ph*) *52* in accordance with
**deambular** (*v*) *88* to wander
**debido a** (*ph*) *8* because of, due to
**década** (*nf*) *6* decade
**dedicar** (*v*) *52* to devote
**dejar** (*v*) *32* to allow
**dejar de** (*v*) *88* to stop
**delincuencial** (*adj*) *88* criminal
**delito** (*nm*) *88* crime
**demostrar** (*v*) *72* to show, to prove
**denunciar** (*v*) *91* to report
**dependiente** (*nm*) *35* salesperson
**deportivo** (*adj*) *12* sports
**derecho** (*nm*) *32* right
**derramar** (*v*) *36* to spill
**desaconsejar** (*v*) *14* to advise against, to dissuade
**desarrollar** (*v*) *12* to carry out
**desarrollo** (*nm*) *80* progress
**descargar** (*v*) *12* to unload
**desconocido/a** (*adj*) *36* unknown
**descubrimiento** (*nm*) *44* discovery
**descuido** (*nm*) *88* negligence
**desempeñar** (*v*) *29* to perform
**desempleo** (*nm*) *83* unemployment
**desencadenar** (*v*) *44* to unleash
**desgracia** (*nf*) *56* misfortune
**desigualdad** (*nf*) *27* inequality
**desinhibirse** (*v*) *16* to lose one's inhibitions
**deslizarse** (*v*) *12* to glide
**desnutrición** (*nf*) *32* malnutrition
**despacho** (*nm*) *92* office
**desprender de** (*v*) *88* to be implied by
**destacar** (*v*) *80* to highlight
**destino** (*nm*) *74* destination
**destrozar** (*v*) *16* to destroy
**detenerse** (*v*) *16* to stop
**deterioro** (*nm*) *48* deterioration
**determinante** (*adj*) *40* determinant
**deuda** (*nf*) *18* debt
**devolver** (*v*) *80* to return
**diariamente** (*adj*) *26* daily

**días de fiesta** (*nm*) *16* weekend
**dibujo animado** (*nm*) *22* cartoon
**dicho** (*nm*) *39* proverb
**diferenciar** (*v*) *29* to distinguish from
**difundir** (*v*) *24* to spread
**discapacitado/a** (*nm/f*) *80* handicapped person
**disfrazarse de** (*v*) *68* to disguise oneself as
**disfrutar** (*v*) *55* to enjoy
**disminuir** (*v*) *88* to reduce
**disputar** (*v*) *20* to fight for
**distraer** (*v*) *32* to distract
**dominar** (*v*) *16* to control
**dominio** (*nm*) *20 36* knowledge; control
**droga de diseño** (*nf*) *16* designer drug
**ducharse** (*v*) *50* to take a shower
**dulce** (*adj*) *28* sweet, gentle
**durar** (*v*) *32* to last

## E

**echar** (*v*) *92* to throw out
**eficaz** (*adj*) *44* effective
**ejercer** (*v*) *23* to exert
**ejercicio** (*nm*) *14* exercise
**emanciparse** (*v*) *92* to become independent
**embajada** (*nf*) *78* embassy
**embalaje** (*nm*) *51* packing
**embarazo** (*nm*) *91* pregnancy
**embarcarse** (*v*) *12* to get on board, to embark
**emisora** (*nf*) *82* radio station
**empezar** (*v*) *15* to begin
**empresa** (*nf*) *24* company
**empuje** (*nm*) *40* drive
**enano/a** (*adj*) *35* tiny
**encajar en** (*v*) *76* to fit into
**encaminar** (*v*) *32* to direct
**encantar** (*v*) *20* to delight
**encargado/a** (*nm/f*) *12* person in charge
**encuesta** (*nf*) *34* survey
**enfermedad** (*nf*) *17* illness
**enfermera** (*nf*) *30* nurse
**enfermo/a** (*adj nm/f*) *30 32* ill; patient
**enfrentar** (*v*) *29* to face
**engrandecimiento** (*nm*) *28* aggrandizement
**enhorabuena** (*nf*) *43* congratulations
**enigma** (*nm*) *76* mystery
**enorgullecerse** (*v*) *64* to be proud
**enriquecer** (*v*) *72* to enrich
**enseñanza** (*nf*) *24* teaching
**enseñar** (*v*) *23 36* to teach; to show
**enterarse de** (*v*) *33* to find out about
**entidad** (*nf*) *32* organization
**entrañable** (*adj*) *64* affectionate
**entregado/a** (*adj*) *94* devoted
**entrevista** (*nf*) *15* interview
**envase** (*nm*) *47* packaging
**época** (*nf*) *76* period, time
**equipaje** (*nm*) *74* baggage, luggage
**equipo** (*nm*) *14* team
**equitación** (*nf*) *34* horseback riding
**erigir** (*v*) *76* to build
**escalada** (*nf*) *12* climbing
**escaso/a** (*adj*) *36* scarce
**escenificación** (*nf*) *84* staging
**esclavo/a** (*nm/f*) *26* slave
**escocés/esa** (*adj*) *44* Scottish
**escoger** (*v*) *10* to choose
**escritura** (*nf*) *37* handwriting
**esfuerzo** (*nm*) *76* effort
**espectáculo** (*nm*) *7* show
**espejo** (*nm*) *58* mirror
**esperanza** (*nf*) *47* hope
**esperar** (*v*) *29* to hope
**espina** (*nf*) *60* thorn
**esqueleto** (*nm*) *76* skeleton
**esquí** (*nm*) *12* skiing
**esquimal** (*nm/f*) *12* Eskimo
**establecimiento** (*nm*) *56* establishment
**estadística** (*nf*) *41* statistics
**estallar** (*v*) *52* to explode
**estar a gusto** (*ph*) *92* to feel comfortable
**estar al acecho de** (*ph*) *68* to lie in wait for
**estar al día** (*ph*) *7* to be up to date
**estar al frente de** (*ph*) *28* to be at the head of
**estar al mando de** (*ph*) *28* to be in command
**estar colgado/a** (*ph col*) *16* to be hooked
**estar de acuerdo** (*ph*) *25* to agree
**estar de moda** (*ph*) *34* to be fashionable
**estar dispuesto a** (*ph*) *32* to be prepared to
**estrecho/a** (*adj*) *60 76* intimate; narrow
**estrella** (*nf*) *15* star
**etiqueta** (*nf*) *46* label
**evitar** (*v*) *12 60* to avoid; to prevent
**excursionismo** (*nm*) *14* hiking, rambling
**exigir** (*v*) *12 52* to require; to demand
**éxito** (*nm*) *15* success
**experimentar** (*v*) *12* to experience
**explanada** (*nf*) *84* terrace, platform
**exprimir** (*v*) *72* to squeeze out, to exploit
**extraer** (*v*) *36* to extract
**extraño/a** (*adj*) *38* strange

## F

**fabricar** (*v*) *44 68* to make; to invent
**facilitar** (*v*) *24* to make easy
**fallar** (*v*) *68* to pronounce sentence on
**faltar** (*v*) *17* to be missing
**falta de** (*nf*) *88* shortage of
**famoso/a** (*adj*) *11* famous
**fantasma** (*nm*) *38* ghost
**fastuoso/a** (*adj*) *84* magnificent
**fatídico/a** (*adj*) *36* ominous
**fecha** (*nf*) *30* date
**fecundidad** (*nf*) *36* fertility
**feria** (*nf*) *26* fair
**fiarse** (*v*) *39* to trust
**fiebre** (*nf*) *38* fever
**fin de semana** (*nm*) *6* weekend
**firma** (*nf*) *28* company
**flotador** (*nm*) *12* float
**folleto** (*nm*) *10* brochure, leaflet
**foro** (*nm*) *24* meeting, forum

**fracaso** (*nm*) *41* failure
**fresco/a** (*adj*) *32* fresh
**frijol** (*nm Lat Am*) *60* bean
**fuegos artificiales** (*nm*) *84* fireworks
**fuente** (*nf*) *6* source
**fuerte** (*nm*) *84* fort
**fuerza** (*nf*) *40* strength, force
**fumar** (*v*) *14* to smoke
**fútbol** (*nm*) *14* soccer, football

## G

**galán** (*nm*) *22* suitor
**galardonar** (*v*) *69* to reward
**gallina** (*nf*) *34* chicken
**ganado** (*nm*) *60* livestock
**ganancias** (*nf*) *68* profits
**gastar** (*v*) *19* to spend
**gastos** (*nm pl*) *92* expenses
**globo** (*nm*) *72* hot-air balloon
**gobernar** (*v*) *30* to rule
**gomina** (*nf*) *56* hair gel
**gorila** (*nm col*) *56* thug
**gorrón/a** (*nm/f col*) *92* freeloader
**gozar de** (*v*) *8* to enjoy
**grabación** (*nf*) *8* recording
**gracias a** (*ph*) *6* thanks to
**grado** (*nm*) *52* degree
**grandes almacenes** (*nm*) *90* department store
**grisáceo/a** (*adj*) *48* grayish
**grupo de presión** (*nm*) *63* pressure group
**guardaespaldas** (*nm*) *21* bodyguard
**guerra** (*nf*) *36* war
**gusto** (*nm*) *44* taste

## H

**habitante** (*nm/f*) *12* inhabitant
**hacendado** (*nm*) *20* landowner
**hacer falta** (*v*) *92* to be necessary
**hacer que** (*ph*) *8* to make
**halagar** (*v*) *59* to flatter
**hallar** (*v*) *76* to find, to discover
**hectárea** (*nf*) *72* hectare (= 2.471 acres)
**hegemonía** (*nf*) *76* hegemony
**herencia** (*nf*) *64* inheritance
**hígado** (*nm*) *19* liver
**hípica** (*nf*) *12* horseback riding
**hispanohablante** (*adj*) *8* Spanish-speaking
**historieta** (*nf*) *9* comic strip
**hogar** (*nm*) *92* home
**hoja de reclamaciones** (*nf*) *93* complaints form
**hojear** (*v*) *68* to leaf through
**hombre rana** (*nm*) *21* frogman
**hombro** (*nm*) *36* shoulder
**horno microondas** (*nm*) *26* microwave oven
**hostil** (*adj*) *31* hostile
**hoy en día** (*ph*) *52* nowadays
**huir** (*v*) *56* to avoid
**hurto** (*nm*) *88* theft

## I

**iberoamericano/a** (*adj*) *8* Latin-American
**idioma** (*nm*) *8* language
**idóneo/a** (*adj*) *12* suitable, ideal
**igual que** (*ph*) *52* the same as
**ilimitado/a** (*adj*) *24* unlimited
**imperiosamente** (*adv*) *35* imperatively
**implantar** (*v*) *88* to introduce
**imprenta** (*nf*) *44* printing press
**inadecuado/a** (*adj*) *32* unsuitable
**incendio** (*nm*) *48* fire
**inclusive** (*adv*) *52* inclusively
**incontestable** (*adj*) *40* undeniable
**inconveniente** (*nm*) *14* disadvantage
**incrementar** (*v*) *88* to increase
**incursión** (*nf*) *40* raid
**incursionar** (*v*) *28* to penetrate
**indebido/a** (*adj*) *88* illegal
**índice** (*nm*) *22* rate
**indígena** (*adj nm/f*) *31 72* indigenous; native
**indiscutible** (*adj*) *40* unquestionable
**informática** (*nf*) *7* computing
**informe** (*nm*) *92* report
**ingresar** (*v*) *17* to admit someone
**iniciar** (*v*) *76* to start
**inmaduro/a** (*adj*) *18* immature
**inmobiliaria** (*nf*) *66* real estate company, estate agency
**intercambio** (*nm*) *17* exchange
**interesado/a** (*adj*) *94* selfish
**intervenir** (*v*) *20* to participate
**inútil** (*adj*) *27* useless
**islote** (*nm*) *72* small island

## J

**jactarse de** (*v*) *36* to boast about
**jamás** (*adv*) *76* never
**jeringuilla** (*nf*) *17* syringe
**jubilación** (*nf*) *92* retirement
**jubilado/a** (*nm/f*) *83* retired person
**jugarse la vida** (*v*) *15* to risk one's life
**juntarse** (*v*) *20* to come together
**jurado** (*nm*) *69* jury

## L

**labor** (*nf*) *80* work
**laca** (*nf*) *48* hairspray
**ladrón/ona** (*nm/f*) *29* thief
**lamentarse** (*v*) *16* to complain
**lancha** (*nf*) *12* boat
**lanzamiento** (*nm*) *41* launching
**lanzarse** (*v*) *12* to throw oneself
**lápiz de labios** (*nm*) *72* lipstick
**lavandera** (*nf*) *92* laundress
**lectivo/a** (*adj*) *10* school
**lejos** (*adv*) *40* far
**lema** (*nm*) *15* slogan
**lesión** (*nf*) *14* wound
**letal** (*adj*) *16* deadly, lethal
**líder** (*nm/f*) *28* leader
**limpieza** (*nf*) *33* cleaning
**lince** (*nm*) *34* lynx

**línea** (*nf*) *28* line
**lirón** (*nm*) *34* dormouse
**llamativo/a** (*adj*) *58* loud
**llevar la peor parte** (*ph*) *52* to get the worst of it
**llevar más razón que un santo** (*ph*) *56* to be in the right
**lluvia** (*nf*) *25* rain
**lobo** (*nm*) *34* wolf
**localidad** (*nf*) *76* place, town
**localizar** (*v*) *24* to track down
**locura** (*nf*) *67* madness
**lodo** (*nm*) *60* mud
**lograr** (*v*) *6* to achieve, to attain
**logro** (*nm*) *31* achievement, success
**luego de** (*adv*) *76* after
**lujoso/a** (*adj*) *74* luxurious

## M

**machismo** (*nm*) *31* male chauvinism
**macho** (*nm*) *32* male
**madera** (*nf*) *13* wood
**madrugada** (*nf*) *55* early morning
**maduro/a** (*adj*) *35* mature
**magia** (*nf*) *12* magic
**mal** (*nm*) *52* illness
**maleducado/a** (*adj*) *56* rude
**maleficio** (*nm*) *36* curse
**maleta** (*nf*) *21* suitcase
**maravilla** (*nf*) *27* wonder
**marquesina** (*nf*) *56* bus shelter
**mascota** (*v*) *32* pet
**materia prima** (*nf*) *51* raw material
**matrícula** (*nf*) *91* license plate
**mayoritario/a** (*adj*) *40* majority
**medianoche** (*nf*) *21* midnight
**medicamento** (*nm*) *44* medicine
**medida** (*nf*) *88* measure
**medio/a** (*adj*) *6 10* half; intermediate
**medio** (*nm*) *12* method, way
**medios de comunicación** (*nm*) *6* media
**mejorar** (*v*) *9* to improve
**melómano/a** (*nm/f*) *17* music lover
**mente** (*nf*) *72* mind
**mercado** (*nm*) *7* market
**merecer la pena** (*ph*) *15* to be worth the trouble
**mesero** (*nm Lat Am*) *54* waiter
**meta** (*nf*) *8* objective
**mezclar** (*v*) *10* to mix
**miedo** (*nm*) *16* fear
**milenario/a** (*adj*) *84* very ancient
**mímica** (*nf*) *53* mime
**misa** (*nf*) *86* mass
**mitad** (*nf*) *19* half
**mito** (*nm*) *40* myth
**mitómano** (*nm/f*) *17* liar
**moda** (*nf*) *11* fashion
**modalidad** (*nf*) *12* kind, variety
**monitor/a** (*nm/f*) *12* monitor
**montar** (*v*) *68* to mount
**mostrar** (*v*) *72* to show
**multa** (*nf*) *90* fine
**municipio** (*nm*) *28* district

## N

**nacer** (*v*) *12* to be born
**nada** (*pron*) *56* nothing
**natación** (*nf*) *14* swimming
**naturaleza** (*nf*) *7* nature
**navegar** (*v*) *27* to navigate
**Navidad** (*nf*) *19* Christmas
**necio/a** (*adj*) *39* silly
**negar** (*v*) *60* to deny
**negarse a** (*v*) *28* to refuse to
**negocio** (*nm*) *68* business
**neumático/a** (*adj*) *12* air, pneumatic
**ni siquiera** (*adv*) *36* not even
**niñera** (*nf*) *55* nanny
**nivel** (*nm*) *10* level
**nivel de renta** (*nm*) *40* level of income
**nocivo/a** (*adj*) *48* harmful
**nómada** (*adj*) *72* nomadic
**nombrar** (*v*) *24* to name
**norma** (*nf*) *14* rule
**notar** (*v*) *59* to observe
**noticia** (*nf*) *6* piece of news
**nuca** (*nf*) *59* back of the neck, nape
**nutritivo/a** (*adj*) *51* nourishing

## O

**obrero** (*nm*) *52* worker
**ocio** (*nm*) *7* leisure
**ocioso/a** (*nm/f adj*) *24 88* idler; idle
**ocultarse** (*v*) *16* to hide oneself
**ocurrirse** (*v*) *20* to cross one's mind
**odioso/a** (*adj*) *16* hateful
**oferta** (*nf*) *28* offer
**olvidar** (*v*) *16* to forget
**opositor/a** (*nm/f*) *28* opponent
**opuesto** (*adj*) *41* opposite
**ordenador** (*nm Sp*) *18* computer
**orientar** (*v*) *40* to direct
**óseo/a** (*adj*) *14* bony
**ostra** (*nf*) *34* oyster
**OVNI (objeto volante no identificado)** (*nm*) *38* UFO

## P

**padecer de** (*v*) *52* to suffer from
**pagano/a** (*nm/f*) *36* pagan
**palmera** (*nf*) *64* palm tree
**pandilla** (*nf*) *89* gang
**papa** (*nf Lat Am*) *9* potato
**papel** (*nm*) *7 10* paper; role
**paraíso** (*nm*) *12* paradise, heaven
**paro** (*nm*) *83* unemployment
**párrafo** (*nm*) *25* paragraph
**pasajero/a** (*adj*) *52* passing
**pasatiempo** (*nm*) *6* hobby
**pasear** (*v*) *32 64* to take for a walk; to go for a walk
**paz** (*nf*) *66* peace
**peinarse** (*v*) *22* to comb one's hair
**peligro** (*nm*) *12* danger
**pelirrojo** (*adj*) *21* red-haired
**pelu** (*nf*) *59* hairdresser's (abbreviation of ***peluquería***)
**pena de muerte** (*nf*) *90* death penalty
**pérdida** (*nf*) *72* loss
**periodista** (*nm/f*) *8* journalist
**perjudicar** (*v*) *60* to damage
**perseguir** (*v*) *12* to pursue

**pertenecer** (*v*) *85* to belong to
**pescado** (*nm*) *25* fish
**pescar** (*v*) *12* to fish
**pese a** (*prep*) *88* despite
**piragua** (*nf*) *12* canoe
**piragüismo** (*nm*) *12* canoeing
**piso** (*nm*) *21 65* floor; apartment
**pisotear** (*v*) *60* to trample
**planchado/a** (*adj*) *56* ironed
**plantear** (*v*) *92* to ask oneself
**plantilla** (*nf*) *80* personnel
**plataforma** (*nf*) *28* platform
**poblador/a** (*nm/f*) *84* inhabitant
**poderoso/a** (*adj*) *30* powerful
**polifacético/a** (*adj*) *64* many-sided
**poner a prueba** (*ph*) *40* to test
**poner de manifiesto** (*v*) *8* to reveal, to make something clear
**por ello** (*ph*) *8* for that reason
**por razones de** (*ph*) *12* for (reasons of)
**por supuesto** (*ph*) *7* of course
**por tanto** (*ph*) *36* therefore
**portada** (*nf*) *70* cover
**porteño/a** (*nm/f*) *64* inhabitant of Buenos Aires
**pozo** (*nm*) *60* well
**prado** (*nm*) *32* meadow
**predecir** (*v*) *37* to predict
**prensa** (*nf*) *6* press
**preocupar** (*v*) *49* to worry
**presa** (*nf*) *6* prey
**prestigio** (*nm*) *8* prestige, reputation
**presumido/a** (*adj*) *59* vain
**pretender** (*v*) *88* to try to
**primer mandatario** (*nm*) *32* head of state
**programa de charla** (*nm*) *24* chat line
**prohibir** (*v*) *18* to forbid
**propiciar** (*v*) *36* to favor
**propietario/a** (*nm/f*) *44* owner
**propuesta** (*nf*) *43* proposal
**prosperar** (*v*) *80* to prosper
**protagonista** (*nm/f*) *20* main character
**próximo/a** (*adj*) *20* next
**prueba** (*nf*) *41* proof
**puente** (*nm*) *12* bridge
**puertorriqueño/a** (*nm/f*) *40* Puerto Rican
**puesto** (*nm*) *29* position
**puesto de avanzada** (*nm*) *76* outpost
**pulmonar** (*adj*) *44* lung
**punto de vista** (*nm*) *24* point of view

## Q

**quedar** (*v*) *40* to remain
**queja** (*nf*) *48* complaint
**quejarse** (*v*) *23* to complain
**querido/a** (*adj*) *28* beloved
**quiromancia** (*nf*) *37* palmistry

## R

**rápidos** (*nm*) *12* rapids
**rasgo** (*nm*) *42* characteristic
**rayos X** (*nm*) *44* X-rays
**razón** (*nf*) *17* reason
**razonar** (*v*) *28* to reason
**realeza** (*nf*) *68* royalty
**realizar** (*v*) *14 20* to carry out; to make
**rebajas** (*nf*) *65* sales
**recaudar** (*v*) *63* to collect
**reciclaje** (*nm*) *48* recycling
**reclamo** (*nm Lat Am*) *28* complaint
**reconocer** (*v*) *28* to admit
**recreo** (*nm*) *69* break
**recuadro** (*nm*) *7* box
**recursos** (*nm*) *24 92* resources; means
**red** (*nf*) *25 66* net; network
**reflejar** (*v*) *21* to reflect
**reflejo** (*nm*) *20* reflection
**refrán** (*nm*) *36* proverb, saying
**regalar** (*v*) *6* to give
**reina de belleza** (*nf*) *29* beauty queen
**relucir** (*v*) *39* to shine
**remoto** (*adj*) *72* remote
**rendimiento** (*nm*) *44* yield
**rendir los honores** (*ph*) *84* to worship
**rentable** (*adj*) *51* profitable
**repeler** (*v*) *37* to repel
**repetir** (*v*) *20* to repeat
**reportar** (*v*) *68 80* to obtain; to give
**requerir** (*v*) *80* to require
**reseña** (*nf*) *43* account, summary
**residir** (*v*) *8* to live
**resistente** (*adj*) *12* resistant, strong
**respaldo** (*nm*) *28* support
**respirar** (*v*) *64* to breathe
**respuesta** (*nf*) *16* answer
**resuelto/a** (*adj*) *94* determined
**resultar** (*v*) *20* to be, to turn out
**resumir** (*v*) *35* to summarize
**revés** (*nm*) *21* reverse
**revista** (*nf*) *6* magazine
**rezumar** (*v*) *64* to ooze
**rincón** (*nm*) *64* corner
**riñón** (*nm*) *19* kidney
**riqueza** (*nf*) *8 51* richness; abundance, wealth
**rizo** (*nm*) *59* curl
**rodear** (*v*) *23* to surround
**ruido** (*nm*) *24* noise
**ruptura** (*nf*) *18* split
**rural** (*adj*) *67* rural

## S

**sabiduría** (*nf*) *30* wisdom
**sabor** (*nm*) *12* taste
**sacacorchos** (*nm*) *21* corkscrew
**sacar** (*v*) *32 40* to remove; to publish
**sacar conclusiones** (*ph*) *48* to draw conclusions
**salario** (*nm*) *36* wages
**salir** (*v*) *56* to go out
**saltar a la fama** (*v*) *28* to leap to fame
**salto base** (*nm*) *15* base jump
**salud** (*nf*) *7* health
**salvaguarda** (*nf*) *44* safeguard
**salvar** (*v*) *50* to save
**sano/a** (*adj*) *19* healthy
**sede** (*nf*) *8* seat, headquarters
**seguridad** (*nf*) *12* safety
**selva amazónica** (*nf*) *63* Amazon rainforest
**semáforo** (*nm*) *21* traffic lights

**semanario** (*nm*) *68* weekly magazine
**semejante** (*adj*) *72* similar
**sensato/a** (*adj*) *35* sensible
**sentido** (*nm*) *36* meaning
**sentirse** (*v*) *16* to feel
**señalar** (*v*) *8* to point out, to indicate
**sequía** (*nf*) *48* drought
**sesión inaugural** (*nf*) *8* opening session
**si bien** (*ph*) *52* although
**siglo** (*nm*) *24* century
**simiente** (*nf*) *84* seed
**sin embargo** (*ph*) *12* however, still
**soberano/a** (*nm/f*) *76* sovereign
**sobrenatural** (*adj*) *38* supernatural
**soledad** (*sf*) *10 18* solitude; loneliness
**solicitud** (*nf*) *32* request
**solidario/a** (*adj*) *61* sympathetic
**solitario/a** (*nm/f*) *27* lonely person
**soñar** (*v*) *28* to dream
**soportar** (*v*) *56* to endure
**sordo/a** (*adj*) *39* deaf
**soroche** (*nm Lat Am*) *78* mountain sickness
**sorprendente** (*adj*) *24* surprising
**submarinismo** (*nm*) *12* underwater exploration
**sueldo** (*nm*) *28* salary
**suerte** (*nf*) *36* luck
**sujetar** (*v*) *12* to hold tight
**sumar** (*v*) *8* to total
**sumergir** (*v*) *84* to sink
**suponer** (*v*) *35* to imply

## T

**tablón** (*nm*) *24* bulletin board
**tabú** (*adj*) *25* taboo
**tal parece que** (*ph*) *32* it seems that
**tala** (*nf*) *48* tree felling
**talentoso/a** (*adj*) *20* talented
**tal vez** (*adj*) *59* perhaps
**taurino/a** (*adj*) *31* bullfighting
**técnica** (*nf*) *12* technique, skill
**telemando** (*nm*) *26* remote control
**telemático/a** (*adj*) *80* telematic
**telenovela** (*nf*) *20* soap opera
**televidente** (*nm/f*) *21* viewer
**televisivo/a** (*adj*) *22* television
**tema** (*nm*) *7* subject
**temor** (*nm*) *44* fear
**temporal** (*adj*) *39* temporary
**tener derecho a** (*ph*) *72* to have a right to
**terapéutico/a** (*adj*) *33* therapeutic
**tercer mundo** (*nm*) *62* the Third World
**terrestre** (*adj*) *12* land, terrestrial
**tesoro** (*nm*) *24* treasure
**testigo** (*nm/f*) *64* witness
**tiempo libre** (*nm*) *6* free time
**timidez** (*nf*) *16* shyness
**tinieblas** (*nf*) *84* shadows, darkness
**tío/a** (*nm/f Sp col*) *56* guy
**tirarse de** (*v*) *12* to throw oneself
**tomar en cuenta** (*ph*) *28* to take into account
**tono** (*nm*) *17* tone
**tontería** (*nf*) *37* foolishness
**toque de queda** (*nm*) *88* curfew
**torero/a** (*nm/f*) *31* bullfighter
**toxicómano/a** (*nm/f*) *17* drug addict
**tragaperras** (*nf*) *16* slot machine
**trama** (*nf*) *20* plot
**tras** (*prep*) *16* behind
**trasladar** (*v*) *36* to move
**traslucir** (*v*) *64* to reveal
**traspasar** (*v*) *40* to transmit
**tratamiento** (*nm*) *44* treatment
**trébol de cuatro hojas** (*nm*) *36* four-leaf clover
**tribu** (*nf*) *75* tribe
**tripulante** (*nm/f*) *12* crew member
**triste** (*adj*) *17* sad
**trotamundos** (*nm*) *72* globe-trotter
**truco** (*nm*) *22* trick
**tumbarse** (*v*) *12* to lie down

## U

**ubicación** (*nf*) *76* location
**último/a** (*adj*) *6 8* last; latter
**una vez** (*ph*) *60* once
**urbe** (*nf*) *64* large city
**usuario/a** (*nm/f*) *15* user

## V

**vacío** (*nm*) *15* void
**vacuna** (*nf*) *35* vaccination
**valerse de** (*v*) *28* to take advantage of
**validez** (*nf*) *37* validity
**valor** (*nm*) *40* value
**valorar** (*v*) *31* to value
**variante** (*nm*) *8* variant
**veintena** (*nf*) *8* about twenty
**vencer** (*v*) *17* to defeat
**ventaja** (*nf*) *11* advantage
**veracidad** (*nf*) *20* veracity
**verdadero/a** (*adj*) *13* true
**verduras** (*nf*) *32* green vegetables
**verter** (*v*) *84* to pour out
**vértice** (*nm*) *20* top, apex
**vertidos** (*nm*) *48* waste
**vestuario** (*nm*) *59* clothes
**viaje** (*nm*) *7 25* travel; trip
**videojuego** (*nm*) *18* video game
**Viejo Continente** (*nm*) *12* Europe
**vínculo de unión** (*nm*) *8* link, bond
**vino** (*nm*) *19* wine
**violar** (*v*) *68* to infringe
**vividor/a** (*nm/f*) *92* opportunist
**vivienda** (*nf*) *65* dwelling
**volverse** (*v*) *23* to become
**vuelo sin motor** (*nm*) *12* gliding

## Z

**zona peatonal** (*nf*) *66* pedestrian area